A Lifetime with Shakespeare

A Lifetime with Shakespeare

Notes from an American Director of All 38 Plays

PAUL BARRY

Foreword by Harry Keyishian

McFarland & Company, Inc., Publishers
Jefferson, North Carolina, and London

LIBRARY OF CONGRESS CATALOGUING-IN-PUBLICATION DATA

Barry, Paul, 1931–
A lifetime with Shakespeare : notes from an American director
of all 38 plays / Paul Barry ; foreword by Harry Keyishian.
p.   cm.
Includes bibliographical references and index.

ISBN 978-0-7864-4953-8
softcover : 50# alkaline paper ∞

1. Barry, Paul, 1931–   2. Theatrical producers and directors — United States — Biography.
3. Shakespeare, William, 1564–1616 — Dramatic production.   4. Shakespeare,
William, 1564–1616 — Stage history —1950–   5. Shakespeare, William, 1564–1616 —
Stage history — United States.   I. Title.
PN2287.B275A3   2010   792.02'32092 — dc22 [B]   2010029401

British Library cataloguing data are available

©2010 Paul Barry. All rights reserved

*No part of this book may be reproduced or transmitted in any form
or by any means, electronic or mechanical, including photocopying
or recording, or by any information storage and retrieval system,
without permission in writing from the publisher.*

Front cover: *Twelfth Night*, New Jersey Shakespeare Festival, 1982 (photograph
by Blair Holley); Shakespeare portrait inset ©2010 Shutterstock.com

Manufactured in the United States of America

*McFarland & Company, Inc., Publishers
Box 611, Jefferson, North Carolina 28640
www.mcfarlandpub.com*

Dedicated to Harry, who said, "Do it";
to Shannon, who said, "Stick with it";
to Ellen, who said, "I'll help you get it right!"

Table of Contents

Acknowledgments ix
Foreword by Harry Keyishian 1
Introduction 3

1. Actors, Plays, and Playhouses — 5
2. *The Taming of the Shrew* — 17
3. *A Midsummer Night's Dream* — 23
4. *Hamlet* — 31
5. *Macbeth* — 43
6. *The Comedy of Errors* — 53
7. *The Two Gentlemen of Verona* — 57
8. *Twelfth Night* — 60
9. *Romeo and Juliet* — 67
10. Shakespeare's Warrior Plays — 75
11. *Troilus and Cressida* — 80
12. *Julius Caesar* — 84
13. *Antony and Cleopatra* — 89
14. *Much Ado About Nothing* — 93
15. *Othello* — 99
16. *The Merchant of Venice* — 107
17. *The Tempest* — 118
18. *As You Like It* — 123
19. *Coriolanus* — 126
20. *Measure for Measure* — 129
21. The Chronicle Plays — 133
22. *Richard II* — 137
23. *Henry IV, Part 1* — 143
24. *Henry IV, Part 2* — 150

25. *The Merry Wives of Windsor*	154
26. *Henry V*	157
27. *Henry VI, Part 1*	162
28. *Henry VI, Part 2*	168
29. *Henry VI, Part 3*	172
30. *Richard III*	175
31. *Titus Andronicus*	180
32. *Love's Labour's Lost*	184
33. *King Lear*	188
34. *Timon of Athens*	201
35. *Cymbeline*	205
36. *Henry VIII*	208
37. *The Two Noble Kinsmen*	215
38. *The Winter's Tale*	220
39. *All's Well That Ends Well*	228
40. *Pericles, Prince of Tyre*	230
41. *King John*	234

Bibliography 237

Index 239

Acknowledgments

Conventional wisdom refers to the theatre as a collaborative art. So is professional wrestling. I am most grateful to my wife, Ellen Barry, and I am reminded daily that I might not have done the book or much else of value without her. She was my partner in the Shakespeare company, almost from the beginning, and she worked with me as co-producer on all of the plays, including all 38 of the Canon, 1965 to 1990. We also managed to raise a family and pay off the mortgage on the house. That should have been enough for any partnership, but she also volunteered to shepherd this book to its conclusion and publication, and we've managed to accomplish that without divorce. In addition to Ellen, I'm grateful to every actor I've ever worked with and every scholar who ever looked on me with tolerance, as well as my extended family — the Barrys, Flahertys, Floods, Fosters, O'Gradys and Yabes — and Morgan Brody, Elise Carper, Robert W. Cook, Paddy Crean, John Cullum, Bela de Tuscan, Frank Daley, Mick Daugherty, Jim DelGiudice, Alex Dmitriev, Richard Dorfman, Phil Dorian, Martin Farawell, Bill Gagnon, Malcolm J. Gregory, Joe Haas, Louis B. Harrison, Shunshin T. Kan, Stan Kenton, Joe Klein, Eleanor and John Kennedy, Josh Logan, Charlie McCue, Ron Meyers, George Mahr, Doug Morse, Aldo Nadi, Vincent Puma, Kurt Remmers, Chita Rivera, Richard Rose, Walter Savage and John Sheehy.

Foreword by Harry Keyishian

I had originally suggested that the title of this book should be "Thirty-Eight by Will and Paul" because that would have suggested both the comprehensiveness of its contents and the singular bond between its author, Paul Barry, and the playwright to whom he has devoted a professional and personal lifetime. While it is true that all theatre is collaborative—the players cannot play without a script and the script does not come into its own until it is played—there is something unusual in this particular collaboration. As a "romance," it went "all the way." By the time he was done, Paul, as artistic director of the New Jersey Shakespeare Festival, had—uniquely among American theater directors—directed all 38 of the plays reliably ascribed, in whole or in part, to William Shakespeare.

It took singular, stubborn devotion to ensure that no play of Shakespeare's would go unproduced during Paul's quarter-century at NJSF, which he founded in Cape May, New Jersey, in 1963 and, at the invitation of Drew University President Robert F. Oxnam, transported to Madison, New Jersey, in 1971. From a commercial point of view, some plays—think *Hamlet, Romeo and Juliet, A Midsummer Night's Dream, Macbeth*—can be counted on to draw an audience. Others—think *Timon of Athens, Troilus and Cressida*, the Henry VI plays, *Coriolanus, Pericles*, and (for goodness' sake) *The Two Noble Kinsmen*—well, not so much. But Paul believed with passion that it was the mission, as well as the business, of a Shakespeare Festival to offer its audiences all of Shakespeare, and the desire of its audiences to want to see it all. If callers to the box office asked for tickets to *Time in a Bottle* (yes, it happened), they would nevertheless be enlightened, enriched, and won over when they got to the theater and actually saw the seldom-staged tale of Shakespeare's greatest misanthrope.

"Doing" the canon was not stunt scheduling, nor a product of statistical yearnings. Committed to Shakespeare's language and dramatic action, Paul was (is) consumed with curiosity about the meanings and mysteries attached to each play. His curiosity is neither idle nor abstract: it is in the service of actually mounting productions, of not only understanding the work deeply but of addressing the host of practical, contingent, often bizarre considerations that arise in running a repertory company performing a variety of plays on an interlocking schedule with a set group of actors. (He is not favorably inclined toward academic critics who come to complex and abstract interpretations of Shakespeare's plays, without a sense of how they might be actually staged.) His preparations were intense, based on lots of thought and research producing tons of notes, which he was happy to share and discuss. As a result, his NJSF productions were strongly conceived as well as vigorous, well-paced, and visually arresting. All in all (in and out of the NJSF), he has so far directed 74 productions of Shakespeare's plays. As an actor, he has played 49 roles, including three Gloucesters, two Iagos, two Tybalts, and two Lord Capulets. In addition, as his own fight director, he staged fights for all 38 plays in the Shakespeare canon. All those people! All that action!

Paul insisted that his actors speak standard American English, not imitation British, unless a specific accent — Welsh or Irish or French — was required. This was by way of demonstrating that American actors could achieve excellence within the framework of their own language, through the sheer power of performance. He strove ever for authenticity: his knowledge of medieval weaponry is extensive, for example, and, when mounting the history plays, he went to great lengths to achieve authenticity — to the point of having halberds and longswords created at a local forge. (It was a treat to see him lugging them on his bicycle through the streets of Morristown, New Jersey.)

This is not to say that Paul was exclusively a Shakespearean during his years at NJSF. He mounted, and performed in, exciting productions from every dramatic era. (I particularly remember his amazing Archie Rice in John Osborne's *The Entertainer* and his *Cyrano*, with its strong romantic yearnings and its dazzling swordplay.) And it should not be forgotten that the NJSF was a collaboration, most strongly with his wife Ellen, who not only served as producing director for the organization but gave some of its most memorable performances, in Shakespeare, of course — Queens Hermione and Constance, especially noteworthy — but also in plays by Tennessee Williams (Blanche once, Stella once), Athol Fugard, Tad Mosel, and G.B. Shaw, among others. (And she, like Paul, had plentiful acting jobs elsewhere, off season at NJSF.) Their actress daughter Shannon, while perhaps not actually born on stage, was pretty much raised there, in a series of juvenile roles.

For me, as a professor of English with the usual academic infirmities, it has been a treat and an enrichment to explore, exchange ideas with, and learn from this brave, resourceful, and gifted man of the theater about his personal search for the essence of Shakespeare. I'm glad that his experiences can now be shared with others. Paul Barry had to write this book because, simply, no one else possibly could.

Department of Literature, Languages,
Writing, and Philosophy
Fairleigh Dickinson University
Madison, New Jersey 07940

Introduction

In 1991, after 33 years as a professional producer/director, I plunged joyfully back into the precarious freelance market, the heady fun of performing without the responsibilities of producing. I was free of the harassment and restraints of a Board of Trustees. Even today, after nearly 60 years of performing, there's no greater joy than the indulgence of abandoning myself to the moment in a live play in front of an appreciative audience. So, writing this book is something I did when I had no plays to perform, and that delayed the completion of the book. Now it's done, and I wonder about it.

Whenever I walk into a library or a large bookstore, I wonder why anyone would write another book. We already have too many. What kind of hubris would lead anyone to write another, especially a book about William Shakespeare and his plays? It seems as if everyone I know has written or is writing a book about Shakespeare. What do I have to add to what they know?

When Harry Keyishian, dear friend and scholar, suggested that I write this book, I immediately agreed and began writing on the spot, without much thought about order or organization. It was only later that I began to question the book's value. What can I bring to the vast Shakespeare book industry that hasn't already been done to death?

I am a director, actor and musician. My professional theatre career has included producing, directing, and acting in all 38 of Shakespeare's plays (several, more than once), a total of 74 productions primarily for the theatre I founded and ran for 28 years, the New Jersey Shakespeare Festival (NJSF henceforth). I've also done fights for productions somebody else directed, and I've acted in a number of Shakespeare plays under other directors. In addition, I've directed over 200 other plays and musicals over 50 years — works of the world's greatest playwrights, notably Molière, George Bernard Shaw, Sean O'Casey, Eugene O'Neill, Arthur Miller, Tennessee Williams, Edward Albee, Herb Gardner, Neil Simon, John Osborne — some carefully planned and thoroughly constructed, others haphazardly mounted under absurd time pressures. Thus my perspective is very different from that of those careful scholars who read not only the plays but also the works of numerous other authors, critics, and scholars.

I've heard many a Shakespeare buff insist that he'd prefer to enjoy the texts in the comfort and calm of the study rather than watch an inept performance. While experiencing the play script as literature, one can ignore the clock. There is abundant private pleasure in studying the words alone in the late afternoon sun, envisioning actors who never were, with the Playwright's imagination influencing mine, envisioning the perfect Juliet embraced by the perfect Romeo. I delight in that intellectual, voyeuristic experience, as I believe most scholars do, peeling the multiple skins of the Playwright's onions, reveling in the infinite possibilities at the bottom of Bottom's bottomless dreams about dreams, then drifting back to the text. (Style note: whenever I use playwright(s) with a lowercase "p," I'm referring to any playwright, or occasionally, Shakespeare in collaboration with others. If Playwright is capitalized, I'm referring to Shakespeare alone.)

Admittedly, the reading of a play demands greater imagination than a novel, but if the plays are perfect, even eternal, on the page, why go to all the trouble and expense to produce them? Another school of scholars concerns itself with the practices employed in performing the works of Shakespeare and his contemporaries, how Elizabethan or Jacobean playhouses were built and decorated, how those buildings influenced their acting companies. This research gets us closer to the plays as plays.

Most of the scholarship is confined to the texts, and I find it fascinating: the minute digging through a thousand debates among "solid," "sullied," or "sallied"; "rack," "wrack," or "wreck"; "Indian" or "Judean"; variations in spelling and punctuation; the correction of scansion or the restoration of initial printings, comparisons of Quarto and Folio texts, the validity of added "Os" or "Ohs." Much praise to the scholars for keeping the flame alive. I enjoy their books and dissertations, enjoy even more the arguments they precipitate, the delightful October afternoons in Harry's living room.

But what can I add to what they've given us? My profession is Shakespeare on-stage, the translation of words on paper into sounds made by actors, the physical realization of the events of the text, the cohesion of a company of actors into seamless action in front of an audience.

Where the director is different from the scholar and where (I hope) this book is different from the others is at the same time simple and profound: the director must set speculation and theory aside to get the play on. The director may begin his/her work as a scholar, but must make choices that the scholar may postpone indefinitely: which texts, which Folio, which Quarto, what edits, which punctuation? We usually end up with a conflated edited text for a number of reasons, some tortuously scholarly, some banal and pedestrian. Then come casting and design decisions: which actors, what doubling, which historical period, which costumes, properties, music, what sets or lack thereof. All in preparation for that awful, wonderful moment when some 40 people will burst into a 20' × 30' space, eager to jump in, scream the words and smash each other into the woodwork.

It is a well-known axiom that the theatre is a collaborative process. It begins with the playwright and the actors, includes designers and technicians, resolves and fulfills itself in performance with the audience. It's not anarchistic and it's not democratic. Everyone in the process makes a contribution and must be allowed a voice but no vote. One mind, one temperament, must shape the whole, making final decisions on all of the above questions, most especially casting. The director has to get the show on. Somehow, this always happens. Lines may be barely memorized, costumes may not fit, weapons may be from the wrong period, properties may not meet the actors' needs, paint on the set may still be wet, but opening night always arrives and is survived. The show is on.

Most of what I know about Shakespeare comes from directing the plays and playing his characters. Most of what I know — not all. I have aspired to scholarship as well, reading many books and engaging in many debates. But the main thing I have to offer is 50 years of practical decisions, mistakes, adjustments, happy accidents, recoveries, of getting the show on. So let's get to it.

CHAPTER 1

Actors, Plays, and Playhouses

In a theatre career spanning little more than 20 years, roughly the last 11 years of the reign of Elizabeth I and the first 10 years of the reign of James I/VI, Master Will Shakespeare wrote at least 38 plays, most of them solo efforts, some collaborations.

He was a shareholder, actor, and co-producer in the most prosperous stock company of his age. Though the company, known first as Lord Hunsdon's Men, then the Lord Chamberlain's Men, finally as the King's Men, changed patrons, James Burbage and his sons, Richard and Cuthbert, had always led it. By today's — or for that matter any day's — standards, Shakespeare's is a prodigious body of work, but then he spent no time selling his plays to producers, no time in negotiation or in promotion, and he did no television talk shows. Most of his career, he lived, ate, and slept within walking distance of his theatre.

The Resident Company

Peter Brook, in his seminal work, *The Empty Space*, wrote:

> I can take any empty space and call it a bare stage. A man walks across this empty space whilst someone else is watching him, and this is all that is needed for an act of theatre to be engaged.

Peter Brook did not invent this postulate. He observed it, articulated it, and acted upon it. It describes the irreducible minimum of the theatrical experience: an actor on an empty stage, observed by an audience. From there, other necessities are suggested, beginning with the script. What further does it call for? A second actor? Properties? Costumes? Please note that I use the term "necessities," not niceties. I mean that which the text demands.

In my opinion, Shakespeare's prolific body of work was made possible by the company of actors for which he wrote: his cry of players was made up of eight to ten shareholders, six or eight "hired men," a few apprentices and an occasional child or two, probably the offspring of shareholders. Such companies had a repertory of 40 to 60 plays, playing short runs, sometimes single performances, over a period of months. Each actor had to learn dozens of roles. Often, an actor was required to go on in a new role at a few hours' notice.

Since the cast lists often numbered many more named characters, plus citizens and servants, than there were actors, even in the largest rep companies, doubling was (and still is) the rule rather than the exception. Even the smaller, shorter plays are large compared to most modern plays. The longer plays, notably the histories, are even larger. My productions of the *Henry VI/Richard III* plays at NJSF in 1983 employed a company of 23 Equity actors and 40 interns, everyone but Margaret playing multiple roles. Most NJSF seasons, three to

Hamlet, New Jersey Shakespeare Festival, 1988: Tim Steiner, T. Ryder Smith, Ralph Lewis, Bob De Luca, Evan Alboum as the Players (photograph by Jim DelGiudice).

six plays in nightly rotating repertory, used 13 to 15 Equity actors and 35 to 40 interns/apprentices. Each Equity actor played at least one lead, one supporting role, and one small role in the rep. Interns played all the citizens, soldiers, and servants, and understudied the major roles. The great advantage of this approach was that it encouraged the audience's perception that they were watching different casts. A beneficial side effect was a happier company in which there were no stars, just good actors supporting each other.

It's difficult to come up with rules on doubling, because every production situation is different. Should doubling be hidden? I believe so, though I've seen enough Shakespeare where the opposite was true, even for the "thematic" doubles. The only thematic double that ever worked for me was actually a triple: the same actor playing the Ghost, the First Player, and the First Gravedigger in *Hamlet.* This triple works well, since these characters echo each other, and if you commit a good actor to it, such a triple gives you three good performances for the price of one.

It is the play that is important, rather than the audience's recognition of individual actors. They want to respond to a stream of events, ideas, and emotional outcries, as if they were actuality. As soon as the audience thinks "actor," they jeopardize the possibility of immersion in the event.

Ask any number of actors, and they'll tell you they want to be completely hidden in their doubles. Or they want to be recognized in one role and hidden in the others.

That wonderful *Hamlet* triple calls first for a month-dead corpse, next a mature, flamboyant professional leading actor, and finally a grubby old workingman. If the roles are, indeed, thematically connected, then having one actor play all three characters helps that connection, but the actor's ego and the play itself are best served if the audience *doesn't* recognize him, if they just watch the scenes unfold. And, as a bonus, there is just enough time to change costumes and make-up, the corpse make-up taking the longest to apply and then remove.

Plays

In Shakespeare's day, plays were considered lesser literature than poetry or essays, and there was no copyright protection until a play was published. The stock company, rather than the playwright, owned the work. If one company had a smash box office hit, there was no legal protection against another company producing the same play across town, if they could get their hands on a working script. There was but one copy of the script, the stage manager's prompt script, which was kept under guard as well as lock and key. Actors were not given full scripts, but rather "sides," scrolls of minimal cue words and their individual speeches, which enabled them to learn lines quickly. Frequently, however, an actor did not experience the entire play until his first run-through, which often did not happen until only a few hours before the first performance.

It's generally agreed that Shakespeare wrote all or most of 38 plays. If he didn't write them, then somebody with the same name did. Or somebody masquerading as him did. The question of who "Shakespeare" actually was is the subject of endless debate, an industry within the vast Shakespeare industry. But this book is not about the authorship dispute.

About half of the Shakespeare plays were printed in "Quarto" during his lifetime. The other half might have been lost to posterity had not three of his colleagues, John Heminge, Henry Condell, and Richard Burbage, collected them and published the First Folio of 1623 (36 plays). Two other plays, *Pericles, Prince of Tyre*, a collaboration with George Wilkins, and *The Two Noble Kinsmen*, a collaboration with John Fletcher, surfaced a few years later.

Over the last four centuries, the actors who have played them, the scholars who have taught them, and the audiences who have enjoyed them, have kept the Shakespeare plays alive. Since Master Will first appeared on the scene, there's scarcely been a time when his plays have been out of the public eye. Shakespeare is the first ten of the world's greatest playwrights. Even those notable chauvinists, the French, declare him to be superior to Molière in comedy and to Racine in tragedy.

Why are we still producing Shakespeare's plays in the 21st century? If you have to ask, why are you reading this book?

The Playhouses

Almost every time I go to the theatre, I'm distracted by how the theatre plant, the space itself, hurts the play. The Globe, Blackfriars, the Rose, and the other Elizabethan playhouses were happy accidents. The inn yards were logical places to do plays, and the playhouses were designed like the inn yards. Initially, touring actors would select a plot of ground, mark out a playing area, and begin a pre-show, which evolved into performance. The audience would gather and surround the action, sitting or standing in circles or semi-circles on the grass. There's no need to go back to your high school geometry book to imagine the validity of the circle as a theatrical form: effectiveness depends on the range of the human eye and ear, as well as the limitations of the actor's voice. In inclement weather, actors would perform in a guildhall or the great hall of a manor. Shakespeare's company often performed at court before the queen or king and select courtiers or foreign dignitaries. Eventually, the Globe and Blackfriars, Shakespeare's theatres, were built.

Elizabethan playhouses served their plays and audiences because of their overall structure, which brought the action close to the greatest number of spectators. A completely accurate reproduction of the Globe built today in an American city would be closed down by the fire marshal.

Shakespeare's playhouses had one significant advantage over today's theatres, indoors and out: the King's Men performed in a much quieter world than we do, as any actor who has ever performed in a New York City park can verify. Burbage's actors did not have to contend with police, ambulance and fire sirens, diesel engines, foghorns, motorcycles, jet planes, helicopters, boom boxes, truck horns, and all manner of mechanical amplification. Because of all this outside noise, today's playhouses must be heavily insulated, and sound designers are needed to create artificial environments to replace what has been lost.

By the very nature of their architecture, the ornate Globe and Blackfriars stages were best suited to interior settings. The Boar's Head tavern scenes are well served, but how about the battlefield at Shrewsbury or Lear's heath? Win some, lose some. The open roof of the Globe was an advantage when the actual weather matched the weather in the play, but a night scene or a storm at the afternoon performances of the time depended, actually over-depended, on the skill of the actors and the coerced imagination of the audience.

I suggest that Shakespeare's plays can be acted almost anywhere. The primary, if not the only, requirement is space: the graveyard scene in *Hamlet* cannot be played on a dime, and there must be room for the audience to sit or stand: otherwise, the performance is but a rehearsal. As many seat-of-the-pants touring companies have demonstrated, performances can happen almost anywhere with but a minimal adjustment in the staging. On the other hand, too large a space, creating too great a distance from performer to audience, will diminish the experience until that point at which the auditor can no longer discern the face nor hear the voice of the actor. The next time you go to see Shakespeare-in-the-Park — any park, there are dozens of them — note the difference in behavior between patrons who sit up as close as possible and those the farthest away.

Plays were performed without intermission. Scenery was non-existent to minimal, although costumes, wigs, beards, weapons, props, and generic furniture, often borrowed on the day of performance, enhanced performances. When Charles II was restored to the throne, he brought back with him the new French scenery, and scenery has influenced, enhanced, and damaged every theatre experience since then. There was a battery of technical effects available, primitive, but effective. Storms in *Pericles, King Lear* and *The Tempest*, for example, were accomplished with minimal sound effects and acting, always the acting; much of the great storm in *King Lear* depends on the ability of the actors to create and sustain the illusion of wet, cold misery.

Over many years I have learned a lot from the simplicity of staging in Shakespeare's day, significantly that stopping to change scenery weakens, and can even destroy the performance. Many problems in the Shakespeare plays can be, must be, solved without scenery, which is the most expensive, cumbersome, and time consuming of the modern tools available to a director and should be used with great caution. In *Measure for Measure,* the prison can be suggested with a few prisoners in rags and manacles who can come and go in no time at all, while the convent materializes with a church bell sounding in the distance and a silent procession of nuns. The Apothecary in *Romeo and Juliet* creates his own shop with a chemist's smock and a few vials of potions hidden on his person. Armed, uniformed soldiers give us an army camp or a castle under siege; mariners on watch conjure a ship at sea. A few books and a candle can bring us into a study late at night. The major problem with scenery in Shakespeare is getting rid of it when it's not needed. Juliet's balcony is very important for two scenes, II.2 and III.5, some ten percent of the play. The rest of the time it's intrusive and distracting.

Trap doors, large enough to hold a corpse on a bier, and constructed to disappear quickly when closed, can solve many staging problems.

Note that I do not suggest projections or elaborate sound and lighting effects. Today, as in Shakespeare's time, most of the best solutions are simple, mechanical, not reliant on modern technology, which has a way of breaking down during the run of a play.

We are overwhelmed today with ever multiplying modes of communication: land lines, cell phones, text messaging, e-mail, CDs, DVDs, Twitter, Facebook, YouTube, cinema technology that can create prehistoric monsters as well as armies of virtual warriors. My accountant is in Bangalore, my bank is somewhere in cyberspace, and I never even met my identity thief who picked my pocket in Huntington, New York, even though I hadn't been there in 30 years. None of this happens face to face. We are moles before blinking consoles.

And yet, despite all of these technical marvels, we do plays today just as the first actors did thousands of years ago, back before Homer, back before literature, back before written language. The first play was probably a retelling of a dangerous hunt with a kibitzer on the side adding comic commentary. The first song was a love song. There's no such thing as acting style. There's life, and there's death. The theatre works, when it works, because the uninhibited observer, the auditor, recognizes on the stage behavior that elicits an emotional response.

What does a play by Shakespeare offer? The performance is life-sized, immediate, and reciprocal. If the producer can resist the use of amplification — "sound enhancement" is the euphemism — a play is as close to "real," to actual human experience, as can be imagined.

Today, there are many attempts at reproductions of the Elizabethan/Jacobean Playhouses all over the world and at least one American reproduction of the Blackfriars, in Staunton, Virginia. Many of the Globe copies lack authenticity because of contemporary fire laws, building codes, disability access statutes. Others miss the point of the Elizabethan playhouse altogether by constructing an outdoor replica of the Globe stage alone, without the surrounding architecture, or by adapting the stage to fit an existing proscenium theatre.

Do we really serve Shakespeare best when we demand an authenticity of playhouse as well as a loyalty to Elizabethan performance practices? How many of those practices were the result of limitations and compromises dictated by the playhouses themselves?

To define the work of Elizabethan/Jacobean acting companies in terms of the Globe, the Curtain, the Rose, and the Blackfriars is equivalent to defining today's theatre in terms of Broadway. Theatre exists anywhere that Peter Brook's "empty space" can be found, where audience and actors can interact. Theatre existed for centuries before the celebrated Elizabethan playhouses were introduced in the 1580s. These playhouses achieved great public acclaim, but perhaps it is more than they deserve. The most important people in the theatre are playwrights and actors. A great play can elevate a mediocre actor, and a talented actor can make a bad play better.

Actors

It is easy to determine the talents of musicians, dancers, and singers: listen to them, watch them. The talent of the actor is more elusive. Who's a good Shakespearean actor? The primary attributes of the actor are believability and passion. The late Davey Marlin-Jones, long-time friend and one of the most talented American directors of the last 60 years, in evaluating actors, always began with the question: "How's his *soul*?" He wanted actors with passion, the ability to feel, the capacity to be moved, to tell the emotional truth of the text.

You can't always tell that in an audition, especially if it is held (as many are) under pressure from the clock. Some good actors don't audition well, because auditions are, by definition, phony. Auditioning is taught as a skill separate from acting. An actor will use audition technique to con the director into hiring him. Many directors hire the second-best candidate for the role; the best actors frighten them, because the directors are frightened to begin with, frightened of failing as well as succeeding in breaking the bad acting mold.

The best actor is also the most believable. If you don't believe that the actor in performance is a living, breathing, feeling, many-faceted being, gasping for breath, fighting his/her way out of a dilemma, then the performance doesn't work. Bad actors don't behave like human beings; the great performances have all been impersonations of possible human beings. Consider Charles Laughton's Quasimodo or Laurence Olivier's Othello or Marlon Brando's Terry Molloy or Anne Bancroft's Annie Sullivan. Possible, but improbable.

The biggest recurring problem the Shakespearean actor faces is to make believable the heightened realities of these poetic texts. A good Shakespearean actor is greater than the sum of his/her attributes. He must have a loud, supple, articulate voice, an athletic body, a strong musicality, and the ability to fight, dance, wrestle, and fence. That's a lot of skills, requiring years of serious, expensive study, for which the actor is usually rewarded with little glory and even less money.

Shakespearean actors act "on the line," meaning that the emotion drives the speech. It's not always natural, but a talented actor learns to do it, and it saves a lot of time. In films, where the director hollers "Action!," the actor can take the time to find the emotion before—or after—she speaks, knowing that if a tight cue is desired, it can be achieved in the editing room. In live Shakespeare performance, acting on the line is an essential. Pauses are expensive in these big, often lengthy, plays.

While Elizabethan blue laws forbade women performing in plays, the laws made little sense, because women were allowed to perform in masques, pageants, and musical interludes. Today, obviously, this is not the case—we improve on the original productions by casting women in the women's roles. Women play women better than men do. We lose a little inside humor in the "trouser" roles, but we gain far more than we lose.

I directed an actor as Coriolanus a few years back who would have impressed 99 percent of the directors in America. He was handsome, strong, athletic, good voice, loud, good anger, made the words work, good fighter, a dedicated First Folio aficionado, but the guy just wasn't an actor. He blocked all feelings, incoming and outgoing. He didn't "take direction" either, but there are many good actors who don't take direction. When a director can't connect with an actor, the director should simply let him do his own thing, and proceed with directing everyone else in the play.

I have always resented producers who hire British directors for American Shakespeare productions out of some misguided notion of British superiority, especially when they try to impose British dialects as "proper speech." Imposed dialects usually fail, because the imposition comes too late in the process and effectively inhibits the actors' emotional spontaneity. The imposed sound is phony and restricting, resulting in an unhappy acting company. The best speech for Shakespeare is that which is most understandable to the audience — American dialects or speech that is as dialect-free as possible makes performances clear and accessible.

Casting

Casting is 85 percent of direction. The director must be the one single person who makes all the casting decisions. He must be right, must ponder, pray to be right. Though the theatre itself is a collaborative art, casting is not. To take this a step further, the director must be empowered to direct, not only the actors, but the production staff as well. The director can't be a tantrum-prone infant or a tyrant although it is essential that he be the captain of the ship.

Those times I felt I failed in directing plays were those instances when I had the wrong people handed to me: I once accepted a job directing *Death of a Salesman* after the original director had been fired/quit. I was handed everybody, including the designers. After the first three days of rehearsal, I told the producers that their Linda was incapable of making the role work, and the set designer was not a designer, but a carpenter. When they replied that neither could be replaced for political reasons, I again insisted that either or both of them was capable of destroying the production, but I was willing to go ahead, as long as my objections were duly noted.

Unfortunately, after the fact, it doesn't help to say, "I told you so." Directors shouldn't invent excuses to justify failures; as the director, he must be willing to fight against conflicting interests. As soon as I'm offered a job, I want to know what strings are attached, including any commitments already made to actors and designers. I reiterate my belief that casting is at least 85 percent of direction, and, further, that a director cannot direct the production he envisions without the power and privilege of casting the play, unencumbered by the opinions of others. The director may be civil, respectful, but not submissive.

Good directors cast well. Occasionally a director will miscast an actor, who may turn in a splendid performance but one that still doesn't work. Whose fault is that? Blame it on everyone: the playwright, the producer, the actor, the actors' parents and teachers, but still accept responsibility. The performance that comes closest to what the playwright envisioned is the result of the right actor in the right role.

Casting to the Text

I attended a lecture/Q and A with Edward Albee, produced by my younger son, Timothy, in 2005. Albee had an important piece of advice for playwrights: write your character descriptions carefully and specifically into the stage directions of your play or into the body of the text. His advice to directors: pay attention to what the playwright says about the character when you're casting.

My conviction that the director's primary obligation is to fulfill the playwright's intention fits neatly with Mr. Albee's advice. Especially in the casting. What does Shakespeare say about casting? What hints has Master Will given us about the people in his plays? In the cast list and text of each play, he may specify not only the characters' gender and age, but also nationality, parentage, occupation, even religious conviction. We are often given explicit and implicit details of complexion, height, weight, athleticism, sexual orientation. Some references are subtle, but many are blatant. For instance, Viola and Sebastian are super-identical twins. Is that such a big deal? What could be bigger?

Even more important are the families. Family members look like each other, combining facial characteristics, skin and hair color, physicality. Reinforcing these biological relationships in the casting and supporting them with wigs, facial hair, etc. helps clarify the text. Costumers should always group families, color-coding or otherwise distinguishing them for the audience — this is especially important in *Romeo and Juliet, King Lear, Macbeth*, and the history plays. The more information that can be conveyed visually, the more liberated the text.

We all recognize and value family resemblance and have since the beginning of time. King Lear has three daughters, and the Earl of Gloucester has two sons. Some directors like to play games with the possibility that Lear might have had several wives, and we know that Edgar and Edmund have different mothers. What is *essential* is that the audience accepts that Lear and Gloucester are both fathers.

Age is important if the Playwright specifies it. According to the Gravedigger's arithmetic, Hamlet turns 30 on the day of his death. Horatio, Rosencrantz, and Guildenstern are his contemporaries, though Laertes can be younger, and Ophelia younger still. Gertrude should be no older than 44; King Hamlet I, the father, is older than his brother, Claudius.

In the history plays, we can research the appearances and historical ages of the characters, but Shakespeare was writing plays, not actual history. When he alters ages, he does so for a dramatic purpose. Hotspur was actually closer to the age of Henry IV when he died than to the age of young Prince Hal. Shakespeare juxtaposes the deaths of Joan of Arc and John Talbot for dramatic purposes. Peter Saccio's book *Shakespeare's English Kings* does a splendid job reconciling historic and dramatic differences.

The text, the lines themselves, often give us detailed physical descriptions. Falstaff is old and fat, Shallow is old and skinny, Sylvia is more beautiful than Julia, Hermia is a short brunette, while Helena is a tall blond. We search for the hints, moving from the specific to the implied. Certainly, physical beauty is important, though not to the extreme that the camera close-up demands; physical capacity is more important. Shakespeare's men had to be able to dance, fight, wrestle, fence. The director hires physical cowards at his peril.

The Playwright informs the director, and the director casts to the Playwright's intent.

I could tell many war stories about the multitudes that descend with ideas, pleas and opinions every time I begin to cast a play. A wise director will consider every suggestion, then retire to his monastic cell to pray and to make the final selection. Any other method courts disaster. I directed two plays for a major Shakespeare Festival where casting was influenced by other directors of the rep, the production staff, favors owed to the faithful, Equity rules, and the ubiquitous stingy budgets, all of which forced compromises. Eventually I just had to lock myself up with the pictures and resumes, shut out everyone's voice except Shakespeare's, then fight for the choices I felt were correct.

Does the director always get the cast he wants? Seldom, but it's important that the compromises and second choices are solely and completely those of the director. Again, my primary artistic responsibility, even my moral responsibility, is to the playwright. If I don't like the play, I have the right to refuse the assignment, but if I do accept it — this is my life and my living, after all — I have to respect the playwright and the actor as the primary artists of the theatre and I must facilitate the process that allows them to fulfill each other. It's my responsibility to protect that aesthetic from what might corrupt it. When I insist on autonomy in casting, I'm not just a nasty little kid demanding his own way: I'm arguing in defense of the playwright's intentions.

If I'm doing a new play with a live author, that's an easier collaboration. If I respect the play, and the playwright believes in my ability to give it the best possible production, then we'll agree on casting. We'll fight it out until we agree.

Directors and Rehearsal

Our Playwright directed plays before there was such a thing as a director — Elizabethan plays were staged the way plays have been staged since antiquity. To be more accurate, it could be said that the plays staged themselves. Movements, kinesics, followed the intuitive rules of human behavior. Kings sat, subjects kneeled, threats were made out of striking distance, lovers embraced, anger escalated to violence. Characters spoke directly to the audience in soliloquy. Occasionally the audience answered back.

That which we call a director today is a relatively recent innovation, a legacy from films. Directors can't be auditioned. You have to see their work. If a performance has left you exhausted and breathless, if no trace of the director has been seen, if the experience felt like a seamless hunk of humanity that just seemed to have happened, then you've just experienced the work of a talented director.

I began directing professionally in 1955 and directed my first Shakespeare play in 1958. Over time, my work as a director has evolved, just as a chemist's work evolves when he analyzes physical and chemical changes. Through a succession of professional productions over a number of years, I've tested my theories, discarded those that didn't work, retested those that proved serviceable, and eventually boiled my rules down until, I believe, only the viable ones were left: keep the action flowing at a pace of 18 to 20 lines per minute, take no breaks between scenes, rely on doubling actors, costumes, props, sound and lights rather than elaborate scenery. I prefer to work in a thrust stage configuration, the audience surrounding the actors in a 216-degree semi-circle. I wouldn't say there's only one way to produce a Shakespeare play — I've been accused of such a stand — but there are precious few ways that maintain the integrity of the Playwright's intent.

The process of play production that begins months before opening is actually two processes: one (the actor's process) is organic, like the growing of a garden. The second (the designer's) is architectural and mechanical in form, like building a house. Both emerge from the text: characters are identified, necessities are defined, scenery, furniture, properties, costumes, sound, light effects created, the simpler the better.

Schedules that respect progressive dependencies could improve most productions. Designers must wait upon directorial decisions, and seamstresses and carpenters must wait upon designers.

Here's where the scholar, the dramaturg, and the director become interdependent, because technology has changed radically in the last 400 years, as have a multitude of customs. What salvages the plays, the practitioners, and the audience alike is the fact that the human condition itself has changed but little in the last 400 years. Indeed, biologically, we are very much the same as we were 100,000 years ago. It follows that the proper approach to Shakespeare production might be one that maintains an awareness of the emotional similarities and differences between his characters and our actors, as well as attitudinal differences between the Elizabethan/Jacobean audience and ours.

After I've decided on the text, even while editing, I start a list of what the play demands. Line by line. It sounds tedious, but it isn't — it's fun. The notes are voluminous at the beginning and then thin out as I get further and further into the play. Research begins. Articulating what I know about the text reveals what I don't know. I must then find answers. Some plays require a lot of research, some a little.

People often wonder what a director does. The answer is ephemeral and sounds evasive. The director's primary function is to make it possible for the actors to respond to the text of the play. In the best of situations, the director just has to provide a safe place for rehearsal and allow it to happen. And the first and last objective of a director is to do whatever he must to get the play on: teach acting technique, build the set, explain meanings, play psychiatrist, coach the football team, romance the leading lady, solve everybody's problems. Compassion is necessary for people who need help. Directing a play, however, requires that the play itself be the primary objective. The production as a whole has to be more important than individual problems or agendas.

Early in the process, the producer and the director must agree on the necessities; budgets must be imposed, and schedules set. Designers and a composer are hired. Casting begins with known actors, and is completed with auditions for new talent. The building of technical elements begins, then rehearsals, with the opening performance a light at the end of the tunnel.

Directors are the most dangerous people in the theatre, especially when their "concepts" ignore or take precedence over the playwright's intent. Scenic designers are the next most dangerous people, especially if the directors are permissive. A director has to learn to say to the designers, "No, we don't need that." The operable word is "need." Complicated designs that distract from the text and demand an elaborate tech always steal precious time (and money) the week before opening, the very time when the actors have to complete the organic growth that will result in a fulfilled performance.

The director's first responsibility is to the playwright — external politics and current fashions out of the process. I'm always amazed when directors go against a playwright's objectives, or worse, try to "fix" the play. If a director doesn't like what the play says, he should turn down the job. How can you serve a playwright if you hate the play?

Editing? If one were going to edit the Sistine Chapel, which of those heavenly little cherubs would be brushed out? What hubris for the director to judge some of Shakespeare's lines important and others expendable! Rather, it's the director's job to make the entire text work, every stage direction work — to stay out of the way of the magic reciprocity between the script and the actor. Many Shakespeare productions are damaged, made unintelligible by clock-conscious directors who cut lines simply because they don't understand them or they don't fit their "concepts." Such directors should be denied access to the works of any playwright not around to challenge them.

But Shakespeare has been dead for nearly 400 years. How do we determine his intentions, his vision of his characters?

In rehearsal, actors and directors define for themselves the action of the plot and identify its elements. Collectively, they define the back-story of each play — what happened before the first scene. As the play progresses, the actors reveal plot points, almost accidentally. Actors need not telegraph the action, hint at it in advance; Shakespeare doesn't telegraph: he plants dramatic possibility early in the plot, and he unfolds action as it happens.

Over the years I've evolved a method for planning rehearsals that has served me well. I begin by determining how many rehearsal hours I can squeeze out under maximum positive conditions, then I divide those hours by five to arrive at a gross rehearsal schedule. I spend the first fifth on the text, the next three-fifths on the evolution of the staging, and the final fifth on tech and dress rehearsals.

Notice that I use the term "evolution of the staging." If we've solved most of the actors' problems in text rehearsals, then the staging comes easily. Text rehearsals (lines being read only, scripts in hand, no movement) are conducted with everyone in a circle, no tables, no separation between actors, directors, and designers.

Is that the only way to do it? Most directors don't spend that much time on text, but as an actor I know I'm in trouble if the director starts blocking at the first rehearsal. I characterize the above method, the whole six months of it, as "organic." The production is allowed to grow.

Every play I've directed involved some 300 hours of preparation, rehearsal, and notes during early performances. Multiply that by the 74 professional Shakespeare productions I've directed, as well as all the plays in which I've performed or staged fights, and you can visualize a mountain of (forgive me!) information and experience. That's my scholarship. It's cumulative, reactionary, biased, but it's informed.

The director's prayer is similar to that of the drunkard: "God, help me to fix the fixable, to leave alone that which will fix itself, to endure the unfixable, and to know the difference among them."

The Virginity of the Audience

At the NJSF we had an excellent madrigal group, directed by Deborah Martin, who would entertain every evening on the lawn in front of the theatre, beginning 20 minutes to curtain time. At five minutes, the Festival Madrigals would enter the theatre and sing a final number or two on-stage. At the stage manager's signal, their concert would end and the play would begin. With some plays, e.g. *The Winter's Tale* and *Twelfth Night*, the final madrigal song would serve as an overture. Beside their aesthetic musical value, the purpose of the madrigals was to relax the minds of the audience and allow them to enter gently into the world of the play. The acclimatization began as soon as they entered the parking lot, and it was continuous. We made no obnoxious pre-show announcements or fund-raising pitches from the stage, before or after the performance.

A director must approach every play with the assumption that the audience has never seen or read it before. As the performance goes along, clarity is essential: the audience must be given all the information they need to understand and emotionally realize the play. The play must be revealed to the audience, word by word, as the playwright wrote it, a linear progression. Ambiguities must be maintained as must the possibility of surprise. Some plays begin with silence, some with music, ambient sounds, winds, waves, the sound of a city at night. Latecomers, by the way, should be penalized. Anyone not in attendance at the beginning of the play risks confusion.

Putting a synopsis of the play into the program is like admitting failure to provide clarity. I've had many fights with educators who argue that the kids need preparation before seeing a play. If they need preparation, let them study another play by the same playwright, not the play they're coming to see. Allow them discovery, the delight of surprise.

One of my happiest memories is a matinee performance of the John Gielgud/Richard Burton *Hamlet* in New York some 40 years ago, packed with high school students. They were noisy, but attentive. More distracting than the teenagers were the teachers attempting to shush them. In IV.7, the long conspiracy scene between Claudius and Laertes is interrupted by Gertrude's entrance and her lament, "Your sister's drowned, Laertes." A young girl right behind me gasped and whispered, "Oh, she died." How wonderful to be present at her moment of realization, to hear her shock at that beautiful, awful moment!

Simplification or translation of poetic language is also a cop-out — if the actor knows what he is saying, and if he's a good actor, the audience will understand. Today's educators bemoan the difficulties that today's students have with language. Today's kids learn to talk from watching television reality shows and some manage to arrive at high school graduation with a vocabulary of barely a thousand words and a hundred clichés, "...like, wow, you know, and he went, and, like, oh my God, I went...." Actors, of course, are all students before they become actors. Directors must remind themselves at the beginning of each rehearsal period how the language has evolved over the last 400 years. Translations, paraphrases, may be valuable in rehearsal to enable understanding, and a good glossary can save many rehearsal hours, but the integrity of Shakespeare's text must be respected and maintained.

What else has changed since the Chamberlain's Men first did the plays? Technology, of course. As I stated earlier, the world is much noisier. Our religions and politics have changed subtly. Many contemporary biographers and scholars of Shakespeare have written about his works from a modern perspective, and have worked to elucidate the moral, ethical and cultural points of view the Elizabethan audience brought to the plays. Primogeniture, the providential theory of history, divine right, social hierarchy, parental matchmaking, private ownership, all must be examined. I will tackle similarities and differences as we go along, as they pertain to individual plays.

CHAPTER 2

The Taming of the Shrew

The first Shakespeare play I ever directed was *The Taming of the Shrew*, at the Keweenaw Playhouse in Calumet, Michigan, in July 1958. I initially wanted to be a scholar, but Leo Kirschbaum pushed me into the theatre, and I began acting in the fall of 1950, directing a few years later. I was fortunate to become a member of the Oregon Shakespeare Festival company in 1951; the four plays in repertory I did for Angus Bowmer, founder and director of the Festival, taught me an ethic of playing Shakespeare: naturalistically, but with a bright pace, good diction, uncut, with a healthy respect/disrespect for the text. This company was made up of the best Shakespeare actors in America; there was only one other such company, in San Diego. Angus and his troupe were not Bardolators: they were good actors devoted to live theatre.

I had directed Cole Porter's *Kiss Me, Kate* at Guy Little's theatre in Sullivan, Illinois, in the summer of 1957. In that wonderful, brutal season — nine musicals in nine weeks!— I was hired as a performer, but ended up directing four of the shows, a gift, a blessing, an opportunity that I seized, squeezed, and exploited. That summer convinced me I was capable of producing/directing on my own.

The 1958 Keweenaw Playhouse season was my first as a solo producer: ten plays in ten weeks with *The Taming of the Shrew* in the middle, which now seems absurd, impossible. I played Christopher Sly and directed the play in a traditional Italian Renaissance setting. There was not much thought or planning behind the production. The actors had signed on for the whole season, we were five plays into it, and nobody was ready to play Shakespeare. We relied on intuition and our collective ability to go without sleep. There were two good Shakespeareans in the company, Addyse Laine as Kate and Frank Nastasi (later to delight a generation of youngsters as Soupy Sales' comic sidekick) as Grumio; but the rest were journeymen stock performers. Subtlety and polish be damned, we plunged in and had fun with it, playing what was there, discovering much, then going on to the next production. In one-a-week stock, you're always playing one show, rehearsing the next, planning the one after that, and trying to forget those you've already done.

Over the next 30 years I directed four more productions of *The Taming of the Shrew*, one in Boston, and three in New Jersey, as well as a second production of *Kiss Me, Kate* in Rochester, New York, in 1958.

I'll begin with a few simple, obvious principles. *The Taming of the Shrew* is a play within a play that could be retitled *The Education of Christopher Sly*. Many who think they know *The Shrew* forget, or have never seen, this framework story because it is so often cut. The story is about a drunken tinker who is thrown out of a tavern and passes out in the street. A nobleman, returning from hunting, carries him home and contrives an elaborate hoax: Sly is told he's a noble lord who has just awakened from a coma, in which he dreamed he was a tinker. To entertain the restored Lord Sly, a troupe of traveling players is hired to perform the comedy of the wooing of Katherine by Petruchio.

The framework play takes place where the audience has gathered, the traveling players perform in English, and the play-within-the-play is set in Padua, Renaissance Italy. Ostensibly, the characters are speaking Italian, but the audience hears English.

The Taming of the Shrew follows the basic rules that differentiate comedies from tragedies. In comedies, nobody dies, the lovers are favored, even blessed, and in the end beautiful people go off to bed to make beautiful babies. The monogamous ideal is assumed from the moment the lovers meet. What is essential to make *The Taming of the Shrew* work? First of all, the Christopher Sly framework must be maintained so that the audience never forgets that they're watching a play. The director must be willing to commit one of the best actors in the company to the role of Sly and keep him on-stage throughout the entire evening. Sly is a first time theatergoer. He's never seen a play before, and he knows nothing of good manners, which can be inhibiting. Sly comments, even intrudes, on the action, eats and drinks when the characters eat and drink; the presence of Sly keeps the proceedings light and comic. The best Sly I ever saw was Christopher Lloyd, who did six seasons for me in the mid–1960s — he is a comic genius. If the comedy is performed straight ahead, it's a wonderful, funny, sexy evening.

Next, the play, obviously, requires a pair of attractive mature lovers for Katherine and Petruchio and another pair of attractive younger lovers for Bianca and Lucentio. Risking redundancy, I repeat: this is a love story. All four lovers fall in love at first sight, and the rest of the play is a classic "boys meet girls, boys lose girls, boys get girls back," leading eventually to marriage.

What complicates the story, and how have mores changed since the play was first written? I submit that the modern feminist spin which rejects this play as misogynistic, even cruel, the reduction of women to chattel, only confuses the issue and diminishes the humor.

In Shakespeare's time, fathers arranged the marriages of their daughters, negotiating with the father of the prospective bridegroom or with the bridegroom himself. If the bride's father was dead, his brother or occasionally his widow would assume this responsibility. This protocol is an important plot point in a number of the plays: even if it is not an obvious plot element, it's still there, just below the surface, influencing, if not controlling, events.

The Taming of the Shrew, **New Jersey Shakespeare Festival, 1987: Madylon Brans as Kate, Jonathan Smoots as Petruchio (photograph by Jim DelGiudice).**

Fathers preferred husbands who would improve or at least preserve the social and financial status of both families. Dowries were important. Marriages often joined two pieces of adjacent property. A compassionate father might not force his daughter into a marriage that frightened or repulsed her, but he'd certainly discourage a love match that he considered doomed. This was not just a medieval British custom — it went back several thousand years, and it still exists today in many of the world's cultures. It's significant that so many romantic plays, poems, and eventually novels, involve daughters outwitting fathers to marry the man they choose.

A related ancient custom figuring prominently in many of Shakespeare's plays is primogeniture, which held that a married man "owned" everything in his home, including his wife and children, and when he died, all of his possessions passed to his first-born son, who then became the head of the household. If the first-born son was underage, he'd still inherit, but the law would appoint a protector to manage his estate until he reached maturity. Daughters did not inherit, nor did widows, but common law assured that they and their children would be cared for all the rest of their lives. If a first-born son died before his father, then the first-born son of that first-born would become the heir apparent. If the first-born son died without a male heir, then his eldest brother would inherit.

There are two primary families in *The Taming of the Shrew:* Vincentio of Pisa and his son, Lucentio; and Baptista Minola and his two daughters, Katherine and Bianca. The younger daughter, Bianca, has a horde of suitors, but Baptista will entertain none of them until he has a husband for the elder, Katherine. Lucentio comes to Padua to study at the university. Petruchio, heir to his recently deceased father, a wealthy man of Verona, comes to Padua to find a wife. All these characters are members of the same socio-economic merchant class, northern Italians, Christians. Shakespeare eliminates extraneous possible conflicts, early in the play-within-the-play, which makes it easier to tie up loose ends at the conclusion.

Lucentio and Bianca are the first to fall in love, at I.1.50, the first entrance of Baptista and his daughters. After Baptista and Petruchio agree that a marriage to Katherine may be possible and negotiate precise marriage terms, dowry, rights of inheritance, all the financial contractual matters, Baptista exits. Petruchio is left to describe for the audience, precisely and minutely, how he will woo Katherine, charming her with all the tricks of courtly love. Then Katherine enters, the ground shakes, and love at first sight, the phenomenon the Italians call "il Fulmine," the thunderbolt, strikes, and the crux of the play is at hand. Note that we are 43 percent of the way into the play-within-the-play. From here on, husband and wife merely do what every husband and wife have to do: work out the details.

This wooing scene is an actor buster. I've seen it played like a wrestling smack down, like a gymnastic event, like a karate match, but it's a wooing scene, for God's sake, a battle of wits between lovers, and all of the physical contact is precisely defined by the Playwright. Some of the verbal duel is witty, and some of it is juvenile, but it's verbal sparring, not physical, which is funnier anyway.

There are threats, maybe some test jabs, and Katherine tries to leave the stage several times. I think Petruchio gooses her at II.1.240, and she swings at him in retaliation, but he ducks. She slaps him where the stage direction indicates, II.1.248, but he doesn't hit her back. He grabs her and restrains her at II.1.271, but he doesn't hurt her. She breaks out of his grasp and kicks him in the shin at II.1.283, but he's wearing boots, and the kick hurts her slippered foot more than it hurts his shin, thus giving credence to the lines about limping. She tries to leave again at II.1.298, and a roundhouse swing would not be inappropriate for her, but again, he ducks and again, he restrains her. The effect of such front-to-front body contact is sexual, not violent. If he pins her arms, she can struggle, but she can't escape, and she can't strike him. The more she struggles, the sexier the embrace becomes. He only releases her at II.1.312.

A director who adds more violence runs the risk of turning Petruchio into a bully or worse. Petruchio's object is sexual conquest, not bodily injury. He's not a sadist or a rapist: he's an eligible bachelor wooing a spirited young woman, and they have a few kinks to work out, but they are a perfect match. They do, indeed, kiss at II.1.364, and the love match is made. The best Kate and Petruchio I ever saw were Madylon Brans and Jonathan Smoots, NJSF 1987, who beautifully realized Shakespeare's ending as a happy couple who have found each other on their own individual terms.

Aside from the dueling lovers, *Shrew* is rich in character opportunities. It is fascinating to see how each minor role, modestly serving the plot in one production, can suddenly leap to prominence in another: Grumio, Tranio, Hortensio, Gremio, Biondello, the Tailor, the Haberdasher, the Pedant. In my 1963 production, Ron Coralian played the Pedant as an octogenarian with not a single organ in working order. He was so hilarious that we used the same characterization in subsequent productions of *Shrew* and other plays right through the title role in *Volpone* in 1980.

What's funny in Shakespeare? The best comedy is the most realistic. Charlie Chaplin's Tramp was a homeless guy who survived against all odds. We laughed at him, rooted for him, and loved him.

Funny is that which elicits laughter. Any subject is fair game: life, love, birth, death, religion, war, honor. The entirety of human experience may be tragic, comic or both, in the hands of a master storyteller. *Hamlet*, a tragedy, has some of the best line comedy in the Canon, and *The Comedy of Errors*, a comedy, some of the worst. *Henry V,* a history, has more bawdy lines than any other Shakespeare play, even more than *A Midsummer Night's Dream*, which is certainly the sexiest play. When I studied with Leo Kirschbaum, in the early 1950s, he told me you had to have a dirty mind to be a good Shakespearean. Wouldn't help? Wouldn't hurt!

All bodily functions are potentially funny. Sex is especially funny, big penis/little penis jokes abound in the Greek comedies, and our Playwright took example from the Greeks. "Petruchio" is the English spelling of the Italian "Petruccio," which is why most actors mispronounce the name. In Italian, "ch" takes a "k" sound, while "cc" is pronounced "ch." Petruchio means "big Peter," and it's a phallic joke, just as is "Benedick." Shakespeare locates 13 of his plays, all or in part, in Italy and two more in Sicily, employing a multitude of Italian names and nicknames, as well as some English translations. I believe the Latin or Italian pronunciations should be used whenever possible. For instance, "Anthony" is the English spelling, "Antony" the Latin, "Antonio" the Italian.

The wooing dance can be especially funny, even with birds and animals. Courtship can be funny, but marriage doesn't seem to be. Shakespeare's sexual comedy is pretty straightforward, heterosexual. There are no gay jokes in Shakespeare. At least I haven't found any, although it's possible there are some buried in the ever-changing language. Venereal disease can be funny, but not its ravages. Adultery and jealousy are funny. Bestiality is funny.

Fat is funny, and skinny is funny. Tall and short are funny. Tall and short together constitute a sight gag, e.g. Sir Andrew and Sir Toby, a tradition carried on by Laurel and Hardy as well as Abbot and Costello.

Age is funnier than youth. Too little education is funny (Sly), and too much is funny (Holofernes). The misuse of language is funny: Dogberry and Mistress Quickly were spouting malapropisms long before Sheridan invented his character.

The French, Spanish, Germans, and Russians are funny. Irishmen, Welshmen, and

Scots are funny, but not after James I/VI became king of England. Social climbers (Malvolio) and hypocrites (Angelo) are funny. Drunkards are funny, and there's a shortage of reformers and prohibitionists.

Violence can be funny, if the recovery from it is quick. Charlie Chaplin falls down a flight of stairs and lies there for a split second. The audience holds its breath until Charlie gets to his feet, dusts himself off, and struts away. The house comes down. The same is true with Sir Andrew Aguecheek, the Porter, and the funny guys in *The Tempest*.

Animals are funny, notably the dog Crab in *Two Gentlemen of Verona*, the ass Bottom in *A Midsummer Night's Dream*, and the bear in *The Winter's Tale*. I like to add a lamb to *As You Like It*.

Food is funny, especially when used as a weapon. In *The Taming of the Shrew*, the action in IV.1 suggests a food fight. A sausage over the head is funny, but the pie in the face is surely the most effective sight gag of all time. Permit me to digress for a bit of instruction on the pie in the face: the audience must see the pie before the stunt, but the stunt cannot otherwise be telegraphed. It must be carried on-stage as part of a feast, and it must appear to be an eating pie. The pie must have substance and must be of the proper consistency: once it hits the face, it must not slide down the target's body too quickly. It should be colored for maximum contrast with the target's face and costume. The pie-thrower and the target must rehearse the stunt until the timing is perfected.

The pie-thrower must pick up the pie, as the target moves toward him. Most importantly, the pie must travel some distance — it cannot simply be slammed into the recipient's face from close range, though this is what usually happens. The greater the distance the pie travels in the air on the way to its target, the funnier, but not if accuracy is sacrificed. The pie must hit full in the face, and the recipient must then freeze, drowning in humiliation as the pie drips down his body. The greatest recipient I had was Charlie Peak in my 1963 production: nobody ever played the humiliation and subsequent resignation better.

If slapstick is the goal, the rubber chicken is funny: it's mandatory in some plays, but totally inappropriate in others.

Shakespeare also uses a poetic device for comic effect: the gentry speak in verse, but the servants speak in prose. The Playwright didn't invent this device, but he quickly became a master of it. As soon as Christopher Sly is convinced that he is a noble lord awakening from a coma, he begins speaking in verse.

Confusion, especially confusion of identity, is funny if the audience is in on the joke. There is a multiple-confusion scene in *Shrew*, V.1, involving several characters, where the comedy is so effective that the laughter is virtually non-stop. It's a volleyball game between actors and audience.

Disguises are funny, but the director must be careful not to presume too much on what Coleridge referred to as "the willful suspension of disbelief." The audience will go along with the gag, as long as the gag doesn't exceed the bounds of credibility.

Running gags, jokes that are repeated over the length of the play, are funny, but they demand no fewer than three repetitions.

The Taming of the Shrew can be a springboard, launching the actors into physical comedy, takes, slapstick, pratfalls, kicks. The Playwright was familiar with Italian commedia dell'arte forms, stock characters, and stock devices, suggesting frequent, often elaborate physical business. For instance, Frank Nastasi, as Grumio, would accompany Petruchio's epic boast at I.2.202 to 214 with elaborate mime and sound effects, playing a lion, the sea, an angry boar, cannons, thunder, trumpets, horses, finally a chestnut in a farmer's fire. This was very funny stuff, especially since Petruchio cooperated, the two actors feeding each other and allowing the audience's laughter to vary the tempo. Biondello's description of Petruchio and Grumio, III.2.46–73, was played at trip-hammer speed with a windmill of gestures, resolving in a faint and a drop to the floor.

But did the Playwright really need such embellishment? He might have been conversant with the elements of physical comedy, but did he need them? Are they necessary today? While *The Taming of the Shrew* was only his second comedy (seventh play), it was a significant improvement over *The Comedy of Errors*, with fewer sight gags and more situation humor, line comedy. For example, one of the biggest laughs in the play comes from an exchange between Petruchio and Baptista. Petruchio asks, "Pray, have you not a daughter called Katherina, fair and virtuous?" Baptista replies, "I have a daughter, sir, called Katherina," with no further elaboration. Because Katherine's character is so well established, all the director has to do is make sure the moment isn't clouded or too busy, and the audience will howl with laughter.

The wisest path to finding comedy is through the reality of the situation: play the text, drive the action along, and the audience will laugh at what they collectively think is funny. I'm not arguing for the elimination of physical comedy, but the audience is always drawn to recognizable human behavior, no matter how absurd. It's easier to identify with human beings than Punch and Judy puppets.

Is Katherine a difficult role to play? I've seen some wonderful actresses founder on the role, because they couldn't chart the progress from frustrated spinster to loving wife. Her final speech, the lengthy "Fie, fie, unknit that threatening unkind brow…" is another actor buster. It's a criticism directed at uncooperative wives, and if taken at face value, it's high praise of a happy marriage effected by a balance of power. If the director wants to go deeper into this final scene, he might discover that the wager among the three bridegrooms could be a conspiracy between Kate and Petruchio, a con job that entraps the other couples. What's Kate's objective? To win a substantial bet with her husband; if he wins the bet, she wins the bet too, and, as he has said earlier, their marriage is between the two of them, and why should they be concerned about the opinion of the rest of the world?

Can Kate's speech be played tongue in cheek? I've seen it done that way at auditions, but in the play nobody calls her on it, and no one interrupts the speech. It concludes with Kate kneeling down and offering to put her hand under her husband's foot. In rehearsals, the actress usually challenges both the director and Petruchio: "Put my hand under his foot? Are you nuts?" But he doesn't step on it: he picks her up, kisses her, and carries her off to bed. They're going to get along fine.

CHAPTER 3

A Midsummer Night's Dream

To become a member of the United Scenic Artists, the union representing scenic, costume, and lighting designers, one must pass a very tough exam. If I were administering it, I'd assign *A Midsummer Night's Dream*— sets, costumes, lights, sound, music — to all the applicants. The play offers infinite opportunities, and it's loaded with landmines. Design decisions that seem right and exciting at the beginning of the play can easily backfire later. The design team needs lots of conference time, because there are many accommodations, even a few compromises, to make.

The epic 1937 MGM movie version of *A Midsummer Night's Dream* was probably the first Shakespeare I ever saw performed, and it was sensational. The play was also my second Shakespearean directorial effort — again at the Keweenaw Playhouse, in the summer of 1959, again in the middle of a ten-play season.

I believe that Shakespeare was writing *Romeo and Juliet* when he was offered a commission to write a comedy to celebrate the wedding of the Sixth Earl of Derby and Lady Elizabeth Vere. The two plays echo each other and the poetics are similar. To accept the assignment, he shelved *Romeo and Juliet*, wrote the comedy and then returned to the tragedy. Difficult? Yes, but possible for any opportunistic pro.

The Playwright was soaring. He took elements of both Greek and Celtic mythology and mixed them with criss-crossed pairs of lovers and a group of amateur community theatre actors. You can do terrible damage to this play, but you can't ruin it. I've seen atrocious productions that the play itself somehow survived.

A Midsummer Night's Dream is Shakespeare's sexiest

A Midsummer Night's Dream, New Jersey Shakespeare Festival, 1979: Frieda E. Henry as Cobweb, Meg Vanzyl as Mustard Seed, Amy Stoller as Peaseblossom, Clarence Felder as Bottom, Mimi Monaco as Moth (photograph by Blair Holley).

play, though others have more bawdy lines. A play written to celebrate a wedding, a fertility rite, could be allowed to come fairly close to pornography. How much more graphic do I need to be?

It's amusing to consider that *Dream* is a favorite of those truncated school tours, where the directors dutifully cut out all the bawdy lines, as well as the essential groping, to get past the PTA censors.

Jan Kott's dark interpretation of the play is fascinating, but it doesn't work. Kott's faeries are demons, hobgoblins, malevolent sprits, the stuff of childhood nightmares and bogeyman threats, which negatively inform productions of this happy, bawdy play.

The play has the greatest number of couplings in the Canon, if we count the lover-swapping back and forth:

Theseus and Hippolyta	Theseus and Titania	Titania and Oberon
Oberon and Hippolyta	Titania and Bottom	Puck and the Faeries
Hermia and Lysander	Helena and Demetrius	Hermia and Demetrius
Helena and Lysander	Pyramus and Thisbe	

Although *A Midsummer Night's Dream* has a stately, formal beginning, the announcement of the royal nuptials of Theseus and Hippolyta, it soon shifts to more familiar ground: a daughter determined to marry against her father's wishes. Hermia's father insists that she marry a husband of his choice, and he demands that the Athenian court support his decision. Theseus gives Hermia the choice of marrying Demetrius, dying, or becoming a vestal, but she wants Lysander, so the plot is off and running. In this play, the Athenian court strolls majestically, the lovers run like hell, the mechanicals stumble and bump into each other, and the faeries fly. The director is well advised to rehearse each group separately to define their individual tempi.

Let me digress for a moment to consider theatrical movement in general. Earlier, I made the brash, unsupported statement that Shakespeare's plays "were staged the way plays have been since antiquity: they staged themselves. Movements, kinesics, proximity and distance followed the intuitive rules of human behavior."

Over the 70 million years of mammalian evolution, our verbal and body languages have developed in tandem, and they're inseparable. While waiting on the ticket line for a Yankees game last summer, I was amused to watch a young woman take a cell phone call from a (presumed) lover. She yelled, cooed, threatened, employed every muscle of her body during the call, even though it was obvious that the person on the other end of the line could see none of her movements. She waved her arms, pointed, jumped up and down, shook her fist, shrugged, danced. Though I wasn't close enough to hear her words, I knew exactly what she was feeling.

Actors are the opposite of people — they've been given words to speak. A person speaks because an instinct or need prompts him to put ideas into words. Movement is generated from the same emotional sources in parallel to the words. We must speak the same language to understand each other's words, but body language is universal — it can emphasize, underscore, or contradict the spoken word.

In contrast to people who are not acting, actors begin with the text, first learning the story and making sense out of the words. Movement then follows meaning: emotion emerges out of movement. Movement in Shakespeare's — or anyone's — plays is suggested or demanded by the text. Following the words, body language will evolve naturally as soon as the actors learn their lines and intentions. As I write this, if I feel thirsty, I'll get up, go to the kitchen, find a glass and turn on the faucet. If I'm too warm or too chilly, I'll take off or put on a sweater. Beware of choreographed movement, however — movement for the sake of movement will soon prove to be superfluous.

But back to the text of *A Midsummer Night's Dream*. Most of the comedy covers four days, but it feels tighter, shorter; time is compressed — what we perceive is a late afternoon, a long night, the next morning, and then the wedding that evening. Since real time, i.e. the time that actually passes during the performance, is the only time that really matters, the audience doesn't stop to wonder where the other two days went.

Speaking of time, another digression on the subject of pauses: contemporary playwrights, like Beckett and Pinter, value pauses and breaks in the action, often writing them into the script very specifically. By contrast, the rhythms of Shakespeare demand that pauses be kept to a minimum. Indeed, directors expend a great deal of energy getting rid of pauses, which are mostly taken because the actor has simply run out of breath. Actors, like athletes, can benefit from running, bicycling or swimming to improve aerobic capacity. A breath should only be taken when an iambic pentameter line ends with a period, question mark, colon, or a semicolon. A pause should only be taken if the line is broken, or an action interrupts the dialogue. The last line in a scene cues the first line of the next scene: this rule demands a playing space that may be entered from all points of the compass.

Each Shakespeare play has multiple entrances and exits. In each entrance, the actor is coming from someplace off-stage to another place, on-stage. The first thing the director and the set designer must decide is where a scene takes place. Many scripts and editions indicate locales, but they should always be challenged.

With 60 percent of the play occurring in the woods at night, *Dream* works wonderfully well out of doors. It was probably first performed on the grounds of an estate, and the actors had to do a lot of running. It's the perfect Shakespeare-in-the-Park show. In fact, without much of a stretch of the designers' imaginations, the entire play can take place outside, first in Theseus' theatre/garden, then an exterior work space of Peter Quince's carpenter shop, and the forest of Athens — all enhanced by a real semi-wilderness in full foliage. Eventually, after sundown, artificial light must be added to the natural setting. Director Stephen Burdman's splendid 2001 production, for example, utilized several square blocks of New York's Central Park, south of 103rd Street. The audience followed the action around, as each scene moved to another locale. The trick was in using all that space without wasting any time in the movement between scenes. At one point, II.1.175 ff., as Oberon and Puck were plotting revenge on Titania, we saw Demetrius and Helena dashing toward us from a considerable distance. It was spectacular. They arrived within shouting distance on cue, and played the "I love thee not, therefore pursue me not!" scene on the run as Oberon and the audience followed them.

Note that all locales in the play exist in both natural form and in a magical dimension. There's the first land mine: designers must create a stage environment that can be altered magically. In an indoor theatre, the design must begin with some kind of scenic device representing the sky. The title of the play instructs us: Midsummer Night is June 21, the summer solstice, the longest day and shortest night of the year. A comedy needs light — if you can't see the actors' faces and hear what they say, you won't laugh. Daytime must be as bright as budget will allow, sunsets and sunrises vivid and colorful, and night must flow from deep shadows to the bright moon Shakespeare calls for. Torches, if the fire marshal approves, will warm up the final scene. Body make-up must be considered along with lighting.

The progress of the play can be quickly summarized. It begins where it will end, in the formal garden of Theseus' Palace. We then go to Quince's shop, where the mechanicals are given roles for their production of *Pyramus and Thisbe*. Nothing unusual so far.

But then the sun sets, the moon rises, and we are in the magic forest of Athens, where we encounter two groups of Faerie Folk: the King, Oberon, and his male spirits, and the Queen, Titania, and her female spirits. Although many directors take perverse delight in mixing the groups, I believe that is a mistake. Putting both males and females into each camp reduces significantly the sexual tension of the Faerie plot.

After the introduction of the faeries, first the lovers, then the mechanicals enter the forest. Now the magic begins in earnest, as the animal spirit, Puck, engineers the switching of partners back and forth.

Realistically, all the forest scenes could be played in the same glade, with Titania's bower nearby, maybe suspended above. Characters exit the scene to travel somewhere else, but like anyone lost in a wilderness, they circle back to the same place.

Anyone who has spent both day and night in the same forest campsite will understand the design problems and opportunities of using just one set for all the forest scenes. The play needs no furniture, a minimum of scenery: trees, rocks, stumps, fallen logs, a sense of distance extending the off-stage area as far as the theatre will allow, with scrims and light employed both realistically and creatively to transform this single glade into many areas. It's even possible to convey the impression of movement in the set itself, as if the audience were moving through the forest. During the story, celestial time passes: sunset, moonrise, stars, moonset, and finally bright sunrise — the appearance of the locale constantly changes. Once out of the forest, we go back to Theseus' garden for the triple wedding, the feast, and the evening performance of *Pyramus and Thisbe*.

I've directed this play three times and acted in it once, having great fun as Puck. In the process, I made a few big mistakes.

First mistake: I cast little kids as Titania's faeries. They were delightful, sweet and they were greeted with audible, "Awws!" from the audience, especially when one little girl stopped on her entrance, stared, walked to the edge of the stage, and asked, "What are all those people doing out there?" The problem is that the faerie plot, an essential element of the play, is filled with sexuality and horny jokes, which can't work with very young children. I've also seen faeries cast as monsters, which doesn't work either. To get the most mileage out of their scenes, cast the sexiest, best-looking young women you can. Costume them and Titania in sheer, diaphanous fabrics to give the impression of nakedness without actual nudity.

The whole play, in fact, is non-stop sexy. The magic flower's juice is the ultimate aphrodisiac. When Puck drips the potion on the eyes of Titania, Lysander, and Demetrius, they not only fall in love with the first creature they see, they awake already boiling with lust for that creature.

Second big mistake, and one I kept repeating: Bottom's asshead. I'm not ashamed to admit this mistake, because most directors I know have also made it, but it took me all three productions to figure out what I was doing wrong. Why an ass's head? The Elizabethans regarded the ass as an oversexed animal. Actually, the great apes, including Homo sapiens, are far more sex-obsessed, but Shakespeare's audience loved their horny donkey jokes. Puck doesn't just put an ass's head on Bottom, he gives him all the attributes of the animal, including his loud bray and alleged voracious sexual appetite, so the Elizabethan audience would have expected a wild orgy to ensue, with the faeries joining in, when the delicate Titania, bewitched by Puck's flower, awakes to discover Bottom as half man/half beast.

In the 1979 NJSF production, we had a delectable bevy of faeries and Clarence Felder as Bottom. In rehearsal, III.1.129 ff. was hilarious, Clarence like a kid in a candy store, incapable of deciding which treat to go after first — his jaw slack, eyes bulging, hands shaking.

Then the ass's head arrived, a beautiful piece of work, accurate, life-like, with movable jaw, eyes, and ears. Unfortunately, although we had gained the appearance of an ass, we had lost Clarence's face and, therefore, much of the humor in the scene.

Consider Bert Lahr's Cowardly Lion costume and make-up for *The Wizard of Oz*. Lahr's expressive rubbery face was not lost, so his performance was never weakened. That's what Bottom needs. While time works against him, with only some 40 to 45 seconds to effect the change, it can be done.

The asshead must be in proportion to the actor's face, rather than to a real donkey. The head should consist of two prosthetic elements used with dark make-up matching the color of the ass's facial hair. About a minute before the transformation begins, an off-stage dresser applies the make-up base and spirit gum to the prosthetic snout. Then the snout is fixed to the actor's nose down to his upper lip, leaving his lower jaw free and unencumbered. This snout, molded on a sculpted model, should be made of the lightest latex, and covered with hair.

The second element in the asshead is similar to an aviator's leather helmet, ears attached. Also covered with hair, it frames the face, hides the actor's own hair, and extends down under his shirt. Ears are attached, which should be built on springs, so they can move in opposition to the actor's head movements.

This design leaves the actor's eyes, eyebrows, mouth, and most of the muscles of the face exposed. We get the illusion of the half-man/half-donkey without losing the actor's performance.

The third common mistake in *Dream* is casting a woman as Puck. Puck is an animal spirit, akin to a satyr, and he's not female. I never saw a Puck who could match Mickey Rooney's delightful dirty little boy. Puck should never be costumed in green. He's not a vegetable.

Speaking of costumes, I've seen this play costumed in many ways, but I found that Greek period costumes, summer clothes, serve the play best. The lovers, the essential plot, should be attractive, sexy, athletic and skillful comedians. If the budget permits, they should be given several versions of their first costumes as they progress into the woods, over brooks, through brambles and a swamp, each version growing more and more distressed and carrying them further toward nudity. The costumes should be designed to endure wind and rain if the performance is outdoors.

Finally, there are the pitfalls in the famous play-within-the-play, which is usually funny even when the rest of the play is not. As a boy, Shakespeare probably attended the equivalent of today's community theatre productions, performances by Stratford craftsmen and merchants. Let's examine what Shakespeare has to say about actors, professional and amateur.

We're aware of Hamlet's famous advice to the Players — I discuss this in the next chapter. It is significant that those professional actors are so willing to cooperate with the man who has hired them to perform before the court, even learning a new speech he has written to be inserted into the performance. None of the Players gives him a bad time.

Contrast them with the amateurs in *A Midsummer Night's Dream*. Peter Quince, a carpenter by trade, assembles his own troupe of fellow craftsmen to perform a classic play at the wedding celebration of Theseus and Hippolyta. Quince will direct, and his star actor, Nick Bottom, a weaver by trade, will play the leading role. Quince has prepared his text, and he proceeds to cast the play. The key to the humor is that he is an inexperienced director, and Nick Bottom is incapable of playing a tragic hero. Bottom is best cast with an actor who obviously isn't a romantic lead. How about a funny little fat guy? Why does Quince think that Bottom is a good actor? Probably because he's loud: loud is good; louder is better; loudest gets the job.

In the original casting, Peter Quince selects the lovers, Pyramus and Thisbe, his father, her mother and father, and a lion. No sooner does Quince assign the roles than trouble begins. Flute, the bellows mender, doesn't want to play a woman. Snug, the joiner, is worried about learning the lion's lines because he's slow of study. Snout and Starveling hold their peace for the time being, while Bottom tries to take over the production: not content to play Pyramus alone, he wants to triple as Thisbe and the Lion as well. Once having agreed to play just Pyramus, Bottom again takes over the rehearsal with a prolonged debate about what beard he should wear. Quince, in desperation, hands out the sides and reschedules the rehearsal for the next night in the Athenian woods.

The rehearsal in the woods quickly degenerates into anarchy as each actor, following Bottom's example, tries to rewrite the play. Shakespeare is making gentle fun here of actors who see themselves as writers and directors, capable of improving whatever play they're doing. The rehearsal never happens. I've had nightmares like this, dreaming of actors, like Bottom, with private agendas, who disrupt every rehearsal. Bottom doesn't even want to listen to the other actors rehearse. He'll be in the green room, and when they finally get to his cue, the stage manager will have to call him.

As many companies do, Quince's troupe gets hung up on technical matters: scenery, properties, and lighting. When Snout is pressed into service to play the wall separating the lovers, somebody has to build a wall costume, and Snout demands new lines to substantiate the impersonation. Once that Pandora's box has been opened, Starveling is asked to play moonshine and demands a dog, a bush, and a lantern to do so. He later identifies himself as the man in the moon. The actors require more lines, more prologue speeches to make the technical changes work. Here's the original cast list and that of the re-write:

Pyramus	*Nick Bottom*	Pyramus
Thisbe, his beloved	*Francis Flute*	Thisbe
Thisbe's Mother	*Robin Starveling*	Moonshine
Thisbe's Father	*Peter Quince*	The Chorus
Pyramus' Father	*Snout*	The Wall
The Lion	*Snug*	The Lion

By the time the play is performed at Theseus' wedding, it has been completely re-written, half the characters have been eliminated to serve the tech, and it's never been rehearsed. The actors have eliminated the families and rendered the back-story absurd. What is Shakespeare telling us here? Actors should respect the play and its writer; the director deserves to be given a chance to make the play work; and encumbering a production with too much tech will waste the budget and suck up everybody's time.

What's genuinely funny in the play-within-the play? Well-meaning but inept amateurs attempting a complex art form. What usually goes wrong in the play-within-the-play? Undisciplined actors who overplay the simplicity of the satire or a director who allows them such license. The mechanicals are tradesman, not professional comedians. Bad actors are often funny because they earnestly overact. Good actors cast as the mechanicals must be reined in by the director and constantly reminded that they are not playing burlesque comedians but craftsmen who are seriously attempting a play for their king and queen's wedding. The young man playing Flute will be funny simply by really trying to play a woman, not a transvestite or an insulting parody of a woman — jokes layered upon jokes dissipate their humor — and to the Elizabethans, this was an inside joke, because all the women's roles were played by young men.

The director of *A Midsummer Night's Dream* is advised to spend some time establishing the mechanicals as craftsmen themselves, before rehearsing the play-within-the-play. Establish the human beings before they attempt to play the classical lovers and their impediments. Certainly, any company of professional actors will have memories, anecdotes of what goes wrong in performance to give *Pyramus and Thisbe* organic humor.

Will Kempe, James Burbage's premiere comic, preceded Shakespeare as a shareholder in the company, later playing major comic roles in his plays, including Bottom and Grumio in *Taming of the Shrew*. Tradition has it that Kempe was a notorious improviser until Shakespeare became the star of the Chamberlain's company and demanded adherence to the written text. Kempe didn't cooperate. He couldn't cooperate. That's not what he did. Would anyone require Milton Berle to stick to the script? Kempe did standup improv, even within the confines of a character in a play. He told funny stories, joked, sang, danced, did imitations, heckled back the hecklers, and did his best to crack up the other actors.

A character in soliloquy is a standup comic, or a standup tragedian or both, depending on the response of the audience. An actor in soliloquy is the character at her most honest. Richard III and Iago may lie to everyone in the play, but they tell the truth to the audience. In standup, the comedy is, at its best, self-deprecating, as in Henny Youngman's:

> My psychiatrist says, "In my opinion, you're crazy."
> I said, "I want a second opinion."
> He says, "All right, you're stupid too."

Am I stretching it to say that the standup tells the truth about the audience to the audience? He not only holds the mirror up, he shoves it down their throats. The standup never works alone: the audience, the many-headed partner, gives him constant feedback.

Consider how Kempe would have played Bottom's awaking soliloquy in V.1.203 to 224. Here is marvelous potential for bawdy implication, imitations, comedic replaying of what the audience has seen before in III.1.123 to 206, and IV.1.1 to 148, as well as what they didn't see in the orgy scene that would have followed III.1. There are also opportunities for heckling in this soliloquy, if the audience is so moved, and the heckling in Shakespeare's day would have had no limits, because there was no producer or director to dampen it. The heckler, like Lear's Fool, was all-licensed: having paid his two-pence, he could do what he wanted, short of violence.

There are several resolutions in *A Midsummer Night's Dream*. The spell on Lysander is lifted, and he returns to his original state, in love with Hermia. Demetrius, however, remains enchanted, and now loves Helena. Theseus overrules Egeus and authorizes the marriages of both couples, so the lovers' plot is neatly home free. Subsequently, Oberon and Titania are reconciled, and early in V.1 we're treated to the triple wedding, the feast, the party, and the play-within-the-play.

Shakespeare has written not only the play-within-the-play but also the audience watching it and heckling its actors. As with the mechanicals' playing, these comments don't need to be exaggerated, merely stated. The lovers apparently behave badly during *Pyramus and Thisbe* but this was either the Playwright's comment on his own bad-mannered hecklers and inept actors, *or* perhaps he was tempting his audience here, encouraging even more heckling of the hecklers.

The play ends with multiple blessings, first from Theseus, then Puck, Oberon and Titania, all celebrating monogamy, the marriage union, "all others forsaking." The wedding, a very public celebration of a very private thing — the sexual union of two people — begins the marriage, but there's little concern over what the marriage will become or how it may end. Only the most cynical would speak of divorce at a wedding. Instead, marriages of sensual joy, bliss without end, are promised, and pretty people go off to make pretty babies. Finally, Puck concludes *A Midsummer Night's Dream* with an epilogue, a speech to the audience in which he again identifies the evening as both a play and a dream. He adds that he hopes they get good reviews.

By the way: Felix Mendelssohn wrote magnificent music for this play, but, except for its scherzo, it doesn't serve the play as well as the score that Carl Orff composed. In my opinion!

Chapter 4

Hamlet

My third attempt at directing Shakespeare was an audacious exercise in hubris. Not the last, by any means. In the summer of 1960, I played Hamlet and directed the play at the same time, again at the Keeweenaw Playhouse, again in a ten-play summer season. Looking back on those years of one-a-week stock makes me want to take a nap, but that slipshod production of *Hamlet* gave me a taste of the great joy in playing Shakespeare described by Eugene O'Neill's elder Tyrone. The joy is immediate, in the moment, the thrill of holding an audience enrapt while demanding their participation:

> Am I a coward?
> Who calls me villain? Breaks my pate across?
> Plucks off my beard and blows it in my face?
> Tweaks me by the nose? Gives me the lie i' the throat
> As deep as to the lungs? Who does me this, ha?

The actor waits for the answer, searches the faces, listens to every sound in the auditorium, breathing, coughs, shuffling, programs rattling, until it all quiets down as everyone waits for the answer, which never comes. Then the soliloquy shifts, and the actor is off again on a sweet orgy of self-incrimination. That's fun. It's more than fun, it's a sensual delight.

I'm describing playing the role, not directing the play. Since that first, naïve attempt, I've done ten more productions of *Hamlet* as director, fight choreographer and actor, playing Polonius, the Ghost, and the Player as well as the Prince himself. Although it's a cliché to say so, *Hamlet*, I believe, is the greatest play ever written. *Romeo and Juliet* and *King Lear* come close to it, but *Hamlet* stands alone, enigmatic, an impossible ideal, the challenge of every great actor.

Directing *Hamlet* is a tortuous drive up a mountain, a dizzying moment at the pinnacle, then an avalanche down the other side. There are a thousand changes of direction, potholes, hairpin turns, impediments, blind spots. Directing is not as much fun in the doing of it, only after it's completed, and you can reflect on the accomplishment.

To begin with, there is the problem of the text. Which text? This primary question can't be ignored, because until it is decided, rehearsals can't even begin. There is considerable evidence that Shakespeare continued to rework, tinker, tweak this play as long as he lived. There were a number of texts in existence in the 17th century alone, before the later editors turned the play into a cottage industry: four Folios, four or five quartos as well as what has been dubbed "the Ur-Hamlet," which Master Will may or may not have written early in his career. The critic Eric Sams is of the opinion that the 1603 Quarto *is* the Ur-Hamlet.

Hamlet, Boston Herald-Traveler Repertory, 1966: Jack Ryland as Hamlet, David Howard as the Gravedigger (photograph by Chris Grant).

In his entertaining and valuable book, *The Shakespeare Wars,* Ron Rosenbaum describes at considerable length the efforts of generations of scholars to identify the real *Hamlet.* For the last 400 years, these scholars have worked in two directions, analyzing and restoring the various 16th and 17th-century texts on the one hand, and, on the other, conflating the various texts into the perfect master script, a hypothetical score, to use the musical term, for the play that Shakespeare envisioned but no doubt never actually saw performed in his lifetime.

To cite but one example, the second Arden edition of the play (first published in 1928 and retaining the best elements of the texts at his disposal) took editor Harold Jenkins over 30 years. This conflated text is exquisitely researched, a monumental labor of love, with copious notes, but still (picky, picky!) a script that Shakespeare never wrote, never saw performed. Jenkins, of course, was not alone. We have dozens of conflated editions in more modest printings, as well as the massive Variorum edition of 1877. Editors have been comparing, and directors have been patching texts together, for the last 400 years in hopes of producing on paper the perfect play script.

What is the contemporary director to do? Just what Jenkins did. Unlike *Twelfth Night* or *Antony and Cleopatra,* for instance, *Hamlet* presents a perplexing embarrassment of riches in these multiple scripts. The director must decide what to cut, what to add, how to mix and match, cut and paste. First Folio fans solve the problem by denying the validity of all other texts. That simplifies matters, but it doesn't necessarily give us the Playwright's preferred script, if there was one.

Some critics argue that Shakespeare's plays were never meant to be played full-length. Today, many producers demand that plays be edited to fit contemporary playgoers' sensibilities and schedules. The first *Hamlet* I ever did (1953), edited by Leo Kirschbaum for a Wayne State University production, eliminated a thousand lines as well as the characters of Rosencrantz, Guildenstern, Fortinbras, Reynaldo, the Second Gravedigger, and the British Ambassadors, all in deference to that stereotypical audience member who had to get up the next morning to go to work.

In his splendid book on playwriting, *Shakespeare's Game*, William Gibson postulates that the structure of Q.1 is probably how Master Will originally wrote the play. The major structural difference between this script and those that followed is the placement of the "To be or not to be..." soliloquy and the "nunnery scene" that follows. I agree with Gibson. The last two productions I directed used the *structure* of the First Quarto, the *text* of the First Folio, and added the "How all occasions do inform against me..." soliloquy at the end of IV.4. So much for purity.

The edit begins with Act II, Scene 2. Note that Ophelia should accompany Polonius when he enters with Voltemand and Cornelius at II.2.61. Polonius proposes that he and Claudius eavesdrop on Hamlet's encounter with Ophelia. Both King and Queen agree. The Queen exits, and the King and Polonius hide behind the arras, leaving Ophelia onstage. Hamlet enters for the "To be or not to be..." soliloquy, followed by the nunnery scene with Ophelia. Hamlet exits, Ophelia does the "Oh what a noble mind..." soliloquy. Polonius and Claudius come out from behind the arras and play their brief three-scene with Ophelia. Claudius and Ophelia exit, leaving Polonius on-stage. Hamlet re-enters, and we resume at line II.2.187, "How does my good Lord Hamlet?" No changes in the rest of the play, except for the addition of the F.2 soliloquy, "How all occasions do inform..." at IV.4.32 to 66.

That most famous soliloquy "To be or not to be..." really doesn't work perfectly anywhere in the play because it interrupts the action wherever you put it. But it's counterproductive where it sits in the Second and subsequent Quartos and the First Folio. The juxtapositions (above) maintain the flow and drive of the play and solve the "To be or not to be..." dilemma. Hamlet doesn't backtrack after he makes up his mind with "The play's the thing/Wherein I'll catch the conscience of the King." To reiterate: this is the structure of Q.1, the way the play was probably first produced.

My 1966, 1978, and 1994 *Hamlets* were edited texts, perhaps two hours and 45 minutes of playing time each. The 1988 production was the one described above, full-length, the structure of Q.1 and the text of F.1.

Interpreting the "bare bodkin" reference in this troublesome soliloquy as evidence of Hamlet's suicidal tendencies only gets actors bouncing off walls and slows down rehearsals. Hamlet appears to accept, in his first scene, that suicide is not an option; it's the unpardonable mortal sin, so it's off the table. Then what? His responsibility is to take back the crown that's rightly his, and that responsibility gives us the arc of the play. He hesitates for a brief time to test the legitimacy of the Ghost and the guilt of Claudius, but the only thing that gives Hamlet pause, slows him down after the play-within-the-play, is the necessity of sending Claudius to hell rather than heaven.

As I wrote in the previous chapter, real time is the only time that an audience perceives. Stage time, the days, weeks, even months or years covered by the events of the play, is an intellectual concept. Aristotle advises the playwright to tell his story in the shortest stage time possible. *The Comedy of Errors* and *The Tempest* each take place in one day. *Romeo and Juliet* takes four days. Both *The Winter's Tale* and *Pericles* have 16-year leaps in the middle of their stories, but they are exceptions. *Hamlet* starts just before Christmas and ends in the spring, but what lengthens it is the travel time between Elsinore and Paris. The action of the play is confined to roughly three days:

Act I: midnight of the first day to dawn of the second day, a little over 30 hours, about 48 minutes of real (audience's) time.

II.1 through IV.4: less than 24 hours, but 98 minutes of real time. A lot happens, but it can still be contained in a continuous day.

IV.5 through the end of the play: again, less than 24 hours, but 54 minutes of real time.

These playing times are based on our 1988 production. One might protest that those are odd places for intermissions, but Shakespeare didn't care about acts and scenes — these are publisher's and printer's concerns. The Playwright wrote continuous action and seldom put in leaps of time.

What difference does it make? It makes a difference to designers, especially costumers, who are relied upon most to indicate passage of time. And it makes a lot of difference to actors, who demand to know sequence, time of day and year, weather, what happens off-stage during time lapses, everything they can find out to help build their characters. Professional actors work very hard to make all abstractions concrete, specific, to fill in the reality that their characters inhabit in order to create reality on-stage. As stated earlier, good acting is believable, indistinguishable from life in all its banality.

Yet throughout *Hamlet*, Shakespeare keeps reminding the audience, through a hundred theatrical references, that they're watching a play. The "fourth wall," that separation of actors and audiences, is constantly breached.

This is most evident, of course, in the Players' scenes. As soon as a troupe of professional traveling players arrives to entertain the court, Hamlet usurps the role of actor-manager of the company, the star who plays most of the leads, does the casting, signs the checks, and directs the other actors. Hamlet not only selects the play he wants the traveling players to perform, *The Murder of Gonzago*, an Italian melodrama set in Vienna — see the chapter on *Measure For Measure*— but he rewrites it, inserting a speech (the poisoner's speech at III.2.266 to 272) designed to startle King Claudius, "catch his conscience," and cause him to reveal his guilt.

That's a lot of chutzpah. I've toured many plays in my time, but no impresario ever tried to rewrite our plays or take over the direction of the company. Still, Hamlet is paying the bill, and he's surely going to be generous.

Hamlet's speech to the Players in III.2 is a director's effort to control actors in early rehearsals, a lecture on acting that has been used in thousands of undergrad actor-training classes. Hamlet is coaching the actor who will play the poisoner, and he's giving him precise line readings, which every actor hates. Hamlet wants articulation, precision of language, no declamation, no "mouthing," sufficient volume, but not too much. He will accept no gratuitous gesticulation. He's asking for naturalistic acting, recognizable human behavior as well — no indication or exaggeration of emotion. Nor will he settle for simple detached statement. He demands nothing more nor less than the reality of a man performing a murder. All of this may be reasonable expectation. Achieving it is something else.

The prince takes some cheap shots at things that annoy him: over-acting and the fans who thrive on over-acting as well as those hecklers who come to the theatre only to laugh and disrupt the performance. Actors should stick to the script and not add "ohs" or "ahs" or "wells" or burps or chuckles. When Shakespeare wants an "oh," he'll write it in. Even screams of agony should be played on the line, not after it.

Perhaps if young Hamlet, the usurping novice director, would just shut up and let the actors rehearse, he might get the performance he wants, but he can't stop talking. He runs out of time, aborts his own rehearsal, and sends the players off to costume and make-up. He has demonstrated his own pitiful ambition and jeopardized the project.

Even in performance, Hamlet won't stop directing. At III.2.238, as the Murderer enters, Hamlet is noisily harassing Ophelia, so the actor judiciously waits until he has a quiet theatre before he begins the scene. This infuriates the Prince, who hollers at him to get on with it, which the actor does, resisting the impulse to heckle back the heckler.

The mousetrap is sprung, Claudius responds, and the play-within-the-play is aborted. Hamlet is satisfied that the vision he saw on the battlements was indeed his father, and his father spoke truth about the guilt of his brother. It's fun to conjecture about what happens to the Players after Claudius stops the play, scattering actors and spectators alike. In *Rosencrantz and Guildenstern Are Dead* (which I've directed three times in repertory with *Hamlet*, the two plays together illuminating each other, giving the audience deeper insights), Tom Stoppard's Players never get paid, and are lucky to get away with heads still on shoulders. Hi diddly dee, an actor's life for me!

An analysis of the famous speech to the Players could fill yet another book, but permit me to spend a little more time on one section:

> The purpose of playing, whose end, both at the first and now, was and is, to hold, as 'twere, the mirror up to nature; to show virtue her own nature, scorn her own image, and the very age and body of the time his form and pleasure.

What does Shakespeare mean by "playing?" Does he mean acting, as in "play-acting," or does he mean the play itself? The "play," not the script. A play is not a play until it's performed, and performance requires players, those who speak the play. Is the Playwright merely requesting realistic acting, or is he promoting the collaborative art of the theatre, which requires an author, director, actors, designers, a composer, technicians, and ultimately an audience?

The best stage Hamlets I ever saw were two I directed: Jack Ryland in 1966 and Eric Booth in 1978. All my Ophelias were excellent, especially Margery Shaw, who played it twice; she also played a splendid Gertrude in 1988. The best Poloniuses were Brendan Burke, Hume Cronyn, and Geddeth Smith, and J.C. Hoyt was a definitive Horatio, playing it for me twice. The toughest role to cast is Claudius. I never saw a really good one on-stage, although Alfred Drake came close.

When my original Hamlet was injured in 1988, the actor playing Laertes moved into the role, and the Laertes understudy, T. Ryder Smith, one of the Players, then moved up, and I discovered one of the best actors I've ever directed. Smith was so good in his original Player role I left him there, doubling in his dippy clown make-up. After this experience, I repeated the Laertes/Player double in the 1995 Iowa production, and I probably will always use it whenever economics demand. I regret that I never had the opportunity to direct T. Ryder as Hamlet.

In determining the final text he will use, the director may ask if there is a unifying theme or themes common to all versions. Does a common thread exist that can protect the play from the lunacy of "concept" directors?

Hamlet is about three sons avenging three fathers and much more, of course. As soon as one starts digging, the number of subjects the play is "about" expands exponentially. Although the *performance* starts with minor characters on a bitter cold, dark night, the *story* of the play begins some 30 years earlier on the day Prince Hamlet was born, the day that his father, Hamlet I, defeated the elder Fortinbras in individual combat, the day the Gravedigger first went to work in the cemetery. Between the beginning of the story and the beginning of the play, a number of events inform the play. Add to that historical events during the Playwright's lifetime, cultural mores, facts and experiences so common to his audience that Shakespeare doesn't even bother to mention them, and the grounding of the play should be complete, until the next peel of the onion.

Shakespeare wrote this play for an audience of Englishmen living in dread of the imminent death of Queen Elizabeth and preoccupied with matters of succession and the responsibilities of the sovereign, a soldier/scholar/statesman. The majority of his plays involved sovereigns. Hamlet, 29 years old as the play begins, a month after the death of his father, is heir to the throne. He has no siblings and has spent his entire life preparing to be king. By the rules of primogeniture, the crown passes from father to son at the instant of the king's death: "The king is dead; long live the king."

Hamlet has been studying at Wittenberg University, where Martin Luther was teaching when he nailed to the door of the Castle Church his famous 95 Theses in 1517. Why Wittenberg? Why not the Sorbonne or Heidelberg or Oxford or the Ecole Militaire? Shakespeare does not mention Luther, but the few, though essential, theological questions that bedevil Hamlet's thinking might imply that the Prince has chosen to study moral philosophy while waiting to assume the throne of Denmark. I do not present this theory as conclusive — it could provide a separate thesis in itself — but pondering such questions as "Why Wittenberg?" is one of the great intellectual joys in doing these plays.

Why doesn't Hamlet act immediately following the encounter with his father's ghost? He can't. He's powerless, a prisoner in a castle secured by a formidable palace guard. He has no followers. He is alone, except for his scholarly friend, Horatio, certainly no soldier, probably not even a Danish citizen. The director must give Claudius sufficient bodyguards and keep them close at hand through all the Hamlet/Claudius scenes so that it is clear that Hamlet couldn't get within 20 feet of Claudius without being chopped down. If this is done, the Prince will not be perceived as timid or hesitant, but simply unable to act without endangering himself.

And there is another factor that delays Hamlet's revenge of his father's "foul and unnatural" murder: he ruminates later as to whether the apparition on the battlements was really the ghost of his father or the Devil. Catholics believed in the Devil *and* ghosts, while Protestants believed in devils, but not ghosts. Hamlet only raises the question long after the encounter, in his "Oh, what a rogue..." speech.

It's certainly an interesting question and an opportunity for extensive midrash but the director of the play, as I wrote in my introduction, doesn't have the leisure of delaying the decision to indulge in scholarly debate. The cast list in the text refers to "the Ghost of Hamlet's father." You can't tell an actor that he's playing a ghost who may be the Devil. That concept is unplayable — i.e., it's an idea, an intellectual concept that can't be translated into behavior. Even playing a ghost is full of traps: movies have taught us that ghosts are transparent, and bad actors are tempted to sing the lines or try to imitate Gielgud's delivery. The safest, most effective, way to play the character is to play Hamlet's father, his dead father come back to life to set his son on a course of revenge. It's a father/son reunion about something that concerns them both deeply.

At the conclusion of this scene, young Hamlet demands that Horatio and Marcellus swear that they will not reveal to anyone what they have seen or heard on the battlements. Horatio agrees, but Marcellus is reluctant because of his oath of allegiance to the king. Hamlet insists they swear on his sword, which is in the shape of a cross: to swear on such a weapon is to make an oath to God. At that moment, the Ghost cries from under the stage, "Swear." Three times Hamlet proposes the oath, and they prepare to swear, but each time the Ghost cries again and changes his position. At this point, Hamlet calls his father an old mole, a pioneer, and questions how fast he can dig a tunnel.

What's going on here? The essential elements for the oath are the acquiescence of Hamlet's companions and the sword itself. Does it make any difference where they're standing? Jan Kott wrote an entire thesis on this business in *Shakespeare, Our Contemporary*, comparing the Ghost to a tragic mole, burrowing in the earth. Like much of Kott's work, this thesis is either genius or nonsense. What I think happened is simply that the ad-libs of two actors putting each other on found their way into the text. It's generally accepted that Richard Burbage originally played Hamlet, and the Playwright himself played the Ghost. If the scene was staged simply, Shakespeare the Ghost was under the stage at a prescribed position, and may have playfully changed position, forcing Burbage as Hamlet to ad-lib to cover the movement. The scene without the moves of the Ghost and the ad-libs that cover them — if they are ad-libs — makes more sense, but as written it may demonstrate how actors' improvisation can become a permanent part of the script. It certainly happens with modern plays.

But to get back to Hamlet's alleged procrastination: the play requires at least four substantial young men, in addition to Marcellus and Bernardo, to serve as guards and pallbearers. They protect the King at all times, they carry Ophelia's bier and place it gently into her grave, they separate Laertes and Hamlet in their fight, and they bear Hamlet's body, "like a soldier, to the stage" at the end of the play. They need not be elaborately costumed; they need not even be actors, though they'll be better actors by the end of the run, but they are, I believe, crucial representations of the power of the state, and again, as I wrote above, they are a practical explanation for Hamlet's initial inaction.

Their protection breaks down, of course, in the chapel scene where Claudius is praying alone. Hamlet enters quietly and argues eloquently with himself about the theological implications of taking revenge on a soul in a moment of grace. This is a brilliant scene that leads Hamlet to the conclusion that such a murder would be "hire and salary, not revenge." The next time he and Claudius meet, Hamlet has been disarmed and his guards again protect Claudius. The impediment remains until Hamlet is sent to England; it exists in the graveyard scene, and it's there in the final scene. Claudius is protected by his guards every moment, until the exchange of weapons puts a lethal sword in Hamlet's hand, and he thrusts home on the line, "Venom to thy work."

The graveyard scene, V.1, and the final (sub)scene, the fencing match, V.2.221 to 408, are two stringent tests of the director's choreographic ability. The first half of the graveyard scene, played by the two Gravediggers, Hamlet, and Horatio, is pure vaudeville, comic relief. Following the heaviness of the plot to murder Hamlet and the death of Ophelia, the audience needs a breather, and the Playwright gives them some jokes, a song, a doubles act about graves and corpses, Hamlet playing Bud Abbott to the Gravedigger's Lou Costello, ending with the eulogy to the long-dead court jester, Yorick. Osric's challenge to Hamlet at the end of the graveyard scene is another vaudeville turn. Notice how skillfully the Playwright keeps humor on-stage throughout in the characters of Polonius, Rosencrantz, Guildenstern, the Gravedigger, Osric, and Hamlet himself. As in the best of Sean O'Casey and Tennessee Williams, comedy and tragedy are in constant close juxtaposition.

The problem of a grave for Ophelia in V.1 is, I believe, best solved with a trap door in the stage floor that can be used in early scenes of the play for access to the battlements. The trap opening must be big enough to allow Ophelia on her bier to be lowered into it with ropes by four soldiers. This business, as simple as it sounds, requires careful drill with Ophelia's participation. The grave itself needs to be about 40 to 44 inches deep. It holds a few bones, one or two secondary skulls, and the skull of Yorick. Give the Gravedigger a shoulder bag to hold his props. Hamlet and Horatio hide when the funeral procession enters.

I've always insisted on a real skull for Yorick — it gives the prop man a bit more work, but it's worth it because of what it evokes in the actor. If Hamlet plays the scene simply, connected to the memory of a departed loved one, the passing of the skull from Gravedigger to Prince is one of the most touching moments in all theatre.

If scene V.1 is rehearsed carefully, building into it from his moment of outrage at seeing Laertes jump into the grave to his declaration "I loved Ophelia," rather than just following the movements by the numbers, it will influence at least his two earlier scenes with Ophelia and bring us back to consideration of Hamlet's relationship with her. Can of worms? Perhaps. How much is planted, how much implied in those earlier scenes?

Ophelia speaks to her father and her brother about Hamlet, and both warn her that he may just be toying with her to get her into bed. Is he sincere? She defends neither him nor herself, but she does agree to be careful, even stingy of her affections. She later reports a bizarre encounter with Hamlet in her bedroom to her father and agrees to cooperate in an interview with him while Polonius and the King eavesdrop from behind the arras. In effect, she is spying on Hamlet and facilitating further spying, but everybody spies on Hamlet, which is why he pretends to be deranged in public. We are a long time into the play before the Playwright gives us a scene between the young couple, the famous nunnery scene where Ophelia returns gifts Hamlet gave her earlier. The scene turns ugly as he challenges both her honesty and her chastity.

Like so much of Shakespeare, this is the stuff of a thousand dissertations. Was this a romance? A love affair? Sexual? There's an apocryphal story that when a grad student asked John Barrymore in his dressing room, "Do you think that Hamlet slept with Ophelia?" He thought for a moment, then replied, "Well, in the Chicago company, he did." Kenneth Branagh's film leaves no doubt that Hamlet bedded Ophelia, giving us a quick cut-away flashback to Kate Winslet and him naked in bed. But the text itself is ambiguous. Indeed, the most famous line in this scene, "Get thee to a nunnery!" maintains the ambiguity, because the meaning of nunnery could be literal, a convent of nuns, or it could be ironic, a brothel.

The insults continue. Hamlet ridicules Ophelia's make-up, her naïveté, her movement, her speech. Then he moves from the specific to the general and belittles all womankind, concluding that there shall be no more marriage. Finally he is gone, leaving her in a puddle of self-pity. Is this love?

The next time we see the young couple together, at the play-within-the-play, the Prince proceeds in full view and earshot of the court, her father, his mother, and the King, to harass her with sexual innuendo, until she shrinks into inconsequence. He then simply seems to forget her as he moves toward the assassination of the King.

Where's the relationship between boy and girl, man and woman? As Claudius says earlier:

> Love? His affections do not that way tend,
> Nor what he spake, though it lack'd form a little,'
> Was not like madness.

Yet in V.1, when Hamlet learns that the corpse is Ophelia, he reveals himself, exploding with rage, identifies himself for a fraction of a second as King of Denmark, then proclaims to the heavens:

> I lov'd Ophelia. Forty thousand brothers
> Could not with all their quantity of love
> Make up my sum.

He offers to prove his love by being buried alive with her corpse, then as quickly as it came, his anger subsides, and he wanders off.

This is the totality of the romance or the fiction of the romance. Did Hamlet and Ophelia love each other? As I've said, the text is ambiguous. Actors can only play what is given them, what is written in the text, yet paradoxically they must resolve ambiguities for themselves in order to realize their characters. Every Ophelia I've ever seen seems to be infatuated with Hamlet, and every Hamlet confused by Ophelia. The Playwright gives them no real love scenes where one may say "I love you," and the other reply "I love you too."

Incidentally, there's a basic lesson in Shakespearean acting in the scene where Laertes first witnesses Ophelia's madness. Any sensitive actor will be destroyed, brought to tears at the sight of her reversion to childhood, playing with dolls and wildflowers. The trick is maintaining the articulation of the words and the meaning of the lines through the devastation. Emotion cannot be allowed to stifle articulation.

I don't think Ophelia's bawdiness in her "mad scenes" is sexual, but rather a reversion to a happy childhood, where all was fun and games, even reflections on death. She alternates a maudlin pop funeral dirge with recitation of flower imagery (see Perdita) with a little girl's nursery rhyme, an early warning against sexual promiscuity. It's "Jack and Jill" and "Little Miss Muffet" stuff, and it's general, a warning about the implication of Saint Valentine's Day (fall in love but stay chaste until married!), little or nothing to do with Hamlet himself. Ophelia betrays Hamlet, then bemoans her loss when he turns on her. When he accidentally kills her father, she blames herself, retreats into childhood and dies as a child would, unable to save herself. She's not a suicide. She just can't swim.

Finally, we come to a moment of clarity and resignation as the Prince ruminates on his own death:

> If it be now, 'tis not to come; if it be not to come, it will be now; if it
> be not now, yet it will come. The readiness is all. Since no man, of
> aught he leaves, knows aught, what is't to leave betimes?

The rapier and dagger technique that Hamlet and Laertes employ is the same one that Tybalt uses in *Romeo and Juliet*. This technique should be taught in acting programs after actors are taught today's competition saber. They should be taught boxing, wrestling, judo, and ken-do as well.

In *Hamlet*, the director/fight choreographer must maintain the tension before and after the match. It's a fencing match, a sporting event, not a duel. Both combatants are skilled noblemen, and both have been in practice. There are three beats to the match — two hits and a third contested hit—before Hamlet is wounded on the arm when he is off guard, at V.2.318. The winner is never decided because the match erupts into a brawl. Laertes dies before Hamlet, because he is wounded in the body with his own weapon, near the heart, and the venom works faster. Lots of wonderful subtleties here. The match itself must be choreographed in private, with Hamlet, Laertes and their understudies. Then the other members of the court are added. The scene that follows, V.2.309–408, must be carefully charted, so it can flow out of the action of the brawl.

Gertrude should be as far away from Claudius as possible when she drinks the poisoned cup, so that Claudius is forced to exert himself to try to stop her.

Throughout the play, incidentally, the director should look for instances where typesetters might have left characters out and add them to the scenes. I make this a habit with all of Shakespeare, for it can do so much to clarify and strengthen relationships. For instance, it doesn't make sense to keep Ophelia off-stage in I.2, even though she has no lines. Osric should be introduced as early as possible, courtier to Claudius, successor to Polonius. It's reasonable to assume that he's in on the poisoned sword plot, making sure that Laertes gets the right weapon.

Anyone who writes about this play is going to end up with a book, because there are so many facets, each of which may tempt the writer into a digression, which, in turn, can grow to a dissertation. By any standards, the play is so complex, treating of so many themes, it is no wonder directors are tempted to shorten it. And this brings us back to the question of editing. As soon as a director has dangerously concluded what the play is "about," he is going to be tempted to cut away all elements that do not support that thesis. Olivier's superb 1948 film is a perfect example. This Oedipal Hamlet eliminated most of the politics, indeed most lines that did not bring us back to a prince in love with his mother. Prominent by his absence was Fortinbras. When the film ended, the royal family were all dead, not a surviving heir in sight. Denmark was headless, clearly a candidate for riot and anarchy. Such a final curtain would have made Shakespeare's audience very uncomfortable—an oedipal prince might have fascinated them, but they were most concerned about the politics at a time when Elizabeth was staring death in the face but still hadn't consented to naming an heir. Even though there might have been an earlier Ur-Hamlet text of the play, directors and scholars alike should be most concerned about the version first presented to the patrons of the Globe.

Because of this, I suggest that the theme common to any and all texts, cut and uncut, that serves all productions of the play best, is that which focuses on Hamlet as the heir apparent, who should have been recognized as King of Denmark upon the death of his father.

Does the audience need to be reminded that Hamlet is the rightful king? An American audience might. It would be reasonable for them to assume that in this fictional Denmark, a king might be succeeded by his brother, rather than his son, *or*, that the king's widow might retain the title of queen, and would then be privileged to remarry, thus creating another king. Reasonable conjectures, but that's not how the British did it, and Shakespeare's audience would have expected the crown prince to be the new king. That audience would have demanded an explanation of why Claudius has been named king, rather than young Hamlet, yet the Playwright gives them no explanation. The fact of usurpation hangs in the air like a bad smell, an aberration waiting to be addressed.

Tom Stoppard deals with it in an hilarious scene in *Rosencrantz and Guildenstern Are Dead*, but Shakespeare did not. Master Will confuses us with that pesky line late in the play in which Hamlet complains that Claudius "popped in between th'election and my hopes."

This phrase has no doubt begat a hundred doctoral dissertations, but I've never found anyone who could give me a satisfactory definition of the term "election," as it is used here by Hamlet. Denmark was a monarchy, like England, and kings were determined through primogeniture, though there is some historical evidence that Denmark was "an elective monarchy," a nation in which a potential monarch had to be approved by his people. That's a theory, not a proof. There certainly was no election in the modern American sense.

If we examine the first throne room scene, I.2, the world appears to be in balance. The King and Queen are on their thrones, with loyal subjects in attendance. In an exquisite poetic aria, Claudius eulogies his recently deceased brother, King Hamlet, introduces his sister-in-law as his new wife, and thanks the court for their cooperation in the "affair." He says nothing about being named (elected) king. Instead, he moves on to matters of state, sending two courtiers to the King of Norway to request that he rein in his nephew Fortinbras, who seems intent on awakening old quarrels. Then Claudius gives permission to Laertes to return to Paris, but he denies young Prince Hamlet permission to return to university at Wittenberg. He admonishes Hamlet for continuing to mourn his late father and declares to the world that his nephew is like a son and, most important, heir to him.

Once again, five minutes into the scene, the questions of inheritance and succession are raised, and, again, nobody objects that young Hamlet should be on the throne, not his uncle. Nor does Hamlet himself complain about the situation within earshot of anyone in the court.

I was surprised to discover, while lecturing on the play at East Stroudsburg University a few years ago, that what I consider a primary objective of Hamlet is not even mentioned in the early scenes of the play. In fact, my good friend, professor and playwright Ron Meyers, urged me to examine Hamlet's first soliloquy, "Oh, that this too, too solid flesh should melt...." In this first scene, Hamlet seems most concerned with the revolting fact that his mother has married his uncle within a month of the death of his father. Her "unseemly haste" appears to torture him more than any other matter. He doesn't complain about the loss of his throne, only about his mother's incest.

The question remains: how did Claudius manage to bypass young Hamlet and enlist the support of the Danish nobility to seize the throne? We don't get an answer. The enigma persists, and only when the Ghost of King Hamlet returns to tell his son that his brother has murdered him is the legitimacy of Claudius' reign called into question.

Fun? This is the stuff of centuries of scholarship. But what does a modern audience perceive, and what did the original London audience of 1601 perceive? What would their expectations be? A modern audience will associate physical things — sets, properties, costumes — with kingship. They'll see two thrones, king and queen in royal robes, both wearing crowns, soldiers/guards with weapons, a show of power, and, amid all the celebratory finery, one person in mourning, and they will, initially, at least, accept this as legitimate, unremarkable. I believe that the original 1601 audience would have instead looked beyond this picture and immediately grown suspicious about why Claudius wore the crown, rather than his nephew, the rightful heir.

What are the responsibilities of an English king? A king must hold his throne against all pretenders and usurpers. He must rule his people justly in accordance with the dictates of the state religion. He must protect the realm against all enemies, foreign and domestic.

So what should young Hamlet's primary objective be? He must expose his uncle as usurper, depose him, and regain his throne. Once the Ghost has convinced him that Claudius is his murderer, Hamlet must avenge his father by killing his uncle. The catch here is that Hamlet may not sacrifice his own life in the process: a suicide brought on by an assassination attempt is not an option.

Whatever else concerns him, personal, practical, or philosophical, his primary objective is to regain his throne. That's the thread, the unifying theme, the super-objective that young Hamlet must play throughout the piece. Whatever else is excised, this straight line must be maintained. Hamlet achieves his purpose in the last moments of the play: he kills Claudius, ascends the throne, and, with his final breath, names Fortinbras as his successor. Directors should pay careful attention to this staging, because it's not arbitrary. The reign of Hamlet II lasts less than two minutes.

For a revenge play, *Hamlet* says a lot about grace and forgiveness. It's a play about the best in the Judeo-Christian tradition. There's a wonderful exchange between a principal and a minor character:

> 1ST. SAILOR: "God bless you, Sir."
>
> HORATIO: "Let Him bless thee too."
>
> 1ST. SAILOR: "He shall, sir, an it please Him."

Coleridge didn't know what this last line means. Other editors spend no time with it. It sticks with me because of the simplicity of the theology behind it. You don't order God to bless the other guy. You ask Him, humbly hoping that the other guy has sufficient grace to be worthy of blessing. But it's still up to God. A prayer truly worthy of the breath it requires is "Thy Will Be Done."

* * * * *

After I played Hamlet in the summer of 1960, I returned to New York and went to work for Joseph Papp, genius producer and founder of both the New York Shakespeare Festival and the Public Theatre. That fall, Joe hired me to play Tybalt and stage the fights in *Romeo and Juliet*, which ran through the spring. I directed no Shakespeare between the 1960 Keweenaw *Hamlet* and the 1963 Cape May *Taming of the Shrew*. I was working almost nonstop, however, as actor, director, and as company manager on two tours of the Austrian concert company, *Vienna on Parade*. I acted on Broadway in *Tiger Tiger Burning Bright*, directed by Joshua Logan, and I produced and directed another season at Keweenaw in 1962, a full season of musicals at the insistence of the Board of Directors. Exhausted and somewhat disillusioned by that season, I took my wife and son to Stratford, Ontario, to bask in the brilliance of the theatre there. Between performances, I read Joseph Campbell's books on mythology. The Stratford experience pumped up my enthusiasm to go back to work. I also did a great deal of thinking about the acting company that would eventually become the New Jersey Shakespeare Festival.

CHAPTER 5

Macbeth

I studied *Macbeth* in high school with a good teacher and later in college with Leo Kirschbaum, but my first encounter with the play on-stage was an early Joseph Papp New York Shakespeare Festival production that toured New York high schools in 1962. Joe had hired Gladys Vaughan to direct and me to do the fights. I attended rehearsals every day, training all the actors in broadsword and shield. Among the combatants were William Devane and Charles Durning. As rehearsals progressed, I gradually took over the staging of entrances, exits, the banquet, all of the violence, military movements, most of the fifth act. It was a great opportunity for me, because I had minimal responsibility for the text: I was in charge of the action. Gladys was happy with the arrangement as well, because her interest was in the psychology and theology of the play, not its militarism. By the time I had the opportunity to direct the play in 1965, I was more than prepared for it. In all, I've done nine productions of this bloody awful play as director, fight director, and actor, playing Macbeth, Banquo, MacDuff, Duncan, Old Siward, and several anonymous combatants in the fifth act.

The First Folio text of *Macbeth*, the only one we have, is seriously flawed and drastically cut. We have no Quarto texts, only the Folio, which is strange in itself. Compared to other tragedies Shakespeare wrote, *Macbeth* is sparse, shorter by half than many of the others. For example, the NJSF full-length *Hamlet* (1988) had a running time of three hours, 20 minutes, while the 1999 Gorilla Rep *Macbeth* ran one hour, 40 minutes. Compare the play with itself: IV.3 seems over-written when compared to other scenes in the play.

I dislike the practice of editing plays, but most Shakespeare texts have some alleged imperfections that tempt directors and dramaturgs into cuts. In *Macbeth*, the entire play, especially Act IV, suffers from revisions, probably from a spectacular revival with lots of special effects and elaborate tech produced by Thomas Middleton sometime after the death of Shakespeare but before the publication of the First Folio. The script also suffers from another impediment, early directorial additions including the addition of Middleton's Hecate scenes. These impositions tempt us further into questioning the efficacy of the script. Please note that I'm not criticizing Shakespeare here, but rather Middleton or other directors who may have corrupted the play and left us with this incomplete text. Directors, as I've said earlier, are dangerous people.

Shakespeare wrote a few Scots into his plays, but he only wrote one play about Scottish kings, and it includes two alleged ancestors of James I/VI, who fancied himself a theologian and a scholar of the occult. *Macbeth* is a play about a usurper, a butcher who kills women and little babies. We start with the impediments not only of an incomplete and corrupted text, but a curse and an actors' phobia as well.

Macbeth, Boston Herald-Traveler Repertory, 1965: Peter MacLean as Macbeth, Curt Garfield as Macduff (photograph by Chris Grant).

Why is *Macbeth* so popular in spite of these things? Why do productions fail more often than they succeed? Why has the title role torpedoed more good actors than any other Shakespearean leading role?

In *Macbeth*, as in all the plays, thematic elements are emphasized throughout. When words are repeated frequently, when statements are repeated, explained, repeated again, if such statements lead to confrontation among characters, then directors and actors are well advised to pay careful attention. In *Macbeth,* the word "blood" appears 38 times, and the word "man" is repeatedly defined. Characters argue about what a man is, what a man does, what is proper behavior for a man. This play is about a Man of Blood, a professional soldier who leads warriors into battle, who kills and destroys in protection of the homeland. Violence is his profession.

To the Elizabethans and the Jacobeans, the ideal king was a soldier, a statesman, and a scholar. A king had to be capable of maintaining his throne against all pretenders and usurpers. He was trusted to defend the realm against all enemies, foreign and domestic. The warrior king was a skillful and courageous combatant: he did not just send his troops into battle, he led them. Further, if a political dispute could be settled by single combat, then the righteous king could justify his crown by defeating his opponent.

The major problem in producing *Macbeth* for a contemporary American audience is their collective ambiguity toward the military hero. Roughly half of our citizens are doves, the other half hawks. When war seems necessary and moral, the military man is held in high repute, a hero, but when a war is considered immoral or unjustified, the military man is labeled a distasteful mercenary. Collectively we are schizophrenic.

Further, Shakespeare believed in the providential theory of history, which held that God controlled earthly events directly through wars, duels, the birth and death of kings. In the medieval world, there was no separation between "supernatural" and "natural." God was omnipresent and active, employing nature, weather, and human events to achieve His purposes. See the chapter on *Henry VI, Part 1*. God was present at the conception and birth of kings. The king was God's anointed, and only God had the right to depose him. "The divine right of kings" derives from this theory. The king is right, because he is the king. To Shakespeare's audience, regicide was the greatest of all sins, because it was, at once, murder, treason, sacrilege, and blasphemy.

Macbeth begins with a two-pronged threat to the realm of Scotland: a rebellion and an invasion. Two generals, Macbeth and Banquo, lead the troops of King Duncan. There is much exposition about characters who have not yet appeared: noble Macbeth, cousin to the king, has not only been victorious against the Norwegian invaders, but also against the rebels, defeating the traitor rebel MacDonald in single combat.

When Macbeth and Banquo finally arrive, seven minutes into the play, it's not clear who is whom. The director is advised to keep the two generals physically separated until the witches identify them. At this point, the audience has heard about MacDonald and Cawdor, they've been told about Macbeth's heroics, but they haven't yet *seen* him do anything. They don't see a hero: they see a man tempted into stealing a crown that is not lawfully his. There's a possibility that Macbeth might be a good king — he would seem to have all the attributes of a king, whereas Malcolm, Duncan's first-born, the heir apparent, is as yet untried and undistinguished as a warrior. If Macbeth is going to be king, he has to get past three people — the king and two heirs, Malcolm and Donalbain, with all their rights and power. Can he do that without sacrificing his soul?

This possibility brings us to a consideration of the Witches. There were only four Christian religions practiced in England during the early reign of James I/VI: loyalists to the Church of England, wary closet Catholics, Protestants (heavily influenced by European sects), and Puritans. Ideologically, they spilled over into each other. All four shared a basic Judeo-Christian dogma and such common beliefs as direct divine intervention, the existence of angels, devils, ghosts and witches, demonic possession, alchemy, faith healing, etc. There was no Judaism, no Islam, no Buddhism, no Hinduism, no Shinto.

Shakespeare's witches are the kind that were accused of all kinds of mischief and burned at the stake in Salem, Massachusetts, during the late 17th century, barely half a century after the death of James. King James himself was much concerned with witches — in fact, the volume entitled *Demonology* (1597) is attributed to King James himself. How is a witch defined here? A witch was a woman who sold her soul to the Devil in exchange for the Devil's assistance in gaining the impossible. Traditionally, witches were old and ugly, the assumption being that beautiful women didn't need the Devil's help to get what they wanted. In exchange for her soul, the witch received, not only the Devil's help, but also long life. The catch was that the witch continued to age, and there might come a day when the ancient crone begged for death.

Aside from her soul, a long-term debt, what immediate price did the witch have to pay? She had to become the Devil's handmaiden, a servant who did his bidding. And she had to be available to the Devil for sex, probably an ancient pre–Puritan association of sex with evil. Most important to *Macbeth*, a witch had to give up her right and privilege to create life. That was no sacrifice for the post-menopausal ancient hag, but if a younger woman needed the Devil's help, then she had to forever relinquish the capacity to conceive and give birth.

It is apparent that many directors who tackle this play don't have that bit of lore tucked in the back of their otherwise fertile brains. Casting the witches is a real trap. The next time I go to see this play, if it begins with three svelte Broadway gypsies dancing about and hollering at me full-voice, or a trio of kid-show witches out of *Snow White*, I will quietly rise, leave the theatre, and go to the movies, where I can, at least, be assured of logical casting. When Banquo addresses the witches, he describes them for us: they're withered, wildly dressed, unworldly, with chapped fingers and skinny lips. They appear to be women, but they have beards — another proof that they are old women, who sometimes grow facial hair as their bodies produce less estrogen. The Playwright is very specific, not leaving much to the imagination of the director or costumer.

Examine I.1: there should be no doubt about the Playwright's intention. The very first stage direction, right out of the Folio, states, "Thunder and lightning. Enter three Witches." Witches. Not manifestations of Macbeth's guilty fantasies, not a bevy of blonde chorines, not vestal virgins, not androgynous all-purpose utility actors, not added characters out of Middleton, but Jacobean witches. The witches' language is all doggerel, incantations with an irregular rhyme scheme, tetrameter, not pentameter (AA, BBB, CC, DD), interrupted by cries from the witches' familiars, and there is something missing in the scene, because they begin with a farewell to each other.

Why are they assembled? To do the Devil's bidding, which, by definition, is evil, but collectively, they don't yet know what it is. The witches are waiting for orders, watching, listening for the Devil's command.

Each one of them solves a piece of the puzzle from some thing, a relic, a scrap of evil. They ask the standard questions, when, where, and why. They will meet again on the heath, the battlefield, a place of violence and death, when the battle's lost and won. There will be no truce, no tie; for every win, there's a loss. They'll meet with Macbeth, the soldier, the man of blood, and when they find him, they'll discover what they have to tell him, but not before. Two of the witches are then summoned by their familiars, demons serving them in the form of animals. Graymalkin is a cat, and Paddock is a frog. The witches will meet again when they find Macbeth. The director must not allow them to laugh. These are deadly serious, miserable, old crones, bent on doing Satan's business.

When they assemble again in I.3, they bring with them more objects of dread to help them define their purpose: a dead pig and a human thumb, cut from a shipwrecked pilot. William Preston was the best Second Witch ever — not only was his playing of the role completely accurate, but he was perfect physically, a thin, grizzled old man with penetrating eyes and wispy white hair. I doubled him as Seton.

In Lady Macbeth's first scene, I.5, she addresses first the audience, then unnamed beings, which she refers to as "spirits that tend on mortal thoughts." This speech is a prayer to the forces of evil, asking their help in committing regicide. If the Lady wants the help of evil spirits, she must be willing to trade something important in return, and that thing is her fundamental feminine nature. She asks to be unsexed, filled with masculine cruelty, her mother's milk turned to gall, bitter bile, unsuitable for nursing a child, and this is the witch's bargain: to give up her ability to bring forth children in exchange for becoming queen through the death of Duncan. She even prays for the courage to perform the murder herself. There is no audible answer to her prayer, but there's also no doubt that she has concluded it. What changes, what happens in that moment between the end of the prayer and the arrival of Macbeth?

There's no greater aphrodisiac for the soldier than surviving a battle. He has escaped death, and he burns to create life. Returning soldiers are the world's horniest. Macbeth comes home to his wife, exhausted perhaps, but flying with his triumphs and new honors, and who greets him? Not an eager lover, but a would-be co-conspirator. What a turn-off! Suddenly, there he is, catching her in the prayer, and there's no reunion — no "Thank God you're safe," no "Good to be home," no "What's for dinner?"— just right into the conspiracy! In this sparse, edited text, we are never shown a happy marriage; just a series of introspective soliloquies and arguments between Mac and the Lady as to whether they should kill the old man or not.

There's no affection, no time for sex. He doesn't suggest it. She doesn't suggest it. Neither makes a pass at the other.

Never again will there be tenderness, love between husband and wife. If there is an embrace, it's empty, cold, impotent. They are not lovers reunited after a time of danger. The Lady has urged her husband to commit murder, and if he should falter at the last moment, we have to believe that she is capable of doing the deed herself. Her prayer to the forces of evil has been answered: she is unsexed, Duncan is murdered, the Macbeths become king and queen, and their marriage is destroyed because she can no longer conceive children. There will be no heir to Macbeth's ill-gained throne.

Shakespeare was obsessed with male heirs after the death of his only son, Hamnet. Macbeth bemoans his childless state in the crucial soliloquy in III.1.52 to 76: he concludes that he has committed an unpardonable sin, and only the children of Banquo will benefit. When Fleance escapes his murderers, Macbeth takes one more step into madness.

At the risk of over-emphasis, I will spell this out again: Macbeth is willing to barter his eternal soul to become king. He'll "jump the life to come." But Lady Mac makes *her* compact with the Devil without consulting her husband. She sacrifices what is most important to him: the male heir. From the moment of their reunion at I.5.58, their marriage is destroyed, over, sterile. The subtext of her remaining scenes is the impotence of their sex life, her inability to conceive a child.

In one of the most expensive, lavish productions of this play in recent memory, the Public's 2006 Central Park offering, there was a total lack of awareness of this crucial fact. An award-winning director, assisted by an able dramaturg, supported by a knowledgeable producer, guiding famous and talented actors, all were oblivious to this crucial element, the unsexing of the lady.

Again, the sparseness of the edited text hinders the director and the actress. Lady Mac is only on-stage for a few minutes before she turns herself into a vicious co-conspirator. From the moment Macbeth arrives home, she's the Fourth Witch, and everything she says and does is all about her complicity. She is obsessed with murdering Duncan until the deed is accomplished, and then she can't forget the details of his butchering, keeps returning to it. The famous sleepwalking scene, V.1, is little more than a guilty, fragmented replaying of earlier events, those of I.7 and II.2. If those earlier scenes are securely rehearsed, then V.1 should stage itself. There is a terrible irony built into the play, hinted at many times, but never directly confronted. Husband and wife outwit each other.

The best Lady Macs I directed were Nina Polan, a Polish actress (good English-speaker though) who did the 1968 South Jersey tour, and Susan Klein, a grad student at Penn State in 1981. They went on, served the text, played what was there, watched from the wings until the curtain call, then put the role on their resumes. No leading diva behavior, no attempts to take over the play. Lady Mac is not a co-star role: it's a fifth or sixth support. *Macbeth* is not *Antony and Cleopatra*. Try telling that to a modern American actress, especially one with a "name." She'll call her agent.

Structurally, Macbeth is simple compared to Shakespeare's other plays: there is only one plot, the story of Macbeth's usurpation of the crown and his ultimate dethronement by the loyalists. Few of the characters, other than Macbeth and his Lady, are fully developed.

Aside from scene IV.3, we don't learn much about the rightful heir to the throne of Scotland, Malcolm. Duncan never addresses either of his sons by name. There's but cursory contact with Malcolm and none with Donalbain.

In I.4, Duncan lavishes praise on Macbeth and Banquo, but spends only seven lines (about 20 seconds) declaring Malcolm to be the rightful heir to the throne, naming him "Prince of Cumberland." Because the modern audience is unlikely to be aware that this title was the equivalent to the British Prince of Wales, that announcement probably goes right over their heads, especially since the play gives neither Malcolm nor Donalbain any lines in response to this honor. Macbeth, in soliloquy, refers to Malcolm's new title as an obstacle:

> ...a step
> On which I must fall down, or else o'erleap,
> For in my way it lies.

Nothing more is said about Malcolm being the rightful king until we get to that detailed and uncut IV.3.

Duncan himself is crucially important to the *main* plot but the text doesn't spend much time in developing his character. In fact, far more time is spent with Macbeth and his Lady debating whether or not to kill Duncan and, later, lamenting his death. We learn more about Duncan from what they say about him than we do watching and listening to him. He is referred to as "the king" but nobody calls him by name to his face. After I.7, 22 minutes into the play, we never see him again, unless the director adds a welcome home party or a crossover after the party, at the beginning of II.1. That doesn't give the actor playing the role a lot to build on. Again, the severe editing diminishes the tension in the play. There are only 24 minutes between the prophecy, "Macbeth, that shall be king hereafter," and the off-stage murder of Duncan that gives Macbeth the throne.

How does Macbeth become king? The parallels with *Hamlet* come to mind. After the discovery of Duncan's murder, not one person points out the obvious, that Malcolm should now be the king and should be addressed as such with the traditional, "The king is dead: long live the king!" Macduff announces Duncan's death, first to the general assemblage, then to Malcolm and Donalbain, but he does not address Malcolm as king. Everyone, including Malcolm, seems to have forgotten that he's the rightful heir apparent, the Prince of Cumberland.

The heavens protest the death of Duncan with a terrible storm. Horses go mad and eat each other, nature itself is in upheaval, in line with Elizabethan beliefs regarding what happens when God's anointed is replaced, but why doesn't Duncan return as a ghost to accuse Macbeth? Banquo does. Hamlet's father does. Why not Duncan? The next time I do the play, I may experiment by adding the Ghost of Duncan to the banquet scene, III.4, by placing him across the stage from Banquo on his stool, so that Macbeth is trapped between them. That might help or hurt.

Macduff, the avenger of the rightful king and heir, also suffers from under-development. Where is he in the early scenes, when Macbeth and Banquo are fresh returned from defending Scotland in Fife against the Norwegian invasion? Although he is not identified as the Thane of Fife until late in the play, he surely would have been involved in protecting his thanedom. When he does speak for the first time in II.3, no one addresses him by name; not until II.4

is he referred to as Macduff. Banquo refers to him several minutes later as "dear Duff," but that is unfocused. Macduff tells Macbeth that he is responsible for waking Duncan up, but we have seen no contact of any kind between Duncan and Macduff.

In my productions I try to establish Macduff more fully by giving him the lines of Angus in I.3 (Macduff is a kinsman to Ross), then keeping him on-stage for the rest of the Duncan scenes. I readily admit that this solution *is* a directorial imposition, but Angus is often absorbed into other characters in productions of this play, as are Menteith, Caithness, and the Old Man in II.4, simply to reduce cast size and thereby save a few bucks.

The future kings plot — Banquo and Fleance — and the prophecy that Banquo "shall get kings, though (he) be none" (their descendants, the apparitions in IV.1) are also thinly developed but can be reinforced in similar fashion by adding Fleance to I.4, and keeping him with his father in all subsequent scenes where Banquo appears.

With such a severely edited, compact text as the Folio gives us, the director may be tempted to indulge in a lot of waves, hugs, handshakes, slaps on the back, locker room guy stuff, family groupings. This play should never be set out of period; the barbaric ferocity of these warriors, akin to the Vikings, is essential. The burden is heavy on the costumer to link families with tartans, and the director may also be tempted to slow down and isolate certain beats to make sure that the audience gets the necessary information. Unlike the other tragedies, there is a conspicuous lack of reinforcement of exposition in *Macbeth*.

The character of the Porter should be planted early in I.5 and in I.6, so we see him getting drunk with the troops. Giving him the messenger's lines at I.5.33 to 39, allows the audience to get a good look at him before he starts to drink. He passes out when the party ends and is awakened by Macduff's knocking at the gate. The primary humor in his famous Hell-gate scene is that he dreams of opening the gate, instead of actually opening it. He opens the dream gate four times before he realizes there's real knocking at the real gate, then when he finally admits Macduff and Lennox after keeping them waiting in the cold so long, he has the gall to ask for a tip. When he doesn't get his tip, he hangs around and tells bawdy jokes, still hoping to pry a few pennies out of Macduff and Lennox. The best Porter I ever saw was Christopher Lloyd, who played him for me three times. As I said in describing his Christopher Sly (*Taming of the Shrew* chapter), he was a superb natural physical comic, and mimed the totality of Hell-gate and the admission of lost souls, as well as the drunken state that created the dream. He squeezed every possible laugh out of his scenes and effectively set up those that followed.

Nevertheless, the Porter's dream is actually a metaphor for a greater reality: there is a hell, and this castle gate leads to it.

Why are the 7th and 8th scenes of Act V structured as they are in the only available text we have? Consider the beats:

a. Malcolm and the loyalists attack the castle.
b. Macbeth kills Young Siward; Macbeth exits.
c. Malcolm, Siward, Ross, etc. enter the castle, then exit again.
d. Macbeth re-enters, encounters Macduff; they fight, then exit; Macduff kills and beheads Macbeth off-stage.
e. Malcolm, Siward, Ross re-enter and mourn the death of Young Siward.
f. Macduff enters with Macbeth's head and proclaims Malcolm king.

Why this structure? Why does Macbeth die off-stage? Most Shakespearean tragic heroes (Richard II, Titus, Romeo, Juliet, Richard III, Julius Caesar, Brutus, Hamlet, Antony,

Cleopatra, Othello, Lear, Coriolanus, etc.) die on-stage, their deaths being the climax of the plot and the penultimate moment of the play: the only other Shakespearean protagonist who dies off-stage is Timon. The only reason I can think of for killing Macbeth off-stage is because you can't cut his head off in front of the audience. Well, you could do it: once.

Mourning Young Siward where it comes in this text is anti-climactic, even embarrassing. It's obvious why the death of Young Siward is in the play but why put his eulogy *after* the big Macbeth/Macduff duel? If the director elects *not* to use the severed head (most audiences don't buy it anyway—they scream with laughter when it's brought out, either from tension or, more often, because it's a bad prop), there is a solution that may correct a Middleton correction and, I believe, restore Shakespeare's initial intent. It's a juxtaposition. Following the list above, move back beat e. so that it follows beat c. The corpse of Young Siward lies where Macbeth left it. Malcolm, Siward, and Ross enter. Ross discovers the corpse on the line, "Your son, my lord, has paid a soldier's debt." Old Siward picks up the corpse of his son, speaks his eulogy over the body, and carries him off. Only one line need be cut: "Here comes newer comfort." Then the play moves toward its climax, the death of Macbeth.

This is the kind of thing that directors do that I really hate, but I think it's legitimate here because Middleton has already compromised the text.

The "Scottish Play," as we saw earlier, has been the undoing of more good actors than any other play I can call to mind. The Oliviers got the worst reviews of their lives doing it. The same with Christopher Plummer and Paul Scofield. There are horror stories about productions of this play. Anthony Quayle said there was only one day in a man's life when he could play Macbeth: the day he's old enough to realize the awful loss, the despair, yet still young enough to fight his way through the last two scenes of Act V. Macbeth, Marc Antony, Othello, Coriolanus, Benedick have to be big tough guys. If you have a short star who wants to play one of those characters, you better hire small people for the rest of the roles.

The only viable Macbeth I ever saw, the only actor who ever made the role work, was Peter MacLean, who played the role for me four times, 1965 to 1968. What was so special about MacLean? First, the obvious: he was a talented, passionate actor who could handle Shakespeare's language. He was big, powerful, good-looking, and actually Scottish, with a wonderful reddish beard. He had a deep voice, a growl. It wasn't pretty—it was frightening. He could bellow and shake the building. He could fight well with sword and shield, and he didn't tire in the Fifth Act, he grew stronger. Most important, he played with an intense ferocity. He convinced you he was a primitive warrior. He made me look like a good director. I have six stitches in my pate as a result of a blow from MacLean's broadsword while playing MacDuff in a television re-enactment of the final duel in Philadelphia in 1966. I am a member of that select, but not small, band of veterans who were dubbed, affectionately, by his cast mates "maimed by MacLean."

On the set of the 1962 Hallmark Hall of Fame television version of *Cyrano de Bergerac*, starring Christopher Plummer, the British actor, George Rose, explained to me the curse of Macbeth—why it's called "the Scottish Play" and considered bad luck to utter the name of the play in a theatre or dressing room or any place other than on the stage in performance.

First, the supernatural: It is believed that Shakespeare used a real witches' curse for the cauldron scene, IV.1, with the result that when the actors say the lines, the demons are actually called down to do service. When they discover they've been summoned for no good reason, they avenge themselves upon the actors. In November 1965, we were doing a student matinee of *Macbeth* in Lynn, Massachusetts. Because two actors were late that day, the show went up 15 minutes late. Just as the soldiers were starting the epic V.6 castle assault, the great Northeast blackout hit, and the play had to be aborted. The emergency back-up lights went on, but it would have been too dangerous to do those fights in such low light. The ancient, dauntless Ed Finnegan, who was playing Duncan, went out into the audience, told the kids the ending of the play and answered questions. The students were deprived of some sensational fights, but they gained a remarkable experience at the hands of one of God's great teachers. Ed was retired from the Boston school system and enjoying a second career as an actor.

There are many, many stories of accidents, mishaps, postponements, replacements, stunts gone wrong — some humorous, some simply annoying — and it's fashionable for actors to roll their eyes and mumble the defensive prayer, "Angels and ministers of grace defend us" when the title of the play is uttered. But, to be objective, similar mishaps happen in all plays. If a fly line breaks and scenery comes crashing down during a performance of *Hamlet*, nobody blames it on the curse of "the Danish play." I suggest that more attention be paid to Murphy's Law, which states, "Whatever can go wrong will go wrong." For more details on the curse of the "Scottish Play," I refer the reader to Richard Hogget's *The Supernatural On-Stage*.

Secondly, the practical: here's where Murphy's Law comes in. This is Shakespeare's most violent play — another good argument for the ideal of the actor as athlete. If you do it correctly, it's inherently dangerous with all those swords, daggers, battleaxes. Since much of it is played in the dark or in low light, stage torches become another hazard. It's essential to provide non-slip boots, helmets, protective gauntlets, and body padding for the actors. They must be trained and drilled as combatants. The fights must be run before each performance, and if the facility is big enough, during the performances, before the actual fights themselves. The actors have to stay warmed up, ready to fight. Lazy actors will create problems for everyone. Most injuries come, not from the swords, but from slips, trips, stumbles that result in sprained muscles or broken ankles. Sword injuries result from actors neglecting to wear helmets or gauntlets. The best helmet in the world won't protect your pate if you don't wear it.

In 1980, the NJSF did 30 performances of this play without a single serious injury: no broken bones, no cuts that required suturing. How did we manage it? We trained the combatants for seven weeks before opening, gave them costumes that protected them as football pads and helmets protect, and paid careful attention to no-slip surfaces, step units, ramps, weapons. I take considerable pride in having developed protective fight gear, training, and a method of performance over the years that have reduced injuries in this play to a minimum. The less power the fight director has, the more likely injuries are to occur. This goes for all the warrior plays, not just *Macbeth*.

I played the Scottish king myself in the summer of 1980, just short of my 49th birthday, and found it to be a Sisyphean exercise, dragging the production on my back. I had a good company, but I felt that the better I got in the role, the greater the antipathy around me became. Hate Macbeth: hate the actor. The play infects its company.

One essential thing was emphasized for me by playing the role: a lot of the evil that Macbeth does happens when he's off-stage, primarily the slaughter of the family of Macduff. If the actor playing Macbeth hangs out in the green room following the cauldron scene that precedes the slaughter of Macduff's children, he escapes the horror of that awful scene and the one that follows, where Macduff is told of it. This is a mistake. Instead, the actor playing Macbeth must remain back stage and listen to those scenes while his dressers equip him for the fights to come, and while he warms up his sword arm, because his performance must be allowed to evolve as the play evolves. The next time we see him on-stage in V.1, we see not a valiant soldier, but a thug who murders babies.

The afternoon of my final performance in the role, we were rehearsing Pinter's *The Caretaker* during the day. At the end of rehearsal, I rode my bicycle home for dinner, and I recall thinking that if a truck hit me on the way home, I'd never have to play that rotten bastard again. I had a good dinner, then drove back to the theatre, dressed, and did the fight warm-ups. Final performance: I was flying. It occurred to me that if any accident happened — if I broke an arm or a leg — it would be part of the performance, and I didn't have to worry about the next: this was the last.

The show wailed. I soared, all the bile and the hate driving me. I fought like a maniac. At the last moment, in the duel with Macduff, I parried a head cut with my sword and hit myself in the forehead. The blood flowed down into my eyes, but I was giddy with the thought that there were only three cuts and two parries left. I finished the fight, fell to the deck, then lay there dead, waiting for the curtain call. In the final blackout, Macduff helped me to my feet, but I couldn't see to get off-stage. During the curtain calls, I waited upstage, then took my call with blood from the wound still flowing. People congratulated me on the spectacular effect, just as they had when I was actually "maimed by MacLean" on the earlier television production.

If asked, I admit that I gave one good performance as Macbeth, after protecting myself (and the play) for the earlier 29 performances. I remember Joe Namath talking about playing quarterback. "The quarterback," he said, "must play without fear, must execute each play in the moment, without memory of the past or concern about the future." The same goes for playing the Scottish king.

CHAPTER 6

The Comedy of Errors

The Comedy of Errors was possibly Shakespeare's first play, inspired by Plautus' *Menaechmi* and expanded for commercial consumption.

I've done this play twice as a director and once as an actor. I don't think it's very good though; it's a one-joke play: super-identical twins cannot be differentiated — they look alike, speak alike, behave alike. Shakespeare does essentially the same thing and does it better in *Twelfth Night* with only one pair of twins, but by then he had another ten years of experience. He had learned to create better comics and to write superb line comedy, which *The Comedy of Errors* lacks.

The good news is that the play is only 1,957 lines long, and it can easily be performed in less than two hours. It doesn't need editing, and it doesn't need an intermission. It's also a great opportunity for good physical comics, if they can be found and cast, to have some fun. The play lends itself to commedia dell'arte slapstick, and there's opportunity for rapid-fire Feydeaux-like entrances and exits. A careful director/choreographer can sustain the running gag by staging the action so that characters barely miss each other as they dash from locale to locale.

The convoluted set-up of *The Comedy of Errors* is that two sets of twins, the Antipholi and the Dromios, born on the same day to a gentlewoman and her maidservant, are separated in infancy in a shipwreck in the Aegean. The father of the Antipholi rescues one of his sons and one of the Dromios and raises them in his home, Syracuse, while the mother of the Antipholi, with her other son and the other Dromio, is rescued by another ship and raises them in Ephesus.

Twenty-three years later, mother and father, both Antipholi and both Dromios find themselves in Ephesus during a war between Syracuse and Ephesus. The father, Egeon, has been arrested as a spy and sentenced to death, but the Duke of Ephesus has given him until sundown to raise a ransom that will buy his pardon.

That's the premise, set forth in an eight-minute expository monologue by Egeon before the audience even has a chance to settle in. Latecomers — fie on them! — will not have a clue as to what's happening, but unless they're held in the lobby until this scene ends, they'll disrupt it and fog up the already elaborate back-story. That back-story must be nailed in with all the craft of the director, the designers, and the actors before the plot starts to roll.

I set my 1980 production in New Orleans during Mardi Gras, opening with a production number set to a Dixieland arrangement of "Tiger Rag," during which the Antipholi, Dromios, Adriana and Luciana chose their Mardi Gras costumes from the racks of street vendors. This not only produced a jovial carnival atmosphere and introduced all the characters in the first scene but solved the problem of making the twins look alike: the Syracusans arrived dressed as travelers, while the Ephesians were dressed like everyone else in the cast. Coincidentally, both Antipholi selected to rent lion-tamer costumes, while both Dromios rented circus clown costumes. Adriana went as Cleopatra, and her sister, Luciana, went as Little Bo Peep. Angelo was one of Sinbad's 40 thieves, and the First Merchant was a pirate, complete with parrot.

That stunt, though it was visually interesting and partially effective, still depended on the audience buying the premise that the Antipholi and Dromios would select the same circus costumes. We helped the odds by depleting the street vendors' rental stock; there were few choices left.

We kept the house lights on, and ushers continued to seat latecomers through the number and the applause that followed. The action of the play itself began as a court of law convened in the street, so that the Duke wouldn't miss out on the Mardi Gras festivities. This was the first play my daughter Shannon ever saw: it opened two months before her fourth birthday. Of course, she loved the crowds and the production number with its clowns, but about halfway through Egeus' long mournful monologue, she piped up in a clear, loud voice, "Mommy, when that man stops talking, will the clowns come back?" This was heard not only by the whole audience, but the actor himself, who was not as charmed by Shannon as others were.

The Mardi Gras setting worked in delaying the beginning of the play and isolating the exposition scene, but it didn't solve all the problems. The lack of funny lines in *Comedy of Errors* is a big problem: It's often difficult to figure out where the joke is. Bill Pitts, a marvelous comic, played Dromio of Syracuse for me in 1980, and we tried to figure out what made the Father Time routine in II.2 funny. It felt like a standard vaudeville routine with Antipholus

The Comedy of Errors, New Jersey Shakespeare Festival, 1980: William Pitts as Dromo of Syracuse, Davis Hall as Dromio of Ephesus (photograph by Jerry Dalia).

of Syracuse playing straight man. We consulted several scholars, other actors, and a few directors, and nobody could help us out. So, Pitts just went out and played what was there, making the lines clear, but each time, he bombed. I'd meet him off-stage after the scene. He'd be bathed in sweat, despondent from a lack of laughs. We never did make it funny.

Pitts did significantly better with his description of Nell, the fat kitchen wench, whom he compares to a globe of the world. I learned, however, that adding an actress to play Nell into the play is a mistake: the character is far funnier if left to the audience's imagination.

What's the director to do with such limited comic material? In my 1966 production, we just played it fast and furiously, let pratfalls land where they might, and the audience loved the action, though I'm sure many were confused by the plot.

This play depends on the credibility of the confusion. Even his brother's wife mistakes Antipholus of Syracuse for his brother. The mistaken identity is so complete that she can take him to bed for a little afternoon delight without discovering her error. Masters confuse servants, and servants confuse masters, even though they've been together for 23 years. What does the audience need? Two sets of super-identical twins.

Coleridge's theory about the willful suspension of disbelief is often invoked as the solution to dilemmas like this, but it's been misinterpreted even more than Thomas Jefferson's line about all men being created equal. An audience cannot be expected to lie to themselves as they experience a play. They see what they see, and they hear what they hear. Wigs, mustaches, beards, and skillful make-up artists can emphasize facial similarities and soft-peddle differences. The director still has to cast actors with similar physiques, but the common mistake that most directors make is to crutch the similarity among the twins with identical costumes. I made this mistake myself.

For the comedy to succeed, however, the audience must be constantly in on the joke. This is so obvious that I'm embarrassed to put it to paper. In each successive scene, the audience must be aware, absolutely sure, of which Antipholus and which Dromio they're watching. The other characters can get them wrong, but the audience cannot. Again, the credibility: Adriana may mistake her husband's brother for her husband, but the audience knows which is which, and is titillated by the sumptuous young wife taking the wrong twin to bed. The audience's enjoyment is derived from their sense of superiority, of knowing more than the characters know.

Am I beating this to death? I have never seen a production of this play, even a commedia-based production with masks at Stratford, Ontario, where the confusions worked a hundred percent.

I'd like to have the resources to do a production with three Antipholi and three Dromios. The first-cast Antipholus would play both Antipholi, and the first-cast Dromio play both Dromios. The second cast would understudy the first, and play the Act V reunion scene. The second and third casts would do crossovers and chases. Egeon, Antipholus and Dromio of Syracuse will always be dressed as Sicilians, foreign travelers, while Antipholus and Dromio of Ephesus will dress like Ephesians. The costumer would need to create a radically distinctive difference between the two looks.

Each Antipholus will have two costumes and a battery of dressers, as will each Dromio. Both Antipholi will be identical, because it will be the same actor playing both, but with different clothes. The same will be true with the Dromios. The effect will always be two sets of twins, narrowly missing each other at each entrance and exit. Figure out the entrances and exits. It will work, and you'd be hiring no more than the four actors and two understudies the play usually demands.

It's certain that Will Kempe played one of the Dromios, but he could have played them both. It can and has been done. Stephen Burdman's 2006 Central Park production utilized two actors for the Antipholi but only one actor, Grant Neale, for the Dromios. He was superb, a gifted physical comic, his Dromio of Syracuse identical to his Dromio of Ephesus, except for turning a baseball cap around, and they were dressed alike. The result, however, was confusing.

Earlier, we've touched on the tradition of heckling between comics and audience at Elizabethan performances. Though we have blessed little information about the heckler, it makes sense to assume that he existed during the heyday of Kempe's career, and that the heckler-comic interchange was wildly improvisational. Today's playgoers are well behaved, but the heckler is still alive and well in the British music hall and panto traditions. While comic improvisation is an entirely separate skill unto itself, every actor must be capable of ad-libbing to cover and adjust to accidents, missed entrances, dropped lines, misplaced props, which happen often. Audiences love accidents and actors' adjustments to them.

Kempe's improvisational skills were as valued as his other abilities, and certainly he must have been encouraged to heckle back at the hecklers, as long as he didn't insult a nobleman or a valued patron. Only when Shakespeare developed the ability to write his signature brilliant line comedy was Kempe squelched. The Playwright had learned to interweave comedy with serious text, and ad-libs could destroy a serious moment.

A playwright can find himself swinging in the other direction. Neil Simon became so skillful at writing sit-com line comedy that he couldn't write a serious play. He almost made it with *The Gingerbread Lady* (1971) but every time he wrote something profound about the human condition, he had to tag it with a one-liner that would bring down the house and shatter the serious moment. Maybe that's his genius, a temperament incapable of taking life seriously.

One other running gag I created helps alleviate a problem in the play, the need to facilitate the costume changes. After his opening monologue, Egeon disappears for another hour and 15 minutes until the tie-up scene. I gave Duke Solinus the entourage of a headsman, a court scribe, and an arresting officer. Every time a little more breathing space was needed, I brought Egeon, the Duke, and his crew back in crossovers, where Egeon continued telling his story, going back to the beginning and elaborating, stretching it out while the scribe kept writing, and the others followed. In the process, Egeon even panhandled the audience to make his ransom. The record of evidence grew, the Duke suffered sore feet, much shtick transpired, but no more than a few minutes were added to the running time.

Incidentally, I don't think *The Comedy of Errors* works in a park. It's a very urban play: the whole thing takes place inside the city of Ephesus, streets between the house of Adriana and the Abby.

Finally, it can't be trusted as other Shakespeare comedies can.

CHAPTER 7

The Two Gentlemen of Verona

The Two Gentlemen of Verona was probably written for Will Kempe, who played Lance. According to tradition, Kempe had a dog named Crab that was never housebroken. Master and dog were inseparable, with Kempe always bringing Crab to rehearsals and performances, where he would raid the lunchboxes of the actors and relieve himself wherever it suited him, indoors or out. The other actors tried to get Crab barred from the theatre. Instead, Shakespeare confided to Kempe that he had written a play about a serving man and his dog. If Kempe could get Burbage to produce the play, Kempe would have a perfect excuse for bringing his dog to work.

There are two scenes in *The Two Gentlemen of Verona* that are standup comic turns, for Lance and Crab. Many solutions have been tried to get around these scenes, including a hand puppet or a small actor in a dog suit, but nothing works but a real dog. To cast Crab for our 1975 NJSF production, we announced in the papers that we were holding auditions on a Saturday afternoon on the lawn of the theatre. Ron Steelman, who played Lance, conducted the auditions, and some 35 dogs of all sizes, ages, and shapes showed up. It was a great afternoon. He ran the dogs up and down the lawn, wrestled with them, cuddled them. We took photographs of all of them, the stage manager recorded copious notes as well as Steelman's comments, and we ended up with a good Crab plus two stand-bys. I recently asked Steelman why he chose the dog he did, and he said he wanted an older dog that would be calm enough not to resist going along with the gag every night. The dog he cast was perfect.

In both scenes, the dog should be led in on a rope, which is then tied off while Lance complains to the audience about him and tells the story of his leave-taking from his family. In addition, Lance needs a hat, easily removable shoes, and a walking staff. He casts his family members with his hat, shoes, staff, the dog, and himself, but has some difficulty with this initial casting and switches characters around. Much shtick is possible with the staff, which has to stand up to work, but, of course, doesn't.

Whatever the dog does during Lance's soliloquy will be funny. The dog is funny just sitting there, ignoring the dialogue, perhaps watching something or someone else in the theatre. If the dog barks or growls, the actor is forced to respond, and that is funny. If the dog yawns or scratches itself, the audience howls. If the dog lies down to take a nap, the house comes down. Of course, the dog will do something different in each performance. Lance can learn and rehearse the scenes as written, but in performance, he has no choice but to go with what the dog does. The dog effectively steals every scene it's in, but a talented Lance never really loses control of the character or the situation.

The myth is that Kempe was upset with Shakespeare for turning the tables on him by giving the dog such focus, but I doubt it. A comic like Kempe would have welcomed the

The Two Gentlemen of Verona, New Jersey Shakespeare Festival, 1975: Ron Mangravite as Speed, Alan Jordan as Valentine and Mark Churchill, Barbi Alison, Tiana Jo Schlitten and Faye Pollock as Punchinelli (photograph by Blair Holley).

opportunity to play those scenes differently each time. Today we tend to sympathize with Shakespeare's rule of demanding that his actors stick to the script, but did he always? I submit that Kempe's improvisational playing style influenced the early comedies as well as comic passages in later more serious plays written between *The Comedy of Errors* and *Henry V*. Shakespeare wrote 20 plays before we hear the admonition about "those who play your clowns..." in *Hamlet*. Even when he had gained enough power to insist on adherence to his script, what he had learned from Kempe continued to influence him.

I can imagine Kempe giving the same kind of performance I saw Mickey Rooney give as Pseudolus in *A Funny Thing Happened on the Way to the Forum*. He stole every minute of the show, even the entrance of the courtesans, which Zero Mostel (who created the role), at least, sat still for. Perhaps it was all those years of film acting, which is often improvisational, or three years on Broadway and on the road with the burlesque review *Sugar Babies*, but Rooney was always on and always the focus, often blowing lines and interfering with the ensemble. The other actors stuck to the script, and they bitterly resented Rooney's theft of the spotlight, but manners, protocol, and star privilege aside, he was brilliant, and the audience loved him.

But enough of Lance and Crab. What's to be said about the play itself? It's a slight effort, like *Comedy of Errors*. The northern Italian setting of *Two Gentlemen of Verona* suggested the commedia dell'arte style of our 1975 production. Shakespeare could have visited northern Italy with Henry Wriothesley, 3rd Earl of Southampton and John Florio, scholar and translator, in the late 1580's. The Playwright seems to know a lot about Milan, Pisa, Verona, Mantua, Padua, and Venice, many seemingly random bits and pieces. He's been taken to task for sending Proteus and Valentine from Verona to Milan by boat, but the canals of northern Italy in the 16th century could have made such a voyage possible.

In our production, we used a chorus of six Punchinelli — interns who could mime, sing, dance and play instruments — as crowds, servants, bandits, orchestra and chorus, minor roles. They also played natural forces, wind, rain, trees, and inanimate objects. We used them wherever possible rather than scenic elements. For instance, the Punchinelli played the gondola Valentine and Proteus traveled in as well as the gondolier. They provided the breath that blew Julia's letter around. Although the principals did not, they wore commedia dell'arte masks, which helped to establish the conceit that they were invisible.

The Punchinelli certainly enhanced the play and provided a great deal of humor, but they worked too hard as individual performers to take focus, causing the principals to complain. As director, I spent more time reining them in than exploiting them. The idea is worth revisiting, but I'd recommend hiring a commedia choreographer to work with the director. By all means, don't cast a Punchinello as Crab.

In *Two Gentlemen of Verona*, Shakespeare introduces the concept of the anti-hero, which he would develop further with Bertram in *All's Well That Ends Well*. In contrast to lovers in his earlier plays, who fall in love at first sight and then stay faithful through thick and thin, Proteus begins the play in love with Julia but goes mad with lust for his friend Valentine's beloved, Sylvia, as soon as he is introduced to her. He will do anything to win the enchantress Sylvia, who does nothing to either entice him or discourage him. Though everyone else in the play, including Crab, behaves in a moral manner, Proteus begins as a simple loser, then turns into a monster. He abandons Julia, betrays his best friend Valentine, almost has him killed, deceives Sylvia, and lies to the Duke of Milan.

The two women are prototypes for many a later comedy: Sylvia should be a knock-out, the kind who renders every male in the house weak in the knees, while Julia must be the girl next door who everyone pulls for. Think Rosalind and Celia or Liz Taylor and Debbie Reynolds.

Despite her innocence, however, Julia's soliloquy with the letter from Proteus is bawdier in the text than most actresses want to play it. When she tears up the letter, then pieces it back together she needs a dress with an open bodice and sufficient cleavage to tuck the mismatched fragments into bed. The letter also presents a clean-up problem. Julia must tear up the letter, but must gather all the fragments before she leaves the stage. Any pieces left will interfere with the next scene.

Does Julia abandon Proteus? Of course not. She's as loving and oblivious to his faults as that other paragon of virtue, Helena, in *All's Well That Ends Well*.

Once again, the play ends with the proper lovers united, and once again, they go off to bed to make pretty babies.

CHAPTER 8

Twelfth Night

What You Will, better known as *Twelfth Night*, is the perfect play. There's only one version available to us, the Folio text, and there's not a single extraneous syllable in it. Produce it uncut, and your audience will love it. It's not foolproof, not foolish-director-proof, but, like *A Midsummer Night's Dream*, it will survive a thousand stupid choices.

One difficulty might be that every actor really wants to play Hamlet, and every director really wants to direct *King Lear*, but the producer wants to do *Twelfth Night*—it will sell more tickets!—and so the director digs through the text for great cosmic meanings and the actor tries to discover murky depths in Orsino. I won't be such a barbarian as to declare that there aren't any great cosmic depths in *Twelfth Night*, but consider this exchange:

Sir Toby: "Does not our lives consist of the four elements?"

Sir Andrew: "Faith, so they say; but I think it rather consists of eating and drinking."

Sir Toby: "Thou'rt a scholar; let us therefore eat and drink. Marian, I say, A stoup of wine."

That's scholarship! Life consists of earth, air, water and fire, but most of all, it's eating and drinking, so let's have another drink. If there are any deep meanings in the play, the Playwright has buried them deeper, and it's wisest to leave them alone to bubble to the surface of the audience's consciousness. If you go digging for them, you will be in danger of obscuring the Playwright's main intent: to present a funny, happy evening in the theatre.

Twelfth Night was written soon after *As You Like It* and *Hamlet*. Commissioned for the Royal Court's celebration of the twelve nights of Christmas, 1602, a few months before the death of Elizabeth, it is structurally brilliant—Shakespeare's best. Three plots are interwoven that parallel and comment on each other, with the major characters in each becoming the minor characters in the others, and Feste, the Clown, acting as a master of ceremonies who bridges all three.

I first did *Twelfth Night* at the Oregon Shakespeare Festival in 1951, understudying Feste and serving as the production prompter. I don't know whether they still do it this way, but at that time, each Oregon production had a prompter who was present at every minute of every rehearsal and every performance. The prompter usually had no other responsibilities. In rehearsal, he would wait for actors to ask for lines, but in performance, he sat in a covered box down center, chin-high to stage level, and listened to the tempo of the play. The moment an actor faltered or hesitated, the prompter would throw, first, a word, then three words. By the time the production closed, I had memorized the entire play.

Angus Bowmer played Sir Toby in this production. He was superb, but he had difficulty with lines. He produced the entire season, directed *King Lear*, and performed as an actor in two productions. He could have been a famous Shakespearean actor, but his contribution as the founder and director of the OSF was one of incalculable worth.

I directed the play twice: in 1965 for the Boston Herald-Traveler Repertory and again in Madison in 1982.

As in *The Comedy of Errors*, Shakespeare gives us the problem of identical twins, and adds the challenge of the disguised Viola being accepted as a male. The director should not trust that Viola's disguise will work simply because it always works. Who said that? Coleridge? That's a literary axiom, not a theatrical one. On the page, it's a given, because that's what is written. There are whole novels built on it, but on the professional stage, directors, actors, costumers, and make-up people work hard to substantiate disguises. I've never seen, directed, or been in a completely successful *Comedy of Errors*. The mistaken identity problems are seemingly unbeatable. With *Twelfth Night*, cast a tall, slim Viola, and then coach her in playing a teen-aged boy. You don't want the audience wondering why Orsino doesn't know she's a she.

I like to set *Twelfth Night* in the Cavalier period, 1640s, because these costumes are just loose enough to hide Viola's body, both men and women wore their hair long, and

Twelfth Night, New Jersey Shakespeare Festival, 1982: Annie Stafford as Maria, Dane Knell as Feste, Ron Steelman as Sir Toby Belch, Zeke Zaccaro as Sir Andrew Aguecheek (photograph by Jerry Dalia).

beards were optional. Viola and Sebastian should be dressed in similar, but not identical costumes. Repeat: similar, but not identical! Both wear rapiers in baldrics without scabbard (the blade is naked). They should look as much alike as hair and make-up can accomplish. The flamboyance of the costumes, hats, and swords, in contrast to Puritan austerity, also helps distinguish Malvolio from the comic servants.

The play begins with music — at the NJSF, our Madrigals ended their pre-show concert by singing a love song on-stage, which seamlessly began the action. The Playwright spends little time on exposition, but plunges headlong into the main plot: Duke Orsino's pursuit of his beloved, the Countess Olivia, who has vowed not to marry but to remain in mourning for seven years for her recently deceased brother.

The introduction of the second plot follows quickly: the twins Viola and Sebastian have survived a shipwreck in the Aegean, but neither knows the other's fate. Viola has managed to make it to shore with her brother's wardrobe chest. To protect herself, she disguises herself as Sebastian, and finds employment as a courtier with Orsino.

If the director decides that the survival of Sebastian should be doubtful, the play will begin darkly. I prefer for the audience to believe that he's alive. But if the Sea Captain convinces Viola that her brother's courage and athletic ability probably saved his life, then the question is resolved too early and eliminated from the list of worries. A brooding Viola, indulging her melancholy about her lost brother or her unrequited love for Orsino, will drag the play down. Considering currents and tides, Viola, the Captain and the mariners probably came ashore within a few miles of Sebastian and Antonio. With a big enough stage, focus can be split and the two groups can be seen arriving at roughly the same time.

The third plot is that of the pretentious Puritan Malvolio and his comeuppance at the hands of the pranksters Sir Toby, Andrew and Maria. Within these stories are multiple combinations of lovers and lusters:

Olivia, pursued by Orsino, Sir Andrew, and Malvolio
Orsino, pursued by Viola
Viola, pursued by Olivia, who ends up with Sebastian
Sir Toby and Maria.

In consideration of our 21st-century American audience, permit me to conjecture and define the probable back-story: Duke Orsino, the ruler of Illyria, is a bachelor seeking a wife and eventual heir. The second wealthiest man in Illyria is a Count, the father of Olivia, and her brother. It is logical to suppose that the Count and Duke Orsino contracted for a marriage between Orsino and Olivia before the Count's death, which left Olivia in the custody of her brother, who shortly also died. I submit that Olivia never wanted to marry Orsino in the first place, but she is bound to her father's contract, so she procrastinates, creating the perfect evasion with a seven-year mourning period. She would not openly violate her father's contract with Orsino, but no one can criticize her for mourning her father and brother. This allows her control of her own destiny. Protocol demands that she receive Orsino's messengers with courtesy, but she's also free to discourage them, because she's in mourning.

When we first see Orsino, he's dutifully following the traditions of courtly romance, writing poetry, daydreaming about his beloved, listening to love songs, sending presents and messages. He's not just lonely: there would be political pressure on him to produce an heir, so he's stuck. He has to marry, and he has to convince all eyes and ears that he's really in love. He's not going to wait seven years for Olivia; he must either convince her to abandon her mourning or find himself another wife.

With the casting of Orsino it is important to bear in mind that he is a head of state, mature, handsome, charming. Though we only see him in his courtly love mode, he is, nevertheless, in command. He doesn't share in much of the comedy, and the role doesn't give the actor many "marbles," but like Don Pedro and Albany, Orsino must have stature and strength. Orsino's court is entirely peopled by courtiers, all males, who take turns carrying messages, written or memorized, to Olivia.

Hire your Viola first, and cast to her. Then, find a good male actor who resembles your Viola to play Sebastian, and the rest of the casting is a cinch. Robin Leary, who played the role in my 1972 NJSF production, was the best Viola I've ever seen. A charming, graceful, tall and slim brunette, Robin had both humor and poignancy — everything the role calls for.

The Countess Olivia's household is made up of her cousin, Sir Toby Belch, a knight in his late 30s or early 40s; Olivia's lady-in-waiting, Maria; Malvolio, the steward of the estate; Feste the clown, Fabian, an all-purpose male servant; a few miscellaneous serving ladies, and a multitude of servants that we never see.

Add to this group Sir Andrew Aguecheek, a wealthy knight "on carpet consideration"— meaning he didn't earn his title: he bought it. He is also a suitor to Olivia, though she's probably unaware of it. Sir Toby encourages Andrew because he pays for the cakes and ale, which would otherwise disappear in a house of mourning. Andrew is a phony who pretends to knowledge he doesn't possess: he claims to be a linguist, which he isn't, and he boasts of his fencing ability, which we find in III.4 is non-existent. He even brags about his bearbaiting ability. What does that mean? Bearbaiting was a gruesome spectator sport, a contest to the death between savage dogs and a starved and enraged bear chained to an upright timber. Fans would occasionally show off to the crowd by moving in on the bear and taunting it. With luck, they'd get away with a scratch or two, but sometimes they were seriously injured. Despite all of the braggadocio, Andrew doesn't have to be played as a moron. What we see is the façade, and the façade is constantly being pricked to expose the great loveable fool beneath. He has the saddest line in the play: "I was adored once."

At least two ladies-in-waiting to Olivia are essential to make sense out of I.5. When Cesario (Viola) enters, he sees four well-dressed women in mourning veils. That's why he asks which is the lady of the house. Olivia wants to keep her identity hidden until she has a chance to examine Orsino's messenger. Does she fall in love with him at first sight? Quite possibly, but the moment is difficult to substantiate with veiled faces.

To cast Malvolio, it is imperative to remember that *Twelfth Night* is a class-conscious play, based on a hierarchical British society, with royalty and nobility on top, then the knights (a military, not hereditary, rank) then gentlemen and ladies, and finally the servants and lower classes at the bottom. Romantic couplings between classes were possible, but discouraged by the in-bred snobbery of the system. It was more likely that a woman might "marry up" than a man. Social traditions implicit in the setup of the first three scenes were so familiar to Shakespeare's audience at court that further exposition was unnecessary.

As Olivia's steward, is Malvolio really a gentleman? A steward was a member of the servant class, in charge of all purchasing, property maintenance, hiring and firing, accounting on an estate. He held the master key to all doors and strongboxes. The bigger Olivia's estate, the greater his responsibilities, but he is still far beneath Olivia, and even her uncle, Sir Toby, in rank, and his behavior, several times, seriously violates social protocol. His airs of superiority are what prompt Maria, Toby, et al. to take revenge on him. His behavior would have seemed peculiar, even perverted, to Shakespeare's audience. He's a social climber, dreaming of becoming Count Malvolio, lusting after Olivia, but more important than his lust are his social aspirations. Unless class snobbery is built into the play from the beginning, the reactions of Olivia and her household to Malvolio may seem bizarre or puzzling to a modern audience. Olivia has given Malvolio a great deal of power in her household, and Toby does not want to jeopardize his meal ticket.

The fact that Malvolio is referred to as a Puritan and is usually costumed as such, all in black or dark grey, deepens his pretentiousness and helps Shakespeare make much of his hypocrisy—especially his sexual hypocrisy. Puritans were a religious sect, so named because they aspired to a simple Christianity, devoid of ceremony and any manner of ostentatious display. They demanded pure behavior from their followers, forbidding secular activities such as singing, dancing, theatergoing, profanity, games, drinking, smoking, and especially sex, except for the purpose of procreation. Olivia's mourning posture suits Malvolio well, because he's able to keep a tighter rein on any and all spending.

The political power of the Puritans increased though the reign of King Charles I until Oliver Cromwell and his parliament launched a Civil War in 1642 and took over the government, sending Charles to the block in 1649. The Puritan Protectorship lasted for 11 years until Charles II was restored to the throne.

Directors and choreographers who conduct actor-training programs at academies and universities will attest to the fact that playing social class differences is inherently difficult for Americans, who are brought up to believe in democracy and egalitarianism and disapprove of class discrimination. Good acting in plays like *Twelfth Night*, which depend on class consciousness, often require the actor to display what he has been brought up to consider bad manners. Inhibitions, manners, and courteous behavior conditioned since early childhood must be eliminated. Unlike the actors who play them, characters in *Twelfth Night* have been bred to observe the differences between the nobility and the "lighter people."

I've seen productions where the roles of Feste and Fabian were combined. Bad idea. They have separate functions and different personalities.

Feste was court fool to Olivia's father and should therefore be cast older to clarify his longevity at her court. Since Olivia places such importance on her mourning, Feste is in danger of losing his job. When we first see him, the text implies that he's been out looking for work, free-lancing as a balladeer, street comic, and panhandler. Like Touchstone in *As You Like It* and the Fool in *King Lear*, Feste is one of Shakespeare's more sophisticated clowns, first played by Robin Armin. I played Feste in 1991 as a baggy-pants circus clown in an Off-Broadway production set in New Orleans in the 1920s. That was great fun, and the play was greatly enhanced by traditional instrumentalists playing on an upper level above the stage throughout the performance. All of Shakespeare's songs were set to Dixieland melodies composed by Peter Nissan. The band played bridges between scenes, defining tempos from one to another. As Feste, I got to play clarinet.

The standup comic is a clown in soliloquy, the irreducible minimum. As we saw in *Comedy of Errors*, the original standup, Will Kempe, had great freedom in his improvisations and in dealing with the hecklers.

Sir Toby and Sir Andrew are an example of the many comic/straight man pairs in Shakespeare, like Valentine and Speed, Petruchio and Grumio, Berowne and Costard, Don Armado and Moth, all models for such later pairs as Abbot and Costello or Laurel and Hardy. Burns and Allen, Sid Caesar and Imogene Coca, Lucy and Desi—innumerable husband and wife domestic comedies merely substitute a woman for either comic or straight man.

The comic double form was standard through the early decades of the 20th century: Gallagher and Sheen, Smith and Dale, for example. Add a third or fourth character, or more, as in the quintet who gang up on Malvolio, and we can detect the genesis of the Marx Brothers, the Three Stooges, the Seinfeld cast, and the loony Parisian artists in the musical *Can Can*, Cole Porter's take-off on *La Bohème*.

Even with the advent of three and four-person acts, the basic comic/straight man form has been maintained in the writing: the straight man does the set up, straight man and comic share the complication, and the comic has the punch line, sometimes a double punch. Shakespeare didn't invent this kind of comedy — it can be found in the works of Greek and Roman playwrights — but Shakespeare raised it to high art.

Such teams were a mainstay of burlesque and vaudeville, popular through the '50s, the former "blue" for men only, the latter clean for the whole family. When I worked as a "houseman" at the Gaiety Burlesque in Detroit in 1955, I was also studying with Leo Kirschbaum at Wayne State University. He used to come to every second show on Thursday, and we'd go out for dinner between shows. He'd go through all the skits and describe their genesis: the Greeks, Terrance and Plautus, commedia dell'arte, medieval morality plays, Shakespeare, Molière, 3,000 years of hand-me-down shtick.

I couldn't have paid anyone or any school for what I learned by working with the genius Scurvy Miller and those other great old comic performers. I did that job for five months, 29 shows a week, and it was exhausting, but after that, one-week summer stock was a cinch. The comics were in their 70s and 80s then, and burlesque was gone a few years later.

Motion pictures are blamed for squeezing out vaudeville, but it survived for quite a time in hybrids. I have a program from October 1925 from the Grand Riviera Theatre in Detroit that featured Cecil B. DeMille's silent film *The Ten Commandments*, supported by an organ recital, a newsreel, a live "educational comedy" (???), the overture to Flotow's *Stradella*, the Six Hassans, acrobats, "comedy characterizations" by Harry Perry, the Billy Wagner dance company, my father, Clement Stanley Barry, singing to a Ziegfeld-like revue of "an astounding array of beautiful girls," topped off by the exit march from *Sonya*. That sounds like quite an afternoon.

But back to *Twelfth Night:* How do you rehearse such material? To my knowledge, nobody has yet written a book on what's funny in Shakespeare, though Eric Partridge has given us an invaluable dictionary of sexual humor, euphemisms, and double entendres, entitled *Shakespeare's Bawdy*. I believe comedy should be rehearsed just like any serious play, by first making sense of the text, defining who is speaking to whom, determining the logic of the lines, eventually specifying objectives, actions, adjustments that translate into movement. All stories begin with "Once upon a time," and all characters begin with "I wish."

Twelfth Night is complex, inventive, often digressive, and yet it's progressive and unerring, a logical line from beginning to end. If the actors play its sense and its action, the audience will define what's funny, i.e. they will identify the punch lines by laughing at them. Don't the actors need to know what's funny in order to play it? No. The actors aren't telling jokes. They're playing characters in situations. Comedians long for laughter as most of us long for love. In fact, laughter equals love, and even the best actors will agonize over the funny parts, wrestling over who has the set-ups and who has the punch lines. They have to be cajoled into trusting the process.

The television productions of the Shakespeare plays produced by the BBC in the 1960s and '70s demonstrate the dangers of attempting to define punch lines without an audience. Many of the BBC comedies are delightful, but some are downright dismal. The most effective television comedies are rehearsed like plays, and then taped in front of a studio audience; the least effective are those with added laugh tracks. It all has to do with the spontaneous reciprocity between performance and audience. Laughter relaxes the actor and feeds on itself, laugh building upon laugh.

Inept directors often complicate *Twelfth Night* by editing the text, then slowing it down with ineffectual comic business. *Twelfth Night* is a sprightly tennis match, each scene spilling joyfully into the next. At the risk of beating this to death, director and actors in rehearsal must patiently search for meaning and the action that meaning suggests. The plot is simple and logical. Early in the play, we see Orsino, Malvolio, and Andrew all in love with Olivia. Viola, masquerading as Cesario, has fallen in love with Orsino, and Olivia falls for Cesario. That's our romantic structure. The addition of Viola's twin, Sebastian, and Olivia's inability to tell the twins apart builds both the sexual tension and the humor. Out of action comes movement, which in turn gives us a continuously changing stage picture that should be able to tell the story of the play even to a viewer who doesn't understand English.

In addition to the running gag of the mistaken identities of Viola and Sebastian, the comedy in *Twelfth Night* is character driven: Toby's drunken bawdiness, Maria's feistiness, Andrew's naïve self-image, Malvolio's social climbing fantasies, Olivia's suppressed sexuality.

Earlier, I described the brilliant structure of *Twelfth Night*'s three interwoven plots. The play's physical settings are similar geometrically, like an irregular open figure, a many-sided form comprising different locales in the city-state of Illyria: a portion of the seacoast, the harbor, the Duke's palace, Olivia's estate, garden, her improvised infirmary, and the streets that connect them. Eventually the form contracts, with the action covering less space in Olivia's estate and surrounding streets. As characters come and go, Viola and Sebastian keep barely missing each other, until they come face to face. To heighten this tension, the director may consider adding a crossover or two.

There are some technical problems in *Twelfth Night* that should be addressed early: the box tree scene requires a device to hold Toby, Andrew, Maria, and Fabian crammed close together several feet above stage level. The box tree is a tree, but I've seen the Elizabethan inner above used quite effectively. The four actors have to play the scene without falling out of the tree, while Malvolio ruminates in a daydream downstage. When Chris Lloyd played Andrew in my 1965 production, he actually did fall out of the tree just as Malvolio obeyed the letter's instruction to "revolve." Unable to climb back into the tree in time to avoid being seen by Malvolio, Chris froze, turning Andrew into a statue of Cupid shooting an arrow. It was hysterical to watch him motionless as the scene progressed.

A second problem is Malvolio's prison, which must keep him confined yet still visible to the audience. Moreover, it must be designed so that Feste can see Malvolio, but Malvolio can only hear Feste, not see him.

The play concludes with the joining of couples: Orsino and Viola; Sebastian and Olivia; Toby and Maria. Malvolio and Andrew are left out in the cold.

When Carol Channing did *Hello, Dolly!* on Broadway, they made her an extra dress, a red ball gown, for the curtain call only. Since the show had a huge cast, she had time to finish the show, make a quick change, and get back on in time for her solo call.

Cesario has time to change into Viola for the curtain call, while Feste sings the final song. Although this means the costumer has to build a wedding dress for her, or at least a beautiful dress that proves she's a woman, just for the curtain call, I think it's worth the expense.

Don't edit this play. Don't change it. Just trust it. Love it!

Chapter 9

Romeo and Juliet

As we saw in *The Taming of the Shrew*, Shakespeare must have believed in the monogamous ideal and the possibility of "il Fulmine," the thunderbolt, love at first sight. If he didn't, he certainly knew how to fake it. There is no more beautiful scene in all theatre than I.5, the meeting of the lovers at the Capulet ball. The language is exquisite, and the structure of the scene is brilliant. It is my opinion that *Romeo and Juliet* is one of the three greatest plays ever written, along with *Hamlet* and *King Lear*.

My first professional experience with *Romeo and Juliet*, as I've said, was Joe Papp's 1961 New York Shakespeare Festival production, playing Tybalt and staging the fights. I toured with that production for five months, so it strongly influenced me. I've done the play eight times, as director, fight director, and actor. I've played Gregory, Tybalt, Mercutio, and Lord Capulet. Shakespeare's play has inspired operas, ballets, films and that definitive Broadway musical tragedy, *West Side Story*, which I've done three times, directing and playing Tony and Doc.

The poetry of *Romeo and Juliet* is superb, and its comedy is hilarious. The Playwright celebrates love just as he ridicules it through Mercutio, the Nurse, and the battling servants.

Shakespeare probably discovered poetry about the time he discovered sex. What better instrument of seduction? He was conceivably writing sonnets when he began writing plays, and he used the shared sonnet form in several of his plays. Though we regard it as a sophisticated artistic form, iambic pentameter is actually very primitive, based on the ta-DUM ta-DUM ta-DUM of the human heartbeat and the five fingers of each hand.

> But soft, what light through yonder window breaks?
> It is the east, and Juliet is the sun

is correctly rendered

> But **soft**, what **light** through **yonder** window **breaks?**
> It **is** the **east,** and **Juliet is** the **sun.**

The five iambs define rhythm and tempo, and tell the actor which words or syllables should *not* be emphasized. Sense and grammar are of primary importance, of course, but they can usually be reconciled with the poetic form. Some directors and scholars prefer that a short pause be taken at the end of each ten-syllable line, but the actor really should not break the thought unless the end of the line corresponds with a period or a semicolon.

The initial meeting of the lovers illustrates the power of the form. At I.5.94, Tybalt delivers a double couplet before he exits, leaving Romeo and Juliet alone downstage. Romeo

Romeo and Juliet, New Jersey Shakespeare Festival, 1981: Robert A. Klein as Page to Mercutio, Stephen McNaughton as Tybalt, Scott Winters and Ken Scherer as Capulet servants, Casey Childs as Benvolio, Ron Mangravite as Mercutio (photograph by Jerry Dalia).

takes off his mask: il Fulmine! They share a sonnet with the rhyme scheme ABAB CBCB DEDE FF. They kiss. They then share a double couplet with the rhyme GHGH. Romeo asks for a second kiss, but I don't think he gets it.

Shakespeare's plays celebrate falling in love more than staying in love. He didn't write many happy marriages. A cynic might describe *Romeo and Juliet* as the perfect marriage: two teenagers meet at a party, exchange poetry for ten minutes or so later that night, marry the next afternoon, and spend that night together. Before dawn the next day, he leaves, and they never see each other alive again. No debates about her career versus his, no spats about religion or politics, no arguments about money, in-laws, kids, schools or where they'll live. The perfect marriage!

But, cynicism aside, the story depends on a maniacal, raging two days of love. In order to work, the play must have a pair of attractive, healthy young actors who are skillful lyricists, capable of making the poetry work, and — most importantly — generous enough to give the play to each other. The moment actor's ego intrudes on either of them the play is doomed. The only couple who really achieved this selflessness for me were Sal Giordano and Tracey Rooney in an otherwise flawed production in Red Bank, New Jersey, in 1997.

I've been blessed with wonderful Juliets, the best being Maureen Padala, but no actor who achieved complete success as Romeo, which I consider the most difficult role in Shakespeare. Romeo requires a highly skillful actor, who must not only make the ideas and the verse work, but must still be capable of maturing from an impulsive teenager to a doomed young madman. There can be no sophistication coloring his passion. He must convince us of belief in the monogamous ideal: Juliet above all other women and better death than life without her. There are three Romeos: the first one in love with the idea of love; the second in love with only Juliet; the third, rising from the ashes of the second, to become an avenging demon on the line "Then I defy you stars" (V.1.24). The best Romeo I ever saw was Bill Ball, who played the role for Arthur Lithgow in Yellow Springs, Ohio, 1954, before Bill's directing career took off.

Ages are important. Ages have always been important. As in all plays, the director looks for the obvious and sniffs out the implied. Juliet is two weeks short of her 14th birthday, and her mother admits to being 14 years older, or 28. We can assume that Lord Capulet is older, not only because that was the custom, but because he gets into an argument with his cousin about how long it's been since they were masquers. It's only logical that all the other kids be teenagers: Romeo, Mercutio, Benvolio, Paris, Tybalt, Valentine, Rosalind, Livia, Helena, the dancers at the party.

I know there have been successful productions of this wonderful play with older stars playing the teenagers, but that's another thesis, the difference between actors and stars, between box office considerations and the realization of the Playwright's intent. As with Viola, the director should begin casting with Juliet, then build around her. Why? It's her play.

Once Juliet is set, cast the young men, all to play around age 17. The best actor should be cast as Romeo, provided he can be matched to your Juliet, and the second choice as Paris/Romeo understudy. Offering an actor the Romeo understudy gives you a better Paris, and this is important, for Paris should be the perfect match for Juliet. The next three actors play Mercutio, Tybalt, and Benvolio. Once you have all your young men, it is most efficient for Tybalt to understudy Mercutio, and Balthazar to understudy Tybalt, Paris and Benvolio. Balthazar's understudy can be pulled from the Capulet/Montague servants. Suddenly, you're offering everyone good jobs, and you'll end up with great bench strength. Chances are the director will have character people already in his rep pool, but they should all be cast to Juliet, then to Romeo.

Although Mercutio is often played seriously, even tragically, that's not his function. He's a comedian, and he's either drunk or hung over during his entire time on-stage. Even his duel with Tybalt is comedic. His intent is to ridicule Tybalt, not kill him. If Mercutio tries to play for tragedy, he intrudes on Romeo's role, and he deprives the audience of the comic relief they need to set them up for the agonizing scenes that follow his death. Mercutio is the easiest role to play. Talk about marbles! Mercutio has everything: comedy, a poetic aria, a duel, and a great comic/tragic death. Ron Mangravite, my Mercutio in 1981, was the best I've ever seen.

On the other hand, I've seen productions ruined by Romeos who try to share the laughs with too much mugging to the audience. Actually, everybody except Romeo and Tybalt are involved in the comedy through the death of Mercutio, when the mood of the play changes radically, but at no time does the comedy ever depart from the naturalistic.

Although the prologue refers to "two households, both alike in dignity," *Romeo and Juliet* is actually about three households:

The Capulets: father, mother, and daughter, plus several cousins;
The Montagues: father, mother, and son, plus a cousin;
Prince Escalus and his three nephews.

I cringe when I listen to the prologue of *Romeo and Juliet*, because it gives the plot away. It's not in the Folio. Why use it? Because it's a neat sonnet?

Any director who ignores ages or family relationships does so at the risk of the clarity and more. Note the stipulation, "households, both alike in dignity." Shakespeare's play is not *West Side Story*. It has nothing to do with racial strife or ethnic differences.

Emphasizing family relationships with costumes, make-up, wigs, etc., is especially important in *Romeo and Juliet*. Because the cast is large, and the family feud so central, the costumer should pay careful attention to color-coding the three families, but, to avoid cruelty from reviewers, should avoid Capulets in red and pink, Montagues in blue. The priests are Franciscans. Every theatre company should have Franciscan robes in its costume bank.

Though the families are divided at rise by an unspecified "ancient grudge," the main conflicts in *Romeo and Juliet* are between the teenagers and their parents. Who can't relate to rebellious teens and dictatorial daddies? As in *A Midsummer Night's Dream*, a father, Lord Capulet, has contracted with a suitor, Paris, nephew of the Prince, for the hand of his daughter, Juliet. Lady Capulet and the Nurse conspire to sell the daughter on the match. At first, she agrees, because she is a dutiful child.

Then Juliet and Romeo meet. The thunderbolt strikes! Love at first sight makes all other possibilities repugnant.

Earlier I wrote about Shakespearean soliloquies as standup comedy (or tragedy). Juliet's "The clock struck nine" speech, II.5, before the Nurse comes on, is at the same time comedic and direct and honest, an expression of real concern and pique, a child's complaint directly to the audience. She doesn't exaggerate for comic effect, nor does the Nurse: her back and knees really do ache from roaming the streets, looking for Romeo. They both can get their laughs without overplaying—Abbott and Costello it's not. Compare Juliet's three soliloquies to see her development, parallel to Romeo's, from petulant schoolgirl to eager not-yet-enjoyed wife to desperate suicide.

Tybalt's death is the toughest in Shakespeare to play. He has to fight a furious duel with Mercutio, leave briefly, gulp some oxygen, return to fight another furious duel with Romeo, then die and lie center stage for another three to four minutes. Death means no movement, no visible breathing (which can elicit unwelcome laughter, especially at student matinees). The trick is to take advantage of the few seconds between the fatal stab and the instant of death to get to his "marks" and roll his body so his stomach is upstage, away from the audience, his knees up, his face cushioned on his arm, his mouth open. He can then die and go into a Zen relaxation to restore the body's oxygen balance. If he does it right, he could fall asleep. Lady Capulet has to make sure he doesn't snore.

Don't make the mistake I've seen of building in an affair between Lady Capulet and Tybalt into the playing. That's a carry-over from the Prokofiev ballet, where Lady Capulet dances at the ball. There's no pay-off and it simply gets in the way. Why does she need a further reason to mourn the death of a relative?

In scheduling rehearsals for *Romeo and Juliet*, sufficient time must be set aside for weapons training and duel choreography, as well as for the dances in I.5. The dances work best with five, then four couples. The first dance is lively, athletic; the second, quieter; the third, soft and gentle. They must be choreographed and drilled, so the music can be played softly enough not to overpower the lovers' meeting. Prokofiev's ballet score serves this scene well, but most available recordings of it are over-orchestrated.

When I played Tybalt for Joe Papp, James Earl Jones played Sampson and I delivered the line, "Fetch me my rapier, boy," to him. In rehearsals he'd respond, "Who you callin' 'boy?,'" which would crack all the actors up, bringing rehearsals to a halt. The venerable Joe put up with this for a while, then got angry and made us quit it.

I had a more serious disagreement with Joe about weapons, arguing that each of the young men should be using different weapons and fighting in different styles. How do I know? It's in the text! Joe's argument for saving money on the weapons was that the audience wouldn't know the difference. "I know the difference," says I, to which he countered wittily, "Who the fuck are you?"

I should not have been such a smart-ass with Joe, but I should not have backed down, either. Most of this play's young men fight, and they use different weapons. Each fight demonstrates not just fencing styles, but personalities, situations, and attitudes. Tybalt, whose weapon is rapier and dagger, fights like a fencing master; Mercutio, whose weapon is an earlier, heavier rapier, fights like a street brawler. Compare Mercutio's contemptuous mocking of Tybalt in II.4 and their actual fight in III.1. The fight should be staged, then modified with forebodings built back into II.4. Tybalt comes looking for Romeo to punish him for his violation of protocol in crashing the Capulet ball by humiliating him on the street. The goal of a challenge to a duel is not the opponent's death, but his humiliation and admission of guilt. The challenge can be satisfied in many ways, all bloodless, and even if blades are crossed, the challenge can be met, and the duel ended, at first blood. A duelist who persists and seriously wounds or kills an opponent can be arrested for assault or even murder.

In III.1, Tybalt first insults Romeo, inviting retaliation, then challenges Romeo. Romeo backs down, apologizes. Tybalt persists. Romeo backs down a second time. Tybalt should be satisfied, but Mercutio takes over the duel, as a second may. But Mercutio isn't out for blood—he simply wants to show Tybalt up as a braggart. Mercutio is having fun, and the duel should elicit laughter as he toys with his opponent as a matador does with a bull. It's only when Romeo tries to stop the fight that it becomes deadly. Romeo grabs the sword wrists of both combatants, and Tybalt inflicts a mortal wound to Mercutio's torso with a thrust of his dagger. Tybalt then flees.

It is essential that the actors not anticipate the tragedy. The first half of the play is a love story, a romantic romp with lots of delightful comedy involving Mercutio, the Nurse, Benvolio, and Peter. It's fun. Even the fight is fun. Blood changes it. It is not until Benvolio, surprised and disbelieving, asks, "What, art thou hurt?" and Mercutio moves the hand covering the wound in his stomach, III.1.93, that the tone of the play alters. Even then, the jokes continue. If the playing before that moment grows serious or deadly, the tension that follows will be dissipated and the dialogue that follows will verge on the operatic.

When Tybalt returns to the stage, Romeo takes Mercutio's weapon and attacks him like a mad man. It's not a duel. It's a fight to the death. Romeo has lost control of himself, and he doesn't stop until Tybalt lies butchered.

Each one of the stage fights in this play is different from the others, as each one of the five young men is different from the others.

The balcony in this play is a good example of the trap of scenery. There are two places in the play where the balcony is essential, II.2 and II.5.1 to 64, a total of some 12 minutes out of a three-hour play. The rest of the time, the balcony gets in the way and distracts the audience. If it's a permanent part of the setting, most directors will be tempted to use it and overuse it, but most of the action in this play takes place on the streets of Verona or in and around the Capulet house.

Don't weaken the power of Juliet's potion scene by putting it in the balcony, far removed from the audience. IV.2 and IV.3 can be played as one scene in the garden. No line changes are necessary. Juliet asks her Mother and the Nurse to leave her alone to pray, and since it's a hot night in July, what better place to pray than in the garden, which traditionally contained the statue of the Virgin or a patron saint? This allows Juliet to play her "dismal scene" downstage, close to the audience. This soliloquy is an actor-buster. I've seen many a good young actress make the mistake of using it as an audition piece and failing. It has many corners, many changes, highs and lows, but if Juliet can play it intimately, with complete faith in the audience as confidant, then it can become a prayer, a lament, a love song to the absent Romeo.

The stage direction about falling on "her bed within the curtains" exists only in Q.1, not in subsequent quartos or folios. It's annoying that contemporary editors include it. If the scene is played on a bed in the inner below or on the balcony, the staging of the discovery scene becomes impossible. But if Juliet drinks the potion and collapses down stage, things evolve neatly. Time passes, but the scene does not change. Lord Capulet raises the household at dawn, but he does not notice the small figure in the shadows down stage. The Nurse comes on and calls up to Juliet to wake her, then discovers her body. The rest of the scene plays out with everyone's focus downstage. Sometime near the end of the scene, Lord Capulet picks up the corpse and carries it off at the Friar's suggestion; the others follow, leaving only Peter and the Musicians. Hire a Capulet strong enough to lift the recumbent Juliet and carry her, though it's possible for other actors to give him some help.

Despite the fact that the audience has been told in IV.1 that the potion is only a draft to induce a deep sleep, everyone must play the scene as one of genuine mourning. Juliet has articulated her fear that it might really be a deadly poison, and those who discover the body believe that she is really dead. With good actors, committed to this belief, the audience will be reduced to tears.

The silly scene between Peter and the Musicians that follows is often cut, because directors don't know why it's there, and they dismiss it as tasteless. Actually it serves an important purpose and should not be cut: it exists to remind the audience that Juliet is *not* dead. With deft comedians, like the original Peter, Will Kempe, this interlude can change tears into laughter. The rubber chicken is strongly suggested for this scene.

Another scenery problem to be solved early is Juliet's tomb, and again the simplest solution is the best. The custom of the time for the wealthy was to bury bodies in crypts, without coffins, sometimes with shrouds, sometimes not. The designer should work backwards from the final tableau where the body of Juliet lies on the body of Romeo. A bier that can be carried at shoulder height by four pallbearers, similar to that used for Ophelia, plus two pedestal feet to support the bier, head and foot, are needed. Customarily, bier and supports would be in one piece made of marble, but turned wood is more practical and will suffice, provided that the assembly is solid, capable of supporting the weight of both lovers. It need not be more than 24" to 28" high assembled to avoid sight line difficulties.

During the Peter/Musicians scene, the pallbearers arrange Juliet on the bier. The mourners intone a Latin Requiem, and the procession enters, led by Friar Lawrence and Friar John carrying freestanding candles. (Note: these have to be smokeless candles, because the scene and the play will be ruined if smoke detectors are set off. Some local fire marshals will allow no flames at all on-stage.) The bier/pedestal device is assembled down stage right, adjusted to sightlines. See Jo Mielziner's essay on scenery and lighting for *A Streetcar Named Desire* if you wonder about this specific placement. Friar Laurence then blesses the "corpse," the candles are extinguished, the Requiem ended, and the mourners exit, leaving

Juliet in shadows. We see Friar Laurence give a letter to Friar John on the way out. Subsequent scenes, V.1, V.2, and most of V.3 should be played to the left and as far away from the crypt as possible. Here, the lighting designer's skill is tested, because in V.3, several locales are implied: the graveyard outside the tomb, the entrance to the monument, and finally the interior, the crypt itself.

I have seen productions of this play where much money was invested in the tomb, but I believe the less scenery the better! Balthazar and Paris' Page can play extreme upstage, and the corpse of Paris can lie extreme stage left. The corpse of Tybalt can be implied off-stage or downstage: it need not be visible. The duel between Romeo and Paris is fought rapier vs. rapier and torch. This is tricky, because the flame of the torch must be small, confined and fail-safe. Why does this duel exist at all? Why do we need yet another duel at this moment in the play? It exists to relax the tension, as violence and comedy always do, so that the audience is willing to sit still for the heartbreaking scene that follows.

Romeo enters the tomb by crossing from the corpse of Paris to Juliet's crypt on line V.3.84, where he lights her candles again, then extinguishes his torch. Romeo is not somber: he's manic. As Lord Capulet did upon discovering Juliet's "corpse," Romeo compares death to a rival, another lover who has stolen Juliet from him. Romeo, speaking joyfully with the voice of the young Shakespeare, rhapsodizes on Juliet's beauty, comparing her to light dispelling darkness; she herself is the source of light, as she was when he first saw her, "teaching torches to burn bright."

As he examines her sleeping form, we may hope he will realize she's not dead, but only in a coma, and hope creates a dramatic tension. Perhaps he can awaken her. We remember that Friar Laurence initially told her that the potion would put her to sleep for 42 hours, and in V.2 he told Friar John that she would wake "within three hours." Though the times are not specific, even confusing, the possibility that Romeo might yet rouse her exists: true love is supposed to be able to effect such miracles. Though Romeo came to the tomb to commit suicide, he cannot help but rhapsodize over Juliet, and so he delays the business of pouring the poison into a cup. Why does Shakespeare specify the cup? To create a kind of sacrament and delay Romeo's death 'til the last possible moment, in hopes that Juliet will awake and stop him. A final pause, then the toast, and the poison works as quickly as did her potion. He convulses, cramps, then tries to kiss her, but fails and slips off the bier in death.

Friar Laurence arrives. Too late. Juliet awakes. Too late. The Watch can be heard in the distance. Too late. Friar Laurence tries to persuade Juliet to leave, but, like her husband, she prefers death to a life without him.

Some misguided American school boards have attempted to ban the study of this play on the grounds that it idealizes teenage suicide, but they miss the point. Shakespeare was writing here about the greatest possible human love, one that transcends death. It's an impossible ideal that's been enshrined in myth for thousands of years, a love so strong that it defeats death by continuing after death, lovers forever joined for all eternity. It defies reason. If the play is done right, the audience cannot help but succumb to it. My daughter Shannon saw our 1990 production 11 times when she was 14. It grabbed her every time, but at no time did she ever consider suicide.

A tourist roaming through Verona today will be touched by how the city has taken Shakespeare's play to heart. One can visit Juliet's Tomb, Friar Laurence's garden, and the House of the Capulets, with its window balcony overlooking a courtyard, to which has been added a statue of Juliet, but I found the marble plaques all over the city that quote an appropriate passage from the play, first in Italian, then in English, especially touching. I'm a pushover, if you haven't already figured that out. My favorite is hung, seemingly at random, on a wall of the city:

> Non c'é mondo fuori dale mura di Verona,
> Ma purgatoria e tortua: inferno.
>
>> There is no world without Verona walls,
>> But purgatory, torture, hell itself.

Chapter 10

Shakespeare's Warrior Plays

The United States Marine is a formidable warrior. He is vigorously wooed by recruiters akin to religious proselytizers, true believers, and receives the best possible training with the best instructors. The primary objective of Marine basic training is the creation of the obedient warrior. The Marine is physically strengthened, supplied with superior weapons, and taught a multitude of skills, but obedience is his most essential attribute. He is humiliated, insulted, degraded by his Drill Instructor, a man whose prime objective is testing and reinforcing that obedience.

Not every recruit makes it through basic training. The D.I.s keep an eye out for the rebel, the thinker who may question a superior's order at a moment of crisis. Such a one is washed out and discharged before he has a chance to infect his fellows.

A Marine is a highly efficient practitioner of destruction. He learns to infiltrate territory, to incapacitate the enemy's equipment, to disable or kill him. A Marine squad, 12 men under the command of a sergeant, is the equal to any fighting unit of equal size in the world. Marines develop a fierce loyalty to their units and to each other. In a firefight, no Marine, alive or dead, is left behind.

There is no such thing as an ex–Marine. Rather, there are two kinds of combat veterans: those who never talk about their experience, and those who talk about nothing else. Their camaraderie is genuine, and their politics are simple and direct, never a negative word against the Corps or the nation or the president.

Warriors like this have been with us for thousands of years. Homer wrote about them. They were at Thermopylae, and they served Alexander the Great, Hannibal, the Caesars, the Vikings, William the Conqueror, Napoleon, Robert E. Lee, Ulysses S. Grant, Dwight Eisenhower, and George Patton. Navy Seals, the Green Berets, British Commandos all aspire to this ideal, the fierce and skillful individual combatant. Among Shakespeare's heroes, Othello, Iago, Coriolanus, Marc Antony, Macbeth, Henry V, and Hotspur are all examples of this warrior.

Wars have always been with us. They preceded language, perhaps even agriculture. Human beings wage war as a consequence of the convergence of several instincts. We are an aggressive, omnivorous, predatory species. As most animals and all mammals do, we hold and defend territories, and we practice social cooperation, defending the "in-group" and expressing antipathy for the "out-group." We are a religious species. We are hierarchical. Those of us with dominant tendencies compete for positions of leadership. The rest of us seek out leaders we can serve. Religion, patriotism, nationalism, dominance, racism all derive from these combined instincts. We continually wage war because we've always waged war.

Many cultures and religions equate the fallen warrior with the martyr. Dying in battle guarantees the warrior spiritual salvation, but no warrior ever believes he's going to die in

Pericles, Prince of Tyre, **New Jersey Shakespeare Festival, 1989 (photograph by Jim DelGiudice).**

battle. He may be frightened, anxious, but he believes he will survive. As George Patton put it, he's not going to win the war by dying for his country, but "by making sure the other poor bastard dies for his country." Hal reminds Falstaff that he owes God a death, and Falstaff replies:

> 'Tis not due yet: I would be loath to pay him before his day.
> What need I be so forward with him that calls not on me?

War was the profession of the medieval nobility. Farming and animal husbandry supplied their income. The children of the nobility were trained in the arts of war from the age of three.

Hand weapons and armor evolved in parallel: the lighter the weapons, the lighter the armor and vice versa. Before the invention of gunpowder, body protection evolved from nothing, with combatants fighting naked, to the full armor of a mounted knight, so heavy that he had to be lifted into his saddle by cranes and pulleys. Weapons and armor were crafted by smiths to fit the physique and strength of the individual combatant.

Though a medieval king, as we saw with Claudius, might have a trained and well-equipped guard protecting his person, his army was comprised of the smaller private armies of his noblemen. Each nobleman's estate was a combination of farm, ranch, town, and army camp. While knights spent much of their time training for battle, foot soldiers doubled as farmers, shepherds, blacksmiths, craftsmen. A yeoman learned the use of the longbow and the quarterstaff as a youth from his father and brothers, but only the nobility were trained in hand-to-hand weapons, swords, shields, battleaxes. Only the nobility were armored combatants. Only the nobility owned horses and knew how to ride them. The longbow and spear were hunting weapons as well as instruments of war.

In many languages, the word "knight" translates as "man on horseback." Knighthood was a military rank, not a title. It could not be inherited. It had to be awarded, and like the Japanese black belt, it was awarded for proficiency in arms. Knights developed and practiced a comprehensive code of moral behavior, the honor vested in the sword.

When it came time to go to war, the nobility and their yeomen left the care of the farms to their wives and fathers too old to fight. Only at harvest time did war go on hiatus. With luck, a common soldier could come home with the ransom paid for a captured enemy nobleman or, at least, valuable contraband. Common soldiers were fed when there were supplies, but more often than not, they had to forage for their dinners. They were encouraged to pillage as reward for the dangers they faced. They had to supply their own weapons or take them from dead enemies.

War was fun. Before the perfection of artillery, warfare was a high-stakes rugby game. Battles and stage fights are often ignored or de-emphasized by scholars and teachers. Witness the thousands of university drama department graduates who can't fence, can't wrestle, can't box, have never studied the Asian martial arts.

Barbara Tuchman, in her book *A Distant Mirror*, points out that medieval armies were made up of teenagers. War was something a wild kid did before he grew up and settled down. With luck, he'd return home with both his eyes and all of his limbs. If he survived as a cripple, his war wounds would probably buy him drinks the rest of his life.

John Keegan's *The Face of Battle* describes the battle of Agincourt (1415), among others. Keegan knows more about Agincourt than Shakespeare did. An astonishing 22 of the 38 Shakespeare plays depict wars and warriors. Another eight include former soldiers in peaceful settings. In writing, rewriting, and staging all these soldier plays, Shakespeare had to possess an affinity for the wars, battles, and duels, then he had to figure out how to put the violence on the stage. Today's directors have the same problems, and the solutions probably haven't changed in 400 years.

The Shakespearean director must analyze and attempt to understand the heart and mind of the warrior. Further, the director and actors must convince the modern audience, disheartened and discouraged by "perpetual war for perpetual peace," that Shakespeare's military heroes are nature's noblemen.

We need not analyze each individual king, general, officer, and common soldier in the plays, but we do need to understand that Shakespeare and the Elizabethan/Jacobean audience held these warriors in high regard. Without this intrinsic respect, Macbeth is just a murderer, Coriolanus a loud-mouthed bully, Othello a wife beater. Morality gets lost in the shuffle. In order to stage the Shakespeare plays, war, like sex, must be viewed as amoral, simply part of the human condition.

In preparing these plays for production, today's director must analyze what the inherent violence does to the play. In that respect, the violence is no different than any other action the Playwright has written. The director must recognize an action implicit in the line, determine the Playwright's intent, then stage the action, as well as the reactions of the bystanders.

In the soldier plays, the great battles are between the lines, not on the page. For instance, the battle of Shrewsbury (1403) begins between Scenes 2 and 3 of Act V in *Henry IV, Part 1* with the stage directions:

"Here they embrace. The trumpets sound. (Exeunt)"
"Another part of the field. The King enters with his power."
"Alarum to the battle. (Exeunt)"
"Then enter Douglas and Sir Walter Blunt."

There's a lot of work for the director and fight choreographer implied by those skimpy few stage directions. These two collaborators must understand why the combat is there, what it accomplishes, how to stage it, how not to stage it.

During the Tudor reigns of Henry VIII and his three children, British religious/political/military thought was heavily influenced by the providential theory of history, which held that the outcome of a battle or a duel was determined, not by the skill of the combatants, but by God's judgment as to whose cause was just. This theory made for curious speculation when two nations, practitioners of the same religion, went to war against each other. Perhaps nowhere in Shakespeare is this theory more clearly set forth than in the case of Joan of Arc: if God favored the English, she was a witch; if God favored the French, she was a saint.

Shakespeare had access to an extensive literature on military history, but there's no evidence that the Playwright himself ever went to war, and I find it unsatisfying to be told that he learned about war as he learned about the law, the sea, politics, etc., by writing about them. If Shakespeare never was a soldier, his idealistic view of battle wasn't sullied by actual experience and the corrupting drudgery and meanness of the grunt's life.

Shakespeare's heroes enjoyed war and despised the "weak, piping time of peace." Othello rhapsodizes on an idealized memory of battle:

> ... the plumed troop ... the neighing steed and the shrill trump,
> The spirit-stirring drum, th'ear-piercing fife,
> The royal banner, and all quality,
> Pride, pomp, and circumstance of glorious war!
> And, Oh ye mortal engines whose rude throats
> Th' immortal Jove's dread clamors counterfeit....

A few definitions here: a duel — Hal and Hotspur, for example — is a combat between armed combatants. A battle consists of hundreds of duels and multiple combats. A war includes many battles. A fencing match, like that between Hamlet and Laertes, is combat with practice weapons, unsharpened and baited. Until the introduction of artillery, there were two kinds of basic weapons, those wielded by a soldier at close range, and those thrown from a distance or propelled by a bow, a slingshot, catapult or other device.

In battle, the object is to capture and hold the high ground and to incapacitate the enemy. There's no time to make sure the enemy is dead. If he's injured and cannot fight on, the combatant will move immediately to the next opponent. In a duel, the object is to humiliate the opponent, then incapacitate him, not kill him. Fights in contemporary stage productions are fought hand to hand with spears, swords, daggers, and shields slightly lighter than the real thing. Naturally, the weapons are not sharpened. Greek and Roman short swords are employed in *Titus Andronicus, Julius Caesar, Antony and Cleopatra, Troilus and Cressida, Coriolanus*, and *Cymbeline*. Long swords, broadswords, and shields are used in the Chronicle plays as well as *King Lear* and *Macbeth*. Rapiers and daggers, cut and thrust weapons, much lighter than broadswords, are employed in *Romeo and Juliet, Hamlet, Othello*, and *The Tempest*.

Museums like the Tower of London, the Hotel des Invalides in Paris, and New York's Metropolitan are well stocked with archaic weapons, and extensive research has produced scores of books on pre-artillery combat.

Much of stage combat is simple physics and muscular efficiency. Human biology and physiology haven't changed much in 100,000 years. Today's fight choreographer, trained in fencing, boxing, wrestling, judo, ken-do, and karate, supplied with research material, can reconstruct styles of combat from any period. A good costumer will provide armor, body padding, footwear, helmets and gauntlets to protect the actor from serious injury. Stage combat must be safe, while appearing dangerous.

Stage fights also have to be possible. Thunder and artillery are often compared by the Playwright. Though artillery on both land and sea was evolving and improving from 1313, it was of no use to the theatre, except as distant noise, off-stage sound effects. So too with ladders, any other siege engines, horses. Shakespeare might have experimented with horses on-stage in the earlier Chronicle plays, but by the time he arrived at Shrewsbury, he had given up on them. On-stage battles were confined to hand to hand combat. Occasional blunt-tipped arrow shot over the heads of the audience from long bows might have been used, but their effectiveness was limited and if they remained on-stage, they could be dangerous. Most injuries to actors resulted from trips, stumbles, falls, not blows.

My own practical experience has proved that the most effective stage weapons are broadswords, short swords, and shields, with an occasional spear wielded like a quarterstaff. Battle axes and maces have limited use. Over the years, my costumers and I developed a protective basic costume, best compared to a football uniform, that gave the actor rubber soled boots for sure footing, hip and knee padding, gauntlets with reinforced knuckles, and light hockey headgear that could be decorated to look like battle helmets from any period.

The primary weapon in my productions was a 36" long steel broadsword with crossbar weighing about four pounds. Shields were built in various shapes, round, rectangular, and shield-shaped, and were secured to the forearm just below the elbow with a strong elastic strap and gripped by the left hand.

Actors were taught a broadsword and shield technique evolved backwards from today's fencing and ken-do, wrestling, karate, and judo. They were trained to aim to hit, not to miss, then to pull the cut at the moment of impact to avoid injury. The nice guy who does not fulfill his movement, but rather veers off at the last moment, thus confusing the parry of his opponent, is the most dangerous combatant.

Actors were trained in a handful of cuts: to the shoulder, the stomach, the back of the thigh, and two cuts to the head. Parries matched cuts. There were two head parries, two parries that protected the right and left midsection, and one low line parry that blocked the cut to the thigh. Actors were taught cuts and parries, one by one, and then shields were added. Every cut could be parried with the weapon or with the shield. Five beat and ten beat patterns were taught as time savers — audiences didn't realize they were watching the same movements over and over, because they were repeated in different combinations throughout the battle scenes. The cuts were then rehearsed for accuracy and efficiency. Some actors love it. Some hate it.

Once some proficiency had been attained, stage fights were carefully choreographed to meet the needs of the plot, then drilled to perfection, and practiced, practiced, practiced.

Chapter 11

Troilus and Cressida

Troilus and Cressida, which I've directed once and played in once (Nestor), is a play cobbled together out of myth and legend. It stands alone in the Canon, neither tragedy, comedy, nor history, and the publishers of the First Folio weren't sure where it should be placed. Is it a faerie tale? Is it satire? A prologue, "armed but not in wisdom," tells us it's a love story that takes place in the middle of a war. Can that be trusted? There's no other play like it. It's either a structural failure or a work of genius. I've never seen it work, though I've seen several productions.

George Chapman published his translation of *The Iliad* in 1611 and *The Odyssey* in 1616. If *Troilus and Cressida* was first published in 1609, did Master Will have anything to do with Chapman's work before it was finished? Since Shakespeare's play ends at the same place and time that *The Iliad* does, it's possible that the Playwright had access to the manuscript of the first book, but not the second. Even if he did, one can dig through *The Iliad* and *The Odyssey* from beginning to end without finding anything about Cressida.

Where did the story come from? The first telling of the tale evidently appeared in the middle of the 12th century in Benoit de Sainte-Maure's narrative poem, *Roman de Troie*, reproduced in Latin in Guido delle Colonne's *Historica Trojana*. From these two works, Boccaccio wrote his *Filostrato*, which gave Geoffrey Chaucer the material for his poem *Troilus and Criseyde*. Shakespeare took the love story from Chaucer, and was clearly influenced by Boccaccio as well, but the material for the rest of his play could have come from Chapman or from any number of poems and tales about the Trojan War. In my opinion, the play is superior to its sources, as difficult as it may be to produce today.

History it is not. In fact, scholars, historians, and geologists still have not determined how many of the events described by Homer and Virgil actually happened. Was there even a Trojan War, or do the tales derive from many wars over several centuries? Homer himself may be a fiction, a composite of storytellers and poets from the beginnings of written language.

Troilus and Cressida probably should have been two, perhaps three plays, and the interwoven plots easily confuse even the best-prepared audiences:

The romance of Troilus and Cressida, engineered by Pandarus
The fading romance of Paris and Helen of Troy
The rivalry between Hector and Achilles
The Trojan war itself, its causes, its leaders and its soldiers.

A supporting character can play a scene, leave the stage for a half-hour, then return to find himself the lead. Except for the smallest roles, doubling is difficult, and it's even necessary to add Hecuba to the cast for clarity, though Shakespeare does not.

Troilus and Cressida, New Jersey Shakespeare Festival, 1972: Kendall March as Cressida, Philip Hanson as Pandarus, Christian Grant as Troilus (photograph by Jay Liebman).

I highly recommend rehearsing the Greeks separately from the Trojans until the last possible moment in order to reinforce the differing identities and personalities of each. This technique also works for *Henry V*, but it is easier to distinguish the English and the French.

Thersites is a continuation of a character type who had been introduced in *Hamlet* (the Gravedigger) and further developed in *Twelfth Night* (Feste): that of the sarcastic fool. Though this clown was still expected to produce laughs, the character was becoming more critical, moving toward the "all-licensed Fool" of *King Lear* and eventually climaxing with the philosopher Apemantus in *Timon of Athens*. It might be fun to put the deformed Thersites in "dress-up" armor and give him the prologue, leading to a running commentary to the audience about the action. Many of the speeches assigned to him could be played as asides.

In the Lancastrian tetralogy, Shakespeare introduced a theme that is emphasized in *Troilus and Cressida*, touched on in the six plays that follow, and returned to with a vengeance in *Coriolanus*: order in society and in the universe. The Playwright argues that all living things in the universe are ranked from God to the king to the lowest peasant to the tiniest unicellular being. Moreover, each is bound to obey the one above him and to rule the one below. In *Troilus and Cressida*, this ranking is compared to the Ptolemaic universe, and in *Coriolanus*, to the organs of the body.

In this play, Shakespeare also reverses himself philosophically from the attitude toward war expressed in the Chronicle plays. War is not noble, a human endeavor of the highest morality—it's mean and dirty, the deadly dull alternating with a ferocious wildness. War is disease, infections, hunger, crippling injuries, prolonged and agonizing deaths. War is seen from the vantage point of the grunt in the trenches.

Take, for example, the death of Hector, a fabled soldier of antiquity killed in a duel by another legendary hero, Achilles. In Homer's telling of the story, Hector runs away from Achilles until he can run no further, and then he turns to fight. Hector hurls his spear at Achilles, but it bounces off his shield. Achilles then hurls his spear at the one unarmored place on Hector's upper body, the space between his shoulder armor and his helmet. The spear pierces his neck, but not his windpipe. Hector is paralyzed, but he can still speak, and he begs that his body be returned to his mother for an honorable burial. Instead, Achilles finishes him off, then ties his body to the back of his chariot and drags it in the dust around the city. A second legend has it that an archer shot an arrow from the battlements that hit Achilles in the heel, causing him to fall off the chariot and hit his head on a rock. Thus the two heroes die.

In Shakespeare's play, there is no duel. Both heroes are engaged in a full-scale battle, where each kills many enemies. Hector withdraws from the battle and removes his armor to rest and refresh himself. Achilles directs his Myrmidons to ambush the unarmed Hector and chop him to pieces with their swords. In our production, they used a net to incapacitate Hector then stabbed him through the net.

There's a second reversal in the play as well, from the moral/ethical stand of *Romeo and Juliet*, the monogamous ideal. It's a 180-degree turn from Juliet, who prefers death to a life without Romeo, to Cressida, who will give herself to whomever will keep her alive.

And yet there's an important similarity between Juliet and Cressida, one that modern actresses may fight against. In the pre–Freudian, male-dominated world of these plays, each takes control of her fate. Neither are victims. If your Cressida believes that she's a victim, not responsible for her actions, you're in for a long rehearsal period.

All the leading figures of this play end in shame. Achilles celebrates a cowardly victory. Troilus mourns the death of his brother and the inevitable fall of Troy. Cressida has become the concubine of Diomedes. Pandarus bemoans the fact that pimps and bawds are not treated with more respect and appreciation. Shakespeare's play ends where *The Iliad* ends, with the deaths of Patroclus and Hector. The Trojan Horse is yet to come.

When the NJSF produced *Troilus and Cressida* in 1972, the war in Vietnam had been dragging on for some ten years, and there was no end in sight. The audience didn't laugh at much, but they seemed to enjoy it, and the critics were kind. The night that production opened, I stood outside the theatre and thought, "If I can direct this monster, I can direct anything."

CHAPTER 12

Julius Caesar

In 1986, I achieved a longtime ambition: I produced and directed the two Marc Antony plays, *Julius Caesar* and *Antony and Cleopatra*, in rotating repertory with the same actors playing principal characters and the same designers for both plays. I had directed *Julius Caesar* twice before, in 1966 and 1967, and *Antony and Cleopatra* once in 1965. Be careful what you wish for.

We began rehearsals for *Julius Caesar* a week early, with Marc Antony, Jack Ryland, and an intern cast of citizens and soldiers, rehearsing the funeral scene, III.2, and other crowd movements. The two previous productions had achieved great success with the excitement generated by the luxury of having large crowds of citizens, and we aimed for that again. The specific lines in the text were assigned, and the crowd was directed to respond to them as well as to Antony's lines.

These two plays are about events beginning in 44 BCE in Italy, Egypt, and Greece. *Julius Caesar* was written in 1599 CE, while the English were obsessed with Elizabeth's health and the dilemma of the succession. *Antony and Cleopatra* was written seven or eight years later, in 1606 or 1607, between *Macbeth* and *Coriolanus*, during the fourth year of the reign of James I/VI.

The schoolboy Will Shakespeare probably knew more about Julius Caesar than he did about his own English kings, because the primary study of the Stratford grammar school was Latin. After basic instruction in reading, writing, and prayers in the petty school, those boys whose parents could afford it attended the grammar school for the next six years, eight to nine hours a day, six days a week, for 46 weeks a year, and all they studied was Latin: no mathematics, no history, no science, no English literature or composition, no music, no sports, only Latin grammar and eventually Latin literature. The student read Latin poets (notably Ovid, Horace, and Virgil), prose (notably the histories of Livy, Julius Caesar, Suetonius, Tacitus, and Josephus), and the plays of Terence, Plautus, and Seneca. Shakespeare draws heavily from Ovid's *Metamorphoses* in his plays and poems, and it was probably in these volumes where he first read of the assassination of Julius Caesar.

After the Latin writers, the Greek biographer and essayist Plutarch, who lived during the first and second centuries CE, had the greatest influence on Shakespeare's history plays, though it is unlikely that Master Will read Plutarch in the original, but probably in Sir Thomas North's 1579 translation of *Parallel Lives of Famous Greeks and Romans*. Plutarch, whose work includes 23 pairs and four single biographies, 50 in all, wrote about contemporaries including Julius Caesar, Marc Antony, Cleopatra, and Caesar Augustus, and, like Homer, he did not differentiate between real historical figures and mythological characters.

He mixed history, myth, and legend freely, and Shakespeare followed his lead and North's in his Greek and Roman plays.

Plutarch's research was as meticulous as his sources allowed. He was cautious, but he was not dissuaded from writing a biography simply because there were insufficient historical facts. The history that inspired the writing of Shakespeare's *Julius Caesar* and *Antony and Cleopatra* was more accurate than that of *A Midsummer Night's Dream*, *Pericles*, *Timon of Athens*, *Coriolanus*, or *The Two Noble Kinsmen*.

Today, when we produce these plays for an American audience with contemporary actors, we have to deal with three different mindsets over some 2,000 years, three different moralities, three different political theories, three different attitudes toward war and warriors: the actual historical period of the events depicted, Shakespeare's own era, and then our own. Each time period has to be examined, compared, reconciled to the others.

Good history or not, *Julius Caesar* is a splendid play that beats like a well-made tragedy. In fact, it *is* a tragedy, designated as such in the Folio (titles are key in Shakespeare), but I'll get to that. Most of the characters are historical and they all have a dramatic function. Notably missing from the cast and the plot is Cleopatra, Queen of Egypt and lover of Caesar, who was ensconced in a villa down the Tiber when he was assassinated. When she heard of his death, she quickly took flight aboard her royal galley, commanding her sailors to haul anchor and row with all possible speed back to Egypt.

It's difficult to direct Julius Caesar today, because American actors are devoted to the tenets of democracy and egalitarianism. Ever since those wonderful, courageous lunatics,

Julius Caesar, **Boston Herald-Traveler Repertory, 1966: Alex Panas as Marcus Brutus, Alan Becker as Caius Cassius, David Howard as Julius Caesar, Bob Neufelt as Mettelus Cimber, Ronald Coralian as Caius Ligarius (photograph by Chris Grant).**

the American founding fathers, signed the Declaration of Independence in 1776 and severed us from allegiance to the English crown, we have absorbed democratic principles as if they were oxygen. We believe that the rule of the people is the human animal's natural way as well as God's chosen system. We long ago abandoned the providential theory of history and the divine right of kings. "Freedom," "equality," "majority rule," are hardwired into our collective conscious and our morality, which makes it difficult for our actors to commit emotionally to several of the Shakespeare plays. *Julius Caesar* is a case in point. Just as the Declaration of Independence uses "tyrant" in a pejorative sense, Cassius calls Julius Caesar a tyrant, and the conspirators fear he will become one. Our actors, therefore, intuitively identify with Brutus.

But *Julius Caesar* is about the protagonist Julius Caesar; the title role is the leading role, not Brutus. In his Shakespeare 101 class at Wayne State University in the fall of 1950, Leo Kirschbaum emphasized the importance of the titles of the plays, which, he insisted, the playwright wrote along with the texts themselves: *Othello* is not entitled *Othello and Iago*. Only three plays, *Romeo and Juliet*, *Troilus and Cressida*, and *Antony and Cleopatra* are about a *pairs* of protagonists.

One theory holds that in *Julius Caesar*, the Playwright wrote a parallel to the political situation among Elizabeth, the Earl of Essex, and James I/VI. If this is so, then it is essential to keep in mind the attitudes of the original audience in September of 1599. The Elizabethans loved their Queen, they believed her to be God's gift to England, and they were terrified because she had never married or produced an heir. Nor would she discuss designating one, though that was a constant subject of gossip at the time. She could have named Essex or James or any one of several noblemen as her successor, but she hadn't, at least not when the play was first produced. At that time, James was a shadowy figure, the son of Mary, Queen of Scots, and Essex was a national hero, though not of royal blood. A year and a half later came Essex's ill-fated Rebellion. No one is quite sure what he hoped to accomplish by that pitiful exercise in hubris, but it's assumed he meant to force Elizabeth to name him her heir. Instead, he appears to have miscalculated not only her, but the English people as well.

How is the assassination of Caesar a parallel situation? Elizabeth had survived several assassination attempts by her countrymen as well as several foreign plots. Might the Playwright have been warning Elizabeth, knowing she had identified herself with his Richard II earlier, as he was deposed and replaced by Henry Bolingbroke? The parallel arises from the political situation at the beginning of the play, not its ending. In effect, the Playwright could have been cautioning Elizabeth about Essex and suggesting that James was safer and no threat to her person.

I've never seen an updated production of *Antony and Cleopatra*, but there have been many productions where *Julius Caesar* has been placed in a different historical period to make it "relevant" to a modern audience. In the 1930s, Orson Welles famously placed the play in Italy with Mussolini as Julius, which was relevant at the time, though the other parallels were not clear. A production in Miami a few years back with Fidel Castro as Julius backfired because much of the audience arrived already opposed to Castro. At his CSC Repertory in New York City, Christopher Martin offered a space age production in which Julius was a computer attacked with screwdrivers and dismantled by the conspirators. A current production is based on contemporary politics and technology, with the Soothsayer a cable news anchor, sending war reports via text message. The capital referred to is Washington, D.C.

Concept productions make up much of the Shakespeare produced in America, based on the cynical assumption that if the plays are traditionally mounted, they won't attract or be intelligible to an audience. Directors often get the flash of an idea, like "any war play can be an anti-war play," and that will launch them into pacifist productions of *Henry V*, or they'll recast Richard III as Napoleon or Hitler. I myself have produced updated (or redated) versions of *Coriolanus*, *The Taming of the Shrew*, *Timon of Athens*, and *The Winter's Tale*, all highly successful.

Are there any rules about transposing time and place? None I can think of that are universally observed. Whatever works, works. But conceptual ideas must be tested scene by scene, line by line, to make sure that every element of the play will work in the new setting. If set in 2010, for example, the tragedy of Romeo and Juliet could be averted by cell phones and modern transportation. Some problems we don't want solved. Baz Luhrmann's 1996 film is a fascinating look at the darkness in the play, but his use of handguns instead of swords and daggers is grating, off-putting, changing accident to murder. Modern weaponry, in fact, works against most of Shakespeare's warrior plays.

The two Marc Antony plays are about Julius Caesar. The assumed rules of the military meritocracy have advanced Caesar to his current position. He should play his early scenes in battle uniform and armor. If the people declare him king, may we not say he has earned the position and the title, and it is the will of the people that he be crowned? Brutus is neither Malcolm nor Henry VII. The director is strongly advised not to load the dice in either direction, but to eschew terms like "hero," "villain," "protagonist," any imposed characterization that might move actors to premature conclusions. Julius must be allowed to play what he was historically and Brutus to play what he can be seduced into becoming. Maintain the blessed ambiguity, and let each member of the audience decide.

Even though he dies some 65 minutes into the play, the presence and authority of Julius are maintained by both Antony and Octavius Caesar. In a 1970 production at Cambridge University, lights by David Hersey, the director Jonathan Miller kept the Ghost of Julius on-stage from the IV.3 tent scene through the end of the play, fulfilling the promise that the Ghost would see Brutus at Philippi. This is the kind of director's stunt that easily elicits laughter, but Miller made it work.

Julius Caesar begins on the Feast of the Lupercal, the Ides of February 44 BCE. The Lupercal was a fertility festival, on which naked young men raced over the seven hills of Rome, while barren wives stood on the sidelines, holding their hands forth to be touched, ostensibly to make them fertile. Caesar is either cynical or ironic when he advises Antony, one of the runners, to touch Calpurnia as he runs by her so she may "Shake off (her) sterile curse." The main reason she is childless is that Caesar has been romancing Cleopatra for the last four years.

The play is similar in structure to a Chronicle Play building to a series of climaxes with the death of Caesar and Antony's funeral oration, topping even those with Cinna the Poet's murder by the frenzied mob bent on revenge. The conclusion of this scene, III.3, is a perfect place for an intermission, for those who insist on intermissions. The second part of the play, the Folio's 4th and 5th Acts, moves out of Rome and onto the fields of battle in Greece. The Battle of Philippi follows the form of the Battle of Shrewsbury in *Henry IV Part 1*, a series of scenes broken up by skirmishes, resolving with the suicides of Cassius and Brutus and the triumph of Antony and Octavius. The story is continued in *Antony and Cleopatra* as if it were a *Part 2*. But in the second half of this play, director and actors will run into difficulty because of choices made early in the analysis of this play.

I pointed out that American actors, committed to the moral superiority of democracy over monarchy, tend to assume that Brutus is the lead or protagonist (dare we call him "hero?"), justified in his belief that Caesar will prove a tyrant and that his removal is necessary. The arguments of Cassius are skillful, and the collection of conspirators is formidable, but is Brutus ever fully convinced, or does he give in to them as the better of uncomfortable alternatives? Would the assassination have taken place without the cooperation of Brutus?

From the very beginning, Brutus is reluctant, conflicted. He argues with himself, not about the practicality of the assassination, but the absolute morality of it. Once the deed is done, his conscience must stand by that morality or admit to a great crime and a greater sin. When he suspects that Cassius has been taking bribes, he argues that the assassination was a sacrifice for the good of Rome, that it was sacrosanct and demanded great purity from the conspirators. But Brutus continues to vacillate right up to the very end. He is in love with his own honor, as he sees it. His honor will not let him admit that he was wrong, much less guilty of a great sin. Even when he decides to end his misery with the right honorable Roman thing, suicide, he cannot commit to the rightness of the act. He cannot do it alone. He asks one of his soldiers, Strato, to hold his sword while he runs on it. Brutus assumes that Strato will guide the weapon to his heart, saving himself the agony of the self-inflicted wound. In retrospect, from the viewpoint of the 5th Act, it's clear he would have been better off if he had remained neutral. But that's not the play we have at hand.

Again, I warn the director to avoid terms like "hero," "villain," "protagonist." Avoid white hats and black hats. Play what's there at every moment.

CHAPTER 13

Antony and Cleopatra

In *Antony and Cleopatra*, the primary conflict is between the two heirs of Julius Caesar. Add his former mistress, and you have a domestic triangle that ostensibly shook the world. This second play begins some two years after the Battle of Philippi. The Triumvirate has divided up the Roman world, and Antony commands the eastern provinces. He and Cleopatra have become lovers. Here again the title defines the primary dynamic in this play. Tradition has it that this love affair was one of ferocious, fiery intensity. If a production of *Antony and Cleopatra* is to succeed, it must work on a visceral level as a love story. All Shakespearean love stories harken back to *Romeo and Juliet*. Love is the greatest morality, and death is preferable to a barren life without the lover. Love is not immoral, and sex is not dirty.

But there's a huge stumbling block: where are the love scenes in *Antony and Cleopatra*? First of all, there is no thunderbolt meeting; that happened before the play began, and that's the first big problem. Romeo, Juliet, Troilus, Cressida, Henry VIII, and Anne Boleyn all fare better, because we witness the meetings of the lovers, the phenomenon of love at first sight. We may be aware that Antony met Cleopatra when she was the mistress of his mentor, Julius, but we aren't shown that first encounter. Then, where are the one-on-one love scenes, the lover's meetings and partings? Shakespeare simply gives us no moments to substantiate the great love story. It remains a myth. Worst of all, it's an off-stage myth.

Just as productions of *Hamlet* have been sabotaged by references to "the melancholy Dane," so too that nonsense about "a mature love story" makes *Antony and Cleopatra* impossible even before it's cast.

That's probably why Shakespeare didn't make Cleopatra a character in the first play. What these two plays omitted so infuriated G. B. Shaw that he had to write his own play, *Caesar and Cleopatra*, but Shaw, being Shaw, never got down to the viscera of it either. Joseph L. Mankiewicz' epic 1963 film attempted to fill in the blanks and was almost a good movie, but it was overpowered by the scandal surrounding it. Ironically, the reality playing out offset was just what Shakespeare's script most needed: Antony (Richard Burton) not only sleeping with Cleopatra (Elizabeth Taylor), but the two of them actually falling in love.

I've never seen a really successful production of *Antony and Cleopatra*, and my two productions, I readily admit, were somewhere between nice tries and failures. The scope of the play, which pops from Egypt to Rome to Greece to the Straits of Messina and back again, simply cannot be realized on-stage. Much of it takes place on war galleys in the middle of the Mediterranean Sea, but what we see are scenes following the battles, rather than the battles themselves. At least Mankiewicz came close to getting the Battle of Actium right.

Earlier I described the director Jonathan Miller's success with *Julius Caesar*. Miller is one of the most learned people I've ever known — medical doctor, theatre director, historian, performer, writer, scholar — but *Antony and Cleopatra* defeated even him. He directed the play for the BBC television series and introduced his production with a speech worthy of a Cambridge Don. Or was he putting us on with a standup sketch à la *Beyond the Fringe*? Listen and decide. There is one scene in this taped epic in which the actors presumably arrive directly from a galley battle, exhausted and war weary. The result is hilarious, because they're all spanking clean, over-indicating, as if they'd just been summoned from their off-set chess games and naps.

Yet the sea battles, far ranging scenes, and sprawling time periods, as daunting to stage as they are, are not what make this play impossible. *Julius Caesar* is about politics, and, like the Chronicle plays, its historical successor might be expected to complete the story of the competition between the heirs of Julius Caesar until one of them becomes Augustus, one of the most powerful men the world has ever known, and the other defeated and dead. Shakespeare might even have been tempted to change the name of the play early in the writing. But the love affair intruded, took over the play, swallowed the politics whole, and gave us almost insurmountable casting and acting problems.

Examine the historical specifics. At the time of his assassination, Julius Caesar was 56, Octavius was 19, Brutus was 41, Marc Antony was 39, and Cleopatra was 25. The myth-makers have it that Antony and Cleopatra did not begin their affair until they met at Tarsus in 41 BCE, but that's unlikely, since Julius brought her back to Rome in 47 or 46. Marc Antony was Julius Caesar's captain of horse, general of the cavalry, a giant of a man with a distinctive red mane and beard, one of the foremost gladiators of the age, another larger-than-life warrior.

We might say that Antony gave up the opportunity to be co-ruler of the world for the love of Cleopatra. Maintaining the affair with Cleopatra despite his arranged political marriage to Octavia, sister of Octavius Caesar, in 39, could hardly have helped him strategically. Certainly the contemporary media never seem to lack stories of politicians who sacrifice their careers to dalliances with mistresses or prostitutes. History usually treats these affairs as simply disastrous lapses in judgment. Some powerful leaders caught in such scandals, like Henry VIII, may prove invulnerable if political opponents don't exploit the affairs. But posterity does not generally call them love affairs; the women involved are either prostitutes or are characterized as prostitutes.

There are two other complications that must be considered in production: though born in Egypt, Cleopatra was a full-blooded Macedonian, a descendant of Ptolemy I Soter, a general of Alexander the Great. She was also one of the wealthiest people in the world at that time, due to the accumulations of the Ptolemys over several generations.

It's possible that Shakespeare was aiming at the love story even as he began *Julius Caesar*. *Othello*, *Much Ado About Nothing* and *The Winter's Tale* are mature love stories, but Antony and Cleopatra are ageless teenagers in the ferocity of their lust. The actors have to be attractive, athletic, healthy, sexy: it's Hollywood casting. The chemistry between the two actors must work, and they must convince us that each scene precedes or follows ecstatic sex orgies, just off-stage. For all the poetry and the political framework of the play, we are one step away from pornography, the best sex that both men and women in the audience can imagine.

The key word here is "imagine." Pornography exists only in the mind's eye. It is vicarious and fanciful, extending beyond experience, but isn't this the essence of all theatre? One might object that this is Shakespeare, not fantasy porn, but the theatre is fantasy. The imagination need never suffer erectile dysfunction.

Antony and Cleopatra, New Jersey Shakespeare Festival, 1986: Robin Leary as Cleopatra, Jack Ryland as Marc Antony (photograph by Jim DelGiudice).

Shakespeare's Cleopatra, observed and enjoyed from the points of view of Caesar and Antony, is a teenaged sexual specialist more akin to Vladimir Nabokov's Lolita than to the historical Egyptian queen. She's younger, more beautiful, more athletic, more exciting, indefatigable, and she can still reel off that magnificent iambic pentameter. In his notorious novel, Nabokov describes "maidens ... whose true nature is not human, but nymphic (that is, demoniac), and these chosen creatures I propose to designate as 'nymphets,'" the underage seducers of susceptible and careless older men. Nabokov reaches back into mythology for a prototype of the ondine, the siren, the Lorelei, the creatures who could lure sailors, driven mad by lust, onto rocks that destroy their ships and drown them.

The nymphet is alluring and available, insatiable, voluptuous, eternally young and always dangerous. In the theatre and films, this quality has created stars, such as Marilyn Monroe and Brigitte Bardot, and uncreated them as they grew older. But the fictional nymphet never ages beyond 13 or 14, and, lest I be accused of imposing a *Playboy* mentality on Shakespeare, note what Enobarbus says about Cleopatra:

> Age cannot wither her nor custom stale
> Her infinite variety. Other women cloy
> The appetites they feed, but she makes hungry
> Where most she satisfies; for vilest things
> Become themselves in her, that the holy priests
> Bless her when she is riggish.

To be favored by Cleopatra is not only to enjoy non-stop sex, but to possess the necessary stamina to keep up with her. The fantasy goes even further: she excites, stimulates her fantasy lover, but never wears him out or belittles him.

This nymphet image is reinforced by the historic specifics: Cleopatra was 31 years younger than her previous lover, Julius Caesar, and when we first see her in *Antony and Cleopatra*, she's still only in her mid–20s. Since the Playwright compresses 12 years into less than three hours of playing time, she does not age. Nor does Antony; at his death he should remain a strong and virile 39. The affair needs actors cast for the beginning of the story, not its end. Although the actors may make subtle changes in their appearances as the story progresses, I submit that Shakespeare does not age them. He introduces them as they were at the time of the death of Caesar, then kills them two and one-half hours later. They do not age over those two and one-half hours.

My second Cleopatra, Robin Leary, slim and gorgeous in her late 20s, an experienced Shakespearean actress, should have been the perfect Cleopatra, but just as a king cannot be created in a vacuum, just as an actor needs his supporting cast to substantiate the fiction by treating him like a king, so too must lovers and admirers create a desirable woman. Jack Ryland played one of the best Hamlets I ever saw on the stage. As Antony, he never fell in love with Cleopatra.

How do you direct yourself out of that kind of dilemma?

CHAPTER 14

Much Ado About Nothing

Much Ado About Nothing has been billed as "a triumph of love," but, more specifically, it's a triumph of love over war, because its two leading men are professional soldiers, mercenaries, who capitulate to love and marriage and eventually become domesticated. The world must be peopled!

Is there anything random in Shakespeare's plays? Must we assume the importance to the Playwright of each name, each locale, each occurrence? We know that characters and events in *Julius Caesar* and *Antony and Cleopatra* are historically valid, that Shakespeare followed both Plutarch and the Roman historians, though he obviously reinvented and expanded their stories. Why two families named "Capulet" and "Montague?" Why does *Twelfth Night* take place on the seacoast of Illyria? Why a seacoast in Bohemia for *The Winter's Tale*?

Shakespeare situated two plays in Sicily, but the Sicilia of *The Winter's Tale* has nothing to do with the historical Sicily, just as its Bohemia has nothing to do with the historical country of that name. In that play, both kingdoms are products of the Playwright's fancy, and he imagines them as maritime countries two days' sail from each other.

The historical Sicily of the 16th century, however, does inform the political/social environment of *Much Ado About Nothing*, filling in some of the blanks of the play's back-story. While history can hardly be defined as the driving force behind the writing of this comedy, the Playwright couldn't have been oblivious to the conflicts among the English, the Irish, the Spanish, the French, and the Papacy, not to mention the ever-present threat of the Ottoman Turks, during his lifetime.

Much Ado About Nothing is set in Messina, Sicily, during a time of Spanish occupation, but many directors ignore this fact and its influence on the premise and plot. It might be of some value, therefore, to go back further into the history of Sicily. For three millennia, this island has been occupied by a succession of conquerors: Greeks, Phoenicians, Carthaginians, Romans, Ostrogoths, Byzantines, Saracens, Normans, Ottoman Turks, Spaniards, Frenchmen, Austrians, eventually the Italians. The primary objective of all these conquerors was to maintain naval bases in the Mediterranean, and they governed by the Roman method, defending the island against invaders, exacting taxes, while allowing the native Sicilians local administration. Messina was the site of an important Spanish naval base during the 16th and 17th centuries.

It's not difficult to get a clear picture of what was important to the Playwright or should be to today's producers. I believe it is essential that Benedick and Claudio be recognized as mercenaries during a brief cease-fire in an ongoing war. We may assume that Don Pedro is based on Prince Philip of Spain, son and heir to the Holy Roman Emperor Charles V, who became Philip II, King of Spain, when his father abdicated in 1556.

Much Ado About Nothing, **New Jersey Shakespeare Festival, 1977: Robert Beseda as Claudio, Eric Tavares as Benedick, Margery Shaw as Beatrice, Robin Leary as Hero (photograph by Blair Holley).**

Phillip's second wife was Queen Mary Tudor of England, elder daughter of Henry VIII. Mary and Philip married in 1554, a union promoted by the Vatican in an attempt to return England to Catholicism. If Mary had succeeded in bearing children to Philip, the history of Europe might have been radically altered, but she died in 1558, and England returned to the Church of England under her younger sister, Elizabeth I.

Charles V also had a bastard son known as Don John of Austria, the hero of the famous defeat of the Ottoman Turks at the naval battle of Lepanto, 1571. See the chapter on *Othello*. Shakespeare's Don John bears little resemblance to this undisputed hero, so why did he select to use this name for the bastard villain of his play? What sense does that make, considering that the legitimate Don Pedro of Aragon is drawn as a good man and a courageous general? Don John of Austria may have been even more important to Shakespeare because of a plot, the stuff of myth and ballads, dubbed "the Enterprise of England," to rescue Mary Stuart, who had been imprisoned by Elizabeth I on charges of treason. Elizabeth's Catholic rival and legal heir, Mary Stuart, was the great-granddaughter of Henry VII, the daughter of James I/VI of Scotland and mother of James I of England. She spent most of her life involved in foreign intrigues, plots between Catholics and Scotch Protestants.

The Enterprise of England plot would not only rescue Mary, but would marry her to Don John of Austria, while Spanish forces from the Netherlands invaded England, defeated Elizabeth and placed Don John and Mary on the throne. Invading forces were to be led by Sir Thomas Stukeley, English soldier of fortune, commander of a galley at Lepanto, reputed bastard son of Henry VIII. Needless to say, the plot was never realized. Don John died in 1578 of typhoid fever, and Elizabeth executed Mary Stuart in 1587.

Shakespeare could have set *Much Ado About Nothing* anywhere, as many contemporary directors have, but if Messina was, to the Playwright, essential to the play, then all elements of the setting, time and place, are potentially important and should at least be examined. Are there hidden meanings in the character names assigned? Don John the Bastard is the big enigma, but what about the others? They're mostly Italian or Spanish forms of common names. Is Leonato a lion? Is Beatrice blessed? Borachio is a drunkard, and the name certainly informs the character and serves the plot. Benedick is not Benedict: Benedick is a bawdy joke, just as Petruchio is; it means "good penis."

As the play begins, the sounds of a battle raging at the harbor may be heard behind the audience: cannons, trumpets, shouts, horses. Leonato, Sicilian governor of Messina, his daughter, Hero, his niece Beatrice, and his brother Antonio are waiting for the Spaniards to return from that battle. We are not told whom they are fighting, but in the 16th century, it would be the Turks. If you place the play later, it could be the French. Directors have placed this play in Mexico and Texas at the time of the Alamo and during the American Civil War. The worst thing about those productions was that they suckered the actors into going for accents and dialects that worked against the rhythms of the text. I prefer placing the play in Sicily in 1808, when Spanish Ferdinand I was king of the Two Sicilys, and the forces of Napoleon continued to attack at regular intervals.

A wonderful production by Joe Papp in the late 1960s was set in America at the conclusion of the Spanish American War (1898), primarily, in my opinion, to justify a delightful musical score. The tuba player was a star of the production, but Kathleen Widdoes and Sam Waterston were the best Beatrice and Benedick I ever saw. Nevertheless, there was nothing Sicilian, Italian, or Spanish about the production.

The opening exposition of the play mentions the battle, then we are quickly told that the Spaniards have prevailed, and then the conversation turns to Count Claudio of Florence and Benedick of Padua, two mercenaries in the army of Don Pedro, Prince of Aragon. The Spanish army also includes Don John, half-brother to Don Pedro, John's followers, Conrad and Borachio, and Balthazar, identified in the cast list as "a singer, attendant on Don Pedro." The rest of the cast are Sicilians. Leonato, his brother Antonio, and "a Lord," are of the Sicilian nobility, as are Hero and Beatrice. The rest of the Sicilians are commoners: the constabulary (Dogberry, Verges, the Sexton, Watchmen) and servants to Leonato. As governor, Leonato administers the municipality, while the Spanish Army functions like a federal government. When the Army first bursts onto the scene five minutes into the play, they are in battle uniform and armor, victorious, grubby, and appropriately horny, thirsty, and hungry.

Shakespeare must have assumed a general knowledge of the times on the part of his audience, and spends little time with either history or civics. He doesn't have to if the director has established the back-story with the actors and designers solidly before the play begins. We are soon immersed in parallel love stories about two young noblewomen and their soldier suitors, but soldiership permeates the play.

Could the love stories exist without these political/military distinctions? Unless the director recognizes that the play is about professional soldiers during a brief time of peace, these essential elements can be (and usually are) completely ignored. Certainly the old hoary differences between a fighter and a lover are dragged out. Benedick describes the decline of Claudio from soldier to lover with appropriate contempt. Who says a fighter cannot be a lover?

Like so many of the plays, the art is in the language. The dueling wits and word play among the lovers in *Much Ado about Nothing* are superb (compare it to the earlier *Love's Labour's Lost*)—and language itself is celebrated, even in the mangling of it, by Dogberry and crew.

The primary plot, of Hero and Claudio, is complicated, ambiguous, and occasionally difficult to follow. The secondary plot, that of Beatrice and Benedick, is actually the more interesting: it appears that they had something of a romance going before the play begins, but we are not told when or how long ago. Unlike Hero and Claudio, who fall in love at first sight and move logically toward marriage, Beatrice and Benedick pretend to loathe each other, but it's a simple matter for the rest of the cast to con them into revealing their true feelings.

The third plot involves the attempts of Don John, the Bastard, to discredit his brother, Don Pedro, by defaming Hero, getting at Don Pedro through Count Claudio. His scheme seems a bit goofy, and it depends on a couple of drunken factotums, Conrad and Borachio, so inept that even Dogberry and his Keystone Kops are capable of exposing them. There's no good reason stated for the dirty trick Don John plays. Some enmity between him and Don Pedro is mentioned early in the play, but they are supposedly reconciled by the time they return from battle. However, Shakespeare's other bastards, notably Falconbridge and Edmund, also appear to lack sufficient motivation. Do all bastards behave alike?

The characters are speaking Sicilian Italian, though we hear English. The Spaniards could be allowed a slight Spanish accent, but Spanish and Italian were closer together linguistically than they are today. Beware of British and American regionalisms. The most trouble I ever had with an actor in this play was an American who had played Dogberry earlier with a Cockney dialect and wanted to use it again. It wasn't his native sound—he simply believed that was the way to play Dogberry, based on the British theatrical custom of using proper speech for the aristocracy and English regionalisms for the lower classes. That might work in a British production, but in an American production, all it suggests is that the director has hired Americans for most of the roles and a Brit for Dogberry.

This play calls for uniforms, and that means many characters should be costumed alike: Don Pedro, Don John, Benedick, and Claudio are Spanish officers; their uniforms can be identical, differing only in insignia. Each needs a battle uniform with helmets and minimal armor, and casual civilian costumes for most of the play. They change into festive garb for the party, but they're back in dress uniform for the wedding of Claudio and Hero. They also need battle swords (similar to American cavalry sabers) as well as dress swords. Period rifles, pikes, if possible.

Benedick needs a fake beard to play the early scenes so that it can be shaved off once he admits he's in love with Beatrice, who does not like beards. "The barber's man has been with Benedick" is a joke based on the fact that dentists were also barbers. He's seen coming out of the barber/dentist's, so he complains about a toothache and hides his face with a towel.

The actors playing Dogberry, Verges, and the Watchmen can be doubled as Don Pedro's soldiers, costumed in standard peasant dress. Directors should be warned to keep the Watchmen in line, because, like Peter Quince's community theatre actors in *A Midsummer Night's Dream*, these roles can tempt inexperienced actors into overplaying and adding shtick. The low comedy in this play comes from Dogberry's erroneous assumption of his intellectual superiority and his insistence on the dignity he feels should be supplied him by his office. The Playwright is lampooning unqualified public servants, who, despite their incompetence, nevertheless manage to get the job done.

The revelers need not be costumed specifically for the masked ball in II.1, but merely provided with carnival masks, as in *Romeo and Juliet* and *The Merchant of Venice*. The dance has some substance, with most of the main cast participating. It must be choreographed so that the characters speaking the five patches of dialogue within it can each be spun-off logically downstage while the other dancers freeze. By using this dance/freeze/dance/freeze technique, moments of intimacy can be isolated in the middle of the wild party. The dance then builds to a joyful frenzy, and all run off, leaving Claudio alone.

Most of the action of the play can be set in the garden of the governor's palace, on a mountainside facing the harbor. Upstage is the rise of the mountain, and downstage (the audience) is the road to the village. Walls, fountains, benches are provided as necessary. At 15 minutes before curtain I like to add a Spanish guitarist who enters, sits downstage and plays a medley of gypsy laments. At curtain time, Leonato, Antonio, Beatrice, and Hero enter with drinks and take seats to listen to the battle and watch. They wait. Some nervous inactivity can be afforded. If the enemy triumph, the Sicilians will have to flee for their lives. They look to the harbor. Latecomers should be seated until the messenger, played by Balthazar, dashes on and the play proper begins.

Once the Hero/Claudio nuptials are agreed upon, the Playwright concentrates on the Beatrice/Benedick plot, using some of the oldest gimmicks in the dramatic tradition, but using them in fresh new ways, with great wit and humor. Most of the characters conspire to convince Beatrice that Benedick is in love with her but is too proud to show it, while she pines for him, just as proud and constrained by custom. The lovers play a delightful hide and seek, each waiting for the other to capitulate.

The third plot is then introduced: Don John's attempt to defame Hero in the eyes of Claudio. Claudio and Don Pedro fall for the subterfuge, and at the wedding, Claudio turns on Hero and throws her back to her father, describing her as a rotten orange. When the wedding party has exited, the Franciscan Friar steps in to suggest that Hero be hidden away, while it is published that she has died. The assumption is that news of her "death" will reveal the treachery of her accusers.

The wedding party then leaves the stage to Beatrice and Benedick. The audience has witnessed the scene and heard the plan. In IV.2, a few minutes later, Dogberry, Verges, and the Watch expose Don John's treachery and exit to carry the news to Leonato. The Sexton tells us that Hero has died.

Leonato and Antonio play the next scene, V.1., *as if* Hero were really dead. These two old brothers play the truth of the lie. We've seen what we've seen, and we've heard what we've heard. Did we miss something? Are they being overheard? Perhaps the brothers are purposely setting up an encounter with Claudio where they will challenge him to duels. In the four-scene that follows, V.1.45 to 109, all four characters play the fiction as if it were the truth.

There is much eavesdropping in this play, and the director is advised to build it back into the action; Conrad, Borachio, and a servant to Leonato spend much time lurking on the periphery of scenes.

Benedick enters on the argument, and he continues the fiction. Though he was present when Friar Francis proposed the subterfuge and knows that Hero is alive, he challenges Claudio to a duel for his part in killing her. Even after Dogberry, Verges, and the watch enter with the prisoners, Conrad and Borachio, to expose Don John's plot, the fiction that Hero is dead is maintained. As penance, Claudio agrees to marry her cousin, and they agree to gather at Hero's tomb that night to sing a song of eulogy and pay homage to her innocence.

The next morning, they reconvene at Leonato's for the wedding of Claudio and Hero's cousin. Through all the scenes from IV.1 through V.4, all the actors behave as if Hero were truly dead, even those who were in on the plot. As the bride lifts her veil and reveals herself, the maligned Hero rises from the dead. It was the defiled Hero that died, but it is the innocent Hero who lives. This is the poetic interpretation; the director should not be tempted to do something spooky.

I've spent a lot of time on this plot recap because it's an excellent example of the argument that there is no subtext in Shakespeare. The subtext would be Friar Francis' plot: Hero lives, and she will remain in hiding until she's proven innocent. What's on the surface and what must be played is the truth of the fiction: Hero was accused of being unchaste, and she died of grief. If the actors attempt to play both surface and subtext, they will confuse both themselves and the audience.

Once Hero and Claudio are united, it's an easy matter for Beatrice and Benedick to capitulate to each other, and love will triumph over all.

In the last few seconds of the play, word comes to Don Pedro that his brother, the enigmatic Don John the Bastard, has been captured and is on his way back to Messina under guard. Benedick promises to deal with him, then leads the company in a wedding dance. Who said that a fighter can't be both lover and dancer? We still do not know the reason for the falling out between the half-brothers, Don Pedro and Don John. We don't know what motivated Don John to harm Claudio by maligning Hero, and there is little explanation of why Shakespeare would use the name of the hero of Lepanto for his villain.

CHAPTER 15

Othello

The Commandment dictates "Thou shalt not kill," but there's something deep in the nature of the beast, the primitive brain, articulated in the early books of the Torah, that qualifies "Thou shalt not kill except the enemy, and that is a higher good." Othello has been a warrior since the age of seven, and he is a general and great hero because of all the enemies he's killed. He's killed with his own hands, and he's led other killers into battle.

Othello is a Moor, a Berber, and a Muslim. To promote his position as a general in the Venetian military, he has apparently converted to Christianity, but he is still a Muslim at heart. His attitudes toward enemies and towards women are those of Islam. His wife is his possession, flesh of his flesh. He worships her, revels in the luxury of her body, then kills her when he comes to believe that someone else is enjoying her. He cannot bear the dull pain, the outrage of such an insult.

Very simple, very primitive, very modern.

Early in the reign of James I/VI, when *Othello* was first produced, Shakespeare had become a star, and he demanded that the audience treat him like one. He catered to no latecomers. The essential premise of *Othello* is laid down in its first five minutes. Show up late, and you'll spend the next hour wondering what's happening and why. It's wise to hold the curtain a few minutes, then delay seating latecomers until the house of Brabantio is awakened, some four minutes into the play, so they won't be a distraction from the opening details.

Directors achieve far more notoriety by doing outlandish things to a play than by going straight ahead, following the Playwright's intent. When Patrick Stewart played Othello for the Shakespeare Theatre in Washington, all the other characters were African American. Sounds fascinating. It was awful. In an earlier production, directed by Hal Scott, Othello, Iago and Emilia were all black — of the four principal characters, only Desdemona was white. The polarity of the play was thrown off because she, not Othello, was the outsider. It wasn't a bad production, and the charismatic Andre Braugher, as Iago, was exciting and wonderful, but it wasn't the play Shakespeare wrote, and it simply didn't work.

Othello is a love story. Critics have referred to it as "a domestic tragedy," but that is a demeaning simplification. During a brief time of peace, the Venetian Senator Brabantio invites Othello to his home, unwittingly giving the Moor and his daughter Desdemona the opportunity to fall in love. Knowing Brabantio will never consent to a marriage, they elope. Brabantio first accuses Othello of using witchcraft to seduce Desdemona, but the imminent Turkish attack on Cyprus resolves the matter temporarily, and Othello and his troops prepare for war.

As is so often the case in Shakespeare, *Othello* celebrates a sacrosanct marriage between passionate lovers. Having established his monogamous ideal, Shakespeare then created Iago to destroy it.

Though I wouldn't group this play among the soldier plays, and we never actually see him in battle, Othello himself begins the play as the perfect warrior. Like Macbeth, Marc Antony, and Coriolanus, Othello should be cast as a ferocious gladiator. If a short actor plays the role, the director is advised to cast small people for the rest of the roles. That's what they did when Olivier, at 5'8", played Othello. They also scaled the set down to 89 percent for him so that he appeared to be well over six feet and at least 200 pounds.

As a Moor, Othello is a foreigner, an outsider, but the Venetians were very liberal in welcoming artisans, physicians, scientists, architects, soldiers from everywhere in the known world. As long as the foreigners obeyed the laws of Venice, they were free to prosper, to come and go as if they were citizens. This is true in *The Merchant of Venice* as well. In 1984, when the NJSF presented the two Venetian plays in rotating rep, the fact that the Doge of Venice was played by the same actor, Richard Graham (the splendid King Lear of my youth), in both plays underscored this important plot point.

In 1471, the Ottoman Turks conquered the islands of Cyprus, Corfu, and Crete, held until then by the Venetians. The plot of *Othello* turns on the I.3 intelligence that a Turkish fleet is preparing to attack both Rhodes and Cyprus, requiring Othello to be dispatched to command the Venetian fleet. This news (all reported, of course, and not seen) is what saves Othello from the prosecution of Brabantio.

How much of this was important to Shakespeare? It was irrelevant to Verdi, whose *Otello* opens with the arrival of the Moor and Desdemona in Cyprus. Verdi's opera isn't Venetian at all. Shakespeare substitutes an off-stage tempest that destroys the Turkish fleet for a sea battle between the Venetians and the Turks. Othello arrives triumphant at Cyprus without ever drawing his scimitar.

To understand Othello's position, it's necessary to first consider the City of Venice itself, which began as a lagoon on the north Adriatic Sea, fed by the Rivers Po and Piave, and contained by a series of barrier islands. The sediment deposited by the rivers in the middle of the lagoon formed some 120 natural islands. Early inhabitants created the city by ferrying stones, sand, and eventually masonry, out from the mainland, sinking foundations to the bottom of the lagoon, and erecting buildings, which were then connected by some 400 bridges. It has to be seen to be believed.

The city could not be attacked by land, and the Venetians built a navy of galleys that doubled as commercial vessels and warships that could match any navy in the world. The Venetian army was not an army, but a marine corps of foot soldiers who fought from the decks of the galleys. Sailors sailed the galleys, slaves rowed, and marines fought the battles. A city built on connected islands, defended by a formidable navy and marines, could not be conquered.

Since the seventh century, the dominant conflict in Europe, North Africa, and the Middle East has been between conquering Muslims and loosely confederated Christian European states. The Holy Roman Empire was a power from the time of Charlemagne through the last Hapsburg, Francis II.

The Holy Roman Emperor, the Hapsburg Charles V, ruled a vast group of territories that included Austria, the Netherlands, French Comte, Spain, Portugal, Sardinia, Naples (all of the south of Italy), and Sicily. During the 16th century, the greatest danger to Christian civilization was the Ottoman Turks under Suleiman the Great, who, when Shakespeare was

Opposite: *Othello*, New Jersey Shakespeare Festival, 1984: Roger Robinson as Othello, Paul Barry as Iago (photograph by Blair Holley).

born, controlled all of North Africa, Turkey and the Crimean peninsula, Greece, and portions of Eastern Europe and Western Asia from what is modern day Iran to the Austrian border. If the Turks didn't invent slavery, they raised it to a high art. They'd overwhelm their enemies, then haul as many as could be carried back to Turkey as slaves. Captured women in harems produced Turkish children to become soldiers of the Sultan, while captured men became rowers for the galleys.

Shakespeare sets most of *Othello* in a Cyprus controlled by the Venetians, but under threat of attack by the Turks. From 1546 on, the Turks fought a series of battles with the forces of Spain, Venice, and the Papal States, a confederation of northern Italian cities under the temporal control of the Vatican. In October 1571, these Christian political entities combined their navies and attacked the Turks at Lepanto, off Corinth in Greece.

Up until Lepanto, slaves rowed Turkish galleys. The development of artillery changed sea battles considerably. Banks of cannons on bigger and bigger galleys could incapacitate the enemy faster than ramming and boarding. Technological advances in sails and rigging eventually made galley slaves obsolete, but this change in technology did not happen overnight. It paralleled the evolution of artillery. The hero of Lepanto, as we saw in *Much Ado About Nothing*, was the dashing adventurer, general and admiral Don John of Austria, half-brother of King Philip II of Spain, who brought the battle to an early conclusion with a head-on attack on the Turkish flagship, killing its admiral, Ali, son of Suleiman. Though the battle continued to rage for another day, the Christian victory over the Turk was decisive.

The Battle of Lepanto was a great turning point in military sea power. Politics and commerce changed too. Both sides concluded that trade was more efficient during peace than during war. The Venetians made a separate peace with the Turks that promoted trade between East and West.

The Spanish armada that attacked England in 1588 was a very different fleet than that which defeated the Muslims in Turkey. What a difference 18 years made!

Why have I spent all this time on history and environment? Because the Playwright does. If the central action of the play is the seduction of the mind of Othello and the deadly results of that seduction, the deaths of Desdemona and Othello, why are we nearly halfway through the play before those temptations begin? To give us the proper back-story and setting against which the tragedy can play out. This is no simple domestic tragedy. It's an inter-racial romance between a Venetian Catholic and a closet Mohammedan at a perilous historic time.

Othello is referred to most frequently in the play as "the Moor," yet the name "Othello" is Italian, not Moorish. In his film, Laurence Olivier used the premise of Othello's conversion to Christianity for some interesting business. From his first appearance, he wore a crucifix around his neck. When he became convinced of Desdemona's infidelity and vowed revenge on her, he tore off the crucifix and hurled it across the room. It's one of those ideas that fill out a production, that give it depth without altering the action or changing the Playwright's intent.

In casting the play, the polarities must be respected. Othello is a North African; most of the others are Italians. Desdemona should be beautiful and sexy, Michael Cassio young and handsome. Directors should be strongly advised against casting Iago as an aristocrat, as I've occasionally seen him played. Iago is the perfect non-com, a professional warrior who knows his place and obeys orders. Only in soliloquy do we see the soul of the poisoner.

Much breath and paper have been expended on the question of why Iago so horribly dupes Othello. Critics don't believe he has any basis for seeking revenge or sufficient reasons to do all that damage. Coleridge, notably, wrote of Iago's "motiveless malignity."

But I don't think these questioners spend enough time examining the first five minutes (100 lines) of the play. Nor do they appear to understand medieval customs of military meritocracy.

Iago begins the play explaining the plot and back-story to Roderigo. If the audience knows how the play ends, they begin by doubting Iago, but ideally, an audience begins the evening with minimal or no knowledge of the play, and is willing to accept what they hear and see as gospel until contradictions prove otherwise.

Iago tells Roderigo that Othello has been promoted to Venice's highest military post and given the privilege of choosing his second in command. Iago has served Othello as personal bodyguard, his "ancient," a rank equivalent to today's top sergeant, for unspecified years in campaigns in Rhodes, Cyprus and "other [battle] grounds, Christian and heathen." "Three great ones of the city" encouraged Othello to name Iago as his lieutenant, but Othello has selected instead Michael Cassio, a well-connected young man, a theoretician and a graduate of a military academy, yet inexperienced in battle.

Clearly, Othello is ambitious, and both Michael Cassio, a Florentine aristocrat, as lieutenant, and Desdemona, daughter of a senator, as his wife, will help advance his career. Nevertheless, we better believe that Othello and Desdemona are passionately in love with each other or there is no play; it's the perfect marriage, one based on physical love, yet advantageous to both husband and wife.

How long has Iago been Othello's faithful follower? The text doesn't specify, but Iago says he's 28 years old, and the Moor would seem to be in his mid to late 30s. Following the traditions of military apprenticeship, it's logical to assume that Iago has served Othello for some 12 to 14 years. Instead of taking Iago with him when he gets his big break, he chooses the society shavetail Cassio. Passed over after a career of serving Othello, what's Iago to do? Send out resumes and look for another job? He's stuck, unpromoted, unrewarded, and this prompts his desire for revenge on both the general and his new lieutenant. So much for "motiveless malignity."

But is the revenge too severe, too horrible in all the characters it destroys? By reducing Iago to a one-dimensional devil, Coleridge and his school ignore his adroit manipulation of events as they progress. Indeed, they ignore Shakespeare's brilliance in this dramatic creation.

Iago's first objective seems to be to disgrace Othello by alerting Brabantio to the clandestine marriage. If Othello can be apprehended and Desdemona "rescued" before the marriage is consummated, their union can be annulled.

But when we first see Othello at the Sagittary, the officers' quarters of the Venetian shipyards, any question about whether the marriage has been consummated is dispelled. Olivier's smug, boastful playing of the scene was that of a man sexually sated. His use of a rose as a surrogate Desdemona was very sensual stuff.

Iago's alternative objective is to disgrace the unproven Cassio, replace him before he can prove his soldiership in the defense of Cyprus against the Turks and vindicate himself as Othello's choice. However, the war ends before it begins, Othello assumes the military protectorship of the island, declares a holiday of celebration, and puts the still unproven Cassio in charge. Manipulated by Iago, Cassio drinks too much, precipitates a brawl, wounds Montano, retiring governor of Cyprus, and is cashiered by Othello. Iago would seem to have accomplished his second objective. The honorable thing would be for Cassio to accept his demotion, and take ship back to Venice to hope for another assignment.

As we know, however, the plot doesn't resolve here. Iago suggests that Cassio employ Desdemona as his advocate, and, foolishly, he takes the bait. At each turn, the Playwright adds another complication to keeps the plot advancing. Having set the engine in motion, Iago hangs on and rides it to everyone's doom.

Othello himself demonstrates Leo Kirschbaum's principle that a character in Shakespeare speaks, not with his own power of expression, but with the Playwright's. Othello tell the Venetian Senate, "Rude I am in my speech, and little blessed with the soft phrase of peace." Then he rips off a few pages of superb poetry in telling his story. Form aside, what does he really say? He tells us he's been a warrior since he was seven years old: he knows nothing of life but death and destruction: fights, sieges, battles, stratagems. He was wounded, captured, and sold into slavery, then escaped. Through his ferocity and courage, he moved up in the Venetian military until he became its general. But where in his history could Othello have learned to read and write, much less create poetry?

Harry Keyishian responds that Shakespeare uses language symbolically, as an expression of Othello's romantic soul. That makes perfect sense, and makes it possible for the actor to reconcile the roughness of the character with his fluid, sophisticated speech. Othello is a warrior with a romantic soul. His eloquence is ultimately derived from Shakespeare, but is also an indication of what and how Shakespeare wants us to think of him.

I directed *Othello* twice, in 1968 and 1984. In both productions, I also played Iago, which I found very satisfying personally. I don't know what I may have lost in giving up the objective eye of another director, but I do know I saved a lot of time by not having to fight a common problem. Too often, the play disintegrates into a duel of two actors upstaging each other with cheap tricks, each trying to undermine the credibility of the other's performance. The best stage production I ever saw was in the mid–1960s, off–Broadway, with James Earl Jones as Othello and Mitch Ryan as Iago. They played the text honestly and directly. There was no attempt on Ryan's part to steal the show. He gave the play to Jones.

Playing Iago was fun in both my productions. Some roles are ennobling, some rewarding, some just fun. Peter MacLean played Othello in 1968, and Tony-winner Roger Robinson in 1984. It was a joy to be on-stage with both of them because they were dangerous. I could never let my guard down, never take my eyes off the Moor, because he could blindside me. Othello tries to choke Iago in III.3. I believed both of them would have strangled me if I had let them. I fell off the stage in the first production and sprained my left ankle, but neither Maclean nor Robinson ever really hurt me. Still, I always woke up the morning after a performance feeling like I had played 60 minutes of football.

I praised the actors playing Iago above for not attempting to steal the play. I believe the trick is to play the truth of the lie. If Iago telegraphs his intent to the audience while tempting Othello, then the Moor appears to be a fool. Othello is not a fool. A selfish Iago can make Othello seem a fool, but directors must be warned of this possibility and must fight to control it.

Othello trusts Iago. In fact, everybody has good reason to trust Iago. How many times is the word "honest" used to describe him? He's a professional warrior, rough, practical, direct. The actor must play everything he says to another character with complete conviction. In soliloquy, Iago tells the audience which things are lies and which are truths, but he should never appear to be lying to another character. The audience will discover what is true and what is not. Politicians do this all the time. They tell the truth of the lie, and when they're caught, they lie truthfully to escape.

For example, Iago speaks of reputation, advising Othello that "good name in man and woman is the immediate jewel of their souls," and he tells Cassio, "Reputation is an idle and most false imposition, oft got without merit and lost without deserving." To earn their cooperation, he tells each what they want to hear. The talented, skillful actor speaks the truth on cue, whether the truth be fact or fiction.

Does Desdemona need to give Othello any reasons to make his jealousy more credible? I don't think so. She is friendly and respectful toward Cassio, as befits the wife of his superior officer, but no more of a relationship need be suggested. Othello is the outsider, the foreigner. He's aware that Cassio might be a suitable lover for Desdemona, and jealousy is deeply entrenched in his nature. Like Leontes, Othello's jealousy is irrational, the stuff of imagination, and the actor has to find the logic of it. The text doesn't need to be helped along.

Some miscellaneous notes: the doubling in this play is simpler than most. The core cast only numbers seven actors, and the Venetians double the Cypriots. There is ample time for changes of costume, wigs, make-up, ethnicity. Even Bianca could be doubled as a waiting woman to Desdemona in Venice.

Othello features one of the pesky technical problems in Shakespeare, like the Ghosts in *Hamlet* and *Macbeth*, Juliet's balcony, Bottom's asshead. It's Desdemona's bed. She has to be strangled in it, but what does it look like? How and when do you get it on-stage? It certainly can't be there, taking up space, until it's needed. This problem must be solved in the initial design, or the director will find him/herself with egg on the face at the end of the play.

What other land mines do we find in *Othello*? The first act takes place in Venice, and the rest of the play in Cyprus. The designers must make the change in locale specific. I found that putting a belly dancer into the Cypriot celebration in II.3 created a sort of instant shorthand for this change of place, and helped kick off a great party that becomes a riot until Othello shows up.

The play has very little comic relief, except for the tiny role of the Clown, and, of course, Roderigo. But Roderigo is not gay, and he's not just a fop; he is propelled by his lust for Desdemona, a man obsessed with a woman he cannot have. His serious function should not be sacrificed to comedy.

Two memories of my *Othello* productions are particularly fond ones. In a 1968 performance, fire provided a spectacular accident. In V.1, the darkest scene in all Shakespeare, an intern, playing a messenger, had overloaded his torch with flammable fluid. He ran on-stage, stopped abruptly, and splashed flaming fluid on my arm. I was wearing fencing gauntlets and a heavy quilted sleeve, so I continued the dialogue, a series of commands to Lodovico, Gratiano, Bianca, and Emilia, while I slapped away at the flames until they went out. After the performance, a breathless young woman came backstage to praise me for the exciting, insightful, symbolic business. It was clear to her that Iago was the devil, and, though he was able to contain the powers of hell much of the time, occasionally they just erupted forth. I thanked her for her good wishes and took the costume to wardrobe for repair.

An even more treasured memory, from the 1984 production, involved a young actor, Herman LaVerne Jones, who understudied Roger Robinson as Othello. Just before a Saturday matinee we discovered that Roger was too sick to perform; he could barely walk. Herman was playing a small role in the production and knew the staging, but he had never had a full rehearsal as Othello. He had only a 25-minute warning that Saturday, and that time was spent on costume adjustments and making him up to look older. He was terrified, but the company was supportive, and we gave him a full-time assistant to handle his props and costume changes and keep him on track between scenes. The cast was excited. A show always gets a lift when an important understudy goes on.

Years later, Herman told me that I told him that day to look into my eyes and hold the stare whenever he was in trouble. That performance was the most fascinating afternoon

I ever spent in the theatre. There were two of me: one played Iago, and the other hovered over my shoulder, monitoring the performance. When Herman lost a line, Iago would cut to the next speech while the monitor mentally checked the text to see whether we could go on or whether we had to go back to retrieve what had been lost. Herman's terror translated itself into a manic energy. He was all over the text, but his confidence grew as the performance progressed. At the curtain call, the house gave him a standing ovation, which he richly deserved. Backstage, he grabbed me and hugged me for a full five minutes.

Herman is still working in the theatre. He produces, directs, and acts in Atlanta, Georgia. When I performed in Raleigh, North Carolina, in Conor McPherson's *The Weir* with the Burning Coal Theatre, he came to a performance and introduced me to his friends as his hero. His memory of that *Othello* performance duplicates mine. Actors are fortunate: the nature of our work, which demands emotional availability, encourages deep friendship, and because of our gypsy existence, the family keeps growing.

CHAPTER 16

The Merchant of Venice

Mel Brooks is one of my heroes. By creating Hans, the Nazi author of *Springtime for Hitler*, Brooks turned the great monster of the 20th century into a clown and his followers into fools. Brooks' 1968 movie, *The Producers*, with Zero Mostel, its 2001 translation into Broadway musical, and the subsequent film version of the musical might have redeemed *The Merchant of Venice* for us. It might have.

Anyone who remembers the Shoah, the Holocaust — three generations of us — is bound to react negatively to the idea of a Jewish villain, especially a comic Jewish villain. Since World War II, every producer of *The Merchant of Venice* has invited a storm of protest because the play is perceived as being anti-Semitic.

I know of several instances where American productions of *The Merchant of Venice* were protested, even picketed. In 1962 George C. Scott played Shylock heroically at the New York Shakespeare Festival for Joe Papp, who would brook no anti-Semitism in his plays. Scott, who was not Jewish, played the role like a tragic hero, a cross between Coriolanus and Lear. The production was heavy, humorless, and certainly biased in favor of the persecuted Shylock. Nevertheless, to Joe's surprise and dismay, the production was maligned because the play itself (not the production) was perceived to be anti-Semitic. If anything, this production sided with Shylock and against Antonio and the Christians. Still, it was protested. Editorials protested and the concerted efforts of a group of rabbis prevented it from being televised by a major network.

Audrey Stanley directed the play for Shakespeare at Santa Cruz in California in 1985 and cut out all references to Jews or Judaism. She substituted a nonsense word.

When Arthur Storch, who is Jewish, produced the play for Syracuse Stage, an affiliate of Syracuse University, he announced the play to the theatre's subscriber base a year in advance. No one protested the inclusion of *The Merchant of Venice*. Months passed and the play went into rehearsal. A week before opening, representatives of the Jewish Anti-Defamation League came to the theatre and demanded that Storch cancel the production. He heard them out, then asked, "Why didn't you object a year ago, or at least while the play could be dumped without seriously jeopardizing the financial health of the company?" The protests continued, but the production played out its run.

When I directed the play in 1984, we received so many letters — most angry, though some applauded us — that my wife, Ellen, as producing director, had to resort to a form letter to keep up with the mail. She also had to endure irate phone calls from the Jewish Anti-Defamation League, and only partially placated them by inviting them to share their views at our annual colloquium. But I'll get to that.

But is the play anti-Semitic? Does the play itself incite Christians to do violence against

Jews? Perhaps it doesn't have to. Anti-Semitism, like any form of racism or bigotry, can manifest itself in a thousand subtle ways.

There are arguments for the existence of Elizabethan anti–Semitism. There's Christopher Marlowe's *The Jew of Malta* and the example of Dr. Roderigo Lopez, a Portuguese Jew, physician to Queen Elizabeth, who was prosecuted by the Earl of Essex, accused of plotting to poison her and subsequently hanged, and drawn and quartered in 1594. However, anyone convicted of conspiracy to assassinate the Queen suffered the same fate. It was a select group, but not a small one. The Jews were expelled from England at the end of the 13th century; those few living in London during Shakespeare's time were bankers, merchants, diplomats, all aliens, privileged foreigners.

However, though both cities appreciated aliens with investment capital, Venice was not London. Despite the ongoing wars between the Ottoman Empire and Christian Europe, commerce never stopped. Venice was the clearinghouse between East and West, and a chain of banks from Hamburg to Amsterdam to Lisbon to Seville to Venice to Constantinople facilitated the trade. Jewish bankers, enjoying diplomatic immunity from all sides, maintained the cash flow. The right-hand man to Sultan Selim II, son and heir to Suleiman the Great, was a Jewish banker named Joseph Micas, who moved freely between Christians and Turks.

Shylock and Tubal are not merchants. They loan money in return for interest, like any banker today. Ostensibly, Christians in Venice were forbidden to loan money for interest, though that law didn't exist in England. Is it worth debating? It's a premise of the play.

The Merchant of Venice, New Jersey Shakespeare Festival, 1984: Ron Mangravite as Bassanio, Albert Corbin as Solanio, Geddeth Smith as Antonio, Cal Winn as Shylock, Alan Jordan as Salerio, Lisa Bansavage as Portia, J.C. Hoyt as Gratiano (photograph by Gerry Goodstein).

Lest it slip through the cracks, let me emphasize one more factoid in the text: Shylock and Tubal are not Venetian citizens. This is an important plot point; in fact, the play turns on it. As I mentioned in the *Othello* chapter, 16th-century Venetians were extremely liberal in welcoming artisans, physicians, scientists, architects, soldiers from everywhere in the known world. As long as foreigners obeyed the laws of Venice, they were free to prosper, to come and go as if they were citizens. The Playwright tells us nothing about Shylock's country of origin, but in Venice, he is a privileged foreigner. As a banker, he provides a valuable service to Venetians. The government determined interest rates that bankers could charge, and protected them against loss of their principal due to unscrupulous borrowers.

I believe—I might be naive in doing so—that the problem with *The Merchant of Venice* today is neither the play nor the genre of the comic villain: it's the context of World War II. Modern audiences, by judging the play in the light of the horrors of Belsen, Auschwitz, and Buchenwald, have rendered the play unproduceable. Leo Kirschbaum wrote the definitive article on the problem, "Shylock in the City of God," and Daniel C. Schiff makes great sense in his 2003 article "Is There a Legal Solution to Resentment," written with a sharp lawyer's eye. But people will continue to abhor *The Merchant of Venice*, not because of what Shakespeare wrote, but because of what Hitler and the Nazis did.

Antonio is often played as reprehensible, nasty, spitting at Shylock or kicking him, but Shakespeare didn't put these actions into the play, only verbal reference to them. If a director adds this business, the dice are loaded.

Jonathan Miller's television production, with Shylock played by Olivier as a wealthy Edwardian Rothschild, also emphasized the ambiguous sexuality in the play, making explicit the ambiguous. Antonio, Bassanio, Gratiano, Lorenzo, Solanio, Salerio are all friends, bachelors, wealthy gentlemen. Three of them get married in the course of the action. We know how Antonio makes his money: he's the merchant of the title. Bassanio is referred to as "a scholar and a soldier." The rest don't seem to have jobs or professions. They hang out and party, and they gossip a lot.

The most satisfactory Shylock I've seen was Warren Mitchell, who used a subtle London East End Yiddish accent, in the BBC tapes. The best stage Shylock I ever saw was Morris Carnovsky's at the American Shakespeare Festival in the 1950s. Carnovsky did not attempt a dialect, but his rhythms were unmistakably American Jewish. I never saw Zero Mostel's Shylock, but I did see him as Max Bialystock in the first film of *The Producers* and on-stage as James Joyce's Bloom in *Ulysses in Night Town* and in *Rhinoceros, Fiddler on the Roof,* and *A Funny Thing Happened on the Way to the Forum*. Mostel was a comic genius. Arnold Wesker wrote a contemporary version of *The Merchant of Venice* in 1976 with Mostel as Shylock, but Mostel died during the out-of-town tryout, and the play failed without him. He died in a Philadelphia hospital in Sam Levene's arms. They were no doubt putting each other on, singing songs from *Guys and Dolls*, and swapping gags, the funniest death in history.

"Zero, Zero, tell me, is dying hard?"

"No, Sam, dying is easy; comedy's hard!"

Rimshot, pa-toom, and the house comes down. What would Zero's Shylock have been? If he had played it like Max Bialystock, he would have knocked the audience cold. Detractors who dismiss Henny Youngman, Sid Caesar, Milton Berle, Red Buttons, Micky Katz, Myron Cohen, Jackie Mason, as mere "Borscht Belt Comics," never saw what these performers could do to a packed house. Yiddish humor is the bedrock of American comedy. What would we have without it? Shylock's early scenes are played with self-deprecating humor, the stock in trade of Jewish comedians. I wish I had traveled to

Philadelphia to see Zero Mostel's Shylock, even though it was Wesker's, not Shakespeare's. Damn! Damn! Damn!

What language are these people speaking? Though, as always, we hear English, all of the characters in *The Merchant of Venice* are speaking Renaissance Italian. All are Venetians, except for the foreigners, the Princes of Morocco and Aragon, and the resident alien bankers, Shylock and Tubal. These characters may use accents to differentiate them from the native speakers.

Shakespeare is playing a language game with Portia when she tells us she can't understand Falconbridge because "he hath neither Latin, French, nor Italian; and you will come into court and swear that I have a poor pennyworth in the English." Not only does she tell us — in perfect English — that she can't speak English, but she uses a British monetary currency as emphasis.

It would be wrong to use an African American dialect for Morocco or a Cuban accent for Aragon — it's been done! — even in a North American production, and it would be equally wrong to play Shylock with a Brooklyn Yiddish accent. Our theatrical libraries provide a veritable treasure trove of accent and dialect tapes and records. We don't have to settle for "British" accents any more — we can get London, London Cockney, Cornwall, Liverpool, Midlands, Northumbrian, upper class, lower class, on and on. Native Algerian and Moroccan English tapes are available to us as well as the English of speakers from Madrid or Barcelona. Skill with dialects is a necessary tool of the professional actor.

What about accents for Shylock and Tubal? Laurence Olivier played Shylock with a multilayered speech that incorporated many sounds, many languages, many cultural influences. To keep up with him, the rest of the actors went way over the top, and Shakespeare's play was buried in the design and performance.

In my 1984 production, Cal Winn, who played Shylock, and I wrestled with this a lot. After much soul-searching, we decided that Shylock and Tubal's first language was Hebrew, and that they had learned Italian later in life. They spoke English with a Hebrew accent, as a modern Israeli would, so we brought in an Israeli to coach them. I know that Hebrew was not spoken as a language of trade during the Renaissance, but neither was American English. This seemed a practical, prudent theatrical choice for a play with many linguistic puzzles.

Back to the play: Shylock doesn't have a really serious moment until he realizes that his only daughter has eloped with a Christian. As a good Jewish father, Shylock should have arranged a marriage for his daughter with a Jewish husband, but he didn't — the Playwright gives us no explanation — and Jessica, who apparently met and fell in love with Lorenzo before the play begins, elopes with him on a night of carnival.

One of the most misunderstood scenes in Shakespeare, III.1, 70 to 115, follows soon after: a scene in which many directors attempt to turn the morality of the play upside down. In most of his plays, Shakespeare celebrates monogamous love and marriage as the ultimate virtue. Daughters who defy their fathers and run off with the boys they love are vindicated. The Canon abounds with examples. Fathers who attempt to hinder the course of true love run the risk of losing the amity of both children and grandchildren.

Directors who attempt to rescue Shylock from his role as villain of the piece can only do so by turning Antonio, Lorenzo and Bassanio into monsters. It doesn't work. The three couples who marry in the play are all young, attractive, nice people, not saintly, but certainly dedicated to each other. Shylock accuses Jessica of theft, but she has only taken the money and jewelry that would have been her dowry if he had responsibly found her a husband. What do the six lovers do to Shylock or anyone else in the play that justifies lowering their esteem in the eyes of the audience?

Further, *The Merchant of Venice* isn't *about* Shylock. It's about the rise of the merchant class and about Venice as the commercial center of the world, where the middle class can become as wealthy as the nobility, can even replace the nobility by buying and selling, importing and exporting. Banking and the stock market have become new paths to wealth, as money itself has become a commodity. None of these new jobs involve actual labor; bankers don't get their hands dirty. Antonio is the title role: he is the Merchant of Venice, and he is the glue that holds the play together. Here are the plots and subplots:

Portia, her suitors, and her marriage to Bassanio
Antonio, Shylock, and the pound of flesh
Lorenzo, Jessica, and Shylock
Gratiano and Nerissa
The servant of two masters, Launcelot Gobbo, and his father.

As we've seen, the custom of fathers arranging the marriage of their daughters is an important plot point in a number of plays: even if the father's choice of husband is not an explicit element, it's still there, just below the surface, influencing, if not controlling, events.

Portia's wealthy father dies before he has selected a husband for her, but in his last will and testament, he stipulates that each eligible suitor must pass a test: he must "choose one of three" small "caskets," one gold, one silver, one lead. The suitor who chooses the chest with Portia's picture will win the lady's hand. To keep the number of suitors manageable, each must be rich or noble to begin with, and each must vow to live single, if not celibate, if he fails the test.

Shakespeare implies that a multitude of suitors has come and gone, some failing the test, others refusing to accept its conditions. Though Portia complains about the imposition of her father's will, it's obvious that she has some choice in the matter and some control over the test. Having observed many attempts, she knows which chests are the wrong ones, and by elimination, which must be the right one.

The text refers to the latest of the suitors, among them a Neapolitan prince, the County Palatine, French and Scottish lords, the baron Falconbridge of England, and the Duke of Saxony's nephew, but we only see the Prince of Morocco, the ancient Prince of Aragon, and Bassanio. Portia does a verbal hatchet job on all but the last.

Bassanio is broke, so he first seeks to borrow money from Antonio to finance his courtship. All of Antonio's money is tied up in international business ventures, so Bassanio borrows the money from Shylock, 3,000 ducats for three months, on Antonio's credit.

Shylock will charge no interest for the loan, and he desires the valuable social advantage of Antonio's association, if not friendship, but Shylock still means business. To insure the loan, he wants a bond, a guarantee: if Antonio fails to repay the 3,000 ducats on time, the forfeit will be a pound of Antonio's flesh

> ... to be cut off and taken
> In what part of your body pleaseth (the lender).

It's a joke, a "merry sport." The three are pulling each other's legs. It's the beginning of a profitable business relationship. Three months must pass, and Antonio's argosies must be shipwrecked before Shylock's bond is due. Without this passage of time, Shylock would not have the legal right to arrest Antonio and take him to trial.

But, as we've seen, in all dramatic forms the only essential time is that which the audience perceives. Shakespeare never wrote flashbacks, but he also never troubled himself with time leaps, except when it was necessary for characters to age. One stretch of continuous action in *Macbeth* appears to cover events from the afternoon of one day to the dawn of the next, perhaps 14 to 15 hours, which can be played on-stage in about 29 minutes.

So when do these three months pass? In I.3, the deal is made. In II.2, Bassanio hires Lancelot, assembles a retinue and a wardrobe, and invites Antonio and Shylock to dinner, where, ostensibly, the ducats change hands. While they dine, Shylock's daughter, Jessica, elopes with Lorenzo, aided by Salerio and Solanio. In II.8, we are told—we don't see it—that Bassanio and Gratiano have sailed to Belmont, just as Shylock discovers that Jessica has absconded with his money and jewels. Shylock suspects Antonio and Bassanio and demands that Bassanio's ship be searched, but Antonio certifies to the Duke that Lorenzo and Jessica were not aboard. During this sequence, there are three cut-aways to Belmont that eliminate all of Portia's other suitors, but these changes of locale don't need time jumps. How far is Belmont from Venice? It's in the mountains, a day or two by boat up one of the rivers that feed the Venetian lagoon.

In III.1, we hear that all of Antonio's argosies are shipwrecked, that he is bankrupt, that Shylock will demand forfeit of the bond. What happened to the three months? In III.2, Bassanio, Portia, Nerissa and Gratiano are married, and they hear the bad news about Antonio's arrest on the suit of Shylock. Jessica and Lorenzo arrive by a second boat and agree to house-sit while the others go to the aid of Antonio.

The action I've summarized above, I.3 through III.4, seems to be continuous, a matter of days, less than a week. What happened to those pesky three months? Shakespeare appears to have forgotten about them entirely. But he also takes away any possibility of credibility for III.1.70 ff., a scene that Stephen Greenblatt makes much of in his *Will in the World*, justifying Shylock and condemning Jessica and Lorenzo.

Let's examine III.1: Greenblatt writes, "When he (Shylock) encounters the fellow Jew he has sent to track his daughter, he asks him for news." Hold it! It doesn't make sense that Shylock has sent Tubal to Genoa to track Jessica. Following the chronology of the play, Jessica and Lorenzo couldn't possibly have traveled to Genoa and back to Belmont, a round trip of some 380 miles, unless they had a jet airplane. Why Genoa? And who in Genoa knows Jessica anyway? They didn't publish her photograph in the paper. Orthodox Judaism forbade portrait painting, along with any "graven image." Tubal might have recognized Jessica, but nobody else could have.

Ostensibly, Tubal has been in Genoa on business, and he arrives back in Venice in time to hear that Lorenzo and Jessica have eloped. Tubal enters, and Shylock asks: "How now, Tubal. What news from Genoa? Hast thou found my daughter?" Tubal replies, "I often came where I did hear of her, but cannot find her." The use of the word "found," which gives some credence to the idea that Shylock sent Tubal looking for Jessica is, admittedly, puzzling. But the idea still doesn't make sense. It's essential that both actors and director put a box around that statement, "I often came where I did hear of her, but cannot find her," because the rest of the scene is gossip, nonsense, hearsay.

What's interesting here is that the audience barely hears Tubal's disclaimer, and, unless they know Italian geography, it doesn't alter the rest of the scene. The scene plays as if Tubal had first-hand information about Jessica's shopping spree in Genoa and the trade of the ring for the monkey. That scene would seem to be important, if it proves Jessica's cruelty and insensitivity, but it's a non-event, a fiction. It never happened. Jessica never went to Genoa, never went on a shopping spree, never traded Leah's gift ring for a monkey. Why does Tubal torture Shylock with this damaging gossip? Beats me. I've always been a big fan of Shakespeare's ambiguities, but this one is tortuous.

Shylock is digging for material to fuel his revenge. Tubal gives him more good/bad news: all of Antonio's argosies are shipwrecked, and Antonio is bankrupt.

In Belmont, all the suitors have failed the test and left except Bassanio. He and Portia are in love, and it remains for her to lead him to the winning casket. Her madrigals tempt him by singing words that rhyme with "lead." Because his love is pure, he scorns the gold and silver and selects the lead casket with the image of Portia. They exchange rings, and their plot seems to be resolved, but Portia has one more test of her new husband's worthiness.

A messenger arrives to tell them of Antonio's misfortunes, that Shylock will have his revenge and his bond because the loan was not repaid on time. Portia to the rescue! Bassanio and Gratiano dash to Antonio's side, but Portia, advised by her cousin, the magistrate Bellario, disguises herself as a lawyer and prepares to defend Antonio in court.

Why does Shylock plan to take revenge on Antonio? Obviously, Bassanio has spent all of the borrowed 3,000 ducats. He has no money to pay back Shylock, but his new wife can pay the debt a hundred times over, as soon as she's asked. Besides the unpaid loan, what has Antonio done to Shylock to justify such revenge? Whenever we see Antonio, we see a mature gentleman, sober, kind, who behaves with courtesy and civility to everyone. Shylock tells us twice in the play that Antonio spat at him, kicked him, called him a dog, insulted his religion, criticized his profession, thwarted him by lending money gratis, and generally offended him with insults and ill reports. But we never see these offenses happen: we only hear about them.

Revenge is "getting even," an eye for an eye, a tooth for a tooth. Are Antonio's supposed offenses justification for cutting a pound of flesh off his chest, torturing and surely killing him? Is that getting even, or is it a petty excuse to express great hate with great injury? When Shylock's daughter elopes with a Christian, he disowns her, but he doesn't seek to revenge himself on either her or her husband. Instead he takes revenge on the only Christian he can attack with impunity: Antonio. Notice that Shakespeare doesn't put Jessica and Lorenzo into the trial scene.

If we can ignore the calendar, as Shakespeare seems to, or bend the time frame, we can presume that Antonio's default coincides with Jessica's elopement. Shylock blames all the Christians for the loss of his daughter and his money, but he has the legal right to take revenge on only one of them. Further, Shylock justifies revenge because Christians give such example: they take revenge on their enemies.

The trial scene is a brilliantly constructed cliffhanger. It plays like great courtroom drama, but also like a burlesque skit — the good news, bad news, good news, bad news kind of sketch. Some productions of *The Merchant of Venice* end with this scene, but such severe editing only serves to truncate the play and turn it into the tragedy of Shylock.

The Doge of Venice, acting as judge, confirms the legality of Shylock's position: because the 3,000 ducats were not returned within the three-month period, the bond is forfeit. Shylock may cut a pound of flesh off of Antonio's chest. Balthazar, the disguised Portia serving as Antonio's lawyer, attempts to negotiate with Shylock, offering him, first, twice the 3,000 ducats, then thrice, then ten times the amount. She argues mercy as a morality greater than justice in a speech that echoes Saint Paul's famous letter to the Corinthians. Adamant, Shylock will have his bond. Antonio bares his chest. But first, a few jokes: Bassanio and Gratiano offer themselves, then their wives, as substitutes. Shylock remembers and curses Jessica. Antonio kneels, and his friends hold his arms.

Shylock raises the knife, time stands still, and then the voice of Balthazar, a Daniel come to judgment, says, "Tarry a little."

Shylock may cut off his pound of flesh, but if he sheds a single drop of Antonio's blood, then all his lands and goods will be confiscated by the state of Venice. Shylock's next line is a big laugh, no matter how he says it, "Is that the law?"

Shylock backs off and offers to take three times the 3,000 ducats, but Balthazar insists he take nothing but the bond. Once again, Antonio and his friends prepare for punishment. Perhaps the pound of flesh *can* be cut off without shedding any blood. Again, Shylock raises the knife, and time stands still. Again, Balthazar stops him, saying this time he may have a pound of flesh, but not a molecule more or less. Precisely one pound, or Shylock dies. A third time, Antonio prepares for certain death. Once more, time stands still, but this time Shylock stops himself, throws his knife down, and says, "Give me my principal and let me go."

Now he is hit with the full force of the law. He is an alien, and because he has sought, "by direct or indirect attempts," the life of a citizen, he must forfeit half his goods to his intended victim and the other half to the state, and the Doge shall have the right to inflict the death penalty or not, as he chooses. Shylock will not beg for his life: rather he says,

> Nay, take my life and all. Pardon not that!
> You take my house when you do take the prop
> That doth sustain my house; you take my life
> When you do take the means whereby I live.

The trial scene turns on the fact that Shylock is not a Venetian citizen: he's an alien.

Portia quotes a law that could not be used against Shylock if he were a Venetian citizen. Ergo, he's not. Shakespeare might be taken to task for not solidifying the setup earlier in the play; I've heard that complaint from audience members many times. Nevertheless, that's the necessary premise. Portia/Balthazar asks Antonio for mercy, and he negotiates the penalty. He asks the court to forgive half the fine, if he may be allowed to use the other half for investments, and upon Shylock's death, to bestow it on Lorenzo and Jessica. Further, Shylock must name his daughter and son-in-law as his heirs, and he must agree to convert to Christianity.

Suddenly, the play turns serious. Arguments are over. Jokes ring hollow. Shylock can become a Christian and embrace his daughter's marriage to a Christian, or he can lose everything and go to his execution. Again, time stands still until Shylock agrees to sign the will, "I am content." He then says he's ill, asks to be excused. After a bravura, flamboyant performance, he leaves, an apparently subdued, sick man.

His exit is not unlike Malvolio's in *Twelfth Night*. Shakespeare, a true British chauvinist, regularly employed characters from out-groups as comic villains: Puritans, Frenchmen, Spaniards, Welshmen, Irishmen, churchmen, magistrates, and old people. Shylock is one with Malvolio, Don John, Angelo, Sebastian, and even the Princes of Morocco and Aragon: comic outsiders, malefactors who are thwarted, judged, sentenced, and then pardoned.

Nobody is punished in *The Merchant of Venice*. Sins are exposed, punishment is suggested then negotiated, and then everyone is forgiven: Bassanio for squandering money, Jessica for disobeying her father, Shylock for attempting to kill Antonio. Dissertations no doubt have been written on Shylock's alleged punishment, but to the Elizabethans, there was none. He could choose to die for his religious beliefs, or he could renounce them, reconcile with his daughter and her husband, and get on with his life and his business. Anyone who lived through the reigns of the Tudors would have recognized this choice as an opportunity for martyrdom. Shakespeare, as a closet Catholic, would have considered the possibility that Shylock might feign allegiance to Christianity, the state religion, but remain privately faithful to his true beliefs. Still, if we confine ourselves to the world of the play, there is no actual punishment. All are forgiven.

In the Miller/Olivier production, the assemblage watched Shylock leave, and then heard him give a loud, high, off-stage wail. It was theatrical, thrilling, but extra-textual.

Following Shylock's exit, we're subjected to a bit of forced humor when Portia/Balthazar demands that Bassanio produce the ring that she gave him as payment for services as defense lawyer. Bassanio briefly resists, and then capitulates. This gives us a cute ending later on, but the main argument of the play has been resolved, and the final act plays out in a series of love duets, a little lame comedy, some music, none of it very satisfying, and a piece of gratuitous good news: Antonio's ships are come safely home. All of the gossip about shipwrecks, like Jessica's trade of ring for monkey, was false.

As with all of Shakespeare's comedies, *The Merchant of Venice* ends with pretty people going off to make pretty babies. The title character, however, ends the play alone, as sad as he began it.

I only directed *The Merchant of Venice* once, and I've never acted in it. I avoided it for most of my professional life but decided to do it in 1984 with *Othello*, a celebration of Venice, that mythic Renaissance city-state. The plays were designed alike and performed in rotating repertory by the same company of actors.

When we first announced the plays, Frank Occhiogrosso, who taught Shakespeare at Drew University, asked me point blank how I was going to deal with the anti–Semitism in *The Merchant of Venice*. He wasn't concerned about racism or miscegenation or the hint of homosexuality in the two plays; he had only one problem: anti–Semitism. The question stopped me cold. When I recovered my wits, I asked him how he thought the problem could be fixed without changing the text. He had no answer to that, and that, as I stated at the outset of this chapter, was my problem.

I decided that the only sane way to do this highly controversial damned-if-you-do, damned-if-you-don't albatross was to remain true to my responsibility to the Playwright. Every playwright. I'm a producer and a director: I serve the playwright, whether he is sitting next to me at auditions or is several hundred years dead.

I do not have the privilege of "fixing" the play or cutting offending material out of it, nor do I have any patience with those "concept" directors who attempt to impose a contrary morality on a play. I am not given to cause du jour digressions like the anti-war *Henry V* or the lesbian chic *Love's Labour's Lost* or the Star Wars *Titus Andronicus*.

I think I spent more private time with the text of *The Merchant of Venice* than I did with all six other plays of the 1984 season combined. We played it intact, not a line cut, and we took great pains to make it as faithful as analysis and logic could make it. The repertory was evenly balanced. Leading actors in each play were supporting characters in the other two. We began rehearsals with the love stories to establish a light and happy tone, only adding Shylock to the mix in the second week of rehearsals.

Cal Winn, Shylock, a Shakespearean actor of considerable experience with the festivals of California, Oregon, and Colorado, was in his late 30s or early 40s at the time. Careful and meticulous in rehearsals, he knew where the laughs were, but he didn't play for laughs, an approach I encouraged. His performance served the play, and he nailed the intricacies of the Israeli accent. More important, his performance wasn't about an accent.

Looking at the ultimate production with as much objectivity as possible, I would say it was safe, perhaps even conservative. We took very few chances.

I repeat: my basic morality is my responsibility to the Playwright; that is my integrity or, as an honest friend observed, "my integrity, as (I) conceived it." If that be a cop-out, then sue me. It's not a religious posture, but it's close.

Yet our 1984 *Merchant of Venice* caught hell from audience and critics alike. My direction and Cal's performance were soundly drubbed. Cal was very funny, reading his bad reviews. He'd read a critic's slam out loud, and then convulse himself laughing. As often happens with "controversial" productions, critics contradicted each other.

The audience recast Cal's performance into the Shylock they brought with them. Response was divided: those who hated the show hated it because of Hitler. I expected that. Those who liked the show — nobody loved it — were responding, in part, to the naysayers. At our traditional symposium night and at our annual colloquium, which drew some 800 scholars and general audience members, participants quickly took sides. As director, I was criticized only for choices relative to Shylock: I should have given him more dignity, and most of all I shouldn't have had him play with an accent.

As I did at the time, I'll answer these criticisms in reverse. Accents and dialects in the mouths of actors are essential to show national or regional separation: the Princes of Morocco and Argon and the Jewish bankers are not Venetian citizens. Everybody else in the play is. Since the plot turns on the fact that an alien seeks to take the life of a citizen, the use of accents is subtle and necessary.

The choice to make Hebrew Shylock's first language and American English his second was a relatively safe one. But our critics and angry audience heard what they wanted to hear, that which fed their outrage. Cal's speech was described, in turn, as "his high-pitched, squeaky dialect," "his eastern European accent," "a Yiddish accent close to caricature," "his broad Jewish accent, forced and anachronistic," "guttural garbling," "a mid–Eastern European accent," "a Yiddish accent," "an out-of-time, out-of-place pseudo European patois," "a falsetto, phony, and presumably Russian accent." Only one called the sound what we intended and achieved: "an Israeli accent."

As for the complaint that I made Shylock undignified: dignity is as dignity does. Most of what Shylock does is negative, often reprehensible. When he says he's going to imitate Christian behavior, he means he's going to take Italian revenge. One colloquium participant argued that Shylock is justified in his revenge because of all the evil done to Jews by Christians over the centuries. But that stance takes us outside the play, back to the pogroms and expulsions, eventually to Hitler and the Holocaust, and to today's threatened nuclear stalemate between Israel and the Muslims. If all racial and religious prejudice can be rationalized by a series of revenges upon revenges, then we're doomed to live in a world of the blind, the toothless, and the maimed.

Many members of our audience were also outraged at Shylock's mandatory conversion, which, again, we played straight ahead with a minimum of emphasis. It is part of the text, part of Shylock's punishment and forgiveness. Today, a forced conversion is obnoxious, but to the Elizabethans, all Christians, salvation was only possible if one believed in the redemption of mankind by the sacrifice of Jesus Christ. Shakespeare's audience believed that his judges were giving him the opportunity for eternal life by demanding that he convert; it was an act of great charity, a blessed gift. Whether today's director believes this or not (cooperation is essential, not belief), it's intrinsic to the morality of this play. This is one of many examples of the differences between the beliefs of Shakespeare's original audience and ours.

One more time: all are forgiven, reconciled. None are punished.

One critic took me to task for ignoring the tradition of the great Yiddish tragedians of the 19th and early 20th centuries, which followed the example first set by Edmund Kean, who played Shylock as a tragic protagonist. Good point, Mr. Critic! Jacob Adler, Josef Schildkraut, Maurice Schwartz, and their schools all did tragic Shylocks (and truncated productions — no 5th Act) in defiance of the German and Russian pogroms that eventually exploded into the Holocaust.

That is not Shakespeare's play. Neither the text itself nor the form, Shakespearean comedy, justifies a tragic Shylock. Edmund Kean got away with it because he was the most famous Shakespearean actor of his age and a matinee idol to boot: he could play any role he wanted, any way he wanted to play it. The only justification for a tragic Shylock today is Hitler, and the closest Shakespeare ever got to Hitler was Mary Tudor. Or Oliver Cromwell, who out–Hitlered Hitler 30 years after Shakespeare's death.

In the fall of 1984, in preparation for the Shakespeare Association of America's Nashville convention, I wrote the feeble disclaimer, "I did not write the play, but I did produce it, and so I am guilty by association, an accessory after the fact. So be it."

Nobody has since offered me the opportunity to direct *The Merchant of Venice* again. There's little chance that anyone will. The play, even with the benefit of Mel Brooks and Max Bialystock, is still a hot potato, it still has the potential to backfire on anyone attempting it, but even without a production to direct, friends, scholars, critics, and show business won't let me leave the play alone.

A passage in Rosenbaum's *The Shakespeare Wars* gave me a chill and some illumination. Rosenbaum quotes Supposnik, a minor character in Philip Roth's novel *Operation Shylock*, who attempts to take Shakespeare off the hook by alluding to a tradition of English anti–Semitism that goes back almost 300 years before the Playwright's birth. Supposnik refers to:

> the abhorrence of the Jew that animated Shakespeare and his era, the long illustrious chronicle of Jew-baiting, the hateful hateable Jew whose artistic roots extended back into the Crucifixion pageants at York, the Jew whose endurance as the villain of history no less than of drama is unparalleled, the hook-nosed money lender, the miserly money-maddened, egotistical degenerate, the Jew who goes to synagogue to plan the murder of the virtuous Christian —*this* is Europe's Jew, the Jew expelled in 1290 by the English, the Jew banished in 1492 by the Spanish, the Jew terrorized by Poles, butchered by Russians, incinerated by Germans, spurned by the British and Americans while the furnaces roared at Treblinka... .

And in the blink of an eye, we're back to Hitler.

Roth's logic is tempting to me, as a humanist and a Shakespearean. If English anti–Semitism goes back to the reign of Edward I, if it's incorporated in the morality plays that preceded all English drama, then how can we say that *The Merchant of Venice* is any more anti–Semitic than all English thought and practice?

Rosenbaum defends Shakespeare by pointing out that he wasn't obsessed with hatred of the Jews. He didn't write a stream of plays casting the Jews as villains. *The Merchant of Venice* is it.

I arrive back at my original conclusion: Hitler has rendered the play unproduceable. It's my hope that time will redeem it, but I wouldn't bet the farm on it. I don't think the play is "about" racial or religious discrimination. I have both convictions and doubts as to what the play is "about," and my ideas, expressed above, are heavily influenced by the genre: Shakespearean *comedy*. Let be. There are other fish to fry.

Chapter 17

The Tempest

The Tempest, the last play Shakespeare wrote alone, is his only play that is not an adaptation from another source. In this valedictory, the Playwright, approaching retirement, in a mood of comfortable reflection, equated the magic of his theatrical art with that of the maligned and deposed Prospero. Master Will probably intended that this play stand alone, uninfluenced by collaborators or creative directors, but the only text we have of it is the 1623 First Folio.

We tend to consider F.1 as the definitive version, but plays are fluid, constantly changing. Directors and editors are forever tinkering, adapting, reconceptualizing. It is assumed that Heminge and Condell used the prompt books of the King's Men, Shakespeare's company, for the Folio scripts, but they could very well have used playing scripts from productions mounted between the death of Shakespeare and 1623. Except for the notorious Middleton production of *Macbeth,* we have blessed little information on such productions. There is a tradition that Ben Jonson edited *The Tempest* and placed it first in the Folio. Its editing and proofreading are accurate, error free, and its stage directions are quite specific, even elaborate.

Jonson continued to produce and promote his own plays after Shakespeare's death, and, encouraged by King James and his wife, Anne of Denmark, he collaborated with Inigo Jones in elaborately designed and staged semi-operatic masques. It is possible that the *Tempest* script we have is that of a Jonson/Jones court production. I don't know where I first read this, and I don't think I dreamed it up, but I've conferred with several scholars about it, and none of them has given the theory any serious credence, so I present it only as a theory, an idea, a possible explanation for what I consider a serious problem in the text: the masque.

I've done this play three times, once as an actor, twice as director. Big budget theatres love *The Tempest* because they can cut loose their design departments and produce a real crowd pleaser. It's only after spending tons of money on special effects that they realize that almost all of the magic in the script is accomplished by the actors. Prospero, with the aid of Ariel, exercises mind control over the other characters; they see and experience only what Prospero wants them to. His hypnotism can replace their reality with his fantasy, which is a relatively simple thing for actors to play. Actors do blind, deaf, drunk, and deluded with ease, and transformations may be accomplished with lines as simple as Oberon's "I am invisible and will overhear their conference."

Even the storm itself, we discover, never really happens. The ships of Alonso's flotilla are on course from Carthage to Naples when they pass close to Prospero's island, and he hypnotizes sailors and passengers alike, creating an imaginary typhoon that ostensibly destroys the ships and drowns everyone but a handful of survivors. Piecemeal, Prospero reveals to us that there was no actual tempest, that the mariners, in a collective coma, anchored in the island's harbor and put ashore the king, his heir apparent Ferdinand, Prospero's usurping

The Tempest, New Jersey Shakespeare Festival, 1970: George Taylor as Prospero, Margery Shaw as Miranda (photograph by Jay Liebman).

brother Antonio, and their nobles, as well as the jester Trinculo and the butler Stephano. Having provided us with plot, subplot, and comic relief, the mariners retire below and sleep it off until Prospero releases them from their dream.

Even if it all is imaginary, however, can today's producer afford to eliminate the storm? I don't think so. It's aesthetically preferable to present what the characters perceive, what the actors aboard ship play, what Miranda sees from a distance, and then explain it away afterwards. The audience doesn't need to be drenched or deafened. A simple device such as rope ladders dropped down from the ceiling, actors swaying on the ropes, can suggest a ship. The storm comes alive as Ariel describes his creation of it, as the audience watches Ariel playing the storm.

Where is Prospero's island? The text mentions Bermuda, which the Elizabethan audience would have responded to, but it lies in the Atlantic between Europe and America, way off Alonso's stipulated course from Carthage to Naples. If you sail this course, you pass close to the island of Stromboli, strange, mysterious, half volcano, half jungle, a perfect candidate for this faerie tale spot.

One big problem with *The Tempest* is its lack of dramatic tension. Prospero is in control at all times. Once he has friends, enemies, and potential son-in-law ashore on his magic island, there's no doubt that he will persevere. Even the plot hatched between Antonio and

Sebastian to kill King Alonso is a red herring. Prospero, invisible, observes everything or sends Ariel to oversee and interfere.

Prospero is the central figure, and the role requires an actor of great authority, but the Playwright doesn't give him much to do. Prospero's a magician, so he should be able to get what he wants easily. Though it's not implicit in the text, some actors will choose to play the magic as if it requires great physical effort, thus exhausting Prospero. For some reason, he never figured out how to magically get off the island — perhaps he wanted to keep Miranda in that pristine tropical paradise, out of the danger of corruption by the court, until she was grown. It worked for Perdita.

Your best actor should be cast as Prospero, even though he'll want to play Caliban, which, like Mercutio, is a great role with wonderful variety. He'll steal the show every time. Any actor who isn't successful as Caliban should consider another profession. His costume is a fascinating challenge for designers, even with considerable hints from the Playwright: his mother was a witch, and his father was the devil, and he has fish-like attributes. His costume shouldn't be clothing, but another body, to which Prospero has added a loincloth for propriety and a blanket for warmth. As with Bottom's asshead, care should be taken not to obscure the actor's face. We had considerable success in the 1976 NJSF production by basing the costume on scuba flippers and building from there. Earl Warren Hindman complained about the flippers initially, but once he got used to them, he appreciated their influence on his movement.

Miranda and Ferdinand, of course, fall in love at first sight, and they are betrothed within the hour. No doubt, no danger, no tension.

I don't think Ariel should be cast with a woman. He's a mischievous boy, more like Puck than a blithe spirit. When women play both Ariel and Miranda the polarity is thrown off: doubling the father-daughter relationship weakens both.

After a stream of nasty cynical fools — Thersites, Appomatus, Cloten — the Playwright returns to the superb comic form of *Twelfth Night* with the clowns in *The Tempest*. Their routines are reminiscent of, and as funny as, vaudeville or the Marx Brothers. Almost an hour passes before Master Will brings on these funny guys. Up until this point, we've seen and heard precious little humor: Ariel is ethereal, Caliban is an angry grotesque monster who resents Prospero's theft of his island, and we are well into a serious romance. Then on comes the jester, Trinculo, to do a standup about an impending rainstorm. Caliban mistakes him for one of Prospero's spirits and hides under his blanket. The audience has already been conned by a non-existent typhoon, so when Trinculo points out a thundercloud about to burst, they probably greet this with some derision. But Trinculo insists that the storm is approaching and crawls under Caliban's blanket, since there's no other shelter in sight. When he discovers Caliban there, he changes his routine, insulting the audience by citing their gullibility: if he had this monster in England to display in a sideshow, he'd make a fortune in admissions.

Now Trinculo and Caliban do a popular routine probably familiar to modern audiences from early Charlie Chaplain or W. C Fields movies: the too-short blanket bit. They face in the opposite directions, their legs pointing at each other, giving the impression of a large spider. Trinculo pulls the blanket up over his head, exposing Caliban's face. Caliban pulls back, exposing Trinculo's face. They repeat the bit as many times as the audience will laugh at it. Finally, it is resolved when Stephano arrives, drinking a bottle of sack he has salvaged from the ship and singing a bawdy sea chantey. He discovers the four-legged monster and gives him wine to drink, then makes a flatulence joke about the monster's two mouths and two voices. Caliban discovers liquor, morphs into a clown, and the three are off on an extended drunk routine, with the monster singing a song of freedom.

When we meet the three of them again in III.2, they have recovered the butt of sack and are in an advanced state of drunkenness. Ariel enters invisible, and the four of them do another vaudeville turn, the invisible man bit: Ariel imitates Trinculo's voice and insults Caliban. Trinculo looks around for the source of the voice. Stephano blames Trinculo for the insult. Ariel repeats the bit. Same business. Ariel does it a third time, and this time Stephano beats up Trinculo. (Three times is funny, and in context, violence is funny too.)

The three clowns devise a plot to kill Prospero and supplant him with Stephano, who will make Miranda his queen and rule the island. Ariel, still invisible, plays a tune to lead them away, and suddenly, Caliban, the comic monster, startles us with a passage of exquisite poetry extolling the "isle full of noises." Though the speech begins in anger, it has its own hypnotic effect on Caliban, who may even pass out, preferring his dreams to reality. Stephano and Trinculo rouse him, and they exit, following Ariel's music.

Their third Marx Brothers scene is IV.1: Ariel has strung a clothesline with "glistening apparel" across the stage, and leads them through a swamp, wet, filthy, and bad-smelling, to find it. Trinculo and Stephano are intent on killing the sleeping Prospero, but the royal clothes distract them. The director and costumer can have fun with this routine—the funnier and campier the dress-up, the better—but it is suggested that the actors be supplied with the clothes as early as possible to refine the resulting routines. While Caliban begs them to stay on task, they fight over the gowns, then they try to load him up like a bellboy with any clothes they can't carry off themselves. Finally, Ariel sics a pack of magic invisible dogs on them, chasing them off. The dogs are created by the reaction and barking of the actors.

When we next see them at V.1.303, they've been tortured by Prospero's goblins until, penitent and hung over, they beg for forgiveness.

Now Prospero is ready to resolve his plots and abandon his magic. But first comes the masque. Let's consider it. In my opinion, the masque effectively stops the play cold and does nothing to clarify it. It has no discernable dramatic function. It's ironic that the lame wooing dance of the nymphs and reapers never resolves: it's interrupted by Prospero, who, as bored as the audience, announces that it's time to get back to the play. We are then treated to the first of Prospero's three valedictory farewell arias, "our revels now are ended," perhaps out of place due to editing, and then we go back to the action.

All the masque does is double the cost of production while adding gratuitous women's roles. Women were allowed to appear in the masques, but were not allowed to perform in plays until 44 years after Shakespeare's death.

In none of the many lectures I've heard about *The Tempest* has a professor or director ever mentioned the masque. It's a non-subject, and unless the modern producer is willing to spend big on it, it falls flat. I've never seen a production that included it that worked. At the moment, I find myself alone in this opinion. Friends and scholars argue for the value of the masque.

Prospero delivers his second farewell, the exquisite "Ye elves of hills, brooks, standing lakes…" aria, breaks his magic wand, and throws his book of spells into the sea. His last request of the spirits who attend on him is for music. He forgives his enemies, rewards the worthy Gonzalo, thanks his friends, confers his blessing on his daughter and her intended, gives the island back to Ariel and Caliban, and prepares to take ship back to Milan.

Prospero has three resignations, abandonments of his magic, speeches that should be compared and considered in parallel. The first begins at IV.1.167: "Our revels now are ended...." The second is Prospero's V.1.39 ff., described above. The third, the weakest of the three, we have as an epilogue, 20 lines of couplets, doggerel written in seven and eight. I'm not even sure that Shakespeare wrote this epilogue; it's certainly not worthy of the mature Playwright. Compare the three, then consider the following flagrant directorial intrusion: cut the masque in its entirety and move "Our revels now are ended" to the end of the play, replacing "Now my charms are all o'erthrown...." The cut would begin after Prospero's line IV.1.34, "Fairly spoke," and continue with IV.1.178, his

>   My old brain is troubled.
>   Be not disturbed with my infirmity.

No further cuts in the play until the very end, where I suggest the doggerel epilogue be replaced with the majestic, "Our revels now are ended...." With this positioning, the actors Prospero then refers to are his fellow cast members waiting to take their curtain calls, and the play now ends with

>   We are such stuff
>   As dreams are made on, and our little life
>   Is rounded with a sleep.

If this be treason, make the most of it.

CHAPTER 18

As You Like It

As You Like It is easy, gentle, brilliantly written, four parallel and contrasting love stories, interwoven with high and low comedy. It's another perfect Shakespeare-in-the-Park show, perhaps too much so; it contends with *Twelfth Night* as the most produced Shakespeare play in America. I hated this play until I directed it in 1973, and then I fell in love with it.

Resist all temptations to impose any concepts or causes du jour on this play. Perhaps it was suggested by the Robin Hood legend, and it works well in that period. The McCarter Theatre did a production several years ago with George Washington as Duke Senior retreating from the British and Hessians. A lot of money was spent on elaborate costumes, props, and scenic elements, and they effectively obscured Shakespeare's story. If you play it straight and uncut, you will be fine. What could possibly go wrong? It's fun for everyone, fun to rehearse, fun to perform, fun to watch.

The best production of *As You Like It* I ever saw was directed by Robin Phillips at Stratford, Ontario, in 1965; the production employed 16 actors, all of whom doubled, except for Adam. The shepherds and shepherdesses were costumed as Mennonites. The second best production was performed by the ACTER company, presented by Homer Swander out of UCSB: five RSC actors performing all the roles. If you didn't know the play, the doubling was confusing, but the acting was marvelous.

Cast the four women carefully. Be wary of broad-hipped Rosalinds. Like Viola, Rosalind/Ganymede should be tall and slim. Whatever choices are made, other than the need for a slim-hipped Rosalind, it must be easy to tell them from each other. Costumes will help, but you need four looks, four voices, four personalities. I was taken by the sweet kid who played Rosalind for Stephen Burdman in the summer of 2005: Genn Schulte. She wasn't knockout gorgeous, and she could be faulted on a lot of technical things, but I was certainly concerned with whether she was going to pull off what she wanted. I was on her side, rooting for her. That Rosalind had soul.

Orlando is not a clod, just a young man crazy in love. He and his brothers should look alike, but the play doesn't depend on it. It is possible to double the two dukes, Duke Senior and his usurping brother, Frederick. They are never on-stage together, there is ample time for changes, and the two personalities are so different that it's an enjoyable challenge for a good actor. Other doubling possibilities will become apparent as the director starts digging.

Touchstone was the first of several notable clowns that Robin Armin played, the tone of playing getting darker and darker, Fluellen to Touchstone to the Gravedigger to Feste to Thersites to Lear's Fool. The foolery had gradually become less physical and more verbal, though, paradoxically, it invited less heckling. It is possible to trace, as I've tried to do in a cursory manner, the transition in the clowns Shakespeare wrote for Kempe and

As You Like It, New Jersey Shakespeare Festival, 1973: Albert Sanders as Touchstone, Joan Ann Fontana as Celia, Gretchen Corbett as Rosalind (photograph by Blair Holley).

those he wrote for Armin — for a modern comparison, think of Milton Berle (Kempe) evolving into Jerry Seinfeld (Armin). What's unusual about this clown is his human side. He doesn't just entertain and fish for laughs: he gets hungry, fatigued, and lustful. The Playwright provides him with the enticing but naïve Audrey, whom Touchstone tries to seduce, but ends up marrying.

Toward the end of the play, Touchstone does a standup routine that still works today, a parody on the protocol of dueling and the seven degrees of insult. The implication is that anything one might dislike or disagree with is sufficient cause to challenge the offender to a duel. Here, the cause is the styling of an offending beard. Touchstone dislikes the barber's work, and the client replies that it's well done, then that Touchstone hated it, then that the barbered one disparaged the judgment of the challenger, then reciprocal veracity, then degrees of honesty. Luckily, the insults and retorts did not go beyond the circumstantial lie. Otherwise, they would really have had to fight and someone could get hurt. I've seen this turn played gently and off-handedly, and I've seen it played furiously. It works either way as long as it winds up with "much virtue in IF." (This routine, by the way, also gives Rosalind time to change into a wedding dress for the end of the play.)

Shakespeare gives his clown a counterpart in the character of Jacques, the quintessential heckler who disparages what everyone else values and takes each argument to a melancholy conclusion. Jacques is not another Touchstone. Touchstone is a professional clown. At times their functions seem to switch, and certainly a good actor could play either role, though they can't be doubled. Jacques' beloved "Seven Ages of Man" speech is wonderful, with more humor in it than actors usually play (probably because they're so worried by the audience's familiarity with it that they try too hard to make it new). And, like the standup routine above, it serves a practical purpose: it gives Orlando time to go get Adam and carry him back.

Watch out for the final scene, the wind-up. There are many plots to resolve, as in *Measure For Measure*, and the Playwright puts his entire cast on-stage at once. As each plot is resolved, the other actors hang out and have nothing to do but become observers, one with the audience. There's a story, probably apocryphal, that the legendary director George Abbott hollered at an actor, "Don't just stand there: do something." Like all such generalities, that's bad advice. There are times when a character should be doing nothing but watching and listening, and that, by definition, is not "doing" but is having something done to him. Beware of the actor who keeps bugging you with, "What am I supposed to be doing now?" He's supposed to be doing bloody nothing but watching and listening.

As You Like It is simple, delicate, and fun. In rep, it's a perfect antidote for a heavy tragedy. Everyone should have a good time with it. Any director who fails with this play should consider another profession.

Just one caution, however: if you decide, as I did, to add Audrey and a baby lamb to the scene where Corin tutors Touchstone on sheep tending, be aware that lambs grow more quickly than you might think. By the end of our ten-week rep, we needed a couple of strong young men in the wings to wrangle the "lamb," pick him up and hand him to our Audrey, Leslie Ann Rivers, just before her entrance. She couldn't lift him by herself anymore.

CHAPTER 19

Coriolanus

The source for *Coriolanus*, as for *Julius Caesar, Antony and Cleopatra, A Midsummer Night's Dream,* and *Timon of Athens,* is Sir Thomas North's 1579 English translation of Plutarch's *Parallel Lives*. It's possible that no Caius Martius Coriolanus ever existed, or, since Plutarch mixed history and legend freely, he could be an amalgamation of early Roman heroes or even a product of myth and Plutarch's imagination.

In *Coriolanus*, Shakespeare creates a Rome that is ruled by a military meritocracy aligned with a wealthy nobility who have attempted to placate the rebellious masses with a condescending nod towards democracy: the commoners are allowed to elect tribunes as their representatives. The tribunes hear out the complaints of the plebians, then submit them to the senators for redress. In this Rome, there is no king, no emperor, only the senators, who control the water and food supplies, administer the courts, supervise the army.

I directed *Coriolanus* twice: a traditional 359 BCE production in 1987 and a concept production in 1973, set in the context of World War II in Italy with the Romans costumed like the United States Army and the Volsces as the German Wehrmacht. This production featured sound tracks of tanks, air cover, and assault weapons instead of swords, but nothing in it compromised the integrity of the text. The 1973 production, with Peter MacLean as Coriolanus, was more successful with the audience than was the later traditional production.

Both times, the play infected the company. Of course, a play always influences a company in some way. The better it's done, the more it permeates the souls of the actors. In repertory it's always wisest to juxtapose a heavy tragedy with a light and happy comedy: each play gives relief from the other. Tours of *Macbeth* are notorious for breeding bitching, sullen, in-fighting companies of actors who stop bathing about the second week of the run.

Coriolanus is a story of rebellion and counter-rebellion. The aristocratic military hero of the title, confident of his entitlements, refuses to submit to the democratic process, and the plebians of Rome banish him. An actor playing the role can come to believe in his own superiority and end up drowning in his own hubris. Earlier, I described the problems I had with the actor who played Martius for me in 1987. His hubris led him to resist any and every direction I gave him. He was also blatant and rude in his criticism of the other actors. I told him that I didn't care whether he paid any attention to me or not, but I wouldn't allow him to direct the other actors. Whenever he acted up, I asked him to leave and rehearsed his understudy in the role. Finally, I just stopped trying to direct him. I don't recommend this technique, but it does work when all else fails.

As an actor fights with the director and criticizes the other actors, he inadvertently gives example to the novice actors, interns or apprentices, who play the Roman crowd. They in turn may begin to examine and debate their lowly estate, and eventually they may rebel as well. When this happens, as it did for me in 1987, it becomes increasingly difficult to get the play on, as each rehearsal turns into an exercise in anarchy. That negative experience left me with little to say about the play, but it leads to some observations on beginning actors.

Even in the best-run repertory companies, there is a wide gap between apprentice expectations and realities. Over a period of 33 years I ran apprentice/intern programs which offered an invaluable combination of classes, exercises, rehearsal, crew work, and performance opportunities. Still, there were always disappointments, bred by overly optimistic ambitions. Every year American colleges, universities and professional schools graduate thousands of drama majors. Except for the graduates of a handful of true conservatories with comprehensive actor training programs, they are haphazardly educated, superficially trained, and woefully conditioned physically. Many have played dozens of leading and supporting roles, but few have received honest, accurate evaluations of their talent and potential. Only a few of them, perhaps one to three percent, have the talent and will to succeed in a life in the theatre.

Nevertheless, these young actors support the resident companies and make plays like *Coriolanus* and the Chronicle plays possible. Without them to play the smaller roles, understudy the larger roles, and provide crews, true rotating repertory companies like mine could not exist and, in fact, fewer do exist each season. Indeed, it can be argued that the theatre itself could not exist without a constant flow of young people, all in love with the theatre, and fueled by belief in their own talents. Even when that belief is misplaced, it still exists, and, for a few years at least, gives them the courage to test themselves.

A director can only judge the interns comparatively in assigning the supporting roles and the understudies. It would be both premature and destructive to discourage any of these kids, and long-term success or failure depends on so many factors that the director cannot afford to play god. Instead, they should be given the same consideration and respect as the leading Equity

Coriolanus, New Jersey Shakespeare Festival, 1987: Ron Mangravite as Tullus Aufidius (photograph by Jim DelGiudice).

actors. Special understudy matinees, where they are given an opportunity to perform for invited audiences of relatives and friends, prepare them for possible illness or injury of leading cast members. Though these understudy matinees create their own problems, they are a valuable challenge for the young actors.

In a larger sense, a director must be able to work with what's on hand: theatre plants, budgets, people. Eighty-five percent of direction is casting. Well, maybe 87.337 percent. It's unfortunate that so many directors don't take the time to cast well, because that's what it takes: time going to plays, time holding auditions, asking actors to perform prepared auditions, read from text, sing, dance, fence, tell jokes, chat, in order to find and secure the best cast available. Is that cast capable of fulfilling the play?

I always begin with what may be little more (or less) than the scholar's ideal of the play, the perfect production that exists only in my imagination. The closer I get to opening, the more choices I have to make, and the more that perfect production gets boiled down to what is possible. That's the name of the game. If you don't want to play that game, then leave the plays on the page, on the shelf.

The first and last objective of a director is to get the play on. It usually gets on. I can remember only one production in my career that was delayed, postponed for five days (I wasn't directing), none that were ever abandoned in rehearsal. You cast the best company you can find, and then you do all that you can to enable that company to fulfill the play. No sense ruminating on actors who got away, who had other jobs, or whom you can no longer afford. It's the actors in front of you at rehearsal who have to do it. The director damn well better convince them they're the best.

Chapter 20

Measure for Measure

Measure for Measure was first performed some months after James I/VI assumed the throne of England and eased restrictions on dissident Christians. It is a very Catholic play, as are *Hamlet* and *Macbeth*. It's possible that Shakespeare was testing the liberality of James and his court, presenting ideas that might have earned him censure during Elizabeth's reign.

At the same time, *Measure for Measure* is a sex comedy. Most of the jokes are sexual or scatological. When in doubt, assume the double-entendre. A company that understands and exploits the jokes will keep the audience laughing. Because death is an abstract, even the jokes about death in this play can be funny too. The play often beats like a tragedy, but put it to the test: comedies end with the continuation of life; tragedies end with death. No principal character dies in this play, and at the conclusion, lovers marry and go off to bed to make pretty babies, except for those who are already pregnant.

I've done three productions of *Measure for Measure*, two as director, one as an actor in the first production of the play that the Oregon Shakespeare Festival ever did, in 1951. Having rehearsed the play seriously, as if it were a tragedy with comic relief, we were surprised on opening night when everybody got laughs, not just the clowns. Philip Hanson, a brilliant actor playing Angelo, was furious and railed against the crass stupidity of the audience. The director, Jim Sandoe, took the play back into rehearsal the next day to lighten some of the moments and build in some breathing room for the laughs.

There are two plays in the Canon that take place in Vienna, this one and *The Murder of Gonzago*, the play-within-a-play which Hamlet orders from the traveling players who visit Elsinore. Hamlet tells us that the play is written in choice Italian and takes place in Vienna, the Italian name for Wien. All the characters have Italian names. *Measure for Measure* takes place in "Vienna" as well, but its characters have Italian, Roman, or English names. There are no Austrians in the cast, nor is there any resemblance to the city of Wien, Austria. Is it possible that Shakespeare saw Vienna as an Italian city?

The first time I directed the play, I set it in the Wien of Franz Josef and opened it at a Hapsburg party with romantic couples in luxurious ball gowns and uniforms swirling gracefully to Strauss waltzes. The actors played the comedy to the hilt: our pudgy, petulant Claudio brought down the house when he whined "thou wilt not do it?" to his prim, nearly manic sister Isabella, and Angelo's seduction was in no way subtle. It was great fun, audiences and the press loved it, but it was wrong. We worked too hard to make it funny. Another sumptuous production, at Arena Stage in Washington, D.C., set in the Wien of Sigmund Freud, was fascinating, but the Freudian implications worked against the play. The second time I directed it, I set it in a northern Italian city, very much like Venice.

Although Shakespeare's plays include a handful of monks, priests, and Protestant ministers, there are only a few nuns, and only one in a major role. I strongly advise directors of this play to take time to consider what a nun is, what a nun does, what a nun doesn't do. We first see Isabella 17 minutes into the play, after most of the other principals have been introduced, in a brief, quiet scene in the garden of the novitiate of Saint Clare with another nun. We learn that Isabella is a novice of the order, committed to her preliminary vows of poverty, chastity, and obedience, but she has not yet taken her final vows. When she takes them, she will be forbidden to talk to any men, except in the presence of her Mother Superior.

For the time being, however, Isabella is allowed to speak, and speak she does. Isabella is a remarkable young woman, intelligent, resilient, courageous. Though her essential vow would seem to be chastity (celibacy in nuns predates that of priests), her primary responsibility is to the laws of God. She obeys. She even throws her vow of poverty up to Angelo, offering to bribe him, not with gold or jewels, but with riches in heaven. She appears to have opinions on everything, and she expresses them at every opportunity. But her opinions are not really opinions at all: they are recitations and articulations of laws and rules of Catholic theology.

Isabella has been described by critics as rigid, puritanical, a fanatic. She's not! She is a nun, and her vows are promises to God. It's logical to assume that Claudio and Isabella grew up in a loving, devoutly religious family. Isabella begins the play sure in her beliefs, happy to become a nun. Claudio is also religious. He's not a libertine; he's simply made love to his betrothed and had the bad luck to be arrested and judged by the harsh new regime Angelo has imposed.

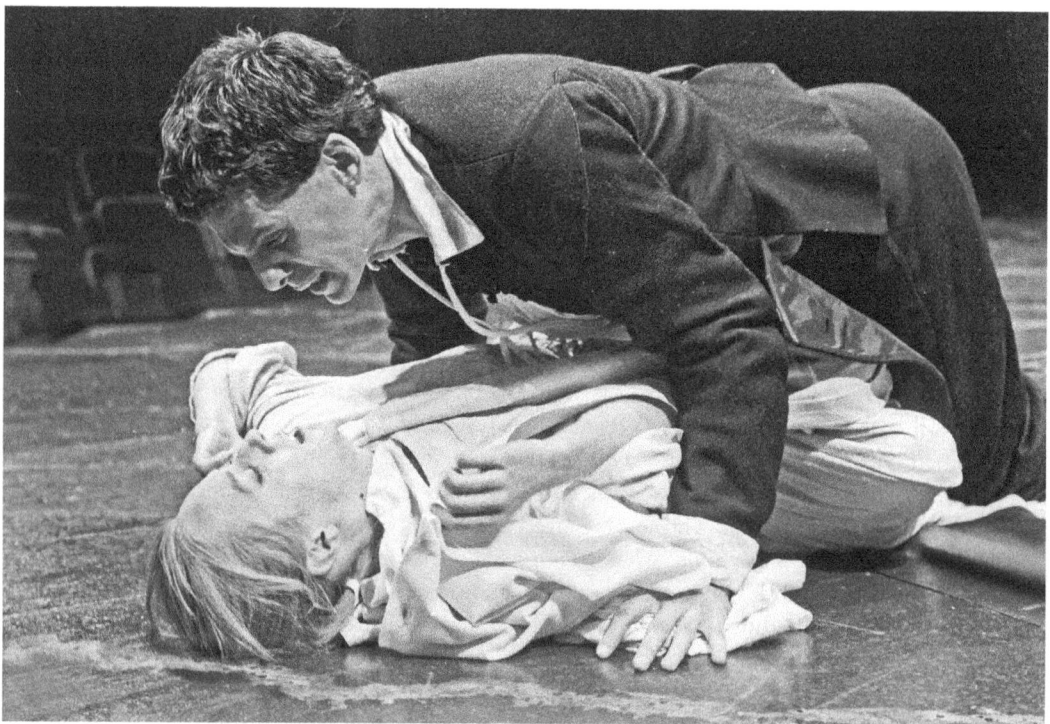

Measure for Measure, New Jersey Shakespeare Festival, 1990: Cheryl Williams as Isabella, T. Ryder Smith as Angelo (photograph by Jim DelGiudice).

The basic plot of *Measure for Measure* is this: Duke Vincentio, ruler of this fictional city, is unmarried and has no heir. Because he suspects chaos would ensue if he were to die, he delegates authority to his deputy, Angelo, and pretends to leave town on a diplomatic mission. Angelo immediately calls for a reformation of the legal system and the enforcement of its stringent morality laws. Isabella's brother, Claudio, is arrested and sentenced to death for fornication. Isabella begs Angelo for mercy to Claudio, and Angelo agrees to pardon Claudio, but only if Isabella will sleep with him. Duke Vincentio, disguised as Friar Lodovico (another Italian name), attempts to manipulate the plot and bring it to a happy conclusion.

The Duke stays outside of the action, for the most part, though he clearly enjoys playing a priest. The central action of the play is the tug-of-war among Angelo, Isabella, and Claudio. Angelo begins the play as a puritan reformer, the image of the perfect, incorruptible prince. Like most of Shakespeare's lovers, he falls in love with Isabella at first sight. But unlike other comic heroines, Isabella does not fall in love with Angelo: she is a nun! His advances insult her. She calls him a hypocrite and threatens to expose him. Of course he's a hypocrite, but he's also been struck by lightning — il Fulmine! — a victim of his own lust.

One of the most touching and hilarious scenes in the play is between brother and sister, Claudio and Isabella. In his prison cell, she tells him of Angelo's proposition, and Claudio argues that the sin of fornication will be no sin *if* it saves his life. They debate morality and theology like two Jesuit lawyers. Isabella insists to Claudio, as she does to Angelo, that because she is a nun, committed to celibacy, sex is not an option.

As he does in *All's Well That Ends Well*, Shakespeare resorts to a staple trick of many plays and stories in *Measure for Measure*: Mariana, Angelo's earlier fiancée, whom he jilted, takes Isabella's place in the clandestine bed. Angelo then unwittingly commits the same crime (or non-crime) as Claudio, consummating his earlier betrothal. That's neat and ironic. Shakespeare's comic argument is that "in the dark, they are all the same." To the Duke, it's simple: they're married, unless Angelo would prefer to have his head cut off.

T. Ryder Smith was the best Angelo I've ever seen, playing every color of a multifaceted character.

Elizabethan/Jacobean marriage customs such as this made marriage and women's rank problems in a number of the plays. What was Angelo's excuse for dumping Mariana? What information does the audience have to have about private and public romance and courtship to understand this?

At 33 minutes, the wind-up scene, V.1, is one of the longest in Shakespeare. The Duke holds court, hears witnesses, passes judgment on everyone, condemns, then forgives. What does a character do when the playwright gives her nothing to do? As I wrote in the *As You Like It* chapter, George Abbott was wrong. Sometimes actors need to just stand there.

Then, in the last two minutes of *Measure for Measure*, with all plots resolved, the Duke suddenly proposes marriage to Isabella. This scene drives actors and directors crazy, because, like Mr. Abbott, they all love action. Certainly, if one of today's ubiquitous celebrities proposed in public, there would be uproar from the crowd, and reporters would descend en masse.

What happens at the conclusion of *Measure for Measure*? Nothing. The wise director will put Isabella where the audience can watch her, and it makes sense to give her and Claudio a moment of reunion, but no more than a moment and no dialogue, before the Duke makes his marriage proposal. Isabella, she of the thousand moral, ethical, theological arguments, says not a word. Time stands still as the audience waits for her answer, but it doesn't come.

The Duke changes the subject to Angelo, then Lucio, back to Claudio, finally to Escalus and the Provost. All plots are tied up. Once again, he proposes, and once again, Isabella says nothing, does nothing. So the Duke postpones the matter, suggesting that everyone follow him to the palace for more chitchat. All exeunt but Isabella; she hasn't said a word in almost five minutes.

Directors can look forward to extended discussions, even arguments, with the actors playing the Duke and Isabella about what's going on here. I recommend conducting these discussions about that last two minutes with the whole cast present; allow everyone to express an opinion — it's good catharsis, lets off some steam — but stand firm with what you are demanding: a specific and unambiguous nothing. Make sure the stage manager, who will be charged with maintaining the performances through the run, understands this as well. The wonderful actress who played Isabella in the Washington Arena production probably began with visible agitation, then a gasp, then an unaspirated "No." By the time I saw the play, near the end of its run, she was left alone on-stage and her "No!" (not in the text, of course) was loud enough to be heard across the Potomac.

In their *Tales from Shakespeare*, Charles and Mary Lamb added a lengthy faerie tale ending to Shakespeare's play. Their book introduced children to Shakespeare's stories before they were old enough to handle the language. That's harmless, but where did they get the right to change Shakespeare's intent, at least in this play? In the Lambs' rewrite, Isabella accepts the Duke's proposal, becomes Duchess of Vienna, and goes on to serve as a shining example of what a wife and mother should be.

Clearly, the Lambs concluded that Isabella was off the hook and free to marry the Duke because she had not yet taken final vows as a nun. A good Protestant conclusion. A nun's vows are not legal contracts: they are promises the nun makes to God, and she can walk away from them, as many have, when she no longer feels bound to the promise. Nobody is going to take her to court for breach of contract. There's also an assumption inherent in Lamb's happy ending that all women really want is a rich husband, a big house, and lots of kids.

Shakespeare wrote no such ending to *Measure for Measure*, nor does the play imply such a possibility. The Duke proposes twice, and Isabella answers not. That's what the Playwright wrote, and that's what he wanted on-stage. His ambiguities must be protected, must be respected. In dozens of instances, Shakespeare lays out incomplete ideas, inviting the audience to draw their own conclusions. If the text does not resolve these enigmas, then the director and actors must cooperate.

Perhaps I'm spending too much time dissecting these two minutes of action, but such careful consideration might save directors and actors much grief in similar moments in other plays. Shakespeare didn't do subtext, not in the sense that Chekhov did. Master Will's intentions are right there on the page. If a character is given no lines by the Playwright, then the actor playing that character is best advised to do nothing more than stand by, watch, and listen.

In addition, the Playwright seldom contradicts facts and principles he establishes early in the plays. The Duke is unmarried, an eligible bachelor with a responsibility to continue his line, but his proposal is inappropriate, given Isabella's profession, her holy vocation.

Isabella really wants to be a nun. No one is forcing her. That's what she wants to do with her life.

CHAPTER 21

The Chronicle Plays

In 1485, as soon as Henry Tudor, Earl of Richmond, defeated Richard III at the Battle of Bosworth and became King Henry VII, he quickly set out to reinforce his position through three separate actions. First, he married Elizabeth of York, eldest daughter of Edward IV, and produced two sons and two daughters with her. Then, he sent out individual assassins, operating clandestinely, to eliminate all possible claimants to the throne. Finally, he selected a team of historians, churchmen, and lawyers to rewrite the history of the previous hundred years to justify the legitimacy of the Tudor line, which subsequently produced Henry VIII, Edward VI, Mary Tudor, Elizabeth I, and the Stuarts.

Among these Tudor propagandists were Polydore Vergil, Thomas Cardinal Morton, Thomas Cardinal Wolsey, and Thomas More, whose revisions were later organized and published by Edward Hall and Raphael Holinshed. Their rewrites whitewashed the Lancastrians, demonized the Yorkists, and created the basis for a great stage villain in the third son of Richard of York: Richard of Gloucester, later King Richard III. The most flagrant bit of Tudor "spin" was the fiction that Richard III defeated Henry VII in single combat.

Today's historians have unraveled many of the contradictions, excised the untruths, and provided us with the facts with which to view the plays, but Shakespeare based his plays on the Tudor version of events.

Isaac Asimov, in his delightful two-volume *Guide to Shakespeare*, takes Master Will to task for writing flawed history, but he wasn't writing history: he was writing entertainment, and where there are discrepancies between the two, the scholar may ponder the differences, while the director must stick to the script. When revealed history agrees with the Tudor vision, it's incumbent upon the director to emphasize the similarities, but there's no third choice. Attempts at comparing Richard III with Napoleon or Hitler are interesting, but ultimately fail as both theatre and history.

What kind of a lunatic playwright would write seven plays entitled *Henry* and two more entitled *Richard*? Was he testing the loyalty of his audience or the skill of his publicists?

The historical sequence of Shakespeare's plays about British sovereigns begins with *King Lear* and *Cymbeline*, but he skips the next thousand years, as well as the Norman conquest, deals briefly with Scottish kings in *Macbeth*, digresses to the kings Richard Lionheart and his brother John in *King John*, then resumes again with the grandson of Edward III in 1399 with *Richard II*, *Henry IV Parts 1 and 2*, *Henry V*. He had already written about the years following the events of *Henry V* much earlier in the *Henry VI* plays, *Richard III* and *Henry VIII*. In the chapters to come, we will look at the plays in their historical order rather than the order in which Shakespeare wrote them.

In 1066 the Norman French under William the Conqueror invaded Britain, effectively annihilated the Anglo-Saxon nobility, and drove the Celts north into Scotland and west into Wales and Ireland. Within a hundred years, the Norman nobility ruled England and much of France, while the Anglo-Saxons barely survived as the English peasantry. The society was feudal, peasants working the land owned by a score of Norman families — a harsh system maintained by force of arms. Property was inherited through primogeniture, and a morality evolved that justified the class system as divinely ordained. Only those of royal blood could aspire to the throne. The nobility formed a parliament to control the commoners and limit the power of the king, but it was many years before a second branch of Parliament emerged, the House of Commons. That was actually something of a misnomer: the House of Commons was made up of knights, clergymen, and wealthy London merchants, not commoners.

Shakespeare's two tetralogies, eight plays spanning 86 years of history, cover the kings of England from the end of the 14th century to the ascension of Henry VII in 1485. The *story* of these eight plays begins with the Hundred Years' war, 1337 through 1453, between the kings of England and France over who had the right to rule the territories of France: the English descendants of the Norman William the Conqueror, the French kings of the House of Valois,

Henry VI, Part 3, New Jersey Shakespeare Festival, 1983: Brett Porter as Edward, Earl of March; Deveren Bookwalter as George, Duke of Clarence; John Hertzler as Richard Plantagenet, Duke of York; Clay Cornog as Edmund, Earl of Rutland; and Michael Tolaydo as Richard, Duke of Gloucester (photograph by Blair Holley).

or the Burgundian dukes. Concurrent with this war were the reign and deposition of Richard II and the rebellions that followed, as well as the civil war known today as the War(s) of the Roses. Note that "War(s) of the Roses" was not Shakespeare's term, though modern directors usually build their designs around the symbols of the white and red.

Prominent characters appear repeatedly in these eight plays: Henry Bolingbroke and his eldest son, Hal, are significant in three plays each. Margaret of Anjou, only 15 when we first meet her in *Henry VI, Part 1*, shows up in three more plays through *Richard III*, finally appearing a year or so after her death, no small feat. That definitive comic invention, Sir John Falstaff, dominates two Chronicle plays and is remembered poignantly in a third. Later, Shakespeare brought him back a third time as the lead in a comedy. Two of Falstaff's followers, Bardolph and Mistress Quickly, are each minor characters in four plays.

Henry IV, Part 1, the three Parts of *Henry VI*, and *Richard III* are similar in structure and treatment, while *Richard II*, *Henry IV, Part 2*, and *Henry V* each differ from the others. *Richard II* plays like a tragedy in verse. *Henry IV, Part 2* is a domestic tragedy in its attempts to reconcile father and son, Henry Bolingbroke and Hal, but is dominated by the Falstaff scenes, which ultimately steal the show. The absence of Hotspur and the nonviolent political solution of the second rebellion tip the polarity of *Part 1* into *Part 2*, putting the comic relief subplot center stage.

Henry V, in which Shakespeare abandoned the means and methods by which he wrote the earlier seven plays, then wrote and rewrote a whole new experimental piece of theatre, is, as we shall see, something altogether new.

Even without the poetry and drama of Shakespeare's genius, these eight plays present a history of English politics: treason and accusations of treason, bribery, influence peddling, nepotism, cronyism, misuse of public funds. Sound familiar? Politics seem to corrupt, whether leaders are selected by bloodlines or by force of arms or by the democratic process. Americans tend to assign a greater morality to democracy, but if elections can be influenced, even bought, with special interest money, then the results are indistinguishable from other political methods.

Shakespeare and his collaborators weren't the only ones writing history plays at the time. The public loved plays about the royalty and the nobility, including *Edward II*, *Edward III*, and *Thomas of Woodstock*, as well as an earlier play about King John, and, of course, the history Shakespeare was covering was in a much more recent past for them than for the modern audience. Today's directors must first educate their actors about these complex events, no small task, then supply program materials that tell the audience the story of the play up to the moment it begins.

The Hundred Years' War begins with Edward III, who was the seventh in an undisputed line of Plantagenet kings going back to Henry II. Edward had seven sons and five daughters, but only five of the sons are crucial to the play *Richard II* and those that follow it. From oldest to youngest they were:

Edward, the Black Prince, heir apparent, father of Richard II
Lionel, Duke of Clarence, grandfather of Edmund Mortimer
John of Gaunt, Duke of Lancaster, father of Henry Bolingbroke
Edmund of Langley, Duke of York
Thomas of Woodstock, Duke of Gloucester

Edward, the Black Prince, was a hero of the battles of Sluys (1340), Crecy (1346), and Poitiers (1356) in the Hundred Years' War. In 1360, the Treaty of Bretigny created an uneasy truce, which was maintained until 1413. The Black Prince died in 1376, predeceasing his father, Edward III. Edward was then succeeded by his grandson, the Black Prince's only son, Richard II. Richard assumed the throne at the age of ten, even though four of his father's brothers were still alive. Such was the rule of primogeniture. Richard married Anne of Bohemia, then, after she died, Isabella of France, daughter of the French King Charles VI. Neither marriage produced an heir; Isabella was only 12 when Richard was deposed.

When a king, like Richard, had no son, the throne could be inherited by anyone with royal blood. Thus Richard was encouraged to nominate an heir according to tradition. Instead of one of his uncles, however, he designated Roger Mortimer, 4th Earl of March, the grandson of his uncle, Lionel of Clarence. In the plays, Shakespeare creates a single character called simply "Lord Mortimer," conflating the historical Roger Mortimer; his son, Edmund Mortimer; and Roger's brother, another Edmund, husband to the daughter of Owen Glendower. As a descendant of Edward III's third son, Lionel, Mortimer had a stronger claim to the throne than Henry Bolingbroke, who descended from Edward's fourth son, John of Gaunt. Richard's eldest living uncle, John had inherited quasi-royal powers for his Duchy of Lancaster, which made him the wealthiest and most powerful man in England after the king.

What facts we have paint a dark picture of the early reign of the boy Richard II, supervised and bullied by counselors and powerful uncles, especially the youngest, Thomas of Woodstock. Historians describe Richard as incompetent, vain, extravagant, a poor administrator.

His reign was marked by social and economic unrest. The bubonic plague, mid–14th century, killed half the English population. A peasants' revolt in 1381 was put down with great severity. Like all such revolts, this one was against taxation, in this case levied to support governmental extravagance: both Edward III and Richard II lived in ostentatious luxury, maintaining expensive armies and multiple castles. The peasantry labored for the material benefit of the nobility, but both were taxed by the Church and by the Crown.

With the Irish, the Welsh, and the Scots continuing to heckle the British, the Hundred Years' War enjoyed a smoldering peace only because the British launched no new campaigns against the French.

In 1388, Thomas of Woodstock, Henry Bolingbroke, Thomas Mowbray, Duke of Norfolk, and the Earls of Arundel and Warwick, led a legal/military action known as the Merciless Parliament. The King survived this attempted coup, but his position was weakened and many of his supporters were sent to the block or into exile. A year later, he attained his majority, dismissed his councilors and neutralized the power of his enemies. Soon after, he issued a proclamation to the nation promising to correct all injustices. Politics as usual.

Though Richard moved clandestinely to strengthen his private army, a military expedition he led to Ireland in 1394 accomplished nothing. In 1397 Richard brought to trial several members of the Merciless Parliament opposition, sentencing Warwick to life imprisonment, Arundel to a traitor's death, and imprisoning Thomas of Woodstock at the garrison at Calais, under the military governor, Thomas Mowbray, whom he had evidently forgiven for his part in the attempted coup. Of the original Merciless Parliament five, only Mowbray and Henry Bolingbroke remained at liberty. In September of 1397, Thomas of Woodstock was murdered, smothered to death by assassins.

At this point in history, the action of Shakespeare's three Bolingbroke plays, *Richard II* and *Henry IV, Parts 1 and 2*, begin. The plays depict the essential action of the next 15 years.

CHAPTER 22

Richard II

Richard II can stand alone as a tragedy or may be grouped among the histories as the first of the Lancastrian tetralogy. The only play of Shakespeare's written entirely in verse, its language is elevated, ephemeral. If a director were willing to postpone staging and begin the rehearsal process instead by exploring in depth the poetry, scansion, the shared verse and its implications for pacing, the effect would be symphonic. The poetry in *Richard II* is so rich that it's sometimes hard to focus on what's happening.

The actors might rebel, of course. American actors, especially, love their pauses and hate the imposition of choral rhythms. Some actors don't feel they're rehearsing if they're not moving and shouting.

I only did *Richard II* once and I'd love another crack at it. Political questions eventually overwhelm the play, but Shakespeare was going for something here that is not immediately apparent: the religious theme of the deposition of a king. Much in *Richard II* elicits the spiritual. There's a Gregorian underscore: Richard's speeches are operatic arias as well as sermons. He always speaks of himself as God's appointed deputy and judge. A child of privilege, smothered in luxury from infancy, he believes that he is more than mortal, hovering between men and the angels, divinely appointed and anointed.

Richard can do no wrong, because the king can do no wrong. This king believes himself to be right because he is incapable of error. He is a celebrity because he was born a celebrity. He is famous because he was always famous. The argument is circular. He invokes the divine right of kings more than any other character in the Canon.

Soon after we opened the play in 1974, Nixon resigned, and our audience saw in his fall a parallel to the much earlier Richard's. A 2004 production elicited comparisons with Jim McGreevey, disgraced governor of New Jersey. Richard II reminds me most of George W. Bush in his hubris. Both believed that they served by the will of God, both believed themselves saintly in the validity of their intuitions, both made decisions instinctively, "from the gut," manufacturing morality on the spot. Hubris can fog the brain, blind the king to evidence, events, arguments that contradict what he believes about himself, the human condition, his kingdom, the world. Opposing viewpoints are rejected out of hand. Opponents are dealt with defensively, contemptuously. Hubris goes hand in hand with paranoia and destroys rationality. To disagree with the king is to be guilty of treason. From Oedipus to Richard to Dub'ya, the seeds of downfall have been sown by hubris.

Richard II explores the two bodies of the king: the body politic, of which he is the head, and the mortal body, subject to the same weaknesses, ills, and passions as the meanest peasant.

> For within the hollow crown
> That rounds the mortal temples of a king
> Keeps death his court; and there the antic sits
> Scoffing at his state and grinning at his pomp.

Too late, he discovers his mortality.

Some conjecture that Shakespeare had planned to write a single play about each of the kings, Richard II, Henry IV, and Henry V, but once into the saga, having added a number of interesting characters, he found it necessary to expand the three plays into four. Though Richard, Hotspur, Falstaff, Hal, Shallow, and the Boar's Head crew are far more interesting and entertaining, isolating the Bolingbroke scenes in all three plays and focusing on them provides an extended analysis of the politics and spin of Bolingbroke's statements.

It's difficult and dangerous to try to sum up in a neat sound bite what a play by Shakespeare is about, easier to state what it isn't. *Richard II* is not about the persecution of Jesus by the Romans, though that's how it was directed and designed for the New York Shakespeare Festival production of 1961, dominated by J.D. Cannon as Henry Bolingbroke.

Richard II is not about gay bashing by the straight establishment. Shakespeare wrote no explicit homosexuals. *Richard II* tradition swings both ways. The splendid 1974 RSC production that toured America, directed by John Barton, alternated two excellent actors, Ian Richardson and Richard Pasco, as Bolingbroke and Richard. Depending on which actor you saw as Richard, the king was either gay or straight.

The BBC television production is blatant, no ambiguity. I.4 is played in "the baths" as Richard gets a massage. Richard and his court are all flamboyant homosexuals, and they are deposed by Bolingbroke and the barons because of it. How much of that is directorial imposition? If we examine the text, the play on paper, where's the homosexuality? There's little on-stage grab-ass even implied, though most actors will be tempted to expand on what is there. The only homosexual implications are Bolingbroke's libels and biased characterizations, as he searches for impeachable offenses. The knights John Bushy, William Bagot, and Henry Green historically were members of the House of Commons, defenders of the king. By having Bolingbroke term them "caterpillars of the empire," parasites of the body politic, Shakespeare gives minimal credence to the tradition that Richard was homosexual.

Bolingbroke's supporters equate homosexuality with corruption, and the ideal warrior king must be a heterosexual who provides the nation with male heirs in between battles. On the other hand, if Richard is as saintly as he sees himself, then his enemies are thugs and rebels.

My advice, that most directors don't take, is to keep the homosexuality ambiguous. Let the audience decide. There's no conclusive evidence either in history or in the play that Richard was gay. He died childless, but both of his wives were very young women, girls actually. We're reasonably sure that Richard I (Richard Lionheart) was gay, despite Shakespeare giving him an illegitimate son, and we definitely know that Edward II was, but the jury's still out on Richard II.

If we visualize the three Bolingbroke plays as one long epic and concentrate on Bolingbroke himself, setting aside the fascinating, entertaining people who distract us from him, then it may be possible to answer the question: when, if ever, is he free of bias, capable of speaking the truth? Conversely, when does he bend the truth to give his listeners what they want to hear in order to enlist their services?

He does what all politicians do, exaggerating, spinning, setting rumors afoot, telling the same half-lies over and over again until they are perceived as truths. How much of what

Richard II, New Jersey Shakespeare Festival 1973: Brian Lynner as Sir Henry Green, Timothy Meyers as Sir William Bagot, Greg Bell as King Richard II, John Greenleaf as Sir John Bushy (photograph by Blair Holley).

he says are out-and-out falsehoods? In addition to the question of Richard's homosexuality, how much of Prince Hal's alleged riot and dishonor is Bolingbroke's characterization rather than reality? I have come to believe that much of what Bolingbroke says and causes to happen is little more than political manipulation, and I suspect that some 80 years later, Henry VII operated in similar fashion.

Shakespeare compresses the first nine years of the reign of Henry IV, which were marked by conflicts with the Scots, Welsh, and French, as well as a number of rebellions, into a continuous flow from the death of Richard II to the ascension of Henry V. This is the same kind of time compression we saw in *Antony and Cleopatra.*

To accommodate this compression of time, Shakespeare changes the ages of several principals, depicting Prince Hal, Hotspur, and Mortimer as contemporaries in their early 20s and King Henry in his late 30s. Henry actually died at 46 of some strange malady, never completely explained. Directors concerned about the time discrepancy can address it by aging Bolingbroke. He ages, but none of the others do.

Again we're faced with the consideration of stage time versus real time versus historical time, and again it's easier to settle for the cop-out: if it didn't concern Shakespeare, it shouldn't concern today's director.

As the action begins in *Richard II*, Henry Bolingbroke and Thomas Mowbray, Duke of Norfolk, accuse each other of treason, embezzlement, the murder of Thomas of Woodstock, and various corrupt practices. Politics as usual. In keeping with custom, both appeal to the king for judgment.

Richard refuses to rule between them, but he grants their request for a trial by combat. Trial by combat was a quasi-religious ceremony, a deadly joust on a level field. Each opponent was given his choice of three weapons and a caparisoned horse. God decided which was the just combatant. The loser was the traitor and his confederates were implicated as well.

In Shakespeare's play, the combatants and their trains, the king and his court, gather at Windsor Castle on the Festival of Saint George. Since designers' attempts to replicate the splendor of the early scenes of the play can easily bankrupt a theatre company, a Brechtian approach is perhaps the wisest. The ceremonies proceed, accusations are read and sworn to, war-horses prepared, combatants armored and armed, stationed at opposite ends of the lists. They close their beavers and wait for the command to attack. At the last minute, Richard stops the proceedings. He confers briefly with his counselors, then banishes both combatants: Mowbray for life, and Bolingbroke for ten years, later reduced to six years.

Why doesn't the King let them fight it out? Note that there's no direct reference anywhere in Shakespeare's play to Richard's own suspected culpability in the death of Thomas of Woodstock. Shakespeare is either depending on his audience to know this historical background, or he's being skillfully ambiguous. Since Woodstock was his uncle, a son of Edward III, and of royal blood, Richard might have been able to arrest him under suspicion of treason, but could never have sent him to the block with impunity. The obvious solution was an assassination, probably suggested to Mowbray by Richard, subcontracted by Mowbray, carried out by anonymous hit men. The widow of Thomas of Woodstock blames his death on King Richard. John of Gaunt and Edmund of York hint at it. On his deathbed, Gaunt comes barely short of an accusation.

If Mowbray loses the trial by combat and is thereby branded a traitor, then Richard himself will be implicated, giving Bolingbroke, a rival claimant to the throne, great advantage. By banishing both appellants, Richard leaves the case open. Mowbray does not confess to his complicity in the crime, and Bolingbroke must accept the judgment of the King because he agreed to it at the outset of the trial.

Here, I must again remind readers that Shakespeare was writing plays, not history. In all of his works about warriors and kings, he used the raw material of history, bending it a bit here and there, combining characters, creating characters out of whole cloth, bringing the relationships among those characters to life, compressing the whole world down to a spectacle on a stage. Plays are always about the human condition.

Now the focus of the play turns to Richard's uncles, the dying John of Gaunt and his younger brother, Edmund of Langley, Duke of York. Both admonish Richard to mend his ways, Gaunt intoning his patriotic aria about "the sceptered isle," an actor's trap if there ever was one. This is one of those celebrated speeches in Shakespeare, like "O what a rogue" and the "Seven Ages of Man" that audiences recognize immediately and actors dread, worrying about how they can make the well-known words fresh. Far too often, these speeches become set pieces, demonstrations of elocutionary excellence, arias sung rather than spoken, pulled outside the play itself. The solution? Concentrate simply and fiercely on *why* the words are being said. The "sceptered isle" actually has elements of humor along with its beauty, a testy elder berating his nephew for fouling his precious inheritance.

But back to the play: Gaunt dies, and Richard commits the first of his major mistakes by seizing all of the Lancastrian lands and goods. This decision happens quickly, so the director must "box" it, somehow emphasize it, perhaps even pause for a few seconds to allow the audience to grasp the enormity of the decision and consider the possible results.

Shakespeare bends history again by putting Henry Percy, the Earl of Northumberland, and the Lords Willoughby and Ross in Gaunt's death scene. The dilemma is dramatized when they observe firsthand how Richard pilfers the enormous wealth of the Lancaster duchy, and this prompts them to turn against the King. They reason that if he can steal those vast lands and wealth on a technical legal pretense, he can steal anything else in sight. If he can steal with impunity, he can also kill. His power will be absolute.

Richard then commits his second big mistake, sailing off to Ireland and leaving England under the command of his uncle, Edmund of York.

The Playwright now compresses time: various nobles rise up to protest the appropriation of the Lancastrian properties, just as the rightful heir to those properties, Henry Bolingbroke, returns from exile to claim them. Bolingbroke insists that his only objective is to regain the lands and title of his dead father, but Parliament, both the nobility and the commons, join together to name him, in effect to elect him, king.

The Playwright tiptoes around his major point here, as well as in other plays dealing with kingship. If God determines who will be king, if God is present at the conception and birth of the king, if regicide is the greatest sin, a multiple sin (see the chapters on *Macbeth* and *Hamlet*), then who has the right to depose the king? Though kings are challenged, not by the voice of the people, but by Parliament, the baronage, and the military, Shakespeare flirts with democracy in *Richard II* as he does in the *Henry VI* plays.

The Percys of the North are Bolingbroke's primary enablers, but the *Henry IV* plays also include other noblemen who first supported his cause, then turned against him when he proved insufficiently grateful for their services: Sir Richard Vernon, Archbishop Richard Scroop of York, the Lords Mowbray, Hastings, and Bardolph, and the Knights Travers, Morton, and Colville. The Welsh under Owen Glendower, and the Scots under Archibald, Earl of Douglas, complete the list. Even though they don't all appear in all three plays, it makes sense to track their influence from the beginning.

Edmund of Langley, Duke of York and uncle to both Richard and Bolingbroke, is loyal to and protective of King Richard at first, and then switches his allegiance to the challenger.

When Richard returns from Ireland, he encounters the combined forces of Bolingbroke and the nobles who support him. Bolingbroke continues to insist that he is a loyal subject, seeking only the lands and properties that are rightfully his. Richard seems to capitulate as soon as he sets foot on English soil. In his "hollow crown" speech (not a soliloquy — he's surrounded by loyalists), he foresees his deposition and death.

Bolingbroke now demands that Richard summon Parliament to restore his rights, and there, in the brilliant trial scene IV.1, Richard tempts Bolingbroke to seize the crown. It is this scene that Elizabeth I objected to, because she believed it dramatized actual plots against her. When she first saw the play in 1597 she demanded that the deposition scene be excised. The unedited play was never again performed during her lifetime, but it was restored to its full length for the 1623 Folio.

Richard is deposed, and Bolingbroke is crowned Henry IV. On his way to close confinement, Richard encounters his Queen in the street. This scene, which plays like a parting of mature lovers, not the historical man of 33 and child of 12, doesn't work at all if Richard is portrayed as gay. Richard and the Queen are allowed a brief farewell, then the Earl of Northumberland interrupts to escort Richard to Pomfret Castle, while she is sent to her father's court in France.

Then follows a scene with the turncoat Duke of York, his wife, and his son, Aumerle, one of the few moments of dark comedy in the play. Aumerle remains loyal to Richard, and his father turns him in to King Henry. Henry pardons Aumerle and makes peace with the Duke and Duchess. The theme of the next two plays, the delinquent Prince Hal and his "unrestrained loose companions" is introduced.

Sir Pierce Exton suggests that Henry had given him a subtle, indirect command when, speaking of Richard, he asked, "Have I no friend that will rid me of this living fear? Have I no friend?" The scene echoes the legend of Henry II: musing aloud to three of his knights, he is said to have complained of Thomas à Becket, "Is there no man that will rid me of this troublesome priest?" So they did. The same device is used in *Antony and Cleopatra*, II.7. The action then moves to Richard's prison cell.

Did Richard deserve to be deposed? If the king is corrupt, so too is the state corrupt. If the king is strong, the nation is strong. If he is weak, so is the body politic. He holds the highest place; to abjure the crown is to admit grievous culpability. The providential theory of history, that the king is chosen by God, is tested several times during the play. Shakespeare either believed in it, or he wrote as if he believed in it; he used it as theme and subject matter of several plays. If Richard failed in his responsibilities as king, then it was God who removed him from office, and God who had him killed. Are his usurpers then guilty of regicide, that multiple sin? Or are they blameless instruments of God's justice?

There is a similar theological debate about Judas Iscariot. Is he complicit in the death of Jesus Christ or was he merely playing his role, hitting his marks, without freedom of choice? If so, can he be condemned?

Scholar Chris Fitter sees the Earl of Essex in the character of Bolingbroke, as well as in Hamlet and Brutus. On the eve of Essex's Rebellion against Elizabeth, Sir Gilly Merrick went to Augustus Phillips, company manager of the Lord Chamberlain's Men, to request a performance of the edited *Richard II* on Saturday, February 7, 1601. Phillips protested that the play was out of the rep, that it hadn't been performed in some years, that the actors didn't know the roles. Sir Gilly made an offer that Phillips couldn't refuse: he'd buy out the house and also allow all the seats to be resold, giving the company the possibility of a 200 percent box office. Phillips accepted the offer, and the actors crammed to learn the roles, ran through the staging in the morning, and then performed the play that Saturday afternoon—all in 48 hours. Such a stunt would be impossible today.

The performance was a signal to Essex's supporters to begin the uprising. The signal worked, but the vaunted Rebellion was an embarrassing failure, resulting in nothing positive, only the loss of Essex's head. Justice was swift when it came to rebellion against the queen. She is said to have exclaimed to the jurist, William Lambarde, "I am Richard Second. Know ye not that?" Essex went to the block on February 25, 1601. There's no record that Shakespeare was accused of any complicity. Gus Phillips was questioned by the authorities, who could well have cut off his head too, but he and his fellow actors escaped punishment.

The historian Thomas B. Costain, in *The Last Plantagenet*, quotes the Duke of Burgundy on the deposition of Richard and the crowning of Henry IV: "Since the English have imprisoned King Richard, they will assuredly put him to death. They always hated him because he preferred peace to war."

The rightful warrior king will always prefer war to peace.

CHAPTER 23

Henry IV, Part 1

Henry IV, Part 1 is the second play of the Lancastrian tetralogy. Though it's impractical to demand that all four plays be performed together, each makes reference to characters and events in the others. Directors and actors must have a working familiarity with all four, if not all eight of the double tetralogy. *Richard II* ends with Henry IV musing about a crusade to the Holy Land; *Henry IV, Part 1* begins with the same subject. Between the two plays, we later discover, there were two border incidents, one a victory by the Welsh under Owen Glendower, and the second the defeat at Holmdon of Archibald, Earl of Douglas, by the son of the Earl of Northumberland, Harry Hotspur Percy.

Glendower captured and held for ransom Lord Mortimer, the grandson of Lionel of Clarence, named by Richard II as his successor. Though Henry Bolingbroke has managed to usurp his cousin Richard, and though he has been crowned King Henry IV, Mortimer remains a valid claimant to the throne.

There are a number of rivalries in the *Henry IV* plays that work themselves out in interweaving scenes. King Henry and Prince Hal compete with each other, each testing a theory of kingship. It may be argued that Henry competes with Falstaff for the soul of Hal, but that's an aesthetic concept, largely unplayable. Henry competes with his earlier supporters, now turned against him, for primacy. In theatrical terms, Prince Hal and Hotspur compete as the "hero" of the piece; the tension built into their rivalry climaxes in their Act V duel.

Shakespeare gives the rebels faces and personalities in his depiction of the Percy family: Thomas Percy, Earl of Worcester; his brother, Henry Percy, Earl of Northumberland; his wife, Lady Percy; his son, Sir Henry Percy, known as "Hotspur;" and Hotspur's wife, Elizabeth (Kate) Percy. The Percys are, in turn, related to the Mortimers, and it is the resultant complexity of these additions (along with the comic Falstaff subplot) that make two plays necessary to tell the story, rather than one.

But it is Bolingbroke's relationship with his son, Hal, which is the central focus of these two rich and colorful plays. Prince Hal was already 12 years old when his father assumed the throne. While he was growing up, his father's ambition was carefully concealed. Hal was not bred to be a king, so Shakespeare concentrates on the son's coming of age and accepting of his newfound responsibility. In the process, Master Will takes liberties with history to build the image of the great warrior who would become King Henry V once he accepted his destiny. Early in the play, Hal tells us, though not too directly, couched in metaphors, that he never agreed to be king. He calls it "the debt I never promised."

Here is where the negative characterizations of Bolingbroke should be challenged. What do we see Hal do that should condemn him?

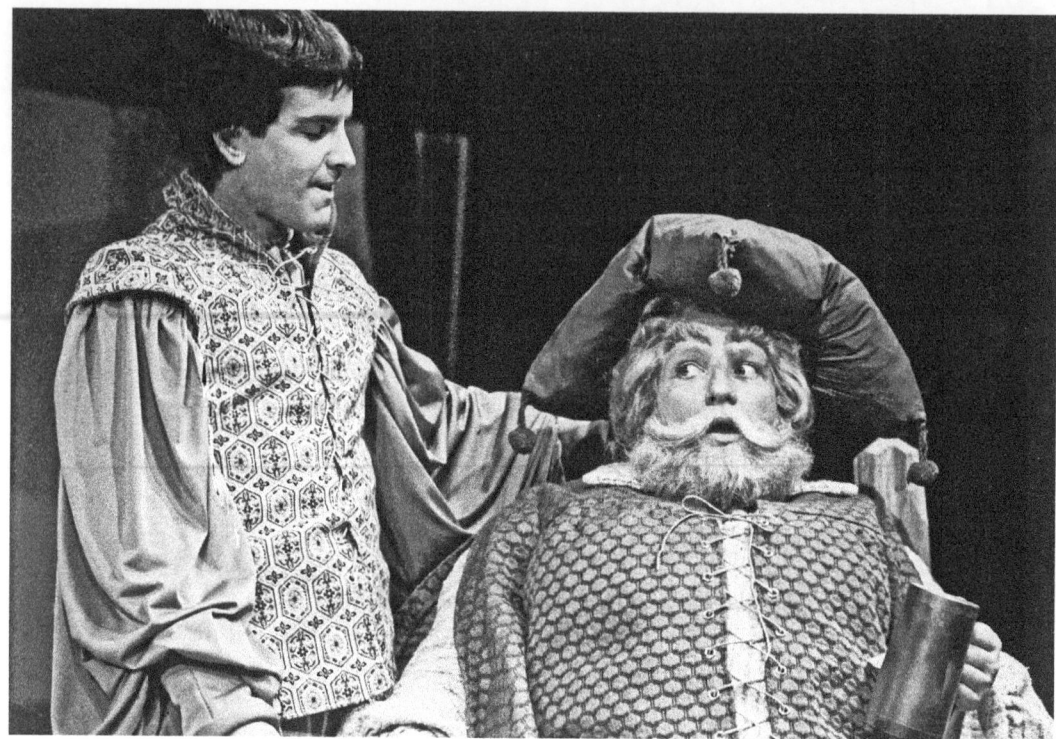

Henry IV, Part 1, New Jersey Shakespeare Festival, 1975: Ron Mangravite as Prince Hal, Clarence Felder as Falstaff (photograph by Blair Holley).

As the play begins, Bolingbroke speaks of his son's riot and dishonor, and later the Archbishop of Canterbury describes Hal's spectacular reformation after his father's death, but what do we see Hal do that is so bad that it requires such reformation? He simply hangs out with Falstaff's crowd, drinks some beer, enjoys a few laughs and the amiable fellowship of a good pub, foils the Gadshill robbery (a minor escapade, of no import), and then goes off to fight valiantly in the wars. Do we ever see him really drunk or even hung over? Do we ever see him with any whores? Is he guilty of influence peddling? Does he appoint his cronies to lucrative positions of power? What does he do to earn his father's condemnation? I think a good argument can be made that Hal wants to be a monarch who knows the real people, not just the pampered jades of the nobility. His behavior in the *Henry IV* plays foreshadows the knowing, sympathetic camaraderie of his pre-battle musings and exhortations in *Henry V*'s "Crispin Day" and "little touch of Harry in the night" speeches.

Isn't his profligate wildness really little more than a figment of his father's imagination? The king complains that he wishes Hotspur were his son, rather than Hal. That's a terrible thing to think, let alone say out loud, and, I believe, a blot on the father's character, not the son's. We are given our children. To compare them negatively to their contemporaries can only do them damage. Our care of them, our example and instruction, can influence them positively or not, but inevitably there comes a point when we must leave them alone to become their own persons.

If Hal truly needs redemption, he has several. The first is when he rescues the king in the duel with Douglas at Shrewsbury in Act V. King Henry IV complains of Hal's dissolute ways, but Hal was raised up in arms in a warrior culture (small Latin and less Greek, but much broadsword and shield and years of horsemanship), and the Hal/Hotspur individual combat is the climax of *Part 1*, so the actors better be prepared to give us a good fight.

Shakespeare places Hal at the battle of Shrewsbury where he kills Hotspur in hand-to-hand single combat. Actually, there is some debate about whether Hal, barely 16 at the time, was even there. The battle was fought on a hot day in a driving rainstorm. Hotspur stopped in the middle of the battle, raised his visor to wipe the sweat out of his eyes, and was struck by an arrow from an anonymous archer right in the forehead. It's ironic that Hotspur's actual historical death vindicates the providential theory of history more dramatically, while Shakespeare's version makes more exciting theatre.

The next redemption is the reconciliation between father and son in IV.5 of *Part 2*. Finally, most tellingly, Hal proves himself worthy as Henry V in the triumph of the French wars.

I don't recall anyone speaking or writing on this question of the validity of Bolingbroke's attitude towards his son. How many performances in the three Bolingbroke plays are based on what is *said* about the characters, rather than what they *do*? I have a strong memory of the early rehearsals of I.2 of *Part 1* in my 1975 NJSF production. Both Hal and Poins wanted to play the scene hung over, with a couple of hookers just hanging out — not participating in the scene, but watching it — thus implying that they had spent the night together. There's nothing in the text to imply that Hal and Poins have been whoring or even drinking. They don't complain of hangovers, no women are mentioned except Mistress Quickly, good naturedly, and the Playwright adds no tarts to the scene. I vetoed the suggestions, choosing instead to simply emphasize the male camaraderie.

While airbrushing Hal's warts can reduce him to a bland Super King-in-training, there's a greater danger in building a character by giving too much credence to what other characters say about him. At the basic actor-training level, we are taught that a character is the result of what he does, what he says and what is said about him. All are important clues; none should be used exclusively in developing an interpretation. If an idea, a line, can be physicalized, if the character can be shown doing something, rather than just talking about it, the impression will be stronger. Character creation is cumulative, working backwards and forwards, the end of the play informing and reinforcing the beginning. The exceptions, of course, are the lies characters tell. I recommend that actors playing Richard II and Prince Hal question what Bolingbroke says about them as he spins and manipulates his way through his reign.

Historicists insist that Shakespeare's life and times informed, influenced all the plays he wrote. Perhaps he was having trouble sleeping when he wrote *Macbeth* or he suffered from the clap when he penned *Timon of Athens*. The death of his young son Hamnet surely was on his mind when he wrote the role of Constance in *King John*. Anti-historicists insist on sticking to the text alone, the text in a theatrical vacuum. Knowing what I do from personal contact with modern playwrights, I don't see how a playwright can possibly escape the influences of his times, especially the pressures of his own success. Arthur Miller couldn't get five minutes into a conversation or a lecture without bringing up the expectations set by *Death of a Salesman*. Edward Albee is clearly political, pro-gay. Shakespeare wrote about what he had just dreamed about.

The comic writing in the *Henry IV* plays is superb. It is comic relief in the true sense of the word, with the Playwright skillfully weaving the comedy into the pattern of more serious matters. As in most comedy, if the scenes are approached realistically, as if the characters are real human beings dealing with real human problems, the comedy will work. If the actors are tempted to play too broadly, there is a real danger that characters in the other plots may be moved to overplay a bit and share some of that lovely laughter. The best

Falstaffs I ever saw were Eric Berry and Clarence Felder, but Falstaff, except for a few soliloquies, is the principal comedian in a gang of clowns, and he needs good support: Bardolph, Poins, Peto, Nym, Ancient Pistol, Falstaff's Page, Mistress Quickly, and Doll Tearsheet. In the 1975 NJSF productions of both plays, Falstaff (Felder), Bardolph (David Howard), Pistol (Eric Tavares), Doll Tearsheet (Y York) and the Page (my son Timothy, then ten years old) played their scenes with the cooperation of circus acrobats.

The Playwright has given us careful and extensive assists in casting these roles. In dialogue and stage directions, their size, age, appearance, physical characteristics, costumes, habits and propensities are described. Note and double underline the Playwright's subtle, but repeated, references about Falstaff's debts. He freeloads off everyone, runs up tabs at the taverns, borrows where he can. This plot point will prove to be very important by the end of *Part 2*.

Falstaff is a knight. His rank is legitimate, but by the time Henry IV becomes king, Falstaff is an old man, grossly overweight, syphilitic, dying (as Henry VIII did) of multiple ailments brought on by a lifetime of indulgences. Though his fighting days are over, he nevertheless goes to war with Hal in hopes of profit. He is skillful at avoiding the actual fighting, then arriving just in time to celebrate the victory. He attempts to take credit for killing Hotspur, but nobody believes him.

The most notable American production of the *Henry IV* plays in recent history was at Lincoln Center in 2003. Unfortunately, realistic box office expectations dictated that the two plays be done as one, a conflation edited by Dakin Matthews, directed by Jack O'Brien, starring Kevin Kline as Falstaff. Much earlier, Orson Welles' definitive film, *The Chimes at Midnight*, was based on a similar cutting. Though the Lincoln Center production was well received, with Kline highly praised, cutting half the text tends to give the whole thing to Falstaff, especially if he's played by the most recognizable star. If both *Parts* are done uncut, on subsequent nights in repertory, as we did in 1975, Falstaff has to exert some effort to hold his own.

Ron Rosenbaum, in *The Shakespeare Wars*, explores two strong influences on Kevin Kline's performance: the scholar, Harold Bloom, and the director, Jack O'Brien. Rosenbaum attended two shows: the third preview and, some weeks later, the final performance. The first appearance of Falstaff follows six minutes of important but bland exposition introducing Bolingbroke, King Henry IV himself, and several matters that concern him. Then, the entertainment begins. Bring on the clowns! Shakespeare gives us the stage direction, "Enter Prince of Wales and Sir John Falstaff," and the first line is a throwaway: Sir John asks what time it is.

Rosenbaum describes the staging of the first moment of this scene in the Lincoln Center production: Falstaff did not enter; he was discovered. The lights went off on the previous scene, Kline entered silently in the dark and took his place on a bench, and then the lights came up on him. A star's entrance applause. Falstaff was alone, no Hal, hung over, exhausted from a night's carousing and whoring on top of some 60 years of such indulgence. He became subtly aware of the audience. He tried to stand up, but this simple exercise required a massive effort of body and spirit. He tried and failed, tried and failed, and each attempt generated howls of laughter from the audience, until Falstaff's cronies finally came to his rescue and got him on his feet. This was classic physical comedy, simultaneously thousands of years of tradition and, at that moment, the invention and sole possession of Kevin Kline. It was a star's moment, the headliner's turn, curtain up, light the lights, and it gave us the summation and present condition of Falstaff. Of course, the crowd loved it.

Kevin Kline put a lot of time and effort into creating the apparent spontaneity of that moment. His costume gave him the appearance of a man twice his weight, but not the feel of that man. He had to work on how it felt to weigh so much more. That opening business, a few moments delightfully added to the text, was well advised and valuable to the production. Anyone who saw the early previews enjoyed the business. I don't know how long it stayed in the play. The worst thing that happens with a piece of business like this is the way it tempts actors to ad-lib. Lines not written by Shakespeare should be not allowed. Grunts, groans, sighs, maybe, but no words.

But at the final performance, Rosenbaum writes, Bloom's Falstaff was gone. Falstaff was still discovered alone on-stage at the top of the scene, but he got to his feet more quickly and easily, and the ensuing performance was sprightlier, less ponderous than that of the third preview. Rosenbaum attributes this change to conscious, intellectual choices made by the actor. I submit that this is the analysis of the scholar, the critic, rather than a practitioner of live theatre. I submit that the changes observed were all organic, subtle, and logical, the result of the audience's reactions to the play over a series of some 60 to 70 performances. Rosenbaum (respectfully) opines that Kline consciously moved to a different performance, but I believe that Kline continued to play the Falstaff he and O'Brien had crafted through rehearsals and previews, and the performance simply evolved.

Is this something new? It always happens in the theatre, given enough performances. Movies are shot in non-consecutive hunks and then edited together, but plays are rehearsed progressively as a whole and it is the audience that completes the performance. It takes some ten to 14 performances before the actors really know the play, through the audiences. Multiple performances are essential to the fulfillment of the play. It's subtle, cumulative, and marvelous. The actors perform, and the audience responds, and then the actor responds to the response, and on and on in a never-ending exchange.

It breaks my heart when kids tell me their high schools only present four performances of a play or musical, and colleges rarely more than seven. The greatest gift I ever gave my company and myself was the opportunity to do uncut Shakespeare in repertory, up to 30 performances of each play, over a period of three to four months.

The positive evolution of a production is a function of continuous performances, up to eight a week, preferably in front of full houses — it's better to perform in a packed 200-seat house than in a two-thirds full 500-seat house. This exquisite happening, this fulfillment, as it evolves in performances, is not intellectual. It's an emotional, sensual collaboration, a reciprocal seduction that can only work if the participants allow it to happen. And it can't be allowed to get sloppy. Ad-libs should be squelched and physical additions scrutinized; the actor must protect herself from letting the thrill of laughter and applause seduce her into indulgent overplaying.

I reiterate: Rosenbaum was writing about two strong influences on an actor's performance, and his conclusion was based on the assumption that actors' choices are rational and conscious. I submit that the most powerful influence was the third one, the living, breathing audience. That's what changes a performance, causes it to evolve over time. That influence is the essence of live theatre, and the best argument I can think of *against* the superiority of films. I suspect Kevin Kline would agree.

There is a comic scene in *Part 1* that requires a skill most actors have, that of mimicry. In II.4, Falstaff suggests that Hal rehearse an interview he has scheduled with his father. They place a joined stool atop a table and use a pillow for the crown. Falstaff impersonates King Henry, and Hal plays himself. Then they switch roles. The actors must watch each other in performance, so each is capable of accurately imitating the other. The imitations need not be exaggerated—accuracy will be funny enough. When the other actors and the audience are added to the scene, the results will be hilarious, and, as with Kline's business above, the scene will grow in performance.

The scene ends with a prophetic moment that is susceptible to milking or "filling." Hal, playing his father, warns Falstaff, playing Hal, of the danger of consorting with Falstaff. The faux "Hal" argues that it might be wise to banish the other Boar's Head companions, but to banish sweet, kind, valiant Jack Falstaff would be to banish all the world. Suddenly, Hal, as himself, says, "I do, I will." He's up on the table on the throne, and he need do little more than assume his own voice and say the line. The moment is startling, and it's followed by a stage direction of loud knocking and the exit of three characters. Falstaff and Hal will be tempted to make something more of this moment, but they should be discouraged. Let the line sit, sink in. Take a short beat then get on to the next extremely active scene. Falstaff never comes back to Hal to ask him what he meant by the line. Let the audience remember and decide.

Who played Falstaff in the original productions of the *Henry IV* plays? There is some, not much, evidence that it was Thomas Pope, who then sold his shares in Shakespeare's company and died before 1604; his replacement played all the Falstaffs. Other scholars insist that it was Will Kempe. Although I have no hard evidence pro or con, I don't think so. Compare Falstaff's soliloquies, his "sitdown" comedy, with Kempe's usual repertoire of comic personae like Lance, Grumio, Bottom, Don Armado, Launcelot Gobbo, and it's evident that Falstaff would have been a departure for him. I'll push my luck even further: I don't think Kempe was capable of playing Falstaff, though he certainly was up to any other member of the Boar's Head gang, and he surely played Pistol in *Part 2*. I refer to Falstaff's soliloquies as "sitdown" rather than "standup" comedy, because each one feels like he's on the way somewhere, and he runs out of oxygen, so he sits down to catch his breath, and while he's there, he talks to the audience.

In addition to his comic scenes, Falstaff has four soliloquies in *Part 1*: IV.2, V.1, V.3, and V.4. They border on sermons or academic lectures, and he refers to the one in V.1 as a catechism. Most important, even though they seek to elicit laughter, they do not seem to invite heckling. He asks questions, but quickly provides his own answers.

But to get back to the larger story of these plays: In previous chapters, I've noted that *Henry IV, Part 1*, *Henry VI, Parts 1, 2 and 3*, and *Richard III* are similar in structure and treatment. This is because their climaxes are strongly physical, depending on the on-stage recreation of actual historical battles, notably Shrewsbury, Orleans, Saint Alban's, Tewkesbury, and Bosworth. That's a lot of fights, as compared to only an imposed minor skirmish in *Richard II*, an aborted battle in *Henry IV, Part 2*, and a comic substitution for the greatest battle in English history in *Henry V*.

Let's take the time to analyze the Battle of Shrewsbury at the end of *Henry IV, Part 1* and the responsibilities of the director and fight choreographer in making this battle serve the text, the play itself. The sequence begins when Hotspur delivers his battle oration. Then he and his army stand their ground while the forces of the king attack. "Alarum to the battle" is the stage direction requiring the director to create a skirmish with actors armed with broadswords, shields, battle axes, maces, spears, accompanied by sound effects: trumpets, neighing horses, the clash of swords on shields, screams, distant cannon, drums. A series of duels follows, each separated by dialogue, ending with the climactic duel between Hal and Hotspur. Here's the list of skirmishes, duels, and intervening dialogue at the end of *Henry IV, Part 1*:

1. V.3 Initial skirmish, all combatants. John of Lancaster fights with Hotspur. The stage gradually empties, leaving only Douglas and Sir Walter Blunt, disguised as the king. Dialogue, then they fight and Douglas kills Blunt. Enter Hotspur, who identifies Blunt's corpse. Hotspur and Douglas exit, presumably to another skirmish.
2. Enter Falstaff, escaping from the battle. He too discovers Blunt's corpse, and tells us that his recruits are all dead or wounded. Enter Prince Hal without his sword (we assume it was broken in battle). He begs one from Falstaff, which Falstaff refuses. Hal takes Blunt's sword and exits to another skirmish. Falstaff soliloquizes again, then exits.
3. V.4. Multiple skirmish: the king, Hal, Hal's younger brother John, Duke of Lancaster, and the Earl of Westmoreland versus several rebels. Hal is wounded and the rebels are driven off. Dialogue. Hal refuses to withdraw for treatment. Westmoreland and John exit. The king brags about how well John fought with Hotspur. Hal exits as Douglas enters from the other direction. Dialogue between the king and Douglas. They fight. The king falls, and Douglas is about to kill him when:
4. Prince Hal re-enters and intervenes, driving Douglas off, saving his father's life. Dialogue between king and prince. The king exits. Several rebels attack the prince, multiple combats. Enter Hotspur from the other direction, fighting with several of the king's men. The stage empties, leaving Hal and Hotspur alone. The climactic duel and the penultimate scene, introduced by some mock courtesy and a bit of boasting. They fight.
5. Falstaff enters, cheers on Hal. Douglas enters and attacks Falstaff. Falstaff feigns death, and Douglas watches as Hal and Hotspur fight. The director has some latitude here as to when Douglas exits.
6. Dialogue between Hal and Hotspur and the death of Hotspur. Hal eulogizes Hotspur, then, discovering the corpse of Falstaff, eulogizes him. He then exits to another distant skirmish, which the audience should not see. At this point, the battle is over, and the Playwright will end the play in another five minutes. Falstaff rises from the dead and plays his grisly scene with the corpse of Hotspur. Later he claims that it was he, not Hal, who defeated Hotspur in single combat.

What has all this accomplished? The obvious: the rebel forces have been defeated by the king without the armies of Northumberland and Glendower. What else? Hal and John of Lancaster both prove themselves as valiant combatants. Had Hal not intervened, Douglas might have killed the king. Bolingbroke's early assessment of his heir as degenerate and unprincely should have been disproved by Hal's triumph over Hotspur. At least we should be sure that God has approved of the future Henry V, because otherwise this would have been a perfect place to kill him off and replace him with the next in line, Thomas, Duke of Clarence.

But there is no time to celebrate. Troubles are brewing elsewhere. The king sends Prince John and Westmoreland north with half the army to encounter the forces of Scroop and Northumberland, while he and Hal head west to do battle with the Welsh and the Marcher barons. There's merely a short breather before *Part 2* begins.

Chapter 24

Henry IV, Part 2

The action continues where *Part 1* left off. Indeed, the Prologue, Rumor, and Scenes I.1, I.3, and II.3 of *Part 2* are continuations of the rebellion that makes up all of Acts 4 and 5 of *Part 1*. Messengers arrive to tell the Earl of Northumberland, Hotspur's father, contradictory stories: that the rebellion has been successful, and both the king and Prince Hal are dead, then the contrary, which we know to be the truth.

Kate Percy, wonderfully playful in *Part 1*, returns as a widow and delivers a spirited diatribe against war. The Hotspurs are one of only two happy marriages in all of the Playwright's works, and here he shatters that marriage. My wife, Ellen Barry, played Kate in both parts, and she was heartbreaking.

At the end of II.3, Northumberland withdraws to Scotland and disappears from the plot. Now the Playwright compresses time again, making a three-year jump to the standoff and treachery that ended the rebellion of Archbishop Scroop, Mowbray, and Hastings in 1405. The Playwright leaps another three years and concludes (off-stage) the opposition of the Percys and the Welsh under Glendower in a few lines. Lord Mortimer, Richard II's choice as his successor, is captured by Bolingbroke and imprisoned; we will see him again in *Henry VI, Part 1*. Shakespeare jumps another six years and goes directly to the death of Henry IV. Nine more years of intermittent peace are disposed of in a matter of minutes, but like the action in *Richard II*, the events in the *Henry IV* plays seem to flow continuously, covering only a few weeks, at best a couple of months.

The Playwright weaves these ongoing events with preparations for a battle at Gaultree Forest (1405). The audience brace themselves for another fierce encounter like the Battle of Shrewsbury, but Prince John tricks the rebels and sends them to the block. The Playwright replaces action with argument and rhetoric, which, after the head-bashing of *Part 1*, is strangely impotent. If the director is tempted to edit the text, here's the place to do it.

Scene III.1, omitted from the Quarto but included in the Folio, recaps the plot from *Richard II* and resolves the Percy rebellion. It includes King Henry's interesting soliloquy about sleep that concludes with the well known, "Uneasy lies the head that wears the crown." It also gives Falstaff some travel time from London to Gloucestershire. Though the remaining scenes include the treachery at Gaultree Forest, the Playwright is aiming at three conclusions: the death of Henry IV, the coronation of Hal as Henry V, and the banishment of Falstaff. Or maybe that's only two.

The early comic scenes in *Part 2* feature the principal comedians from *Part 1* plus Mistress Quickly and Doll Tearsheet. In the latter half of the play, the Playwright gives the ladies a rest and introduces the Justices Shallow and Silence, thus enabling Falstaff to steal even more of the show.

I haven't spent much time discussing the comic scenes, Falstaff and his rep company of clowns, because they're so brilliantly written that they depend primarily upon good casting and the director's willingness to let them work. With scenes like these, the director is extremely important in his capacity as casting director, but serves rehearsal best by providing a safe space in which the actors can explore and fulfill the text, then staying out of the way.

If this is a cop-out, sue me. I remember a performance in 1975, in scene II.4, when Pistol stood on a table pontificating and flourishing his sword, only to have it break and go flying across the stage. No one was hurt, but the dialogue stopped, and the audience screamed with laughter. There ensued a round robin of takes, eye rolling, shoulder shrugging, and more takes from the Boar's Head cronies as the laughter continued. The actors were such accomplished comics, and had established such personal bonds, that they were funny doing nothing. Or next to nothing. This hysteria continued, it seemed, for an eternity until the small Page retrieved the broken sword blade, which precipitated another round of laughter. This could have gone on all night, had Doll Tearsheet not taken charge and driven the scene on toward the exit of Pistol and the next beat. I'll repeat my advice: cast these plays well and stay out of the way.

Henry IV, Part 2, New Jersey Shakespeare Festival, 1975: Clarence Felder as Falstaff, David Howard as Bardolph (photograph by Blair Holley).

The last third of *Part 2*, after the non-battle of Gaultree Forest, pops back and forth between Hal (without Falstaff) and his father, Henry Bolingbroke, and scenes of Falstaff (without Hal) and Justices Shallow and Silence. Hal and Henry attempt reconciliation through manipulation, each trying to convince the other of his own point of view of kingship. Henry IV is dying of a peculiar ailment that is never explained, neither by history nor by Shakespeare. He is only 46 now, but he's already an old man, burdened with his own guilt in the death of King Richard and bemoaning former fellow conspirators now turned enemies. He advises Prince Hal to renew the Hundred Years' War with the French to distract the English people from problems at home. Father and son reconcile, the other sons are called back in for a rare family gathering, and they all exit to the Jerusalem chamber. Henry recounts a prophecy that he would not die but in Jerusalem; we do not witness his actual death. These scenes are very low-energy, gentle, with few fireworks, and the audience can get restless. Nevertheless, this is the play. They can't be rushed.

Meanwhile, back in Gloucestershire, a more amusing pair of scoundrels attempts to manipulate each other to use the future King Henry V to their personal advantage. Justice Shallow has managed to conjure up a close friendship with Falstaff out of a few chance encounters in brothels some 40 years earlier, when Shallow and Silence were studying law at the inns of court and Falstaff was page to Sir Thomas Mowbray. Falstaff does not discourage Shallow's "old buddy" overtures, because Shallow can provide him with recruits, some of whom will pay him bribes to escape impressment. It's possible that Shallow might be a means to even greater riches for the deeply-in-debt fat knight. When Falstaff's tavern-hopping mate, Prince Hal, becomes king, surely there will be advancement for all his friends. Shallow dreams of a seat on the royal bench or an even more lucrative appointment.

The plots converge on a loan of a thousand pounds Shallow makes to Falstaff, but we don't learn about this loan until Shallow, Falstaff, and his cronies arrive back in London for the coronation near the end of the play. The first mention of the loan is V.5.12, and the speech is constructed in such a way that one may believe that Pistol, not Shallow, has made the loan. But that's not possible—Pistol has no money. The loan is too important to the climax of the play not to plant it earlier in the audience's mind, so I suggest the addition of business to show the loan being handed over in V.3 (though it may strain the prop budget if historically accurate—a thousand pounds in coins in 1413 weighed between 500 and 1,000 pounds!). The director should assume that the deal has been struck sometime earlier, but it's contingent upon Hal becoming king. Shallow has advised Davey to collect the money in anticipation of the death of Henry IV. Although they call it a loan, it could be argued that it's a bribe, Shallow buying influence which will surely pay off with a cushy, lucrative high judgeship.

Pistol arrives at Shallow's in V. 3 and, after some teasing, announces, "Henry the Fifth's the man." Falstaff advises Shallow to choose whatever office in the land he wants. Shallow is speechless. Silence passes out, and Shallow gestures to Davey to bring out the money, which he does. The bags or chests are loaded into Falstaff's saddlebags by his cronies, and off they go to London. Falstaff pays his debts, meets his payroll for the first time in months, puts up the bail money for Mistress Quickly and Doll Tearsheet. The money left unspent is then squirreled away all over London, as Falstaff prepares for his warm reunion with Hal.

Here's where traditional interpretation confuses the play and demeans the rascally magnificence that is Falstaff. Now transformed into the perfect king, Henry V, Hal openly rejects his former companions, especially "the tutor and feeder of (his) riots." Note that Poins, Hal's former fellow reveler, is long gone from the plot, probably to double as another character.

Hal orders Falstaff to keep ten miles' distance, but gives him the opportunity of reform and even advancement. Then he exits with his brothers, his nobles, his train. Falstaff is shot down. Or is he?

Traditionally, actors and directors go for a tragic conclusion, assuming that the rejection leaves Falstaff defeated, shattered, on his way to death. But here's where the plant of the loan/bribe from Shallow comes into play, and the addition of the earlier business, allowing the audience to see the transfer of heavy funds, will pay off. We can afford a pause here as the king's entourage exits the stage, covered by drums and trumpets. Shallow, Falstaff, and the Boar's Head gang stand with egg on their faces, waiting for someone, anyone, to speak. Then Falstaff turns the somber moment into one of glee with the simple statement, "Master Shallow, I owe you a thousand pounds." Falstaff has paid off all his creditors, is out of danger of being sent to debtors' prison, has money left over, and Shallow is stuck with the tab.

Shallow sputters, asking for the money back, even half of it, but there's no remedy. Shallow is the patsy, left holding the empty bag. The chief justice and Prince John return with officers to arrest Falstaff and his men, but they run away, except for Shallow who is left to explain that he's an officer of the Crown and guiltless.

And Falstaff survives.

What is lacking in the play, or is severely obscured by other elements, is a true, heartfelt reconciliation of father and son. Perhaps the form and the formality got in the way. Parental relationships change when human beings and their circumstances change. Father and son became different people when Henry Bolingbroke became king. Fourteen years of overpowering pressures and anxieties later, on his deathbed, could the man he had become simply hold his son to him and say, "I love you and I'm proud of you. You'll be a far better king than I was?" Was he capable of such humility? And was the new king capable of believing him?

Shakespeare might have carried Falstaff over into *Henry V*. Indeed, the Playwright wrote an epilogue for *Part 2*, which promises to bring Falstaff back for Hal's French campaigns. But sometime later, something dissuaded him. Audiences who flocked to *Henry V* in hopes of seeing Falstaff as clown advisor to the young king discovered they had been conned by Master Will.

CHAPTER 25

The Merry Wives of Windsor

Legend has it that Good Queen Bess was so taken with Falstaff that she commanded Shakespeare to write another play for him, showing the fat knight in love. Detractors insist that the result, *The Merry Wives of Windsor*, is third-rate Falstaff. But even though it pales in comparison to the superb *Henry IV* plays, this play is superior, when well done, to a lot of what passed for comedy in Shakespeare's time or, for that matter, ours.

We are not sure of the sequence in which Shakespeare wrote *Henry IV, Part 2*, *Henry V*, and *The Merry Wives of Windsor*. It's possible that he kept right on writing the story of Prince Hal, planning to bring Falstaff back, but detoured due to concern that he might steal the thunder of the Super King. Perhaps fellow shareholders in the Chamberlain's Company demanded another kind of play, as *Henry V* eventually became. The Playwright may have written *Henry V* first, then gone back to write *The Merry Wives of Windsor* in response to demand from Falstaff's fans. It's also possible that he wrote the two plays at the same time, as he did *Romeo and Juliet* and *A Midsummer Night's Dream*, which might explain some of the convolutions in *Henry V*.

Falstaff arrives in Windsor with some of his Boar's Head gang, notably Bardolph and Mistress Quickly, though Shakespeare barely uses them as he does in the other plays, and Ancient Pistol is a shadow of his former (and future) self. If Will Kempe played Pistol in *Henry IV, Part 2* and *Henry V*, it's unlikely he was wasted on such a small role as the Ancient becomes in this play. It's more likely that Kempe played Dr. Caius, a wonderful, flamboyant role in the hands of the right actor. *The Merry Wives of Windsor* picks up where *Part 2* left off, with Master Shallow complaining that Falstaff has cheated him and threatening to take him to court to recover the loan, which was actually a bribe. Shallow's cousin, Abraham Slender, also complains that Falstaff's men got him drunk, then rolled him. As in earlier comedies, the action begins with three suitors for the hand of one fair damsel. Young, handsome Fenton is Anne Page's choice, though her mother prefers the prosperous French physician, Dr. Caius, and her father the wealthy naïf, Slender.

Slender appears so totally ignorant of women, so thoroughly incapable of even a simple conversation with one, that it is easy to pull lots of laughs by playing him gay. Wrong. He's a naïf, a fool, and as phony as Sir Andrew Aguecheek, but he's straight.

Sir John is still the happy freeloader of the earlier plays, still trading on some obscure moment of glory lost in the distant past. He never picks up a check, never gets his purse out in time. The essential difference is that this Falstaff is a would-be lover who assumes that two happily married matrons are sexually available. On the contrary, the Pages are one of the two happy marriages in Shakespeare; Mistress Page shares the audience's amusement at Falstaff's presumption and enjoys leading him on. Mistress Ford is equally uninterested

The Merry Wives of Windsor, New Jersey Shakespeare Festival, 1985: Jane Moore as Mistress Page, Robert Machray as Falstaff, Thea Ruth White as Mistress Ford (photograph by Jim Chambers).

in a later-life extramarital affair, but she enjoys the game of duping him as well. The two matrons conspire against him. Falstaff's motives are mercenary, rather than romantic. He harbors the absurd Falstaffian assumption that the way to a man's wallet is through his wife's bed. The fat knight usually has the game figured out. Not here.

If the audience can get by the outrageous premise of the main plot, then the play is smooth sailing, but there's a lot of establishment to be done in the first few scenes. We've seen the fat man before, and we've heard Poins' question, "Is it not strange that desire should so many years outlive performance?" Falstaff is old by Elizabethan standards, diseased and dissolute, but the merry wives are vigorous and healthy. What could he do even if he did manage to get one of them into the sack? Maybe that's the funny part, along with his presumption that his charm will be enough of an aphrodisiac for both of them. Or all three of them.

He sends similar love notes to both wives, and they compare notes and decide to go along with the gag. They confide in each other, not their husbands, but Master Ford suspects Falstaff with his nightcap and attempts to lay a snare for him. Falstaff is trapped in Ford's house and escapes by hiding in a buck basket of soiled laundry, which Ford's servants dump into the river. The fat knight survives drowning and delivers a typical sitdown soliloquy with rich opportunities for shtick and sight gags, seaweed on his head and fish in his pocket. He arranges a second assignation with Mistress Ford, is again trapped, and this time escapes in drag, dressed as a fortuneteller, suspected by Ford of being a witch. Drag is always funny, as long as it isn't overused.

The minor characters here also offer plenty of comedy. Dr. Caius is funny because of his French accent and mangling of English. The Welsh school master Hugh Evans, brother to Holofernes in *Love's Labour's Lost*, also has a comic dialect and also manages to make hash of English as well as Latin. The Latin lesson, where Hugh Evans tutors young and innocent William Page while Mistress Quickly heckles him and gives obscene meanings to the Latin, is a great burlesque sketch, but the Playwright could have put it into any play wherever he needed comic relief. That is to say, it's not organic to this play.

In Master Ford, Shakespeare gives us a parody of the jealous husband whom he later takes deadly seriously in *Othello*, *Cymbeline*, and *The Winter's Tale*. Ford has two excellent soliloquies where he bewails his suspected cuckolding, which should elicit heckling from the audience but never seem to do so today. Ford suspects Falstaff and his wife, but the audience sympathizes with him, rather than ridiculing him.

All the plots are concluded using the now familiar mistaken identity device, which allows the preferred suitor, Fenton, to elope with Anne Page while Falstaff is beaten and pinched, Caius and Slender are humiliated, and Master Ford is reduced to quiet submission for suspecting his virtuous wife. Note that Justice Shallow never gets his money back. Falstaff escapes again.

In the final analysis, *The Merry Wives of Windsor* is pretty thin stuff, but if played by a skillful company of Shakespeareans, audiences love it.

CHAPTER 26

Henry V

I can't remember when I first saw Olivier's film of *Henry V*. I think I saw his *Hamlet* first. The *Henry V* film was a double miracle: in the skill and talent that went into it and in the fact that the British government was actually convinced to provide the money for it as a propaganda film during the dark days of World War II. Somebody was a great salesman.

Olivier won Academy Awards for both films, *Henry V* in 1946 and *Hamlet* in 1948. Both knocked me out long before I ever considered acting or directing Shakespeare.

Olivier's *Henry V* begins with overhead shots of London circa 1600, then dives into the Globe Theatre as the audience gathers for a performance while vendors peddle oranges and ale. The camera wanders backstage to catch the actors preparing, making-up and dressing, boys donning wigs, last-minute running of lines. Then the play begins: as a play, not a film, with the audience a loud and vociferous presence. Olivier maintains the tradition of the prologue, Chorus, advising the audience they'll have to use their imaginations because of the limitations of the playhouse. I have a memory of a line that triggers a mental image:

> Think, when we talk of horses, that you see them
> Printing their proud hoofs i' the receiving earth.

But the camera shows us no horses. Of course. You can't use horses on-stage. They may use an occasional horse in the summer operas in Verona; they even use elephants and camels in *Aida*; but plays usually stick to humans.

Olivier's *Henry V* evolves from play to movie. The moves are surreptitious, gradual, the transition occurring in subtle steps. The first takes place during the second Chorus speech, as the scene actually moves away from London, and, more important, the Globe audience disappears. The scenery is still architectural, still the same dark grays and browns of the playhouse, but we see a Mass being said next to the mast of a sailing ship. The scene approaches the naturalistic.

The next change comes when Mistress Quickly relates the story of the death of Falstaff. We see a bit of the dying old knight in bed, dreaming his fevered memory of his rejection by Hal at the conclusion of *Henry IV, Part 2*. Earlier we saw a boy dressed up as Quickly, but we go further into film here as she becomes a mature actress recounting in quiet detail the end of the Playwright's great comic creation. At this moment, Falstaff fans realize they've been conned by the Playwright: Falstaff won't be back. The Playwright now replaces his cohorts Poins, Peto, and Gadshill with Corporal Nym, a distinct voice from the others, as counterpart to Bardolph and Falstaff's Page. Ancient Pistol becomes the dominant comic.

Further steps into film are taken with a shot of a stormy English Channel and then soldiers on the beach. The transformation is complete when Olivier, in full battle armor, arrives on a war-horse. Now, we're into film with all its possibilities, and we stay in film until the very end where we return to a filmed play, which almost seems gratuitous.

The film is fulfilled with the Battle of Agincourt: hundreds of French and English knights on elaborately caparisoned horses, a full charge to Isaac Walton's symphonic march, and yeomen launching thousands of arrows from behind pickets of ground pikes.

Despite the Chorus' admonition that the only horses we'll see will be in our imagination, 46 minutes into the Olivier film, we see real horses. Within minutes we see hundreds of horses. Horses surround us. Was Olivier saying that film had made the playhouse obsolete?

Now, consider the play, not the movie: everything about *Henry V* is different from the soldier plays that lead up to it. It's as if Shakespeare looked back on those earlier plays, his success as a star Playwright, the possibilities of the new Globe, and decided he could do better if he could cut loose some baggage, abandon some traditions, and begin anew. First, he dumped Falstaff, because Falstaff no doubt would steal the play from Hal as he did in the *Henry IV* plays. Then, Shakespeare examined the structure of the earlier plays and decided that what he had been doing with the battles hadn't ever worked, and it was time to try something new.

This was a gutsy move. If all the Chorus speeches are examined together, his plan becomes apparent. Shakespeare begins by telling us that the play can't be done. He apologizes for the limitations of the stage, for the ineptitude of his actors, the inadequacies of the playhouse, the penurious budgets that make a joke out of famous battles. What

Henry V, Boston Herald-Traveler Repertory, 1965: Christopher Lloyd as Lord Scroop, Melvyn Weinstein as the Earl of Cambridge, Jon Ogden as John Bates, Peter MacLean as Michael Williams, Robert Hazleton as Sir Thomas Gray, Nicholas Kepros as Henry, Michael Randolph as the Herald, Joseph Lo Grippo as Alexander Court (photograph by Chris Grant).

will be his plan, his style of production in *Henry V*? The actors will do what actors always do: they will impersonate human beings in a particular situation, speak of two mighty monarchies, the English channel, ships, thousands of soldiers, the fights themselves, and horses (!!!) while the audience simply imagines all these things. Risky! And for the Elizabethan audience, a whole new way to do a soldier play! Of course, all theatre depends on imagination, empathy, emotional identification between character and audience, but in this play, Shakespeare puts all the crucial action off-stage, even the most famous battle in English history.

In his film, Laurence Olivier used the Crispin's Day speech as a battle oration, brilliantly delivered in full armor from the back of a bucking steed. But that's not what the speech is. The Playwright wrote no battle oration here. Kenneth Branagh, in his later film, plays the speech as I believe the Playwright intended, as a gentle pep talk, while Henry wanders among shivering soldiers in the dawn's first light, those anxious last moments before the battle.

In the play, Shakespeare abandons the literal battles and duels that featured so prominently in *Henry IV, Part 2* and in the *Henry VI/Richard III* plays. What is accomplished by doing this? Instead of violence, we are given the heart and soul of the soldier. The Playwright, in a miracle of doubling, gives us a cast of English and French royalty, nobility, knights, captains, and foot soldiers. Each is given his opportunity to describe the warrior's essence, to praise its noble intentions, to badmouth it, to bemoan it. Though the British government financed Olivier's film during World War II for propaganda purposes, the play does not promote war, nor is it an anti-war play, as a number of my colleagues have conceived it.

Neither pro– nor anti–, *Henry V* is a play *about* war, about the men and boys who practice war. It goes deeply into the causes of wars and questions of the legitimacy and dangers of the warrior's profession. Most importantly, it gives us all sides of the question, insights into the soldiers themselves. No one ever did it better. The play is deeply complex, often convoluted. If produced full-length, the audience can experience the full range of its arguments. Directors can slant it one way or the other with editing, but this will deny the audience the privilege of reaching their own conclusions about the play.

A normal-sized theatre company, however, is hard put to do the play uncut. There are just too many characters, calling for too many costumes and weapons. Directors can create essential differences in style by separating the French from the British, but the cast is so huge that even with an ensemble playing the crowds, the first problem a director has is in the doubling.

Then there's the problem of language. As always, the actors speak English, and we hear English, but what various dialects of English! Some characters are Gaelic speakers, whose English has Irish, Welsh, or Scots accents. Some characters are French who sometimes speak French and other times speak English.

In my 1976 production, I was presumptuous in attempting to communicate more precisely and clearly this variety of language and dialects. When the English and French were on-stage together, they all spoke English, the French using a slight French accent. The Katherine/Alice English lesson scene and the Katherine/Henry wooing scene remained as written. But when the French were alone, they actually spoke French. The text was translated and the actors laboriously (and often reluctantly) learned it. This use of more French angered some audience members, who felt that they were being robbed of plot points (examining the scenes, I disagreed — I felt the playing made the meanings clear). But by and large, the production was very successful, very popular. Eric Booth was a splendid Henry, making all the colors work.

Again: the essence of the play is in the way it reveals the soul of the warrior. The early scenes in *Henry V* argue the politics of the conflict and tie up elements left over from *Richard II* and *Henry IV, Parts 1* and *2*. The invasion itself follows with sieges of several towns and the French response.

The essential scenes dealing with the Battle of Agincourt, before the battle and after, begin with a long preparation, III.7, played by the French nobility, in which they discuss horses, armor, their low opinion of the British. Most directors either cut this scene altogether or edit it severely, but it serves an important purpose in describing the inadequacy of the English forces and the French underestimation of their enemies.

Then the Playwright resumes his playhouse magic, bringing the Chorus back to describe the preparations for battle in the opposing camps. The soliloquy is rich with visual images, with sounds, descriptions of campfires, nervous souls trying to catch a few minutes of sleep while others check and double check equipment. King Harry, himself, does not sleep: he wanders from tent to tent, joining prayers, sharing jokes and words of comfort. He plays a comic scene with Pistol, listens in on another between Gower and Fluellen, and finally arrives at the meager campfire of three foot soldiers, Michael Williams, Alexander Court, and John Bates. Though this is one of many examples of the difficult casting and doubling problems in this play, still the scene must be played by good actors, each arguing a point of view. The soldiers do not recognize the king, and he does not reveal himself to them. They discuss not only the dangers facing them in the upcoming battle but the morality of it. The soldiers wish themselves quit of it, while the King argues for its moral validity. Soldiers obey their superiors. They don't question direct orders. Even if the war is unjust, then their obedience to their king, to their superiors, absolves them of any possible sin: the sin is on the head of the king, and all those who suffer and die in the war will return at the last judgment to bear witness for or against him.

King Harry argues, over-argues, that no man goes to war to die, but to win the battle and return home. The king must proclaim a just war, and all who follow him must agree with him, otherwise, they should not go to war. But try to tell that to a draftee or some poor peasant pressed into service. That Marine mentality I wrote about earlier makes the battle possible. Kings and presidents ponder the morality of the cause. Warriors obey. Harry tells his campfire companions, "Every subject's duty is the king's, but every subject's soul is his own."

The argument grows more heated until Williams and the King almost come to blows. They agree to postpone their quarrel until after the battle, and they exchange gauntlets to wear in their hats, so they will recognize each other if they survive. Bates hauls Williams off, and the King is left to soliloquize on kingship, the man and the office. Compare this speech with Richard II's "graves and worms" reflection. King Harry reflects on what the three yeomen have said about the duty and the fate of the common soldier. He remembers, muses, speaks honestly to the audience. He does not pity himself. He compares his state with that of his peasant soldiers, and this theme carries forward. Erpingham interrupts him momentarily, and then he prays to the God of battles that his father's usurpation of Richard II will not curse this field of Agincourt.

The scene briefly cuts to the French camp then returns to the English army nervously preparing for the beginning of the conflict. They tally up the odds. The English are outnumbered by the French five to one and they are tired, sick, undernourished. Westmoreland wishes that he had a few more men from the ranks of the unemployed in England, and King Harry, entering, hears his comment and chides him for not selfishly hoarding the glory. The King concludes the argument he began with Williams the night before in the "Upon the king" soliloquy. The time for debating the morality of the war is over. The battle will happen. He speaks of the glory this day's battle, on the feast day of the Roman brothers Crispin and Crispianus, will bring to all who die and all who survive. He predicts an evening's drinking in the future where the survivor will show his wounds, bragging of those who fought here, and perhaps earn a pint on the house. The king includes his real brothers, Bedford and Gloucester, then embraces the entire host as his brothers,

> We few, we happy few, we band of brothers,
> For he today that sheds his blood with me
> Shall be my brother; be he ne'er so vile,
> This day shall gentle his condition.

Is he promising them promotion? Or merely lowering himself to their social status?

King Harry rejects the offer of terms of surrender from the French Herald, Montjoy. The Duke of York (Aumerle from *Richard II*) begs to lead the vanguard, and Harry gives him the honor, which costs York his life. Harry then leads his troops off-stage with a last minute prayer, "And how thou pleasest, God, dispose the day." Alarum. Excursions. They all exit, then, while the most famous battle in English history is raging in the wings, Shakespeare gives us a comic scene played by a coward, a braggart, and a boy. For a description of the battle itself, see John Keegan's book, *The Face of Battle*.

There's some evidence that Will Kempe's final performance for the Burbage company was in *Henry V* playing Ancient Pistol, as he had in *Henry IV, Part 2*. If you subscribe to the theory that Kempe played Falstaff, then this theory is blown out of the water. There is no conclusive evidence to substantiate either conclusion. All I can add is my opinion: Falstaff is not a typical Kempe role.

Historically, after Henry V conquered the north of France, a three-way truce was effected among the English, the French and the Burgundians. The Treaty of Troyes (1420) stipulated that Henry would marry the Princess Katherine, daughter of French King Charles VI, and their first-born son would be named heir to the throne of France. This treaty disinherited the Dauphin Charles, the rightful heir by descent.

In *Henry V*, the Playwright brings to fruition his image of the great warrior king. There is no instant realization, no "Eureka!," only an awareness that gradually builds within the audience and within Harry himself as he discovers what it means to be king.

Actors are always susceptible to the times, especially its politics. The actors in our 1976 *Henry V* were so soured by the Vietnam war that they couldn't get their chops around Hal's patriotic rhetoric. They found it emotionally difficult to portray what was in the play. It was a little easier in our 1965 production.

*****

This story may be amusing. It was to me. At the NJSF, we followed our summer classical repertory with straight runs of contemporary plays and, rarely, musicals. The actress who played Alice in our 1976 *Henry V*, Marilyn Cervino, also played one of the twins in *Stop the World! I Want to Get Off* in the fall. At the time, we were still doing two performances on Saturday nights, with only an hour's break between them. One Saturday during the break, the chorus gypsies were complaining vehemently about having to do two shows in one night. Marilyn pointed out that we had done two performances of *Henry V* on Saturday nights all summer, to which one of the chorus girls replied, with conviction and a strong Brooklyn whine, "Yeah, but ya don't hafta' sing and dance in Henry tha' Fifth."

CHAPTER 27

Henry VI, Part 1

It is unfortunate that when the *Henry VI/Richard III* plays are done at all, a tradition has arisen of doing only conflated versions in three evenings, rather than as four full-length plays. John Barton began it in 1963. The fear is that the audience may be willing to sit still for three evenings of plays on the same subject, but not four. To be more precise, Barton left *Richard III* relatively intact, while he boiled the eight hours of the three *Henry VI* plays down into two evenings. Barton's editing is masterful, and he even wrote a few scenes, Shakespeare style, to bridge events or develop characters who seemed slim to him. His director, Peter Hall, referred to Barton's work as "the ultimate literary heresy."

The New York Shakespeare Festival followed suit in 1970 with Stuart Vaughan directing, and the NJSF did it again in 1983, in repertory, calling the three evenings *The Wars of the Roses*. I directed all the plays, using my own cutting, even though I was in possession of John Barton's editing and probably could have gotten permission to use it.

Henry VI, Part 1 was the first play produced with Shakespeare's name on it. It was probably a reworking from an earlier play, surely a collaboration.

Henry VI was crowned King of England at the age of nine months, and soon after, upon the death of Charles VI, the infant became King of France as well, disinheriting Charles the Dauphin, in accordance with the Treaty of Troyes. *Part 1* covers the time from Henry V's death at the age of 35 in 1422 to the betrothal of his son, Henry VI, to Margaret of Anjou in 1444.

A practical matter here: Since the *Henry VI/Richard III* tetralogy covers the entire life of Henry VI, it could have presented us with a difficult casting problem. Certainly, a skillful actor can play the king from age 14 through his death at the age of 50, but another actor, a child, is needed to play him pre-age 14. The playwrights solved the problem by keeping young Henry off-stage while subplots were developed, notably the rivalry between Humphrey, Duke of Gloucester and the Archbishop of Winchester; the establishment of the conflict among the houses of York, Lancaster, and Neville; and the war in France. Sequence is difficult to pinpoint here, because the playwrights juggled and juxtaposed important events. Suffice it to say that the actor who will play Henry VI through the rest of the tetralogy does not make his first appearance until III.1 of *Part 1* at Parliament, where he names Richard Plantagenet Duke of York.

In Barton's adaptation, the first of the three evenings, called *Henry VI*, ends with the death of the Earl of Surrey. I felt that this division, with Margaret lamenting over the severed head of her lover, put too much importance on Surrey and on their affair. The second play, called *Edward IV*, begins with a scene written by Barton, summarizing intervening events. In my restructuring of the three plays into two, I ended the first evening following *Part 2*,

Act III, which put a greater emphasis on the deaths of Gloucester and Winchester. Our second play, also called *Edward IV*, began with Surrey's capture by pirates.

We began rehearsals for this epic undertaking working out of sequence to establish rivalries and competition in the English court before introducing the French. We didn't perform the play that way. We stuck to the playwrights' chronology wherever possible, beginning with the funeral of Henry V and moving progressively to the victory of Henry VII at Bosworth. I remember the whole season as spending three months at a funeral.

Shakespeare includes in *Henry VI, Part 1* one of the strangest people who ever lived: the young peasant woman who called herself "la Pucelle," the Maid, known to us today as Joan of Arc. Volumes have been written about her, her victories, her trial and conviction, the subsequent trial that reversed her earlier conviction, her ultimate execution, and the laborious process that eventually led to her being named a Saint of the Catholic Church, replacing Saint Denis as Patron Saint of France.

Joan has been dramatized by such luminaries as George Bernard Shaw, Maxwell Anderson, Jean Anouilh, and Bertolt Brecht. Shakespeare's Joan, a decidedly English chauvinist creation, is very different from any of these, and it is worth reviewing the historical facts to better appreciate the difference. Born in 1412, Joan was 17 when she began her short, spectacular career as savior of France. Charles the Dauphin was 26, and Henry VI was a child of eight.

The premise of Joan's mission was a blend of religion and patriotism. She believed that God spoke directly to her through two saints and an archangel, and God's justice ordered that France belong to the French, that France should be ruled by a French king. This interdependency of faith and nationalism was certainly not a novel idea, and it is still with us today. What better example than the modern state of Israel, which dates its foundation from the Book of Exodus?

Henry V had conquered the north of France and his brother John, Duke of Bedford, had laid siege to its second largest city, Orleans, some 60 miles south of Paris. If Orleans fell to the English, there was no way that Charles the Dauphin could be crowned king at the Cathedral of Reims.

Why did all those Frenchmen so eagerly follow her, scarcely a woman, an unknown peasant child who overnight was hailed as a military genius? First, France needed a hero, a leader. The Dauphin Charles did not seem willing to fight for his rights. He was well off, comfortable, and the British and Burgundians seemed content to leave him alone. After several years of renewed hostilities with the English, French morale was at its lowest ebb. The siege of Orleans had lasted 210 days. The English were starving the defenders without having to sacrifice any of their own men.

From the time Joan first came forth, her message was simple and direct. She was sent by God to rally the French, drive the English back to the Channel and deliver Charles for coronation as the rightful king of France, in defiance of the Treaty of Troyes. There was nothing timid or hesitant about her. She presented herself not as a saint, but merely as a messenger, and she was absolutely certain of the rightness of her cause. Men followed her, emulating the ferocity of her enthusiasm, because they believed in her.

The soldiers outfitted her in fighting gear, armor, and the sword of Saint Catherine, and they gave her a good horse. Joan refused to leave military decisions to the generals and captains. Her orders were practical, but courageous, and she insisted they were God's decisions, not her own. Noblemen, captains, and soldiers alike marveled at her military acuity. She was either divinely inspired and blessed or simply lucky: the first miracle attributed to

her was little more than a wind shift that allowed French supply barges to move upstream to Orleans before the English could stop them.

Joan led troops into battle with unwavering courage, but she herself did not fight. She carried Catherine's sword, but she shed no enemy blood. Indeed, there were tales of her gentleness and mercy in caring for the English wounded as well as the French. During the battle for Orleans, she was severely wounded by an English arrow, but did not withdraw from the assault until she collapsed from loss of blood, and she was soon back in the battle. Under her direction, the siege was lifted in nine days and she eventually effected the coronation of the Dauphin as Charles VII.

Her campaigns continued after the coronation until she lost the battle of Compiegne, was captured by the Burgundians, and sold to the English. Through an absurd trial, Joan defied the hierarchy of the established Church, which branded her as a witch and a blasphemer. She was said to have been convicted of heresy on her own testimony.

If it was a mystery why so many followed this simple peasant girl in her quest in the first place, it was equally strange that, after her capture, no one came to her rescue. There were no offers of ransom. The king she had raised to the throne, Charles VII, had absolutely nothing to say about her capture or her trial.

Joan was burned at the stake May 30, 1431, in the city of Rouen. The coronation of Henry VI as King of France took place the following December in Notre Dame Cathedral, Paris. John, Duke of Bedford, died in September 1435; Charles VII reconciled with the Burgundians three months later, and they moved jointly against the English. In the spring of 1456, the Church convened a second trial to reexamine Joan's condemnation to death 25 years earlier. On July 7, 1456, 136 years before Shakespeare wrote his play, she was declared innocent of all charges. She was canonized in 1920, nearly 500 years after her death.

These are the facts about Joan of Arc, the basis of all the books and plays written about her. Almost without exception, these works take the French view that Joan was saintly. But this is not Shakespeare's Pucelle. His Joan, following the British hard line, is indeed a witch, a mad woman, and a tart. I repeat my earlier warning: any young actress hired to play Joan is likely to resist Shakespeare's characterization and try to play G. B. Shaw's lyric Joan, which, of course, will knock *Henry VI, Part 1* off balance.

Shakespeare's Pucelle is a witch in every sense of the word as the British understood it (see the *Macbeth* chapter). In *Part 1*, V.3, deserted by Charles and the French loyalists, left alone with the audience, she calls upon the Devil, lordly Monarch of the North, and his fiends to assist her. They appear, but do nothing. She refers to nursing them with her blood and offers to cut off a breast in appeasement. They hang their heads. She offers her body. They refuse. Finally, she tells them to take her body, soul and all. They desert her, leaving her unprotected, before Richard of York and the English capture her. In V.4, she rejects her father, a gratuitous addition by the playwrights, insisting that she is of noble birth. She first insists that she's a virgin, then confesses that she's with child by the Duke of Alençon, then changes her story yet again to blame her pregnancy on Reignier, King of Naples. When York assures her that no unborn child will save her from the stake, Shakespeare gives her a moment of dignity and resignation, which she squanders to prophetically curse the divided England to darkness and death. In Shakespeare's play, we do not see the trial,

Opposite: *Henry VI, Part 1,* New Jersey Shakespeare Festival, 1983: Lisa Barnes as Joan of Arc; William Pitts as Charles, the Dauphin (photograph by Blair Holley).

execution and death of Joan. In our production, we yielded to the temptation and put her burning at the stake on-stage. The effect was, at best, symbolic.

Aside from the scenes of Joan and the French wars which continue the story begun in *Henry V*, a familiar problem is re-introduced in the *Henry VI* plays, echoing the back story of *Richard II*: that of a child king supervised and controlled by powerful relatives. In this case, the young Henry VI is the pawn of his uncles, Humphrey, Duke of Gloucester, and Henry Cardinal Beaufort, Bishop of Winchester, and his cousin, Richard Plantagenet, Duke of York, grandson of the inept Edmund, Duke of York. The rivalry among the three carries over into the next two plays, and explodes into civil war between the Lancastrians and the Yorkists for the throne of England, which ultimately costs the English those French territories won by Henry V.

In *Part 1* characters first introduced in the *Henry IV* (Bolingbroke) plays resolve their plots and die, notably John of Lancaster, Duke of Bedford, who first distinguished himself at Shrewsbury. Richard of York replaces him as Regent of France. As the rivalry continues, the English strength is sapped in battle. Among the dead are the heroes John Talbot and his son.

Toward the end of the play, a new plot development is introduced. The Duke of Gloucester suggests that King Henry VI ensure peace by marrying the daughter of the French Earl of Almanac. Henry reluctantly agrees, but in the same battle of Angers where la Pucelle is captured, the Earl of Suffolk captures Margaret of Anjou, daughter of Reignier, King of Naples. Suffolk falls in love with Margaret and proposes that she marry the English king, while taking himself as her lover. He negotiates with her father, agreeing to return to him the provinces of Maine and Anjou if he agrees to the marriage. Note that Suffolk has yet to propose this marriage to Henry. He's playing a dangerous game.

The play concludes with a truce between Richard of York and Charles VII breaking off the betrothal agreement of the young King Henry VI and the daughter of Almanac, which clears the way for his betrothal to Margaret of Anjou. Suffolk compares himself to Paris of Troy, kidnapper of Helen, and promises us that Margaret shall be queen and rule the king, while Suffolk rules them both. The Treaty of Troyes is out the window, Charles VI is King of France, and Henry VI sits uneasily on a throne challenged by Richard of York and his followers.

Any director editing the three plays into two must simplify, combine characters, and juxtapose scenes. Long before casting began, over six months before the first play opened, I had to construct a character by scene chart suggesting how doubling could be done. The chart took up half a wall in my dining room. Because of Equity rules on doubling, I had to know what the doubles would be before offering jobs. I wound up hiring an Equity company of 23 supported by an Intern company of 40 for the *War of the Roses*. Even after eliminating and consolidating characters, my cast list included the following:

12 named characters from the House of Lancaster,
11 from the House of York,
three from the House of Neville,
20 from the English nobility,
plus 13 knights, four churchmen, seven of the English gentry, 17 commoners,
and ten from the French royalty and nobility.

That's a total of 98 named characters, all with lines, many requiring both court and battle costumes. Even though tights, boots, helmets, gauntlets, armor, and leggings could be doubled and tripled, and our costumer, the talented and resourceful Kathleen Blake, relied on color coding to keep things as clear and simple as possible, consider the number of tabards, shields, and doublets for the nobility on both sides that were built for that company! We had to add a portable dressing room to house all the soldiers and equipment. The usual theatrical devices of clarification are difficult to employ in the *Henry VI/Richard III* plays. There are too many battles and individual duels. A scene packed with English is followed immediately by a scene packed with Frenchmen. These plays are an epic effort even for a large, well-endowed company, and were certainly a triumph for us, with our modest budget and 238-seat theatre. Is it possible that they were originally done with a company of only 16?

One positive result of that 1983 season was my resultant disgust with severe editing. From then on, I pushed for full-length productions. As usual, the philistines objected, citing the audience's lack of tolerance and bowing to that stalwart of the community who complains that he has to get up the next morning to go to work.

How many theatres in America have the capacity, the sheer volume of resources, to attempt the *Henry VI/Richard III* plays in the winter time? At least in the summer, we could spread out on the side lawn.

CHAPTER 28

Henry VI, Part 2

If I were ever to tackle the *War of the Roses* again, I'd schedule *Henry VI, Parts 1 and 2* one season, take a long winter vacation in the Caribbean, then do *Part 3* and *Richard III* the following season. Never again such severe editing as in 1983. I began with original texts running to 11 hours of playing, cut some three hours out of them them interlineally, then rehearsed and played what was left in a straight line for three months. Now, some 27 years later, I'm trying to reassemble the four plays as if they were about to be produced as first written, full-length.

The *Henry VI* plays suffer, as do *Julius Caesar* and *Antony and Cleopatra*, from the playwrights' fidelity to their historical source. Many characters appear in these plays simply because they lived during the time and were included by the chroniclers. It was then up to the playwrights to work them into the story and give them a dramatic function. On the other hand, many of the characters are fascinating enough to hold center stage in their own plays, their own stories, but the four plays are primarily about the rivalry between the houses of York and Lancaster, and everyone else became a functionary.

The vacillations of Richard, the Earl of Warwick, "the kingmaker," for example, his victories and defeats, and the eventual fate of his daughter, Lady Anne Neville, deserve a play or novel of their own. Instead, the *Henry VI* plays keep him in the cast lists for all three parts, but give him insufficient importance. The rivalry between Humphrey of Gloucester and Thomas Cardinal Beaufort over the young King Henry VI smolders and sizzles and gives us a bit of excitement throughout *Parts 1 and 2*, but a cynic might ask whether they'd be in the plays at all if John of Gaunt had not had two wives and many children.

The romance of Margaret of Anjou and the Earl of Suffolk promises some good racy scenes, but delivers little. His death at the hands of pirates seems gratuitous, and the only solid dramatic payoffs are the scenes where she plays with his severed head as if it were a newborn child. Luckily for all the plays, the playwrights fell in love with Margaret too and gave her much stage time over the course of all four plays.

Henry VI, Part 2 starts immediately after *Part 1* ends and covers the ten years from 1445 to 1455. I reiterate what I stressed in the Chronicle Plays chapter: that Shakespeare was working from the revised history of England written by Tudor propagandists employed by Henry VII. In writing these plays, the original playwrights made further revisions for dramatic purposes. Today's directors must construct their own calendars and genealogical charts that will make casting, doubling, and staging possible.

The Hundred Years' War comes to an end sometime during the final scenes of *Part 1* and the early scenes of *Part 2*. Since the playwrights' focus was on the politics and personalities that created the rivalries among the families of York, Lancaster, and Neville, the actual end of the war is fogged in the plays, and the director is tempted to alter scenes and events to make some sense of the chronology. The deaths of Joan La Pucelle and John Talbot, for example, are juxtaposed; history and the plays do not match up. The French retook Normandy from 1449 to 1450 and would have taken Calais as well had not a separate truce, in 1453, bowed to commercial interests and allowed Calais to remain a free-trade zone, a cynical, pragmatic decision if there ever was one.

Not with a bang, but with a whimper did the Hundred Years' War end. Even the name is inaccurate: it actually lasted at least 115 years. But only well-made plays neatly begin and end. In reality, events cross, blend into each other. Once again, I urge directors to approach the eight plays of the double tetralogy as one long epic, no matter how many of them are actually planned for production.

Henry VI, Part 2 begins with the marriage of Henry VI to Margaret of Anjou, engineered by Margaret's lover, the Earl of Suffolk. Soon after the British withdrawal from France, the political wrangling between the Yorkists and Lancastrians degenerated into armed warfare. For the common grunt in the trenches, the time of peace was indeed too brief. Any person (male or female) could become sovereign of England if they could claim one drop of royal blood, no matter how far back in their ancestry. This meant that at any given moment there were many contenders for the crown, and since the royals were given to marrying distant (and not so distant) cousins, some of them might base their claim on multiple royal ancestors. The sons of Richard of York were a good example: descended as they were from two sons of Edward III, they could argue that their claim was greater than

Henry VI, Part 2, New Jersey Shakespeare Festival, 1983: Annalee Jefferies as Margaret of Anjou; Davis Hall as King Henry VI; Jeff King as Clifford; J.C. Hoyt as the Earl of Northumberland; Brett Porter as Edward, Earl of March (photograph by Blair Holley).

that of the sitting Henry VI. The counter argument was simpler: Henry VI was the only son of Henry V, who had been the eldest son of Henry IV — a clean, direct line.

Unlike the unrelenting heaviness of *Part 1*, this play gives us some comic relief. The rivalry between the Duke of Gloucester and Henry, Cardinal Beaufort, should have resolved itself now that the boy king has reached his majority, but it continues and becomes an annoyance to other factions at court. Gloucester's wife, Eleanor, enlists the aid of sorcerers and witches to harm the Cardinal, but she is exposed by a confidant, the priest John Hume, arrested, convicted, and made to do public penance. In I.4, spirits are summoned and questioned about the future. Compare this scene with *Part 1*, V.3 in which Joan bargains with the Devil, and the chapter on *Macbeth*. Though James I/VI's *Demonology* was not published until 1597, his interest in the subject began with the witch trials of 1590 in Scotland, and Shakespeare, writing this play in the early 1590s, could have had access to James' earlier writings.

Before they show us the punishment of Duchess Eleanor, the playwrights give us a genuinely funny scene, in which a man, allegedly blind since birth, has his sight restored at the shrine of Saint Alban. King Henry, in his piety, believes the man's story, but Humphrey of Gloucester puts him to some tests and exposes a hoax. While this scene scarcely advances the larger plot, it is true situation comedy, played naturalistically, resolving in the running escape of the con man.

Eleanor is brought to trial and convicted of treason and witchcraft. She will be required to do three days' public penance, then banished for life to the Isle of Man, while her accomplices, the witch Margery Jourdain and the priests, are convicted and sentenced to death. Duke Humphrey resigns as Lord Protector. The public penance of the Duchess reads as a tame scene, almost dignified, in the text, but the custom of the times was for the common people to take boisterous and cruel revenge on the repentant sinner. All protocol was suspended. They could insult her as they liked, throw rotten fruit and vegetables at her, yank at her gown, spit at her, anything short of real violence. That's what we did.

The playwrights next give husband and wife a gentle farewell scene, but Gloucester is arrested soon after for treason, imprisoned and murdered by assassins. To keep things neat, Cardinal Beaufort commits suicide, and the Earl of Suffolk is killed by pirates soon after.

The question of democracy, rule of the majority, is raised in the treatment of Cade's Rebellion, which follows. Is this examination unbiased? Certainly not in a country ruled by Elizabeth. However, there is no evidence that Elizabeth objected to the Cade scenes or anything else in the plays until she saw the abdication scene in *Richard II*. Then she registered her objection. The primary function of Cade and his followers might be structural and utilitarian, but they are akin to the mechanicals in *A Midsummer Night's Dream*, and they provide effective comic relief as well. Will Kempe may have played Cade; we have no evidence either way, though Kempe and his hecklers would have had a heyday with Cade's scenes, challenging the audience to join the rebellion, then playing his campaign speeches directly to them. Cade's platform as he hucksters cross-country, picking up followers by promising political reform and "lower taxes, greater benefits" for the lower classes sounds like something straight out of recent American campaigns. Look what that platform promises: a 70 percent reduction in the cost of bread and beer, fountains that run red wine, ultimately the elimination of all money, account keeping, schools, and printing. He promises free food and clothing at government expense, the death of all lawyers and the elimination of all written contracts. Cade wants to bring down the jails and enclosures, free all prisoners, open all lands common for hunting and grazing. Though these scenes may tempt actors into overplaying, there is definitely fun to be had by giving Cade and his followers free rein, in contrast to the formality of the proceedings so far. The playwrights were not ridiculing the commons so much as giving the audience an opportunity to question democracy itself. Cade's Rebellion, like all rebellions, is a reaction to the oppression of taxation. Yet, without taxation, there would be no government benefits, no roads, no armies, no courts, no protection of the old and infirm. Cade's followers see no advantages, only the taxman with his hand out. They have yet to learn that there's no such thing as a free lunch.

And Cade, claiming to be descended from Lionel, Duke of Clarence, the third son of Edward III, would be king of this chaos. As just reward for abolishing all the laws of the land, his followers would restore to him the custom of droit de seigneur. Finally, the rebellion blows up in his face. He escapes the wrath of his own followers, only to die a few days later at the hands of a Kentish squire, who then sends his head to the king.

Then comes an exciting moment: the arrival of Richard, Duke of York, in full battle armor and chain mail, surrounded by his four sons, Edward, George, Richard, and Edmund, as they will appear throughout the rest of the tetralogy. Finally we have an out and out battle for the crown at the first battle of Saint Albans, won by the Yorkists, supported by Warwick. Margaret appears on the field of battle in armor, a more formidable warrior than her husband, Henry. We are introduced to young Richard of Gloucester, the future Richard III, in his first battle, defeating John Beaufort, Earl of Somerset, while York kills Clifford, and Young Clifford helps King Henry and Queen Margaret escape. Time to tally up the corpses and determine who is left to fight their way through *Part 3*.

Anyone who saw our 1983 repertory would remember all the battles, especially the frequency of them. It seems we spent every play alternating between shouting matches and head bashing. In the chapter on the Warrior Plays, I mentioned the training of combatants for broadsword and shield. Basically, the actors were taught five cuts and five parries, and then combinations of those moves. For the *War of the Roses* repertory, we developed three basic combats, which everyone learned. The first was the one-on-one and involved up to 20 cuts and parries. Then, the three-way involved one principal combatant fighting two opponents in a 20-cut sequence. Finally, the most elaborate of all involved first one-on-one, then two versus one, then three versus one, until one of the multiple opponents was killed and dropped out of the action; then we were back to the three-way, which could be aborted at any time while the combatants raced off-stage. Each principal learned three fights, but they were the same three fights over and over again. The foot soldiers who constituted all the armies learned the one-on-one and the same corner in the three-way and the four-way.

These fights were first taught for technique, then choreographed, then drilled. A foot soldier could, in effect, be plugged in anywhere. Those who worked the "death corner" could die over and over again without being recognized by the audience. Phil Prestamo told me that he died seven times in the three evenings.

*****

We had a faithful subscriber, Mrs. John Fleming, who held the same seat downstage right in the first row over many seasons. I always made sure the fights dropped a strapping young man at her feet in every soldier play.

CHAPTER 29

Henry VI, Part 3

Henry VI, Part 3 begins where *Part 2* left off. In our shortened version, we didn't even take a breath, as if the battle of Saint Albans continued on into *Part 3*. But re-examining the original text, we see that the Yorkists won the first battle of St. Alban's, then chased the Lancastrians back to the House of Parliament in London, where Richard of York assumed the throne and demanded that King Henry abdicate. After a hollering match, during which the opposing arguments about who is the rightful king are again dragged out and debated, they come to a compromise, similar to that of the Treaty of Troyes of 1420: Henry shall continue as king, but Richard of York shall be his heir, disinheriting Henry's son by Margaret, Edward, Prince of Wales. Margaret, of course, protests and goes off to take command of the Lancastrian army, leaving Henry alone. The sons of Richard of York debate the compromise until we're ready for another battle, then off we go.

In the ferocious "handkerchief" scene engineered by Queen Margaret, Richard of York is captured, humiliated, and put to death. The sons of York rally, proclaim Edward their leader, exchange insults with Margaret and her confederates, then charge back into yet another battle. Suddenly there is a quiet moment where we are given a glimpse of the master dramatist to be. In the second battle of Saint Albans, Margaret and Young Clifford take King Henry out of the battle and force him to wait and watch until the fight is over. Henry meditates on what his life might have been had he been born a shepherd, not a king. This soliloquy and the touching scene that follows are breathtaking in their beauty.

Some time, somewhere during *Part 2*, Shakespeare became a playwright: no longer an apprentice, not yet a master craftsman, but certainly a respectable journeyman. He was born a poet, and he now became a dramatist, able to combine facility with language with the actor's double sense of the visceral and the theatrical. All around him, he had vivid examples for his soaring iambic pentameter passages, notably the works of Christopher Marlowe, all written in the few years before Marlowe's untimely death in 1593. The soliloquies in *Henry VI, Part 3* are superb poetry and effective character studies as well, notably those given to King Henry VI and Richard of Gloucester.

I wish I knew how a playwright emerges. To say one is born is only to perpetuate the mystery in poetic fancy. A child learns letters, then words, then language. The process is as old as the human species. Many playwrights begin as actors. Actors must be able to improvise, adjust when a mishap occurs on-stage. A playwright hears dialogue in his head, then writes it down; when he reads it back, it changes, moves away from the writer. Shakespeare was probably acting in these history plays as he was collaborating in their writing. It was like what we term today a workshop process: a group collectively writing a dramatic work as they went along, much as the musical group memoir, *A Chorus Line*, was created. The

Henry VI, Part 3, New Jersey Shakespeare Festival, 1983: Annalee Jefferies as Margaret of Anjou; John Hertzler as Richard, Duke of York; John Hoyt as the Earl of Northumberland; Jeff King as Clifford (photograph by Blair Holley).

play doctor then takes the mish-mash back to the drawing board and crafts a structured play out of it.

In Master Will's time, any play that had any value would probably get produced — the Burbage company was always hungry for new works. Eugene O'Neill's plays were produced at the Provincetown Playhouse in Massachusetts where he lived and worked. He wrote 64 plays over 40 years, varying wildly in length and complexity. Most critics agree that the first ten or 12 were garbage; if he were writing today, the market probably would force him to quit after the first five. Shakespeare and O'Neill could learn their craft by seeing their plays performed and hearing audiences react to them. Sadly, in the current economy, playwrights are seldom given the opportunity to move beyond the endless, even counter-productive, workshop discussions and on to the stage.

As Shakespeare became more adept at connecting words, speeches, and emotions, he was given more to do. The Henry VI soliloquies are certainly his. It's possible that he returned to the these plays in later years and improved on them, especially *Part 3*.

Back to the field, where the playwrights have combined the battles of Ludlow, Northampton, Wakefield, and Towton, and covered the events of five years in a few minutes of stage time. The Yorkists triumph, Young Clifford dies, King Henry is banished, and York's eldest son seizes the throne as Edward IV. Edward takes the widow Elizabeth Grey to wife, and his younger brother, Richard of Gloucester, in a long soliloquy, confides his ambition and plans to steal the crown. The treaty of 1460 had given the House of York the right to succeed Henry VI at his death, but not to usurp him. Nevertheless, Henry went into exile, and Edward ruled for nine years before the combined forces of Margaret and

Warwick restored Henry to the throne in 1470. Shakespeare covers these nine years in less than a half hour's stage time. Warwick deserts Edward IV to join with Margaret and her forces from France. He marries his daughter to Prince Edward, son of Margaret and Henry, and Henry is restored to the throne. Within the year, Edward of York returns from the Continent with an army, defeats and kills Warwick at Barnet, then defeats Margaret and her forces at Tewksbury, where her son, Prince Edward, is butchered by the three York brothers in a scene that calls to mind a ritual sacrifice.

Henry is removed to the Tower, and Edward IV returns to Parliament to reclaim the throne. V.6 of *Part 3* is a scene worthy of the mature Shakespeare: the final debate between Henry VI and Richard of Gloucester on the primary argument, who shall be king, and then Richard's taunting and murder of Henry. It is brutal and exquisite. There remains one more scene, the re-coronation of Edward IV, which can either end *Part 3*, or, my preference, open *Richard III*.

CHAPTER 30

Richard III

Just as the Bolingbroke plays might be seen as prelude to the saga of Super King Henry V, so too do the *Henry VI/Richard III* plays lead up to the victory and crowning of the first Tudor, Henry VII. Earlier, I described the efforts of Henry VII and his propagandists to legitimize his claim to the throne by rewriting history. In so doing, they characterize Henry VI as a saint and the Yorkists as usurpers.

The play *Richard III* was probably Shakespeare's alone. Thomas More, lawyer, jurist, theologian, later Lord Chamberlain to Henry VIII, was one of the principle Tudor revisionists. In his book entitled *The History of Richard III*, More pictures Richard as a monster, deformed in mind and body. There are two distinct versions of this work, one in English and one in Latin, that do not line up exactly. Neither can be said to be a translation of the other, and the work was never finished. The English version probably served as Shakespeare's source for his play, though he was capable of reading the Latin version as well.

Shakespeare went More one better by giving Richard some of the longest soliloquies in the Canon, in which he takes responsibility for and gleeful satisfaction in every dirty deed done during his lifetime. In one of the early soliloquies, Richard compares himself to "the murderous Machiavel" even though Nicoli Machiavelli didn't write *Il Principio* (*The Prince*) until 47 years after Richard's death. The first three acts of Shakespeare's *Richard III* are based on More's work; Acts 4 and 5 are the Playwright's own invention.

I directed three productions of *Richard III*, the first in 1964, the second at the Asolo Theatre in Sarasota, Florida, in 1978, and the third as part of the NJSF's *The War of the Roses* in 1983.

As we've seen, Shakespeare first introduces Richard, along with his brothers, at the first battle of Saint Albans, V.1 of *Part 2*, where Richard's first line has to do with "speaking" with his sword. Richard's alleged deformity is first referred to in a line of Young Clifford's at the conclusion of this scene. Richard kills the Duke of Somerset at this battle, quite a stunt because Richard was only four years old when it was fought. When we next see him, at the beginning of *Part 3*, he's carrying the severed head of Somerset.

The third son of Richard of York, this Richard is redrawn as a crippled homicide, the personification of pure evil. He's bloodthirsty, hungry for power, and when he becomes king, he doesn't know what to do with it. An examination of Richard's three soliloquies — two in *Part 3*, III.2.124 to 195 and V.6.61 to 93, and the opening of *Richard III*— provide a full blueprint of his deformities as well as his intentions. It's become fashionable for actors playing Richard to take patches of the earlier speeches and combine them with the "winter of our discontent" speech. According to Thomas More, Richard of Gloucester was born prematurely, a breech delivery resulting in significant birth defects. He's a hunchback. One

175

arm is shrunken "like a withered shrub," and his legs are of "an unequal size." He is disproportioned "in every part" and too ugly to be a successful lover like his lecherous brother Edward. Alec Guinness played Richard with a damaged left eye as well. Actors and costumers should be warned about not inhibiting his sword arm, and his armor should be built like a turtle's shell. The "bad" arm and hand should never be used except for holding a prop or a document between elbow and body.

As I overemphasized in the chapters on the Chronicles and *Henry VI, Part 2*, an audience that comes to *Richard III* without knowledge of, at least, plot points of the two plays that precede it is bound to be hopelessly confused for the first 45 minutes of the action. Just as there is no break between each of the *Henry IV* plays, so too does *Richard III* continue the plot and characters of *Henry VI, Part 3*. It begins with a reference to the concluding events of *Part 3*: the wars are over, and the sun (son) of York is once more on the throne.

Richard III is performed more than all the other Chronicle plays combined, due chiefly to the fact that its title role has been a favorite of every famous actor of the last 400-plus years, simply because it's so much fun to play. The role has everything: humor, deformity, athleticism, violence, sex. Audiences love Richard, and he loves them, disclosing his plots with a wink and a strut. Unlike Richard II, Richard III does not struggle with himself. He begins as pure evil and sustains it through his final victim. Though it may be treason to say so, I don't think that *Richard III* is a very good play. *Macbeth* tells the same story, but is far superior in defining personality and psychological motivation.

Like Iago, Richard confides in the audience early and keeps returning to them to ask, "How am I doing?" Having murdered King Henry VI and his heir, Prince Edward of Lancaster, Richard lines up all those relatives that stand between him and the throne and proceeds to demolish them. It's almost too easy. He contracts out the death of his brother, George of Clarence, to a pair of comic murderers, precipitates the death of elder brother, King Edward, eliminates Earl Rivers, brother to the Queen, and seizes the throne from his nephew, the child Edward V, on the pretense that his father's marriage to his mother was invalid, and the children of that marriage are illegitimate. There were strong political reasons for the boy's removal as well. England had suffered under child kings manipulated and bullied by powerful uncles, and 40 years of civil wars had weakened the government and drained the treasury.

Richard tells the truth to the audience, and they know when he lies to other characters in the play. Everyone believes Richard and trusts his altruism except, of course, Henry VI's widow, Queen Margaret of Anjou. Margaret, by the way, had been dead for several years before she appears in *Richard III*, but such niceties didn't seem to bother Shakespeare. However, if the audience has no knowledge of the *Henry VI* plays, they have no idea who Margaret is when she shows up in I.3. Directors tempted into eliminating her from the play, as many are, deprive the audience of some marvelous scenes, notably the concerted lament of the widows in IV.4.

I put an interesting piece of business into my 1964 production that leads to a favorite story. Tyrell comes to tell Richard of the death of the children in the Tower, then exits so that Richard may catch the audience up on a couple of plot points, including the death of his queen, Lady Anne. I decided to do double duty with this soliloquy by using it to kill Tyrell, although this does not actually happen in the play. I grabbed him in a one-armed strangle hold, broke his neck, dropped his corpse to the deck, opened the trap door, then kicked his corpse into the cellar while delivering the speech. What made this bit of business chilling was that it was performed so off-handedly, with no reference to Tyrell: all the business described was performed with one good arm within the space of 25 seconds. One night someone stepped on the ring that controlled the trap door and jammed it. I dropped the corpse of Tyrell to the floor, reached

Richard III, New Jersey Shakespeare Festival, 1983: Michael Tolaydo as Richard III (photograph by Blair Holley).

for the ring, but couldn't unjam it with only one good arm. I glanced at the wings, and there was Allan York, playing Catesby, waiting for his entrance. I finished the speech and called to him, "Catesby, ope thou the trap." He was surprised, but he did what he was told. He got the ring to work, opened the trap, and helped me push the corpse into it. If you ask Phil Dorian, my associate producer that year and a co-founder of the NJSF, he'll tell you that his favorite Shakespeare line is "Catesby, ope thou the trap."

The battle of Bosworth follows the form that the Playwright employed in *Henry IV, Part 1*, with orations on both sides, an initial clash of every actor within miles, then a series of skirmishes interspersed with patches of dialogue. Just as the King did in the earlier play, Henry of Richmond utilizes the device of dressing several combatants like himself in order to draw Richard to him. By the time they actually come face to face, Richard has fought five false Richmonds and has lost his horse. He delivers the famous line, "A horse! A horse! My kingdom for a horse!" with all the oxygen he has left in his body. Actor and character become one, the aerobic capacity of the actor determining how well the duels are fought. Then he has to fight one on one with the fresh Richmond. Here's the best example of how the Tudor propagandists loaded the dice. The real Henry VII was not a warrior and could never have stood up to the real Richard III in single combat. Richard was actually mobbed by his own rebellious soldiers and lynched upside down, while, like a 20th-century general, Henry of Richmond directed the battle from behind the lines and never broke a sweat. A perfect illustration of history versus theatre.

Of my three productions of *Richard III*, the 1978 Asolo production is in one sense the most memorable to me because it provided some important cautions about power and its uses in the theatre. That theatre's schedule, eight plays in rotating rep, and its complicated business and artistic staff made it almost impossible for a guest director to get a play on, but the show did get on, and I managed to escape with my reputation intact. I didn't think the Asolo production was very good, but Ellen, my wife, did.

Back to the *War of the Roses* rep. One great advantage of doing the plays as we did is the illumination of the back-story of *Richard III*. No need to load the program down with background information, because we could assume that every customer had seen the earlier plays. This was presumptuous, but it was a relief to be able to simply do the play without the usual concerns. Though I champion producing Shakespeare uncut, I must admit that *Richard III* is over-written, almost as if the Playwright wrote alternate passages that ended up in the published text. The Richard/Lady Anne seduction scene is a good example. Both of them say what they have to say two or three times over, and despite the pleasure of listening to Richard's spellbinding manipulation of Anne, the auditor is tempted to holler, "Come on, get on with it!" The best productions I've ever seen kept Richard active and the plot direct, linear, and crystal clear. Richard may be allowed some moments of introspection, but no more than the Playwright intended.

Our 1983 Richard was the splendid South African actor, Michael Tolaydo, who had just broken his leg while understudying one of the two roles in the Broadway *K-2*. Tolaydo rehearsed most of the *Roses* plays with a hip to ankle cast, but it came off before the plays opened, and the subsequent limp fit in fine with Richard's deformity. Tolaydo, however, did not want to wear a helmet for his many fight scenes, preferring a shoulder-length wig, which he insisted would protect him from injury. On one of our two-performance Saturday nights, we played our second play, which included all of *Part 3*, at 6:00 pm, with *Richard III* scheduled for 9:30. At the Battle of Tewkesbury, Richard took a head cut to the pate, resulting in a nasty gash under the wig. He didn't realize he was hurt until the blood ran down into his eyes, but he finished the performance. We gave him rudimentary first aid, but we knew the wound would have to be sutured. We also knew the local hospital's E.R. wouldn't consider it a priority. I called Dr. Donald Kent, one of our trustees and a skillful physician, interrupting his quiet evening at home. He immediately drove to the theatre and sewed up Richard of Gloucester's pate, while the costume people devised a bandage colored like the wig that would be hidden under it. Once again, a performance was rescued by the aid of a generous friend.

I wrote earlier that doing these plays was, to me, like spending eight weeks at a funeral. It was no fun. I subscribe to the premise that the operable word is "play," but I fear that I was so immersed in my world of charts, doubling, tabards, swords, and shields that I didn't take the time to realize what the audience saw. These four plays of the first tetralogy are a miracle of achievement by a team of writers and actors, the young Shakespeare among them. The four plays make a sprawling whole, the picture of a turbulent time in history. To have done them all together, even edited, was monumental.

We had a core company of very strong leads, notably Davis Hall as Henry VI, Annalee Jefferies as Margaret of Anjou, John Hertzler as Richard of York, and Michael Tolaydo as Richard III.

Lisa Barnes was our Joan of Arc. Her courage in learning broadsword and shield and plunging into battle — as the historical Joan did not — was admirable. She put some of the men to shame. Despite our efforts to present Shakespeare's Pucelle, the historical Joan came through, perhaps influenced by the authors who had lionized her over time, and the audience who brought with them the Joan they'd always known.

The real heroes of this epic were my old guard, the reliable Victoria Boothby, Ed Dennehy, J.C. Hoyt, Dane Knell, Don Perkins, Bill Pitts, and Margery Shaw, who played multiple roles, often spending more time changing costume and make-up than they did on-stage. To play the one seven-minute scene of the dying Edmund Mortimer, for instance, J.C. Hoyt spent an hour making-up, then another half-hour undoing that make-up and changing into his next character. Casting the plays had been an especially difficult process, simply because many actors don't know the plays. Ellen had to spend considerable time convincing reluctant New York agents that roles like Jack Cade were terrific opportunities.

On one August Saturday during the run, we did a marathon, the entire eight-hour epic in one day, beginning at 2:00 P.M., with a dinner break between the first and second plays and a shorter break between the second and third. We sold box lunches to the patrons and set up a non-stop buffet for the actors in the green room tent on the lawn. Festival Guild volunteers with cars stood by, ready to take actors to the local hospital's E.R. in the event of more serious injury or heat prostration. Among our many challenges with *War of the Roses* was a very hot summer; we'd been trying to raise money to upgrade our inadequate theatre air-conditioning for years. The marathon was harder on the audience than it was on the actors, but everyone loved it. Around 1:00 am, at the marathon's end, the company received a standing ovation that went on longer than any in my memory. The marathon was an enormous hit.

The *War of the Roses* also inspired our first colloquium, three days of lectures and discussions in conjunction with the performances by nationally known scholars Maurice Charney, Peter Saccio, Samuel Schoenbaum, Homer Swander, and Charles T. Wood, thanks to the efforts of staff member Deirdre Jacobson, in her last season with us. Under Ellen's direction over the next seven years, the colloquia received national recognition, growing to the point where they attracted over 800 participants from across the country and internationally.

Considerable ingenuity went into mounting these huge plays on a limited budget. We received support from such a wide range of businesses that the Festival was honored in Atlanta with a Business Committee for the Arts citation. Toys 'R Us, for example, contributed dozens of kids' round sleds that were ingeniously converted into shields by our heroic costume shop. Despite full houses, rave reviews, and increased contributions, however, the project put us considerably in debt, especially because of the significant increase in actor salaries.

Everyone seemed to have been impressed except for the officials at Actors' Equity. In the fall, soon after *War of the Roses* closed, faced with red ink and cutting all possible corners, Ellen called the union to protest when we were denied our request for a minor concession, that we be allowed to exceed the non-professional quota and use an intern in a tiny role in *Born Yesterday*. "We carried 23 contracts all summer, more than our quota required," Ellen argued. No luck. "Nobody asked you to do *The War of the Roses*," the union staffer replied.

CHAPTER 31

Titus Andronicus

Shakespeare's first tragedy, *Titus Andronicus*, is right up there among plays people hate without knowing anything about them. *The Merchant of Venice* runs it a close second. Potential customers stay away in droves because they've heard that one play is violent and the other anti–Semitic. The problem is not in producing these plays, but in selling them.

My 1977 NJSF production of *Titus Andronicus* was heavily influenced by research materials on religious ceremonies supplied by Harry Keyishian, Frank Occhiogrosso, and a Basilian priest in Michigan. My second production, in 1989, was informed by what worked and what didn't the first time around. Obviously, the more a director does a play, the greater his pile of experience, the narrower his idea will be of what makes a play work and what gets in the way.

Both times I conceived the play as a Roman religious ceremony describing an iconic series of events, just as the Catholic Mass re-enacts the life of Jesus Christ. *Titus Andronicus* became a funeral Mass taking us from the death of an emperor through a trial of fire — the reign of an evil ruler — to the emergence of a just one. The son of Titus, Lucius, is tested by time, deaths, and horrific events until he is strong enough to merit the garland and govern Rome.

Our Roman Mass was celebrated by a high priest, Marcus, assisted by the rest of the cast, who served as acolytes and vestals. The set was a ruined Roman temple. Its primary entrance, a yawning hole dead center, brought the actors up steep steps to stage level. The play began with the entire cast, dressed in identical simple white robes tied at the waist with cinctures, entering from the center cavern. Humming a single tone, "ummmm," they took seats at extreme upstage right and left. Subsequent entrances were not really entrances: actors simply rose from their seats to play their scenes, then returned to these seats when they exited, except when a character died. Corpses were carried off-stage, and the seats of characters who died were left empty — actors did not return to them.

Shakespeare created a Roman political system in this play to which he returned in *Julius Caesar* and *Coriolanus*. It is neither republic nor empire, but more closely resembles a participatory democracy. Upon the death of the emperor, his elder son does not automatically ascend to the throne, as in the British system. Rather his two sons, Saturninus and Bassianus, campaign like small-town hucksters for the votes of the people. Instead, the people elect the triumphant returning general, Titus. Compare this to the opening scenes in *Julius Caesar*. Titus refuses the throne and chooses Saturninus, elder son of the deceased emperor, citing the principle of primogeniture. The people appear willing to accept Saturninus as a second choice. Once confirmed as emperor, however, Saturninus behaves like a tyrant.

This is neither the British nor the American system, so it's essential to present it clearly in the staging. We added fragmented costume pieces to the acolytes' white robes as they became characters in the story. When Saturninus was named emperor, he donned a purple

Titus Andronicus, New Jersey Shakespeare Festival, 1977: Geddeth Smith as Titus, Robin Leary as Lavinia (photograph by Blair Holley).

robe. When he chose Tamara as his bride, she dressed a second time as a Roman matron. Properties were kept to a minimum but were as realistic as possible, especially swords and daggers. Wherever possible, properties were built into the set, preset or concealed.

A big problem came up early. With so many killings, mutilations, and other atrocities, how do a director and costumer deal with the blood? Today's audiences are accustomed to realistic blood. In films, an actor will wear a special undergarment with blood capsules sewn over a small explosive charge; when the actor is "shot," the charges are activated, throwing the blood out and away from the body. Special effects people give us the illusion of blood exploding out of exit wounds and splattering the wall behind the actor. Actors will also conceal non-toxic blood capsules in the mouth, then bite down on cue, sending blood running out of the mouth.

But in the theatre, even if you can find a way to produce the blood, the laundry between performances can become an even bigger problem. One celebrated solution to the gore in *Titus*, in the Olivier production, was the use of scarlet ribbons, ingeniously streaming from wounds.

We decided to eliminate the blood altogether and substitute a ritual from the Mass. Every time there was a death, Marcus moved to center stage with a large chalice. On each side of him, acolytes poured water and wine from cruets into the chalice. Marcus elevated it, as at the consecration of the Mass, then drank a small amount. As bells solemnly rang, the vestals and acolytes hummed. This device freed the actors to play the violence, the wounds, and deaths without having to worry about the blood.

We were initially concerned that the ritual would elicit laughter, especially since it was repeated so many times in performance. However, the audience members understood the symbolism and were moved by it. We did not hold the action for the business. Marcus moved independently of the action. The symbolic consecration he performed was coordinated to the violence, rather than the violence to the symbolism. In 1977, in the grave and venerable person of Richard Graham, it worked beautifully. Geddeth Smith played it in 1989, a very different performance but equally effective. Geddeth had played Titus in the earlier production, the first performance of many to come in the next 13 years. Margery Shaw, Tamara in 1977, first worked for me in 1966, eventually playing over 50 other roles for me, from Ophelia to Gertrude. What luxury when such long-term relationships are built!

But I digress. Instead of severed heads, we used plaster masks built on the actors' own faces, then painted and decorated. Lavinia's severed hands were created with flesh colored bandages, easily wrapped and unwrapped, and a second costume, identical to the first, but distressed and with longer sleeves.

We also added a flash of total nudity to the rape scene, which proved extremely effective, eliciting shock but, again, no laughter. At Tamara's exit, II.3.203, Chiron and Demetrius each grabbed a sleeve at Lavinia's wrist and yanked it out and away from her body. Her entire garment ripped in half, leaving her completely naked. She turned and ran off-stage, where she was redressed quickly in a second distressed costume. The ripping of the costume and the flash of nudity took but a few seconds. It was not telegraphed, and the audience was not prepared for it. There it was and then it was gone. Chiron and Demetrius pursued her, then returned with her at the beginning of II.4. In the 1977 production, Robin Leary, as Lavinia, had no objection to the nudity and did it easily. However, in the 1989 production, Diana LaMar did object, strongly, insisting she could play the scene just as effectively without it. I agreed, because at the time it seemed a deal breaker, but the rape was weakened substantially.

As in much of Shakespeare, the actors had to adjust to ethical and cultural differences between today's mores and the world of the play, in this case pre–Christian Rome. This society was heavily influenced by the Roman militaristic philosophy and the principle that the word and rule of the paterfamilias were supreme in his household. If his wife or children disobeyed a man, he was free to punish them severely, even kill them. There was no challenging his authority, though one could still beg for his mercy. In early rehearsals, the actors were comfortable with the conception of the play as ritual, but the extreme emotions of the characters were difficult to play.

In the violent scenes, there was no time for thought, only reaction. Even the killing of the rapists Chiron and Demetrius was done with dispatch. Their ankles were tied together and a pipe thrust between their legs, then military pressed to a height of six feet by four strong men of equal height while their throats were cut. The famous pie Titus feeds to Tamara and Saturninus actually was a large potpie, meatless to accommodate the actors' diets, baked nightly and served warm, but not hot. The multiple deaths at the end of the play were accomplished quickly as well. Any delays or overplaying would have elicited laughter.

Though *Titus* was a very early effort by Master Will, heavily influenced by the "blood and thunder" revenge plays of the preceding era, and much of the writing is rough, even primitive, and on a level with the *Henry VI* plays, there is evidence that the Playwright must have done some rewriting, perhaps after he finished *King Lear*, because certain passages in *Titus Andronicus* show considerably more sophistication than others. Since there are three quartos as well as the First Folio text, directors are tempted to pick, choose, and edit in search of a usable playing script. III.2, which I included, does not appear in any of the quartos, only the Folio. Whatever final script is used, I strongly believe that the play should be performed straight through with no intermission. Naturally, the audience must be warned, but there's really no place to put an intermission. *Titus*, which plays so much better than it reads, needs to blaze its gory path straight through to the end.

As I wrote at the beginning, the problem with *Titus* is not producing, but selling it. I still don't have the answer, although the dilemma reminds me of a favorite cartoon that hangs in my office. A well-dressed couple are leaving the theatre, the wife complaining, "Sex and violence! Sex and violence! All they show is sex and violence." Behind them one can see the Globe Theatre marquee advertising *Hamlet*.

The sex and violence angle did work, however, with at least one person when we did the play in 1977, a security guard at Drew University, home to NJSF. Not normally a theatergoer, when he heard about Lavinia's nudity he began to sneak into the back of the house at every performance to watch it. One night, his walkie-talkie came on while he was standing there. He tried to turn it off, but couldn't find the right control, so he turned to leave and noisily fell down a flight of stairs in the dark. That was the last we heard of him.

Chapter 32

Love's Labour's Lost

Please don't edit this play, please, I beg you. It's very special, a poetic gem, like a book of sonnets, but underrated, seldom performed. A few years ago, a study was undertaken of all the Shakespeare plays to determine the size of the Burbage acting company. Most of the plays demand multiple doubles, and the casting problems dizzy the imagination. Some doubling is thematic, some merely convenient. In recent years, tight box offices have forced resident theatres to use smaller companies, but in *Love's Labour's Lost*, when we arrive at the play-within-the-play scene, there's the full company: 16 actors and a boy, and the play cannot be doubled or edited further without damaging both structure and language.

So, if you cannot afford to assemble such a company, don't do this play.

Shakespeare's earlier dramatic use of the shared sonnet in *Romeo and Juliet* is eloquent, but in this play, he uses the device with a vengeance, building and revealing the love matches of the primary plot on it, one of the main reasons the play is so hard to rehearse. A great deal of time must be spent on the language, balancing sense and emotionality against the requirements of the verse. Actors hate this. Actors hate having to sit (or stand) still and drill the verse until it's right. Actors like to get up on their hind legs and move around and yell a lot.

You have to have four attractive couples in love to make the body of the play work, no small task, and those eight actors must all have a superior command of the text. Though Berowne is the flashier role, the precursor of Benedick, the King is most crucial and demands an actor of authority and dignity: his wooing of the Princess of France is the dominant love story; the Playwright intends it to be taken it seriously. Berowne's wooing of Rosaline starts off as a dalliance, but ends with them ensnaring each other. The casting of the other two couples should balance these four principal actors. Pedestrian as it may seem, a primary objective is clarity. It should be easy to differentiate among the King, Berowne, Longaville, and Dumaine.

I saw an awful production in California a few years back where the director had decided that all the young women were secretly lesbians. It was mean, misogynistic, and the production mocked itself: given the twisting of ideas, the conclusion made no sense. It made my flesh crawl. I was virtually squirming in my seat, not in response to the homosexuality itself, but because the destruction of the romance in the play managed to deconstruct it into a cold evening's waste of time.

The RSC came to America some 20 to 30 years ago with Ian Richardson playing Berowne, and that was delightful.

The play celebrates young love and mocks the practical likelihood of celibacy. Four young noblemen agree to withdraw from society to dedicate themselves to the pure asceticism of academic studies. They will fast, sleep little, take little exercise, avoid distractions, and, especially, abjure the company of women. They will have their books, tutors, time to study, contemplate, and write, but they're going to do it on the grounds of the Royal Palace of Navarre, just in case the King is needed for affairs of state. It's a laudable goal, but as any college freshman can attest, it's impossible. Before the first day of their monastic life ends, the Princess of France and three ladies-in-waiting arrive, supposedly on a diplomatic mission, and easily tempt the men into the wooing dance. All the young ladies behave alike, and all the young men behave alike, and they appear to be well on the way to a multiple wedding, the usual comedy conclusion, but this piece has a twist that makes it unique.

The company must play *Love's Labour's Lost* as if it were on the way to a happy ending, joyfully charging along, until the surprise arrival of M. Marcade, the messenger of death, dressed in black. The costumer should avoid black in the other costumes, even the academic robes. Brown or grey will work as well, and shades of blue can provide accent, but no one should wear black except Marcade. There is no warning. The party would seem to go on forever, and suddenly there's the spoiler.

This play in particular illustrates the necessity for control of the rehearsal process. The early beats of a play are much more difficult than the later beats, because the early ones are doing multiple service, establishing place, mores, characters, weather, time of year. Actors become acquainted with this essential information slowly, and so does the audience. However, many actors believe that all parts of a play should receive equal rehearsal time, which is simply not true. Tony and Oscar-winner Mike Nichols insists that the first third of a play should receive twice as much rehearsal as the last third. Further, he insists that there is no sense in moving on to the second scene until everyone is comfortable and solid in the first

Love's Labour's Lost, New Jersey Shakespeare Festival, 1978: J.C. Hoyt as Berowne, Robin Leary as Rosaline (photograph by Blair Holley).

scene, and so forth. If the play is staged too quickly, the later scenes will have too great an influence on the early scenes.

I firmly agree with Nichols and would even add that actors are at times unable to fulfill later scenes until they've fully realized and been informed by the early scenes. Adhering to this principle, I often began rehearsal at the beginning of the script, going forward and adding a bit more each day. Sometimes we would do "double backs" where each scene was repeated twice as a new one was added. This practice drove some actors crazy. I'm convinced it worked.

Love's Labour's Lost is a happy-go-lucky multiple love story until the last ten minutes. Then it switches, changes direction. Because of the death of her father, the King of France, the Princess dictates that she and her handmaidens will mourn for a year. Only if love still remains at the conclusion of those 365 days will there be the conventional "ever-after" ending. The play concludes with a song about the length of the year, the imposed time of mourning. The song may be rehearsed in advance, but rehearsing that last ten minutes should be avoided as long as possible. The actors may complain, but those last ten minutes need very little rehearsal: they are the undoing of what has come before. Here, the wooing dance does not end with love and pretty babies. If fully and honestly received, this sudden realization will allow the ending to play itself.

Still, the director better figure out what the statement of the play is before the company arrives at that last minute twist. Is this a love story? Of course. Following the Playwright's tradition, each of the eight lovers falls in love at first sight, but with an appropriate object of affection. I understand that penguins do the same. Naturally, the King of Navarre falls in love with the Princess of France. No populist social statement here. If they eventually marry, it will be a public political union involving territories, millions of people, and untold riches. As the Tudors demonstrated, royal marriages take a lot of negotiation.

Berowne falls in love with Rosaline, or rather they rekindle an earlier flirtation. Longaville and Dumaine easily manage to fall in love with the remaining two young women. It's all quite neat, like a quartet of bachelors hitting a singles bar on Saturday night. There's no competition, no fighting over the remaining women, but they're not looking for world-without-end bargains either. What would happen to the story if three of the four men fell for the same woman, say, Katherine? No, it's all neat and ordered, each Jack to his Jill, and the tradition of the thunderbolt is maintained. By definition it's true love, but only for the King and the Princess.

The minor characters and their subplots comment on the four parallel love stories. Holofernes and Nathaniel are ostensibly hired as tutors, but they quickly find themselves with nothing to do but write poems and discourse on idiosyncrasies in Latin and English. The comic Spaniard Don Armado, the retired soldier, parodies courtly love, the "I pine, I swoon" school—he could speak English with a Spanish accent, especially the Castilian "th" substituting for the "s" sound.

Notice again how quickly the gentlemen abandon their vow to disdain the world and devote themselves to academic studies. Their good intentions barely last a day. The women, having made no such monastic pact, go along with the four-way wooing dance, until the coup, the cut, the arrival of the deus ex machina. The King tries to argue the Princess out of her year of mourning, but this is a tradition that goes back centuries; we saw it in *Twelfth Night*, though Olivia's commitment to seven years of mourning for her father and her brother is more than a little excessive. The Princess scarcely has a choice.

The conditions meted out by the Princess and Rosaline are often criticized as being too harsh. Upon examination, however, we see that they are not of a kind, and that they're not really punishments. Instead, they're penances, non-mandatory, and the first is little more than a suggestion by the Princess that the gentlemen return to the King's original intent of monastic study. Her suggestion, that it last for only a year, is easier than the original vow of three years the gentleman scholars imposed on themselves. Actually, the Princess suggests an improvement on the plan: a removal from the cares of the world, into a monastic existence far from the palace grounds. I am reminded of the bunker J.D. Salinger allegedly built at the back of his New Hampshire property, an all-weather building with all the tools he needed to write, but no telephone, radio, television. Salinger could work there as long as he wished, and he couldn't be easily interrupted. Agents, critics, reporters needed good snowshoes to get to him in the winter.

Rosaline's penance is more unusual and creative: not just solitary study, but public service for Berowne, ministering to patients so ill they cannot speak for themselves. This clown, he of many words, shall spend the year making poor wretches laugh. Not likely. The King's wooing, as befits a king, may have been sincere, but Berowne, Longaville, and Dumaine were only playing the game of courtly love. Will they return to their scholarly plan? The Playwright gives us neither answer nor hint.

The director may decide to use the song which ends the play to cover the time needed to strike the set that has been used for the play-within-the-play and to pack for the trip back to the funeral, or for the final exit itself, or the song could be used to underscore the curtain call, though the tune may be too somber for that. The play is essentially over with the speech,

> The words of Mercury are harsh after the songs of Apollo.
> You that way: we this way.

Though these final lines are assigned to Don Armado, this could be a typesetter's error. They make more sense if spoken by Marcade or even Boyet, and they refer to the Princess and her entourage going off toward Paris (stage left), while the men remain in Navarre (stage right).

I've seen productions where these directions are ignored, but a conventional happy ending where the couples exit arm in arm is not what Shakespeare wrote. At the end of *Love's Labour's Lost*, like life itself, we don't know what will happen. Once again, the Playwright is ambiguous.

CHAPTER 33

King Lear

King Lear is about love lost, love regained, love and life lost. The text is maddening in its complexity, its labyrinthine turns and reverses. A director faced with the task of mounting it begins with a precarious no-win choice: who will play Lear? A younger man will stand up to the rigors of the play more easily, but a great deal of what the play says has to do with the process of aging, of growing old, rotting, slowing down, stiffening, and fighting mental confusion. Beyond the specifics in the play, Lear does things and suffers ailments the same as every older person. Theoretically, the best Lear is a healthy older man who has been an actor all his life, who has learned the role before rehearsals begin. Putting in the woodshed time to learn the words while rehearsing the play is just too much. The role is too long and complicated. The producer and director should relieve his Lear of all personal concerns: feed him, transport him, clean his room, give him a dedicated dresser and prop master, and daily prompters to assist him.

Lear can't really be played until one is over 60. Over 70 is better. When asked what kills Lear at the end, Sir Donald Wolfitt replied, "Playing the role." Wolfitt was a famous 20th-century actor/manager of the old school, one of the last of his breed. His tombstone reads, "Well roared, Lion!"

Lear seldom concentrates, rarely sticks to the subject. His eyes and ears are going. He addresses several people at once, even those who are absent. He asks questions, but doesn't wait for answers. He interrupts others like a spoiled teenager. His speeches go in circles. The actor must build lapses in concentration and memory into his performance, and that's dangerous for any actor, because in the moment there is only a thin line between performance and reality.

Lear may be dying, as Paul Scofield played him. His division of his kingdom may be a deathbed bequest, but this is not necessary. The direct choice, that Lear is not dying, is simpler to play and more logical — he's dividing the kingdom because Cordelia is getting married.

I've done this play six times. I played the soldier who kills Cornwall at Oregon in 1951, directed it three times, and later, played Lear once and Gloucester thrice. (If the numbers are confusing, twice I did double duty.) Of all the productions I've seen, the 1963 mounting at Stratford, Ontario, starring John Colicos, directed by Michael Langham, was the most fully realized over-all. Rather than a star turn with supports, it was balanced, the actors performing like the fingers of one hand. The most recent production I directed, at the San Francisco Shakespeare Festival in 2001, was the most fulfilled emotionally, thanks to the chemistry among Lear, Cordelia, and the Fool: Ray Reinhardt, Shannon Barry, and Jerry Haiken.

In my own productions, I've been blessed with some superb actors. My first and second Lear, Richard Graham, was the best: he first played the role in Oregon in 1951 when he was

38, a performance honored with a commemorative statue on the Oregon Festival grounds, and he played it much later for me in New Jersey when he was 66. Jerry Haiken was the best Fool. My daughter, Shannon, was the best Cordelia. Daniel Nelbach was the best Gloucester.

Daniel played Gloucester for me at Marywood University in Scranton, Pennsylvania. When he died in the spring of 1997, the friends who eulogized him remembered Gloucester as his last acting job, and reminded me of how he bragged about it. That touched me deeply, because it was a college production with but two Equity actors, the rest students and locals. It was, however, a triumph of courage, trust, and patience by the actors and unstinting hard work by the Marywood faculty. That's what theatre friendships are about. We do the plays. We share those great half-hours in the dressing room, but, when we're inside the action, we have no idea of whether the thing we do is good or not. It's only the banter, the gentle insults, the tolerant bitching that we remember. As far as performance, we remember the screw-ups more than the triumphs. We're unaware of the triumphs. Are there ever any triumphs?

According to myth and history, King Lear came to the throne of Britain six centuries before the birth of Christ. In Shakespeare's play, the value system is Christian, but the only gods mentioned are neither Judaic, Celtic, nor Norse, but Roman. Lear prays to a few Roman gods and to forces of nature — thunder, lightning, winds, fogs.

The culture is patriarchal and feudal. The royalty and nobility are warriors, trained in the arts of war from childhood. All of the peasants are serfs, serving at the pleasure of the nobility. The nobility have the power of life and death over the peasantry. The king has the power of life and death over everyone.

This play has three main plots and several subplots. There are four possible parental relationships in nature, and Shakespeare wrote this play about two of the four. There are no mothers in *King Lear*. If the mothers were important, Shakespeare would have put them into the play. What is essential is that the audience accept that Lear is the father of the three daughters, and Gloucester is the father of the two sons. The proof has to be right up on the stage, evident, no confusion, no ambiguity. In order to express everything he feels about fathers and children, the Playwright must tell the same story twice: once with a father and his daughters, a second time with a father and his sons. What happens to one physically happens to the other psychically. Each of the fathers gives us insights into the soul of his counterpart. Gloucester says things about Lear that Lear would never say about himself, and vice versa. Crucial ideas are reinforced by every poetic and dramatic device in the Playwright's armory.

We begin with simple playable details: two of Lear's daughters have not yet borne children, and the third is unmarried. In his early 40s when he wrote this play in 1605, Shakespeare had married young and fathered three legitimate children, two daughters and a son. The son, Hamnet, died in 1596 at the age of 11 and the daughters presented Will with no grandsons. The text of his last will and testament indicates that he was obsessed with grandsons, for he bequeathed all his considerable estate to male heirs who never materialized. In his personal life, his politics, and his art, Shakespeare sought the male heir, but the entire Shakespeare male line came to an end with his death in 1616.

As we've seen repeatedly, primogeniture had determined all inheritance for all of recorded history. God was believed to be present at the conception, birth, and death of a king. The surviving first-born son inherited everything: title, lands, wealth. Daughters were pawns used to cement political alliances and could easily be disinherited.

As *King Lear* begins, three actors peruse a huge map that's on the stage from the time the house opens. If they wish, audience members may come up and examine it before the

King Lear, New Jersey Shakespeare Festival, 1979: Richard Graham as Lear, Clarence Felder as Kent, Albert Sanders as the Fool (photograph by Blair Holley).

play starts. It's a map of the main island of Britain with rivers and mountains delineated, but only a few cities or towns. The map has been divided into three equal sections. The actors move around the map, studying it. They are waiting for something to happen. No hurry. Then one speaks, describing characters yet unknown to us. A second joins in. They discuss the division of the kingdom, but the language is stilted, indirect, cautious.

A third, younger character is introduced as son of the second speaker. A minute and a half into the scene, we discover that the first speaker is "my Lord of Kent." A nobleman! The son is addressed as "Edmund," but there seems to be a problem involving another son. Edmund's mother is referred to as a joke, not as the speaker's wife, and Edmund is called a knave and a whoreson. Gloucester has a legitimate son, Edgar, who will inherit all; Edmund is the bastard son who will receive nothing; King Lear has a parallel problem.

Suddenly the stage fills with another 20 or more characters, including the three alluded to in the very first speech of the play. The Playwright feeds us information gradually, piecemeal. He introduces the main plot of the play immediately, but quickly switches to details of the second plot. Subtly, surreptitiously, all plots are established by the time the title character enters.

King Lear is 80 years old, with no male heir, so he decides to divide his kingdom evenly among the husbands of his three daughters to avoid the possibility of civil war when he dies. Somewhere, in the back of Lear's mind, in the back of Shakespeare's mind, there is the possibility of a grandson, perhaps named after his grandfather, who will someday reunite the kingdom. Lear has chosen the day of his youngest daughter's betrothal to announce the division of the kingdom. What we see here is not the event itself, but the ceremony, the formal proclamation of the event. Lear has already decided on the specifics of the division: Goneril and Albany will get the north, Regan and Cornwall the southwest, and Cordelia and her husband the southeast, all very reasonable and logical. As he describes the bequests, he crowns each daughter, naming her princess. He isn't really going to give the biggest hunk to the daughter who says she loves him most; he's just devised this ritual to put a symbolic seal on the political fact. If there's any question to be probed and examined in this first scene it's why Cordelia won't play Lear's ceremonial game, so we can get on with the next essential event: the naming of her husband.

To make Cordelia's task a little easier, I put Kent downstage and to her left so she could address her asides, I.1.61 and I.1.75 to 77, to him.

The first two scenes of the play, 25 minutes of playing time, are compactly written. Even if a production is to be edited, the director is advised against any cutting in these two scenes, where the Playwright lays down the rules, the premises the audience needs to understand. We should assume that Lear has discussed his plan carefully with his sons-in-law and with Cordelia's suitors. They have employed cartographers to determine territories and boundaries. Lear is not abdicating. Nail that in: Lear is not abdicating his throne. He's going to retain the title, the name of "king," with its perks and privileges, but he is proposing a new political organization by assigning the actual business of governing to his sons-in-law. Lear will be king until he dies, but each of his three daughters and their husbands will rule and tax a third of the country.

Lear adds one other condition: he's going to spend a third of each year with each daughter: a month with one, the next month with another, the third with another, then back to the first. He's going to bring his 100-knight bodyguard with him, and each knight has a squire, horses, retinue. That's a significant company to entertain, even if it's only for one month out of three. Nevertheless, that's the contract, the bargain between Lear and his daughters' husbands. It should be emphasized that this is a good and fair agreement. Each son-in-law will rule and tax a vast area of productive real estate. Even if an additional hotel has to be built to house Lear's train four months out of 12, the cost will be insignificant relative to the potential revenue.

The ceremony goes well until Cordelia is called upon and then Lear's world starts to crumble. Why does she do what she does? Why doesn't she dutifully ape her sisters in the infantile "I love Daddy more than you do, nyah, nyah, nyah!" charade? Perhaps she doesn't understand the game, or maybe she thinks she's been asked a trick question, and that the answer she gives is really the one Lear wants to hear: that she is ready for marriage, that she will love her father and her husband equally. Whatever the actress decides to play in this crucial beat, she should avoid appearing contemptuous of her father. She may be confused, off balance, but she loves her father.

At Cordelia's first "Nothing," the play stands still, then erupts as Lear disowns her, abandons her, almost casually divides her portion between Albany and Cornwall, and throws her, dowerless, at whichever suitor wants her, then threatens Kent for defending her and banishes him. The only moment of tenderness breaking up the fury of the scene is the King of France's saintly proposal of marriage. Lear roars on and leaves the stage with a final cheap shot at his youngest daughter:

> Therefore be gone
> Without our grace, our love, our benison.

The opening scene of *King Lear* is the most specific setting in the entire play. It is Lear's throne room, the place from which he rules his domain. What the audience sees when they enter the theatre is the image they will hold the longest. It is the visual metaphor of the play: what is necessary, the minimum, is the map of Britain divided, a throne for Lear, and several crowns, symbols of royalty. We see two kings, three dukes, three princesses, a number of lesser nobles, knights, soldiers. This image remains from the time of the audience's arrival until it's augmented, then altered, by the action itself.

When Lear leaves the stage, 16 minutes into the play, the importance of his throne has been reduced. When the King of France and Cordelia leave the stage a minute later, it is further reduced, and when Goneril and Regan leave, the throne is rendered superfluous. It has no further function. The concrete becomes abstract.

Only Edmund is left behind. Where is Edmund? Some editors identify this as "Act I, Scene 2, the Earl of Gloucester's castle." But what does that serve? There is no indication of passage of time or movement from one place to another between the scenes. Edmund was in attendance on his father at the ceremony. Why not Edgar? I use Edgar to escort Cordelia in the first entrance of the daughters. When Lear bellows, "Call France. Who stirs? Call Burgundy!" it makes sense for Edgar to exit and inform his father of the King's wishes. Gloucester returns with France and Burgundy, and Edgar trails after, again standing quietly, waiting for instruction.

I don't think Edmund ever leaves the scene. Certainly his prayer, "Thou, nature, art my goddess..." is informed by the earlier conversation between Gloucester and Kent, and there is no need to play this speech and the scene that follows anywhere else but in Lear's throne room. Do we need Lear's throne? Not at all, but it won't interfere with the scene if it's left on-stage. We are going to have to get rid of it eventually. This second scene is the first of many examples in this play where time and place are irrelevant. All we need are three actors and a prop letter. The scene ends with one actor alone, boasting to the audience of the plot he's just set in motion. When he leaves, we are left with nothing, a void.

There is a bit of fuzzy chronology here, resulting in a slight structural weakness. In I.2, Edmund shows Gloucester the fake letter, and Gloucester immediately takes the bait, gullibly believing that Edgar intends to betray and kill him. Edmund, a few minutes later, warns Edgar to stay out of Gloucester's way. That's the setup, but the Playwright leaves it for some 23 minutes audience time to concentrate on the main plot before he returns to the phony Edgar conspiracy. Shakespeare then just picks up the second plot where he left it at the end of I.2.

Despite the printed text's delineation of Acts and Scenes, the early action of *King Lear* takes place in three blocks of time, three days: the ceremony of the dowries; another day, some weeks later, when Lear leaves Goneril's home; and the third, the night of the great storm at Gloucester's castle. Each of these three sequences could begin with concrete design specifics: walls, banners, furniture, gates. But each ends with a character alone in an empty universe.

In this play, specificity of locale is only intermittently important. The Playwright is more particular in indicating time of night/day and weather. Distances between locales are important only in terms of travel time. A healthy man can travel 20 miles on foot in a day and 30 miles on horseback. Everyone in the play travels by horse or horse and carriage, except for Edgar and Gloucester on foot in Act IV. Much of the action takes place either at Gloucester's castle or on the way from Gloucester to Dover, a distance of 160 miles as the crow flies. Nobody makes it to Dover.

Costumes and properties: I see no great advantage in pinpointing the years of Lear's reign. We don't have the archaeology, images, paintings for reference that we do for the later kings. I prefer a simple Celtic warrior/peasant look for this play: leather armor, wools, furs, and a minimum of metal, except for weapons. As always, casting is of primary importance, and costuming should identify and reinforce family relationships. Lear, France, Burgundy, Cornwall, and Albany are warrior chieftains. Goneril's costume should tell us that she is Lear's daughter and Albany's wife; Regan's that she is Lear's daughter and Cornwall's wife. Cordelia's first costume should tell us that she is Lear's daughter, but it shouldn't telegraph who her husband will be. Gloucester and Kent are earls. Edgar and Edmund should be identifiable as Gloucester's legitimate and bastard sons. Kent should begin the play in nobleman's court finery, with a full-faced beard, maybe a wig; in I.4, he tells us he's razed (double entendre) his visage and borrowed other accents. He's dressed like a yeoman looking for employment.

Another costume consideration should be addressed early, because without sufficient building time, it can be lost to compromise. Lear begins the play at his most opulent and royal, a king at a ceremonial event. When we next see him, in I.4, he is still a king, but at his leisure, dressed for hunting, perhaps carrying a boar spear. He'll wear this costume plus a traveling cape as he travels from Albany's castle to Cornwall's, back to Gloucester's, where the storm begins. Over the next few scenes, the wind and rain beat on these clothes, and Lear himself tears them and throws some of them away. By the time he gets to IV.6, he is in rags, but they are the rags of the costume we first saw in I.4.

Gloucester can wear the same elegant costume from the first scene through II.4, and then get soaked by the wind and rain. His captors tear his clothes off in III.7, where he is blinded and thrown out of his own home to "smell his way to Dover." The journey further deteriorates his costume, a distressed version of what he wore at the beginning. Though it will strain the budget a bit more, several stages of Lear's and Gloucester's costumes must be built, and care taken to show the progression of their deterioration.

Edgar exchanges clothes with a Bedlam beggar in II.3 and subjects himself to the cruelty of the elements over the next several scenes. As Poor Tom, the text requires him to be naked, filthy, dreadlocked, with pins, slivers, and thorns stuck in him. Some actors will resist this, because naked means cold, but naked or not, it is essential that nobody recognize him, not even his father. The only time Poor Tom encounters Gloucester before he's blinded is during the storm on the heath, with only a torch for light. By the time Lear, Gloucester, and Edgar meet again at IV.6.80, they are all dressed or undressed alike, in torn and bloodied rags, the meanest of wretches.

Back to sequence. In the second day, designated in most scripts as Act I, scenes 3, 4 and 5, the action takes place within the Duke of Albany's castle. We are a considerable distance from Lear's palace. The change in locale justifies the assumption of a passage of time. Lear has made good his promise: he's going to spend a month at Goneril's with his hundred knights, and then he's going to move to his second daughter, Regan's.

The dispute that begins the scene is less than cosmic. It's homey. It's trivial. Petty quarrels have been building. Goneril's carping breaks into open warfare. She berates the Fool and dismisses half of Lear's train. Lear then trashes the banquet hall and storms out, declaring his intent to go to Regan. Anything that can be done to solidify the look of Albany's castle will help this scene, but, as with the setting that began the play, we have to be able to get rid of it, all of it, logically and quickly, when the castle is no longer essential.

Lear storms out of the castle and into the courtyard as his followers prepare his horses for the journey to Cornwall. He surveys the world that he commands, focusing on *his* stars. He and his Fool are alone in a void, darkness, lit only by the stars. The universe that remains is silent, vigilant, ominous. The Fool exits, and the scene again comes down to man alone in nothing, nowhere.

Another time/place confusion here is easy enough to correct with a simple line change. Lear fights with Goneril and leaves for the supposed safety of Regan's castle in Cornwall, sending Kent on ahead with letters to advise Regan of his intentions. When Lear arrives, he finds she has gone to meet her sister at Gloucester, which is a halfway point between Albany and Cornwall, so he turns his train around and heads back north. This all happens off-stage and is explained in several passages, but an audience without a map of England to consult can get lost. To clarify matters, change the word "Gloucester" to "Cornwall" in line I.5.1 and specify to actors and designers the time/place leap between I.5 and II.1.

Scenes II.1 through IV.1 take place at the Earl of Gloucester's castle and nearby. All the action is continuous, no time breaks, and takes place at night, the Playwright moving from the concrete to the ephemeral. First he returns to the plot he left at the end of I.2 to reinforce Edmund's lies about Edgar, and eventually establish Edgar's disguise as Poor Tom. Here, Curan should be played by an older actor and combined with the Old Man who leads Gloucester in IV.1; despite its brevity, this is an extremely important role.

The longest of these scenes, II.4, is an interesting exercise in staging. Because it involves nine major characters and a number of soldiers, servants, functionaries, the scene itself is unlike the majority of contemporary scenes we direct today.

Early in the action, Kent is set in the stocks. Edgar plays his soliloquy on the other side of the stage, and Lear and the Fool discover Kent when they enter. The early beats are logical enough until Regan and Cornwall enter, II.4.124, and Kent is set free. Then the director must remove characters who are momentarily out of focus to remote positions to give emphasis to the action. Lear rages at Regan, and she holds her ground, logically, even gently. Then Goneril enters with Oswald, and we arrive at a point where directors can founder and the staging can break down. Regan crosses to greet Goneril as Cornwall challenges Lear about Kent. If the director allows Goneril and Regan to remain together, reinforcing each other, shoulder to shoulder, then the rest of the scene will be lopsided, static. However, if Regan crosses back to get between Cornwall and Lear at line 199, then Goneril is left on the other side of the stage with Oswald, and Lear can play the remainder of the scene moving back and forth between the two daughters.

Though the scene involves a number of actors, some with lines, others with practical functions, it still remains a fight between Lear and his two daughters, broken up a couple of times with prayers to the gods. What do the others do while the three shout it out? They simply watch and wait and prepare for the next time the Playwright involves them in the action. Cornwall actually controls the movement of the scene. He orders Kent set free, directs the stocks to be removed, orders the gates shut. Except for Lear, whose authority is challenged, Cornwall is the highest in command from II.1.84 through III.7.96.

What do we need to substantiate Gloucester's courtyard? The stocks are mentioned often. These can be simple double beams of timber holding Kent's legs at the ankles, forcing him to sit or lie down because he can't walk or even stand in them. When Lear leaves this courtyard, Gloucester is told several times, "Shut up your gates." The king has first been driven out, and now he is to be locked out, prevented from returning. From this point on, once the gates are locked, scenery is not only unnecessary, it's an impediment.

I did a severe editing and juxtaposition of scenes here, cutting all of III.1, following II.4 with III.3, then III.2, cutting the lines III.2.79 to 96, segueing into III.4, so that the two appear to be one continuous heath scene. Much of III.1 is reiteration, exposition and a couple of red herrings. I cut the Fool's doggerel soliloquy at the end of III.2, because I don't think Shakespeare wrote it. Lear needs time to make costume adjustments before his heath scenes, but 27 lines at the end of II.4 plus the 27 lines of III.3, about two and a half minutes, will have to serve. The heath scenes take place a short distance from the castle.

The storm, thunder, lightning, wind, rain of III.2 and III.4 overpower the scenery. On such a night, in such a storm, it would be impossible to see anything anyway, except during flashes of lightning. The text supports this: many times characters are identified only by their voices. These heath scenes are among the most famous in all dramatic literature, so much so that their familiarity itself can be distracting.

What is Lear up to besides showing off his lung power? Having been disobeyed for the first time in his life, Lear is testing his authority. His daughters have ignored his instructions; servants have defied him; his knights have followed Goneril's orders rather than Lear's; Cornwall faces him down; and even the loyal Gloucester tries to talk Lear out of issuing a direct command. Lear prays to the gods, but his prayers are not answered. Have the gods deserted him too? Perceiving a conspiracy afoot to usurp his authority over his family and kingdom, he heads out into the storm to see if he can command the elements.

Do they obey? Lear behaves like a field general commanding his troops. Someone has to determine cues for the guy on the thunder sheet and the lightning flasher. Usually, the thunder and lightning respond to Lear's lines, but should they? What if Lear gave an order and nothing happened? Do the elements obey Lear any better than his daughters? If Lear demands lightning, and he gets lightning, then this may prove to him that he's still the king. If he tries to command the elements and they ignore him, just as the gods seemed to earlier, then there's an opportunity for an expression of greater frustration, which can inform and drive the next speech. Or Lear could holler for lightning down right, and a bolt could hit him from up left. The director and the actor playing Lear need to take the time to chart these commands to determine where the sound and light effects go. Lear's performance should inform the tech, not the other way around, though involving the designers in these decisions early can be both fun and creative. Ultimately the director must set the cues. It's always a mistake to stop or slow down a play to accommodate business or to make a prop or technical effect work.

Though Shakespeare had primitive technical effects that passed for rain, wind, thunder, and lightning, today's sound and light effects are extensive, versatile, and relatively inexpensive to use. Instant sound and light changes are possible.

Lear's intent must be maintained in this scene, as loony as it might seem. He's the king. He gives orders.

We move toward that astonishing image of the man alone, the center of the universe, under attack, surrounded by hostile forces. It's my opinion that the storm scene is far more interesting if the elements do not obey the commands of the king.

There is no scenery, only total darkness alternating with blinding flashes of light and crashes of thunder. Then the scene gradually becomes naturalistic again, as Gloucester attempts to lead Lear back to his castle. The locale of the short two-scene between Cornwall and Edmund, III.5, is a problem, but it can be played in limbo, leaving Lear and the others upstage dimly lit. The attempt fails, and Lear, Edgar, the Fool, and Kent find shelter in a hovel in III.6, where the homeless have retreated to get out of the storm. It could be a chicken coop or a pigpen, but it's also the banks of the River Styx, a morgue, a court of law, whatever Lear's imagination makes it. Seven actors play the scene. Four others enter to finish it. Yet this is the smallest, most confined setting in the play.

Lear's so-called "madness" is displayed here. Certainly the sanity of anyone who seeks to order around the elements should be questioned, but there's always a logic in Shakespearean madness. In II.4, Lear has experienced the collapse of his authority. He must get it back. Failing to command the universe, he tears off his clothing, the last remnants of his kingship, and begins from scratch as unencumbered man, a poor, naked wretch, advised by a fool and a madman.

Through the storm scene, the Fool urges Lear to return to his daughters and ask their forgiveness, but once Lear is convinced that Poor Tom, his new counselor, is a wiser philosopher, the Fool is ignored. The Fool returns to something of his old form in the hovel scene, but he is clearly tiring. Gloucester brings a small horse cart to the hovel to convey Lear to Dover. The last reference to the Fool is Kent's order, "Come, help to bear thy master. Thou must not stay behind." But there is no response: the Fool is given no further lines. The next time we see Lear, he's wandering through the woods recruiting an army, but the Fool isn't with him. Where does the Fool go when he's not there any more, when the Playwright has ended, resolved his function? Shakespeare doesn't even bother to explain.

As in the final moments of *Measure For Measure*, directors and actors are tempted to resolve moments like this, but Shakespeare's ambiguities should be respected, left alone. I think it's wrong to resolve the Fool's function, especially to give him a death. Despite Kent's order, the Fool simply remains behind. If there's to be an intermission, place it here.

The blinding scene, III.7, follows the hovel scene (or the intermission) with great urgency. It's logical to play it back at the courtyard. The storm has ended, and it's early morning, pre-dawn. Goneril and Regan have discovered that Gloucester facilitated the escape of Lear, so they punish him for his treachery by gouging out his eyes in one of the most horrifying scenes in all Shakespeare. It must be played coldly and methodically. I suggest that Gloucester not be tied to a chair, but be held with ropes in a kneeling position, his back to the audience. When Gloucester's blinding is complete, all the scenic elements disappear into a bright painful gray and become the road to Dover, IV.1, a blind man's world.

Gloucester and Curan (the Old Man) need not leave the stage. They cower in plain sight, Curan silently ministering to his wounded master as III.7 resolves, as Cornwall and Regan exit, as Edgar enters for his IV.1 soliloquy. Curan helps Gloucester to his feet, and they move toward Edgar. This delicate, gentle scene should never be cut or edited. Edgar takes responsibility for his blinded father; from this point on, Gloucester only moves when Edgar moves. When Edgar releases himself from Gloucester's grip, Gloucester must stand where he's left. In Scranton, Daniel Nelbach broke this rule and fell right off the stage.

In IV.2 we see Edmund and Goneril as lovers. Not only are they lovers, but they're contriving to kill the Duke of Albany, Goneril's husband. Stephen Booth lists Albany among his "Kamikaze roles," those that critics always pick on, that actors are virtually doomed to fail in. Still, like a handful of generals in Shakespeare's soldier plays, Albany must have size, presence, an unmistakable authority; he is not the "milk-livered man" whom Goneril describes. That's the language of an unfaithful wife demeaning the man she has betrayed. Of those left alive at the end of the play, Albany is the highest ranked.

Now we return to Gloucester led by Poor Tom. Gloucester's blindness is real: his eyes have been gouged out. Edgar's madness is feigned: he pretends to be a Bedlam beggar to disguise his true identity.

Shakespeare's audience, accustomed to the Elizabethan playhouse with its non-representational thrust stage, was used to being told where they were. In that box office smash hit, *Henry V*, for example, the Chorus, the voice of the Playwright, asks the audience for their trust, directing their imaginations:

> Piece out our imperfections with your thoughts ...
> And make imaginary puissance.
> Think, when we talk of horses, that you see them....

That's fair enough. The audience, after paying the price of admission, has no responsibility other than response. Safe and relaxed, they are free to react to whatever they see and hear.

In IV.6 of *King Lear*, this principle is tested to the extreme. The stage is empty. It's neutral. It's neither night nor day, but it's bright enough to see two actors entering, a madman and a blind man. Where are they? The madman tells us they're climbing up a hill. The blind man says the ground is even, no hill. The madman hears the sea. The blind man hears nothing. The madman tells his companion that they've reached the very verge of the cliff, within a foot of the edge. He describes the beach below and the sea beyond. They are so high up that the fishermen on the beach look like mice. In fact, the height of the cliff explains why the blind man can't hear the sound of the surf. It's too far below. The madman complains of dizziness.

The blind man accepts this explanation, gives him a tip, and asks to be left in peace so he can drop over the cliff to his death. We remember that the blind man described this place earlier as

> ... a cliff whose high and bending head
> Looks fearfully in the confined deep.

So far, the "trust us" principle is working. Gloucester's blinding has apparently impaired the rest of his senses. He and Poor Tom *are* on the edge of a precipice, and the audience believes it because they are used to believing what they're told, even though the limits of the playhouse might demand that they question, disbelieve what they're seeing. The performance contract remains valid.

But then the madman tells us in an aside that he does "trifle thus with his despair ... to cure him." "Trifle?" What is he talking about? There's no time for an answer. The blind man kneels, prays for his son, bids the madman farewell and falls forward. He falls from his knees to a prone position and lies still. The madman addresses the audience again:

> ... had he been where he thought
> By this had thought been past.

Where did we think he was? We were told that the hill was real, the cliff was real, the beach and surf and distant sea were real. The blind man lies still. Did he fall off the cliff to his death, or didn't he? The madman then assumes another persona and runs down the "beach" to the "corpse" of the blind man. And he revives. He's not dead. It's got to be a miracle, because otherwise a drop of some ten masts' length would surely have killed him. The Playwright has conned the audience. The madman has lied to the blind man and to them as well. Where are we? We know where we're not: we're not on the cliff nor the beach. That fiction has been exposed.

Then another madman enters, dressed in rags, wearing a garland crown of flowers. What is this second lunatic doing? He is a king of nothing, recruiting an army, paying out press money, auditioning archers, rounding up mice as beasts of burden or war-horses. The newly arrived king challenges an opponent to single combat, bragging that he's David to any Goliath. He watches an arrow fly straight to the bull's eye. There is a moment of lucidity as he remembers the terrible storm that refused to do his bidding. Then he's off to court to render judgment on a man indicted for adultery, Gloucester's offense, and on and on and on. The first madman, Poor Tom, has already fooled the audience. Are they going to believe this second one?

There is a continuity of purpose in Lear's actions. He is dressed (or undressed), as are Gloucester and Edgar, like a beggar, but his mission is clear. From the time his authority is defied at the end of II.4, he is intent on taking back his kingdom, and if he lacks followers, money, equipment, horses, he'll figure out a way to find them. Lear never relinquishes his crown.

Is there a guiding principle of design that will work at least most of the time, in each and every play? When the Playwright specifies a setting or a state of nature, day or night, it makes sense to reinforce that specificity. If time and place are not specified, or if the Playwright is ambiguous or patently deceptive, as in Gloucester's non-fall off a non-cliff to his non-death, it is the responsibility of the director and actors to maintain the ambiguity or support the deception. But the director and designers better be on the same page from the beginning, or much time and money will be wasted on technical devices that do not add to the play. From this point on, Lear's escape at IV.6.200, the question of scenery is irrelevant. Geography is irrelevant. Interior/exterior are irrelevant. The blinding of Gloucester has altered the way we all see.

There are several resolutions in *King Lear*. Two main plots converge at IV.6.180, a tableau of three wretched creatures, when Lear reminds us that we are watching a play performed on a great stage of fools. The universe stops for a moment: it would be gutsy to put in a Samuel Beckett grand pause here, before the play charges on again. How long can an audience endure a stoppage of the action, silence and stillness?

At IV.7, we come to what appears to be the happy ending, the reconciliation between Lear and Cordelia that will be echoed in several other plays yet to be written. Father and daughter forgive each other, and they exit arm in arm. If the play ended here, the audience would go home content. But it doesn't. I suggest that IV.7 and V.3 be *rehearsed*, but not played, together, because the second continues the first. Lear has awakened from his nightmare of madness to be reunited with his lost daughter. This is no dream. She's really there, and they can be loving friends again. Perhaps, soon, she'll present him with the grandson he wants. A quiet, frugal life near Cordelia and her children will be kingdom enough.

Now we come to one of the strangest battles in all Shakespeare. Cordelia has returned from France with an army to rescue her father. The French are surrounded and forced to fight. The British forces are combined, Albany leading his own army, Edmund leading the army of Cornwall. Albany, as general, outranks Edmund. But why a battle? Though Goneril and Regan may wish their father dead, Albany is not a part of their conspiracy, unless he has been convinced that the French force is an invasion, and there's little evidence of that. The battle does not do what Shakespearean battles usually do: demonstrate God's favor as the righteous triumphs over the traitor. The prudent director is advised *not* to put it on-stage. War is too strong an image. *King Lear* is a tragedy, but not because the English defeat the French.

The battle brings us to the second chorus of Lear/Cordelia's gentle love duet of reconciliation, only interrupted by Edmund's impatience. Father and daughter go off to prison to "sing like birds i' th' cage."

A duel to the death then resolves the third plot, the rivalry between Edgar and Edmund.

The audience is, by now, exhausted and impatient, but they must still endure one of the most heartbreaking scenes in all literature, the arrival of Lear carrying the body of the hanged Cordelia. Lear announces his own entrance with "Howl, howl, howl!" staggers down stage, then collapses and lullabies his daughter's corpse, as if she were a sleeping child. Shakespeare surpasses his own genius in this unbearable scene. The director and other actors are well warned to stay out of Lear's way and let him play the scene quietly and delicately.

Lear's final moment is one of great joy, for he imagines that Cordelia has begun to breathe again. His heart leaps, and he dies. Though Albany, Edgar, and Kent have a few more lines to give the play a neat ending, this is the final image, the dead Lear with the dead Cordelia in his arms, again alone in the universe. Nothing has come of nothing.

The 1608 Quarto gives us an entirely different final scene than the 1623 First Folio above (my preference), almost creating a different play. Some critics argue that these two endings actually resolve two different plays. It's worth consideration, but the director has to choose one or the other, and I suggest that both texts be studied carefully before preparing the working script. Quarto ending or Folio ending, the death of Cordelia must work the same dark magic on enough of the audience to make them subtly aware of their collective emotional involvement. If they are not moved, then the conclusion is negative. The play hasn't worked.

An older actor, after three hours of playing Lear, has just enough fire left in him to play the last scene. Picking up and carrying Cordelia on is too much, impossible. Within that one speech, "Howl, howl, howl!" Lear has to come into view with Cordelia in his arms, carry her downstage to his "mark" where he'll end the play (lights must be considered), arrive at a pose that will be comfortable enough to play the rest of the scene, then adjust that pose again when he dies. It's my opinion that he should be in his final position by the time he begins, "Lend me a looking glass." I find it unsatisfactory for Lear to put the corpse down, kneel beside her, then pick her up again and cradle her. He would have to perform this whole sequence alone. Cordelia can't help him out.

The movement is possible if the director uses the other actors available to him: Kent, Albany, Edgar, and the officer (Lear's Knight), whom Edgar sends off. It requires another strong man, an actor or stagehand, off-stage to pick Cordelia up and hold her in a mirror image of Lear's carry. Lear positions himself for the entrance. On the cue, "Bear him hence awhile," the strong man hands Cordelia to Lear, who begins his "Howl, howl, howl!" on cue, while the Knight backs up Lear and keeps him steady. Lear moves onto the stage where he is met by Edgar, Kent, and Albany. They spot him, guide him, steer him down to his mark, then support the weight of Cordelia for a moment, as Lear collapses into position, and give her back to him for the pieta. The Knight has followed, watching carefully to see that Lear's costume does not entangle him as he collapses into the pose.

The illusion must be Lear carrying Cordelia until his legs give out, then collapsing to his knees (he's actually sitting on his right hip with both legs to his left) while still holding her. The brief assumption of Cordelia's weight by Kent and Edgar should go unnoticed.

The attention of the audience must be on Lear and Cordelia from the moment Edmund confesses to giving the order for their death. Nothing that follows after must interrupt that concentration. Even the lines of the other actors (which shouldn't be cut) must be delivered in a spirit of resignation, agreement, no conflict among them. In his film, Peter Brook juxtaposed the dead Cordelia with a live Cordelia, impossible intercutting that can't be duplicated on-stage, but Brook's editing, cinema magic, informed the meaning of the scene by reinforcing Lear's confusion.

Don't bring the bodies of Goneril and Regan back onto the stage. Since there are several quartos and several folios, each dealing with this stage direction differently, there is some latitude. Let be.

The final image is reduced to the minimum number of players: Lear, Cordelia, Edgar, Kent, Albany, and Lear's Knight. If there's an unobtrusive way to get Lear's Knight off the set, strike him too. Otherwise, open up the staging so Lear and Cordelia are in focus, loosely framed by the others.

In my introduction, I noted the different challenges Shakespeare's plays pose to scholars as compared to directors. I bemoan both jobs here. No matter what the final choices, the scene depends on the emotional commitment of the actors and protection from any outside distractions. Bad actors can't make it work, and impossible environments can kill it. An insensitively played curtain call can destroy it as well. The stage must be quiet during the final speeches. The lights dim to blackness, and *nobody moves.* No one in the wings moves or speaks or even breathes. The final silent absence of light is part of the play, the "nothing" that we've returned to so many times, but here there is no ambiguity: the deaths of Lear and Cordelia are irrevocable, the very definition of nothing. Our play is done. Everyone must wait for the applause to begin before anyone moves, because the curtain call must not be allowed to damage that final moment. The more effective the play, the more mesmerized the audience, the longer the time between final word and applause. Then, in the darkness, Edgar and Kent help Lear and Cordelia to their feet, and they move quietly upstage away from the audience, as the lights come up, and actors off-stage enter to begin the curtain call.

It's always difficult to get this play on. It wears actors out, tests the patience of even the best of them. The September 11, 2001, terrorist attacks came on a dress rehearsal day for my San Francisco production, scheduled to preview for an invited audience two days later. The producer's sister woke me up at 6:00 that morning, screaming, "Turn on the television. Turn on the television." Everyone in the company had friends or family in New York. My younger son, Timothy, lived two miles away from Ground Zero. My wife, Ellen, was at home alone in New Jersey. All the *King Lear* actors spent the day on cell phones or pay phones trying to get through to New York and New Jersey. The rehearsal was a shambles: suddenly, all those talented professional actors were brought to the realization that our play was not the most important thing in the universe. Just before he died, I told Davey Marlin-Jones this story, and that wonderful, great heart took issue with them in absentia. Davey protested that the actors were mistaken: the play *was* the most important thing in the universe. No one who didn't believe that could possibly perform it.

I've mentioned my daughter, Shannon, several times in this book, but please indulge me in one more story. My 1979 production of *King Lear* was a bear to get open, and we went immediately into rehearsal for *A Midsummer Night's Dream* the day after. A week later, just before Shannon's third birthday, I came to see another *Lear* performance. I was frazzled, over-extended, too critical of my own work. Then, the play grabbed me, dragged me along with it. It was agony. I watched that final scene, stifling my own sobbing, waited until the curtain call began, then stumbled out of the theatre and drove home, much too fast. I dashed into the house and up the steps to Shannon's room and listened to her sleep. She breathed. I hugged her. She lived. My poor fool was not hanged.

CHAPTER 34

Timon of Athens

The best production of a Shakespeare play I ever saw was *Timon of Athens*, directed by Michael Langham in 1963 at the Stratford Festival of Ontario. Starring John Colicos, in modern dress, with a score by Duke Ellington, it envisioned Timon as an Aristotle Onassis with Alcibiades as a Fidel Castro. It was an example of how good Shakespeare can be with enough talent, enough money and enough time. It was lavishly produced, superbly cast, and brilliantly directed, and, as the flaks would have it, "torn from the headlines."

In 1982, I placed the play in 1929, in a *Great Gatsby*-like setting on Long Island, New York, with costumes by Heidi Hollmann. Timon made his first entrance in traditional fox hunting "pinks," led by two greyhounds. It was the "snob hit" of the season, garnering rave reviews. I've never seen a successful Athenian version of the play. The productions that work all seem to be set in other times and places.

Timon of Athens was a collaboration between Shakespeare and the rising star Thomas Middleton, who would later do such damage to *Macbeth*. There is no evidence that *Timon* was ever produced during Shakespeare's lifetime, and the First Folio text reads like a first draft with several instances of repetitive passages, i.e. alternatives to speeches, on the same page. I can imagine Shakespeare presenting the manuscript to Richard Burbage (whose father, James, had died in 1597) and Burbage reading it quickly, then advising Shakespeare to shove it under the bed and take a vacation for a few weeks. The play is negative to the point of being suicidal. It's paranoid, misogynistic, and obsessed with venereal diseases; the high points dramatically are wild, insulting tirades hurled at the audience.

On the other hand, it's easy to chart and rehearse, provided the director pays attention to and deals with an early structural problem. Shakespeare might have set out to write a play about the rebel warrior, Alcibiades, with Plutarch's chapter on him as inspiration, but Alcibiades is reduced to a bit player as Timon immediately becomes the focus of the play.

Timon of Athens begins in a world of wealth, luxury, and benevolence. Timon is the perfect billionaire, a wealthy altruist. He is not evil; quite the contrary, he believes in his own virtue as well as the goodness of mankind. He finances business enterprises, subsidizes artists, provides a dowry for the bride of a servant, bails a friend out of prison, pays off everyone's debts and is the perfect host at a non-stop party. Everyone is welcome, even the philosopher Apemantus, who warns Timon that he is merely buying friends who will disappear when his money is gone. But Timon believes that will be never. The market will always be bullish, his wealth unending, his cornucopia bottomless, and generosity his only vice. Gifts fly back and forth, chorus girls dance and sing, everyone laughs at Timon's jokes, and the banquet never runs out of champagne.

Timon of Athens, New Jersey Shakespeare Festival, 1982: Tim Quinn, Lewis Musser, Van Santvoord, Chet Hood as followers of Alcibiades; Robin Leary as Phyrnia; Annie Stafford as Timandra; J.C. Hoyt (center) as Alcibiades (photograph by Blair Holley).

Then something happens. It's not explained in the text, but suddenly it's there at the top of Act II: Timon is broke, and he owes everyone. How did this happen? Here's the problem referred to above. Certainly, this sudden reversal in fortune must be built into the design of the production. In the Langham production, it was the collapse of the world oil market. In our 1982 production, it was the stock market crash of October 1929. Today we may (cautiously) make comparison with the crash of 2008, surmising that Timon has led friends and acquaintances into speculative investments, sub-prime mortgages, and underfinanced enterprises. It could be a play about Bernard Madoff's clients. Timon himself could be played as a benevolent and optimistic Madoff who naively invested his and everyone else's money in ventures that he honestly believed would make money as long as the economy kept improving. Someday, I'd like to do this play in the London of Charles Dickens: Timon as a reverse Scrooge.

This reversal of fortunes comes on slowly and has been building for years. In a novel it can be explained, spelled out, built over several pages. In a play, however, that's too slow a process. The director needs something visual to represent the bursting of a massive economic bubble at the beginning of Act II. We used a snowstorm of shredded ticker tape to signify the instant trauma of Black Friday, 1929. It took some effort to clean up the paper — several interns quickly sweeping the debris off-stage while Apemantus, a Jimmy Breslin-like reporter, casually watched, smoking a cigarette — but the effort was well spent. That visual metaphor, that memory, remained in the audience's mind for the rest of the evening.

The next several scenes play out the catastrophe as Timon's creditors hound him and he asks friends and colleagues to repay loans, then for investments, even handouts. But the crash is universal, a pandemic. Any audience member who ever experienced an economic downturn can relate.

What is unique about this play is the absence of a major woman's role. We changed one of Timon's investors, Sempronius, into a female CEO, Sempronia, and two of our leading women played Alcibiades' camp followers, but the balance of the play remained male.

One after another, friends, investors, creditors turn out empty pockets to Timon, leaving him bankrupt and in danger of debtors' prison. The rejections and refusals build over some 40 minutes of real (audience) time, only digressing for a moment to establish that Alcibiades is an enemy of Athens because a friend of his has been, in his opinion, unjustly executed. Then we arrive at the banquet scene. Timon has invited all his friends and creditors to a feast that promises to be as opulent as those of the old days. They conclude that Timon was just testing them, pretending to be in need. He gathers them at the banquet table and says an ambiguous grace, which could be insulting or not. On comes the feast, which proves to be warm water and stones. Timon explodes, drenching them with water and hurling stones and utensils at them as they scramble to exit. III.6 segues into IV.1 as Timon curses first his former friends, then all of Athens, and finally the audience when the guests are gone.

His curses all refer to the false worship of riches, an enduring theme adaptable to any era. He wishes on his friends the worst illnesses of men and animals. He suggests that he'll burn down his own house and hopes for an earthquake to take down the city. He prays for incontinence, disobedience, theft, murder, anarchy, patricide, the transformation of virgins into prostitutes, impiety, unbound sexual license, riot, plagues, lust, airborne diseases, and the abandonment of industry. He denounces all friendships as contagious, poisonous, and all human contact as merely a source of venereal disease. Though Timon has been basically sexless up to this point, he reveals himself to be overly concerned with sexually transmitted diseases, a theme he'll return to again and again throughout the play. As Timon's house burns down, his faithful steward, Flavius, shares what petty cash is left with Timon's servants, then sets out to find and serve his master, whom he insists had only good intentions:

> Poor honest lord, brought low by his own heart,
> Undone by goodness! Strange, unusual blood,
> When man's worst sin is he does too much good!
> Who then dares to be half so kind again?

If the director wants to schedule an intermission, the logical place for it is between IV.2 and IV.3.

In IV.3, Timon has abandoned all civilization and found shelter in a cave near the seashore. The wilderness is barren, inhospitable. He wishes to die, and he needs little to sustain life. He is in rags, unshaven, filthy, living on roots, berries, herbs, whatever he can pull out of the sterile earth. With luck, he'll find a plant that will poison him, some infection that will hasten his death. Failing that, he has rigged a hangman's noose on a convenient tree.

As he digs, he continues his litany of curses, invoking the sun and moon, assailing the audience as representative of all mankind. Instead of roots, he finds a treasure trove, a fortune in buried gold and jewels, enough to solve all his financial problems and those of his friends and associates. But it's too late — by now Timon has abandoned materialism as evil, unworthy of his new philosophy. Midas has learned his lesson and turned misogynist.

The discovery of gold should bring a big laugh. The play continues its downward slide as Timon contrives to use his newfound treasure to do the greatest damage to the most people. He will have the prostitutes infect everyone with venereal disease. Ultimately, he exits the stage and hangs himself, unique among major Shakespearean characters as an off-stage suicide. The play ends, not with a bang, but with a whimper. I'm sure the playwrights would have come up with a better ending if the play had had a theatrical life. But it didn't, and they didn't. Let be.

I wish I could do *Timon* in 2010. It resonates particularly just now.

Chapter 35

Cymbeline

Shakespeare wrote a string of monumental tragedies, progressively meaner and more angry, over a period of five years, 1604–1608: *Othello, King Lear, Macbeth, Antony and Cleopatra, Coriolanus,* and *Timon of Athens.* With the latter play, never produced during Shakespeare's lifetime, the Playwright hit a wall, and his next four plays were radical departures from the tragedies.

Susanna, Shakespeare's elder daughter, married Dr. John Hall, Stratford physician, in 1607, and in 1608 she presented her father with his first granddaughter. The child, Elizabeth Hall, evidently changed her grandfather's life and his work forever. Her arrival dazzled him, and it suddenly dawned on him, that old cliché that politicians haul out every four years: *families* are the most important of all treasures. Master Will began writing faerie tales, all featuring lost little girls who were eventually reunited with their fathers: *Pericles, Cymbeline,* and *The Winter's Tale.* From the near hysterical vitriol of *Timon of Athens,* these three plays, plus *The Tempest* and *The Two Noble Kinsmen,* shifted to themes of repentance and forgiveness, following the admonition of Saint Paul in his famous 1st Letter to the Corinthians, and extolling the greatest of virtues. The word Paul used was the Greek word "agape," which English translators have rendered as "love" or "charity." Actually, the meaning is more complicated, combining charity, love, and forgiveness into one linguistic concept, echoing the Sermon on the Mount: "forgive us our trespasses as we forgive those who trespass against us."

Each of these plays contains a Yom Kippur, the day on which we forgive and ask forgiveness. And when each of the errant fathers and brothers is forgiven, the sun comes out and the faith of the audience is awakened. If King Cymbeline can get away with what he did and still have another chance at heaven, surely the rest of us have some hope.

Here's a disclaimer: my theories about the familial influence on Shakespeare's later plays, those that modern critics and directors characterize as "romances," as well as my theory about the Christian origins of *Cymbeline,* are mine alone and can only be proved or disproved by viewing the plays. I have collected shreds of evidence from the religious liberality of James I/VI, through a time of great Shakespearean anger, through a perceived reconciliation with his wife and daughters, through the onslaught of grandfatherhood, all bearing on the writing of those five romances. Whatever the cause, something significant must have happened to the Playwright between *Timon of Athens* and *Cymbeline.* Fatherhood might have passed the young Master Will by, obsessed as he was with success in the theatre, but with the arrival of his granddaughter, I believe he became a new person. Grandfathers take the time to stop running and really observe their grandbabies.

Cymbeline, New Jersey Shakespeare Festival, 1981: Peter Burnell as Posthumus Leonatus, Chris Weatherhead as Imogen, Richard M. Davidson as Cymbeline, Stephen McNaughton as Arviragus, Ron Mangravite as Guiderius (photograph by Jerry Dalia).

Theories, theories, theories, not to be bought, but rather argued. But how else is it possible that the same poet who wrote *Timon of Athens* could have written *Cymbeline?*

I only directed *Cymbeline* once, and I never played in it, although I have seen several productions. I'd love to tackle it again. My 1981 production played in repertory with *Romeo and Juliet* and Molière's *Tartuffe*. I had played Macbeth the summer before, and I directed *Macbeth* again at Penn State University in January and February of 1981. I spent six days a week in State College, Pennsylvania, but I drove back and forth to my home in New Jersey each weekend, a four-hour trip each way. I taped the Caedmon Records *Cymbeline* (with Boris Karloff in the title role) and played the tapes on each trip. By the time *Macbeth* opened, I had heard *Cymbeline* ten times, but I still couldn't figure out what the play actually said. Even today, I'm not sure, but I'm getting there.

When we went into rehearsal with *Cymbeline* that summer, I admitted as much to the actors. I said that I didn't know what the play was about, what it meant, what it said, but I did know what each word, each line, each phrase meant. So we'd start from the beginning and try to figure it out together. We proceeded to go line by line, fulfilling each moment, each beat, physicalizing the text. At the final rehearsals, we were still uncertain, dispirited, and suspicious that we might have a "turkey" on our hands.

But the process had worked. Audiences and critics loved it, and, fed by their enthusiasm, the actors relaxed. It turned into a marvelous production, the hit of the New Jersey theatre season, with many people returning to see it more than once.

Clearly, this story is of little help to a director preparing this play for production. What can be said that will help? The play is a departure from form. It is neither tragedy, comedy, history, nor pastoral, though it contains elements of all of these. It's a faerie tale: "Once upon a time, there was a king of Britain who had two sons and a daughter. The sons were kidnapped in infancy, and the King's wife died of grief. The daughter grew up to become a beautiful princess. The King married again, a wicked widow with an evil son, whom she hoped to marry to the princess. But the princess was in love with another, an orphan whom she secretly married. When the King and Queen learned of the marriage, they banished the princess' husband and confined her to house arrest in the castle. The husband returned to Britain in disguise and distinguished himself in battle against invading Romans, thus earning the King's forgiveness. The two lost sons were reunited with their sister and father, and all forgave and were forgiven."

This is the basic bedtime story plot, but the playwright added many sophisticated elements to his tale: an ill-advised bet on Imogen's chastity between her husband and an unscrupulous would-be seducer; the Queen's son Cloten's planned rape of Imogen; the death and beheading of Cloten by one of the King's lost sons; a sleeping potion that creates a death-like state; and some murky history about the conquest of Britain by the Roman forces of Octavius Caesar Augustus. Like *Othello* and *The Winter's Tale*, *Cymbeline* dwells for a while on the theme of jealous husbands of chaste wives.

Much has been written about anachronisms in *Cymbeline*, and designers will attempt to resolve them, but such efforts only serve to confuse the audience and hide an element that I believe to be important in understanding the playwright's intentions.

It is widely accepted that William Shakespeare was a closet Roman Catholic, carefully hiding his religious beliefs, as well as political theories, by setting his plays out of his own time and place. In *Cymbeline*, I believe that Shakespeare makes a strong religious statement with his characters and then skillfully buries that statement in the action. The play begins at the time of the birth of Jesus Christ, which influences everything that follows, finally resulting in the multiple forgivenesses that rejoin the King and his children. The birth of Christ changes the whole world for the better: it sanctifies the just and the moral, and punishes, then forgives, the immoral.

If directors attempt to put the Roman scenes into a Machiavellian Italy, for example, the importance of this essential event is lost. The play must remain in Britain and Rome during the reign of Caesar Augustus, and the design must reinforce this time. Modern dress or out-of-period productions only weaken the Playwright's intent and further obscure the already subtle moral of the play.

CHAPTER 36

Henry VIII

For the 1985 NJSF rep of *Henry VIII* and Robert Bolt's *A Man for All Seasons*, I went back to my research for earlier productions of Hermann Gressieker's *Royal Gambit* and John Osborne's *Luther*, as well as new books about Thomas More, Erasmus, Thomas Cardinal Wolsey, Archbishop Thomas Cranmer, Henry and his wives.

In *Shakespeare's English Kings*, Peter Saccio argues that this play by Shakespeare and John Fletcher isn't about the historical Henry VIII at all. I quote Saccio, because I couldn't say it better:

> ...the historical king whose egocentricity is perhaps unmatched elsewhere in the records of human personality, who changed from a splendid young athlete into a gross and diseased hulk, who destroyed the English monasteries and wasted the money he gained from their dissolution, who married six wives and executed two of them, who struck down saints like Thomas More and statesmen like Cardinal Wolsey and Thomas Cromwell, who was once described by Charles Dickens as a "most intolerable ruffian, a disgrace to human nature, and a blot of blood and grease upon the history of England," is not here. Instead Shakespeare gives us an embodiment of benevolence, wisdom, virtue, and majesty, a dream of a semi-divine king.

Although the history upon which this play is based has been the subject of unending books, novels, television series, indulge me while I summarize it, for to evaluate the play it is critical to bear in mind what Shakespeare *didn't* tell.

The heir apparent to King Henry VII was his first-born, Arthur. When Arthur died, Henry, his younger brother, became the Prince of Wales. Arthur had been married at age 15 to the Spanish princess, Katharine of Aragon, but when he died six months after the wedding, his father and her father, Ferdinand V, petitioned Rome for dispensation for Katharine to marry Prince Henry. They argued that her marriage to Arthur had never been consummated. The appeal to Rome dragged on for years, as discrepancies in the teachings of Leviticus and Deuteronomy were debated, but eventually pressure from Spain and England prevailed, and Pope Julius II consented to the necessary dispensation. Still, the prince didn't marry Katharine until after his father died in 1509 and he took the throne as King Henry VIII. She subsequently bore him several children, but only one survived, a daughter, Mary Tudor, later Queen Mary.

Shakespeare's play begins when Mary was four years old and covers the years 1520, when Henry was hailed as "Defender of the Faith" for his dissertation against Martin Luther, through the birth of Elizabeth I in September, 1533. The play is a romanticized version of the love story of Henry and Anne Boleyn. To understand and direct it, it is necessary to view it with the same optimism that exists at the beginning of *Romeo and Juliet* or *Troilus and*

Cressida. Indeed, in the play, Henry and Anne first meet at a ball in 1526, and Shakespeare again employs "il Fulmine," the thunderbolt.

Anne's elder sister, Mary, had been Henry's mistress earlier, but Anne herself allegedly resisted his advances until he promised to marry her. In order to marry Anne, Henry petitioned Rome to have his marriage to Katharine of Aragon declared invalid, on the grounds that he had sinned by wedding his brother's widow. He insisted that God had cursed this marriage — that the deaths of all Katharine's male offspring were evidence that God wanted him free of this marriage so he could beget an heir to the throne, who, by definition, had to be male. Although he acknowledged Henry Fitzroi, his son by Bessie Blount, a previous mistress, by conferring the titles of Dukes of Richmond and Somerset on him at age six, he stopped short of proclaiming Fitzroi his legal heir. England had to have a legitimate male heir. Katharine was past childbearing age. Henry insisted he had to cast her aside and find a new wife.

Pope Clement VII refused to grant an annulment or divorce for a number of political reasons, but his stated public argument was refusal to overturn the earlier dispensation granted by Pope Julius II. In defiance of the Pope and with the support of his bishops, Henry declared himself supreme head of the Church of England, divorced Katharine, and married Anne Boleyn, who then became queen and bore him a daughter, Elizabeth. Shakespeare's play concludes with the baptism of Elizabeth by Cranmer, the beginning of a golden age.

It is instructive to consider what and whom Shakespeare includes in *Henry VIII* and what is left unsaid. Just as *King John* omits any reference to the Magna Carta, *Henry VIII* does not mention the break from Roman Catholicism and the creation of what we know as the Anglican Church. This break can be pinpointed to February 7, 1531, when Henry addressed Parliament and demanded that he be recognized as supreme head of the Church of England: king and pope in one.

Among the important figures absent from the play's cast of characters are William Warham, Archbishop of Canterbury, Sir Thomas More, Bishop John Fisher, Sir Richard Rich, and several women essential to the bigger story. Archbishop Thomas Cranmer is present in the play, but is not accorded the importance he deserves: Cranmer was the theologian who first told Henry that, as king, he could do as he liked: change and enforce the laws, burn heroes and traitors alike at the stake, divorce and execute wives, assume the power of an emperor. According to Mark Twain, during the 38 years of Henry VIII's reign, 72,000 men, women, and children were judicially put to death for crimes as serious as murder, rape, and treason down to those as petty as stealing a chicken. Henry's reign was not unique in this regard; the death penalty had been in use at least since the Middle Ages, but Twain emphasized how far-reaching was the cruelty of this man.

In Cranmer's theology, the conscience of the king was the ultimate arbiter of God's will, pretty heady stuff for any man, but especially for one overladen with ego and self-righteousness. Henry considered himself a theologian, "the Defender of the Faith," and went to his grave believing he was a devout Catholic. He never saw his church as Protestant, nor did he change the liturgy or abolish the sacraments. Without intending it, however, he facilitated the infiltration of the doctrines of Luther, Calvin, Zwingli, Knox, etc., which eventually resulted in Oliver Cromwell's rebellion and the civil war of 1649. Cause and effect. Obsessed as he was with a legitimate male heir, Henry gave little thought to the far-reaching implications of his actions.

Thomas Wolsey, a cardinal of the Catholic Church and a candidate, however remote, for pope, was an important man in the England of Henry VII and Henry VIII. Some historians insist that he actually ran the country until Henry VIII dumped him. When Henry

declared himself both king and pope, Wolsey didn't have a chance: he had to choose between loyalty to the new religion or martyrdom, an impossible dilemma for a materialist. When he was arrested for treason, Wolsey said to his accusers, "If I had served God as diligently as I have done the king, He would not have given me over in my grey hairs," which Shakespeare rewrote into the more elegant:

> Had I but served my God with half the zeal
> I served my King, He would not in mine age
> Have left me naked to mine enemies.

Wolsey's role in history is certainly given significant importance in the play. He served Henry well, but he failed him in his "Great Matter": he could not effect the divorce of Katharine of Aragon.

In contrast, Thomas More attempted to remove himself from the divorce problem and was beheaded; although it took 400 years, the Catholic Church eventually named him a martyr and a saint. The best book about both Wolsey and More is Richard Marius' *Thomas More*, a book I own and treasure. Marius was a wonderful, decent human being and a brilliant scholar. Bishop John Fisher, the most outspoken and adamant in defense of Queen Katharine, lost his head along with More, but not before the Pope named him a Cardinal. He too was canonized.

Within two years of his marriage to her, Henry divorced and beheaded Anne with trumped-up, ill-advised accusations of adultery, incest, and treason. Jane Seymour, Henry's third wife, presented him with his only legitimate son, who became King Edward VI upon Henry's death. Thomas Cromwell engineered Anne Boleyn's fate, but lost his head when he botched the king's fourth marriage, to Anne of Cleves.

Edward died in his teens (probably due to the same genetic weakness that killed Prince Arthur and Henry's bastard son, Henry Fitzroi) and was briefly succeeded by Lady Jane Grey, a distant cousin, and then by his elder half-sister, Mary Tudor. For his service in the divorce of her mother, Katharine of Aragon, Mary had Cranmer burned at the stake, along with 300 other churchmen she deemed heretics. During her reign the nation briefly returned to Catholicism, but reverted again to the Church of England when she died childless in 1558, and her younger half-sister, Elizabeth I, became queen. Elizabeth would rule for 44 years.

Considering the doctrinal differences among Catholics, Church of England loyalists, Lutherans, and Puritans, it is essential to consider how the various forms of Christianity were affected during the reigns of the Tudors. To the Church of England, which had annulled Henry VIII's first marriage to Katharine of Aragon in order to validate his second marriage to Anne Boleyn, Elizabeth was legitimate. To the Catholics, she was a bastard.

In 1570 Pope Pius V put forth a bull excommunicating Queen Elizabeth and releasing all subjects from allegiance to her. Pius blamed the moral laxity of his predecessors for the Protestant Reformation and was obsessed with returning England to Catholicism. Looking at that bull objectively, it seems absurd. Was the Pope really so naïve as to think his edict would motivate all the common people of England to simply rise up and holler, "We're off the hook: the Pope says we owe no allegiance to the Queen?" On the contrary, the Pope's bull effectively supplied her ministers with justification for burning, hanging, and quartering the occasional outspoken closet Catholic.

Opposite: *Henry VIII*, New Jersey Shakespeare Festival, 1985: Thea Ruth White as the Midwife, Dion Anderson as Henry VIII (photograph by Jim Chambers).

After Pius V's death, his cause was taken up by his successors Gregory XIII and Sixtus V. In the spring of 1588 the Catholic Alliance pushed Spain to attack. The Spanish Armada, under the command of Don Medina Sidonia, sailed to invade England with 130 ships and 30,000 sailors, galley slaves, and marines. For the next two months, battling storms, the Armada sailed up the English Channel, around the tip of Scotland and south along the western coast of Ireland. More storms off Ireland destroyed most of the fleet, and Sidonia limped home. Naturally, the English gave credit for the defeat of the Armada to their sea captains, including Sir Francis Drake and Walter Raleigh, and to God, who supplied the bad weather, a solid argument for the providential theory of history.

Elizabeth's primary concern was a united England with herself as sovereign. Once, when Sir Francis Walsingham, head of Elizabeth's Secret Service, was asked the purpose of English education, he promptly answered, "To create loyal subjects to the Queen." If religion had been truly important to her, she would have chosen her father's Church of England or her sister's Catholicism. Instead she cobbled together a compromise liturgy in English that sounded Catholic and an ethic based on Calvinist articles of faith, a national church calculated to appeal to the overwhelming majority of her subjects. Only the right and left extremist fringes could possibly feel slighted. Unlike her sister, Elizabeth promoted no religious reign of terror, no burning of dissenters. Her church held onto the Hebrew Prophets, their Holy Books, the Christian Gospels, Jesus and his Apostles, while Elizabeth herself replaced the Virgin Mary by assuming the persona of the iconic Virgin Queen.

Elizabeth was supported by skillful politicians: Walsingham, the Cecils, Raleigh, Essex. In her long, brilliant rule, she maintained the civil reforms of her father and grandfather, fostered international trade, avoided war, and allowed education, art, literature, music, and the theatre to flourish.

The end of this story, if there ever is an end to a story, was a brilliant dirty trick, perfectly legal, allegedly approved by Elizabeth on her deathbed: revenge was taken on the Scots and Mary Stuart by declaring her son, King James VI of Scotland, King James I of England. With this action, the British nobility effected a bloodless conquest of Scotland that had eluded them for centuries, though it took the politicians another century to effect true union, what we know today as the United Kingdom.

Now, with the historical summation behind us, let's get to Shakespeare's play. In the simplest terms, *Henry VIII* is Shakespeare's attempt to curry favor by legitimizing Henry's second marriage, the birth of Elizabeth, her reign and that of her successor, James I/VI. The play, especially in its overwritten, purple prediction of Elizabeth's greatness, insists that the Virgin Queen justified all that came before.

Having dismissed it so perfunctorily, let me note some of the problems and joys of directing it. In addition to the love story between Henry and Anne, the play has echoes of *The Winter's Tale*, not in story and structure, but in the ill treatment of a queen by a tyrannical husband and the twin trial scenes of Katharine and Hermione.

The Playwright spends some 35 minutes establishing historical elements and characters, notably Henry himself, Katharine, Cardinal Wolsey, the Dukes of Norfolk and Buckingham. The action beats like a Chronicle play, condensing 13 years into two and one-half hours of stage time, and the first five years go by before we arrive at the masked ball (shades of the Capulet party) where Henry meets Anne, and the domestic tragedy/comedy begins. Themes of love, lust, fertility, and morality soon bubble to the surface. From their meeting through the birth of the Princess Elizabeth seven and one-half years pass. Two and one-half years later, Anne was beheaded, but Shakespeare leaves her full story to future writers. His play is an homage to his late queen, not a history. The validity of the English Reformation, the politics of the time, nothing but the divorce of Katharine and the romance and marriage of Henry and Anne concerns the Playwright here. The actors and the characters better conjure up respect for that romance or there's no play.

Just as modern American actors would prefer to play Shaw's or Anouilh's Joan of Arc rather than Shakespeare's, so too do they lean toward the self-indulgent Henry VIII, the obese beast of the late Holbein paintings, as performed by Charles Laughton rather than the sexy young man of Shakespeare's play. But as in the Chronicle plays, when history and the play agree, the director should align them in production. When they don't agree, then the play must win out. The Playwright's vision must supplant recent historical discoveries and revisions. We can still do this play accurately. We don't have to bend the text, but everything else we know or think we know about these people and this age will be there as the play is designed and built and rehearsed, as inescapable as the humidity.

Doing *Henry VIII* in rep with Robert Bolt's modern masterpiece *A Man for All Seasons* exposed its bias and that of Bolt's play as well. Even today, it's difficult not to take sides about the man Henry VIII. Athletic or obese, charismatic or obnoxious, a great king or a despoiler of the nation, what was he, and what were those around him? Books about Henry, his wives, and his age could fill up a library. Can we distill the truth out of all those books? Even if they collectively give the lie to Shakespeare's play, we still have only that play, its characters, to put on the stage.

Perhaps the most ambiguous scene in the play, V.1, involves what would have been an earth-shaking moment to Shakespeare's audience. Henry is awaiting news of the birth of Anne's first child. She is in labor, and he busies himself with the loyalty and religious orthodoxy of Cranmer and Cromwell. Busy, busy. At this point in the story, does anybody in the audience really care about them? Of course not. Everyone is waiting to find out whether the baby is male or female. The tension of the scene depends on that question. Ten minutes pass before the silliest midwife in creation comes fluttering in, giggling and blessing the king. An impossible scene to play follows: Henry says,

> Now, by thy looks
> I guess thy message. Is the queen delivered?
> Say aye, and of a boy.

We wrestled with this a lot in rehearsal. It's not a simple Q and A moment. The king asks this woman a simple question, and then, before she has a chance to answer, he gives her a direct command. He's the king, and she can't disobey him. She replies,

> Ay, ay, my liege;
> And of a lovely boy: the God of Heaven
> Both now and ever bless her!

He has told her what to say, and she says it. We hear what we know is wrong, but he hears what he wants to hear and his wildest dreams are fulfilled, his desperate prayers answered: he has a son! Then something happens. The midwife contradicts herself, continuing:

> 'Tis a girl,
> Promises boys hereafter.

Leave it up to the actors, and give them free rein in rehearsal until they find the logic here for themselves. Has she first obeyed out of fear, telling him it's a boy? Is she now forced to cower and correct herself? She has now pronounced the truth, followed by an evident apology, and the truth is unbearable. As Shakespeare has shown us and as all audiences know, Henry has risked his very soul, changed his whole world because of his insistence on a legitimate male heir. He has sanctified his desire for Anne Boleyn, given his lust spiritual significance: she must give birth to the savior of England. The silly midwife continues with a fulsome compliment,

> 'Tis as like you
> As cherry is to cherry.

He can't bear to speak to her, has nothing to say to her. He dismissively commands Lovell to give her 100 marks as he storms out on the way to Anne. These are traveling lines, their purpose simply to take him off-stage. His great joy at the midwife's single word "boy" has been aborted and reversed by her single word "girl." Unlike 99.9 percent of Shakespeare, here the emotional reaction happens off the line. The playwrights gives Henry no soaring declaration of sorrow but only a moment of impotent apoplectic silence before he exits, leaving the foolish messenger to complain that 100 marks is a lousy tip.

It is not what the playwrights have given the actors here, but what the actors have *not* been given that defines the reaction of the actor playing Henry. If the play were about anyone else, a fictional king like Cymbeline, for instance, or a beloved national hero like Henry V, the audience's sympathy might be with this husband and wife, but maybe life in this play is one big filthy joke, one obscene punch line after another.

If I have failed to describe the production I directed or to define the object of this play, please examine its last five minutes, excluding its gratuitous epilogue, which is silly enough to be delivered by our friend the midwife. V.5 depicts the baptism of Elizabeth and Cranmer's prediction of her accomplishments. Written in 1612, nine years after Elizabeth's death, it omits all of the unpleasantness of the previous 80 years: the execution of Anne Boleyn, Henry's subsequent marriages, the death of his great hope, Edward, the bloody reign of Mary Tudor, and the execution of James' mother, Mary, Queen of Scots.

One more thing. Like *Antony and Cleopatra*, this play presents us with a problem in the aging of the actors. *Henry VIII* covers 13 years in two and one-half to three hours of performance. The director has to cast a sumptuous, fertile Anne of 25, a healthy athletic Henry of 34, and a mature beauty as Katherine. Characters who die early in the 13-year period make the job easier.

There is much in this play that a modern audience might find offensive. The playwrights have shamelessly whitewashed the historical Henry and Anne in order to sanctify Elizabeth. The parents of Good Queen Bess were rotten human beings, selfish and manipulative. In the final analysis, not even their storied love could redeem them: they exploited each other, betrayed each other. I suppose, like a conscientious novelist, I could come up with a few obscenities to describe them, but why bother? Unless a company is committed to producing all of Shakespeare, as we were, as few are, the producer might well question whether to do the play at all. If you don't like it, don't produce it.

CHAPTER 37

The Two Noble Kinsmen

John Fletcher must have had a good horse. Born in 1579, he first appeared on the scene as the author of *The Faithful Shepherdess* in 1609, but is best known for collaborations with Francis Beaumont that continued for seven years until Beaumont's death in 1616. Fletcher allegedly collaborated with Shakespeare on at least three plays, *Henry VIII*, *The Two Noble Kinsmen*, and *Cardenio*, which was probably lost when the first Globe burned down in 1613. There is evidence that he collaborated with many other playwrights as well, the last being Philip Massinger, with whom he produced *The Spanish Curate* in 1622. Between 1610 and 1613, he appears to have had a hand in as many as a dozen plays. Clearly, he did a lot of traveling.

Though *Henry VIII* was included among the 36 plays of the 1623 First Folio, *The Two Noble Kinsmen* was not. It first appeared in print in a 1634 Quarto, where it was attributed on the title page to John Fletcher and William Shakespeare, and it was included in a 1647 Folio of the works of Beaumont and Fletcher. Critics were skeptical of the work when it first appeared; both Beaumont and Shakespeare had been dead for 18 years. Today there is general agreement that Shakespeare did have a substantial hand in its writing, but opinion differs widely as to what can be attributed to him and what to Fletcher. *Henry VIII* is easier to decipher.

The direct source of *The Two Noble Kinsmen* is the *Knight's Tale* from Chaucer's *Canterbury Tales*, which were, in turn, derived from Boccaccio's *Teseide*. Plentiful earlier sources exist as well as from Greece and Rome: the gods Mars, Diana, and Venus; the warrior Theseus and his bride, Hippolyta; Oedipus and his brother-in-law Creon; the Seven against Thebes and the Widows of the Seven; and finally an earlier version of the two Theban youths, Arcite and Palamon, who fought for Creon, were wounded, and were then brought back to health and imprisoned by Theseus in Athens. Act I of *The Two Noble Kinsmen* brings on a number of characters we never see again and makes reference to dozens of others from all corners of history and mythology. All this to get us to the beginning of the story. Could the author of the precise, easily accessible, and lovely play, *The Tempest*, have written this convoluted muddle?

When I directed this play in 1986 in repertory with *Julius Caesar* and *Antony and Cleopatra*, I decided to do it out of period in a 19th-century Greek setting reminiscent of Shaw's *Arms and the Man*. Looking back on this decision some 20 years later, I can find no good reason for it, but I do know that the designers welcomed it, the actors went along with it, and our madrigal/musical director, Debbie Martin, composed an original score inspired by Greek folk music that provided a lot of fun after the heaviness of the Roman plays. We rounded up every intern who could play a musical instrument, borrowed horns and drums, and enlivened what otherwise might have been a perplexing, even tedious, evening.

The Two Noble Kinsmen, New Jersey Shakespeare Festival, 1986: Kia Christina Keith as Luce, John Pietrowski as the Wooer, Don Perkins as Gerrold, Geddeth Smith as Pirithous, Margaret Emory as the Gaoler's Daughter, Raye Lankford as Nell, Joyce Dudeck as Maudline, Cal Winn as the Jailer (photograph by Jim DelGiudice).

I suggest that the director of *The Two Noble Kinsmen* begin work with the Second Act, then go back to consider how much of the First Act helps set up the story and how much of it actually impedes the story. As with the masque in *The Tempest* and the Hecate scenes in *Macbeth*, I'm inclined to seek out the non–Shakespearean passages and question them before committing budget to them. That first act can cost a lot of money and take up a lot of rehearsal time before the body of the story is ever reached. I decided to cut most of it and get rid of dialogue probably written by Fletcher.

The playwrights give us a Greek myth as a prologue, then duplicate it in the main plot and mirror it in the subplot: a three-way battle among the deities Mars, god of war; Diana, goddess of chastity; and Venus, goddess of love. In the main story, two Theban knights,

Arcite and Palamon, the noble kinsmen of the title, are imprisoned together and fall in love with the same beautiful woman, Emilia, sister of Hippolyta. A second young woman, the Jailer's Daughter, falls in love with Palamon but not Arcite, and she is loved, in turn, by a young man known only as the Wooer. From there, although the plot wanders a bit, there is a direct line to the end.

Hovering over these events as a constant presence are the feuding interventionist gods and goddesses — Mars, Diana and Venus — championing one or another of the principals, who are at once pawns and free souls with free wills. The Gods are prayed to, thanked, and given credit for every event, especially the accidental. A director of the play who is tempted to put them on-stage, however, will be looking for trouble. Ubiquitous deities who watch worldly events unfold for a while, then move in to make a decisive move that changes the course of action are found in many religions. Greek history/mythology and the history of the Jewish people as recorded in the Bible not only demonstrate this principle, but stress it; the principle is present in pantheism and monotheism, probably in all religions. The custom of prayer is based on it. We ask, we receive, and we thank the Giver of all Gifts.

The Two Noble Kinsmen was the first Shakespeare play my daughter Shannon, aged nine, appeared in. When I offered her the role of Freckled Nell, her first question was,

"Will I get paid?"
"You'll get room, board, and transportation," I replied carefully.
"How about a salary?"
"How much would you like?"
She thought for a while, and then said "Thirty-seven cents."
"Is that 37 cents per performance or for the whole run?"
"For the whole run."

We shook on it.

At first reading, *The Two Noble Kinsmen* feels like a dreary progression from a funeral to a deadly duel. There is an uncomfortable tension created by the presence of those three gods, watching, watching, waiting for one of the characters to make a wrong choice. As a result the humor remains at the periphery and never gets a chance to lighten the mood. Partially because we were doing *Two Noble Kinsmen* in rep with the Marc Antony plays, we determined to bring this humor to the fore and soften the heaviness wherever possible. For example, we exploited not only the performance of the festive morris dance, but its rehearsal as well, which included rehearsal accidents and the frustration of its director/choreographer. We brought the wrestling on-stage (it is off-stage in the text), where one of our heroes, Arcite, takes on a series of opponents, each bigger than the last, and, naturally, defeats them all. The aborted duel was funny as the two combatants help to dress and arm each other, and its potential deadly conclusion was postponed by Theseus' insistence on a formal joust.

We decided to treat even the madness of the Jailer's Daughter with humor — perhaps a dangerous choice, but we had a gifted comedienne, Margaret Emory, playing the role, with a sensational bray of a laugh which sounded like it came from some creature other than this diminutive teenager. We counted on the audience's sympathy for her to vindicate us. Playing any script for laughs has its perils. The director has to watch out for bit players inventing shtick to get in on the action: too many little laughs usually rob you of the big ones.

The character of the Jailer's Daughter should be examined carefully as her subplot plays and occasionally drops in on the main plot. It's possible that her story was an afterthought, added because the original script was too short or too heavy. Rehearsals can be simplified by working the Jailer's Daughter scenes separately from the rest of the play.

Do not change the structure of the play, just rehearse her scenes separately, giving focus to both her plot and the main plot. She begins like a teenybopper mooning over a celebrity, but she's totally rational. She knows who she is, who he is, where they are. In her second soliloquy she tells us she's in love with Palamon, and she reasons that, if she helps him escape, he'll be so grateful that he'll return her love. She doesn't seem to consider that her father will probably lose his job, perhaps even his life. Nothing matters except her love for her hero.

I added the escape of Palamon into my staging, just before her II.5 soliloquy, which seems to be drifting a ways from reality. The Daughter has prepared a love nest for the two of them, complete with food and files to get rid of his handcuffs. Her fantasy is becoming stronger than reality: she's begun to believe that he's already in love with her. When we see her next in III.2, she tells us that he's lost his way, maybe been killed by wild animals. She'd rather die than live without Palamon, so she sets out to find him, no matter what the danger. In III.4, she has lost her orientation, cannot tell day from night, and thinks she's on a leaking ship at sea, seeking direction from a frog. She comes upon a rehearsal of a morris dance for the entertainment of Theseus and Hippolyta, where she's recruited to replace an absent dancer. She rehearses, then performs with them, then goes off with the troupe, just missing Palamon.

When she returns in IV.1, she is imagining her wedding day, complete with gown, bridesmaids, musicians, and is ready to forgive her bridegroom, Palamon, for getting all the maids of the town with child. Then she reverts to an earlier fantasy, employing the dancers to form a ship, casting her father as the captain and sailing off to the woods where her lover is waiting. In IV.3, she's in a vision of hell, beginning with a funeral, singing one of Ophelia's dirges, fearful that Dido will give up Aeneas for Palamon, describing an inferno where lechers and adulterers are punished for their sins. She seems to accuse her beloved of deserting her for others, while she remains a virgin. Since they cannot coax her out of her fantasy, her father, her Wooer, and a physician decide that the Wooer will take on the persona of Palamon and marry her.

In V.2, the playwrights give us one of the most tender, gentle love scenes in the Canon with the Jailer's Daughter as the bride, the Wooer in the guise of Palamon, and others substantiating the charade. We know it's a charade, but directed and played simply, it's heartbreaking. At its conclusion, it parallels Emilia's love story.

The Act V conclusion, following that of Chaucer's *Knight's Tale*, tells the story of how Arcite, champion of Mars, defeats Palamon, champion of Venus, in a duel, initiated by the two of them and later formalized by Theseus. Emilia has prayed to Diana that the victor be the one who loves her most; after the duel proves which of the combatants is the braver warrior, Diana intervenes with what appears to be an accident that mortally wounds him, and leaves Emilia free to marry the loser. In a sense, both Mars and Venus are satisfied, because one champion wins the duel and the other has won the hand of the lady. Diana wins too, because her handmaiden is rewarded with the suitor who loves her the most.

Now, having rehearsed the two plots separately to define their specificity, put them back together, and see how they reflect each other. Then define for yourself who is the more lunatic, the Jailer's Daughter or Emilia.

******

Only after it opened did we learn that our production of *The Two Noble Kinsmen* would have the longest run in its history: 28 performances. I don't know if that record has been broken, but I salute anyone who may have done so. By odd coincidence, the Royal

Shakespeare Company also presented the play that season, and our photographer, Jim DelGiudice, visited London and saw their production. He was excited to meet a publicist from the RSC staff and to tell them about our achievement, but had to add that he'd been so concentrated on the photography in New Jersey that he hadn't really seen the play. Asked how he liked it when he saw the RSC version, he ruefully admitted that "a lot of it kind of went over my head." "Yes," replied the Englishman, "we don't care much for it either."

CHAPTER 38

The Winter's Tale

The morning we began rehearsal for *The Winter's Tale* in the summer of 1987, word came that Laurence Olivier had died during the night. In attendance that morning were some 30 actors, from Shannon Barry, age 11, playing Mamillius, to Richard Graham, in his 70s, playing Antigonus, which would prove to be his last Shakespeare role. We reminisced about the continuity of actors playing Shakespeare, all the way back to Burbage's troupe, each actor passing lore and traditions on to others, the eldest learning from the youngest, the youngest learning from all the others, a family in the best sense of the word. And then we went to work.

I was wary of *The Winter's Tale* before I directed it. I suppose I had seen too many bad productions, and it was a chore to read the piece. I agreed with the play's detractors who say this is really two plays — the first an inferior *Othello* with parallels to *Henry VIII*, the second a pale *As You Like It* — and that it is both a comedy and a tragedy. For a long time, you could tell if one of Shakespeare's plays was a comedy if nobody died, if every character survived to the curtain call. When did the Playwright first break his own rules?

Having directed *The Winter's Tale* twice — a traditional production at NJSF in 1987 and a concept production at the San Francisco Shakespeare Festival in 2002 — I've come to love the play by doing it. It contains one of the most poignant moments in all literature, the reunion of mother and daughter at the play's conclusion. Of course, the impatient ones won't stay for the end of the play. If you put the intermission anyplace before the 16-year time jump, you'll risk losing the philistines even earlier to the local pubs.

The Winter's Tale was the third of a string of faerie tales after *Cymbeline* and *Two Noble Kinsmen*. Like most faerie tales, it contains elements of cruelty, wild beasts, death, resurrection. The protagonist, Leontes, commits terrible crimes against his wife and children, but he repents, does penance, and is forgiven. If this monster can be forgiven, then there's hope for Shakespeare and for all of us.

Doubling in *The Winter's Tale* is tricky because there are two casts, two countries, and the establishment of each depends on keeping them separate. At times, actresses — the renowned beauty Mary Anderson among them — have doubled Hermione and Perdita, seeking to attract attention and to impress audiences with their versatility. I strongly protest this idea — it seems to me a cheap trick, displaying a lack of sensitivity, and it deprives the audience of the play's greatest moment.

In the Watermill/Propeller's all-male production at BAM Harvey Theatre, directed by Edward Hall in the fall of 2005, Mamillius also played Perdita, which might have worked as a thematic double if the actor hadn't been the tallest person in the company. A tall Mamillius doesn't work, and a tall Perdita is equally awkward. Like so many of Shakespeare's plays, we can do them better today because we don't have to rely on boys, but have skillful actresses available to us.

Hall's production was extremely well staged with some interesting performances, but a cast without women does considerable damage to the romance of the play! All the roles ended up androgynous, and the homosexual implications were inescapable. The best performance was Adam Levy as Paulina, who, dressed in an off-the-shoulder black pants suit, came across as a roaring dominatrix. It was not a low budget production by any means, though the director completely blew off the Bear, which created confusion in the audience. I'm a great fan of the principle of redemption by bear.

> There are three families and two kingdoms in *The Winter's Tale*:
> Leontes, his wife, son, and daughter;
> Polixenes and his only child, a son, Florizel;
> The old Shepherd, his simple son, and the foundling child.

My concept for the 2002 San Francisco Shakespeare Festival production came right off the front page of the *San Francisco Chronicle* the morning after *King Lear* opened in September of 2001. It reported that a recent United States census showed that Hispanics were no longer a minority in California, and Asians, Indians, and middle–Easterners were significantly represented. I decided to do a *Winter's Tale* that reflected this ethnic diversity, but we didn't

The Winter's Tale, New Jersey Shakespeare Festival, 1987: Timothy Boisvert as Leontes, Shannon Barry as Mamillius, Ellen Barry as Hermione, Jonathan Smoots as Polixenes (photograph by Jim DelGiudice).

want to do the obvious flower children in the woods production. A good thing too, because the Oregon Shakespeare Festival did a 1960s hippies version which opened a couple of weeks before ours did.

Ignoring geographical logic, the mythical kingdom of Sicilia was placed in Hapsburg, Vienna, circa 1880; its music was Strauss and Lehar. The kingdom of Bohemia was frontier Spanish California, a three weeks' sail away (please don't look at the map); we added a couple of shepherdesses and three songs from *As You Like It*. We worked hard in the casting to preserve the integrity of the families, i.e. parents and children resembled each other. Polixenes, Florizel, the Old Shepherd, his Son (the Clown), and Dorcas were Chicano. Mopsa was Japanese, and another shepherdess was Korean. Autolycus and yet another shepherdess were African American. The rest of the cast were European Americans.

The music in our Bohemia reflected the mix: a blend of Mexican, calypso, Japanese, African, and country-western. Everyone sang and danced, and many of the performers played instruments: guitars, guitaron, banjo, trumpet, Latin rhythm. We translated a few random passages into Spanish. *The Winter's Tale* opened with the cast singing "Blow, Blow Thou Winter Wind." The song, lyrics by Shakespeare, created a perfect mood, and established the atmosphere for the farewell party for Polixenes. The Playwright creates a happy, balanced world, then proceeds to smash it to smithereens. Shakespeare doesn't give us much time to enjoy the contented family of Leontes, his pregnant wife Hermione, his son Mamillius and his long-standing close friendship to Polixenes. Only eight minutes into the play, jealousy takes over, and the imagination of Leontes carries the action toward multiple disasters. Leontes' jealousy is as volcanic as Othello's, though Leontes has no Iago to stoke his fires. Indeed, everyone he speaks to tells him he's mad, that Hermione has never been false to him, that her unborn child is indeed his. Does the director need to give Leontes grounds for his suspicions? The text provides little time and few opportunities to observe any dalliance. Hermione dances with Polixenes and with Mamillius, perhaps with other courtiers, before she leaves to take the air with Polixenes at I.2.185. The director is well advised to examine the text carefully and be careful to include the movement and business that Leontes describes and later remembers. Nevertheless, Leontes' jealousy is irrational: it's up to the actor to create its reality, and that's no small task. Each actor must find his own logic for it.

In an unbroken action that only hesitates for a moment to indicate the travel time between II.1 and II.3, the play careens downhill, sending Polixenes running for his life, Camillo following, planting the plot point of the illness of Mamillius, and dispatching Antigonus to murder the infant Perdita. The action then lurches into the trial of Hermione, an echo of Katharine's trial in *Henry VIII*. Hermione is forced to defend herself against charges of treason, adultery, and conspiracy. In rapid succession, events unfold: the Oracle at Delphi proclaims Hermione's innocence; Leontes defies the Oracle; word is brought that Mamillius is dead. Hermione faints, and Paulina says,

> This news is mortal to the queen: look down
> And see what death is doing.

Hermione is carried off, Leontes prays for forgiveness, he trashes his courtroom, and in less than a minute Paulina returns to tell him Hermione is dead, berating, beating and cursing him. Leontes accepts her abuse, asks to be taken to the dead bodies of his queen and son, and vows to bury them together, visiting their graves each day to keep his repentance alive. The stage empties as all leave for the double funeral.

For more than an hour, the Playwright has hit us with powerful, awful images, and the audience is braced for a third death in five minutes, that of the infant Perdita. If this play follows the form of the six bloody tragedies that preceded *Pericles*, the audience will either be facing a stage strewn with corpses, or they'll be on the way out of the theatre, kiddies in tow.

Instead, the play moves to the desert seacoast of Bohemia. Enter a Mariner and Antigonus, carrying the infant Perdita. They're dressed for a sea voyage, and we see and hear a gathering storm, but our big scenic problem here is getting rid of the castle of Leontes in Sicilia—the play makes a big leap in distance before it makes a bigger leap in time. Antigonus recounts at great length a dream he had about Hermione, whom he supposes dead. In the dream, he is instructed to name the baby Perdita and to abandon her in Bohemia. That's the last we hear of Hermione and Leontes for 16 years.

Now, to the Bear, my favorite Shakespearean technical problem, a major stumbling block for many directors, and the best example of the advisability of keeping the tech simple. What does the Bear do for the play? For its first half, *The Winter's Tale* appears to be a tragedy—heavy, nasty, and humorless, with death following death. We are teased for a moment as Antigonus ruminates on the horror of his deed. Antigonus has tucked the infant into a basket with letters, a fortune in gold, and gifts. His doubt and self-recriminations are agonizing. He hesitates, starts to leave, comes back, starts to leave again, and then says,

> A savage clamor!
> Well may I get aboard! This is the chase:
> I am gone for ever!

Then the famous stage direction: "Exit, pursued by a bear." Note that we are not given an entrance for the Bear, nor are there any stage directions as to what the Bear does. Enter the director, afflicted with choices. Antigonus' "savage clamour" is the roar of the Bear. The Bear comes on looking for dinner. To be more precise, the Bear suddenly appears; it should not be seen before its roar.

The Globe Playhouse was in close proximity to the bearbaiting pits, as well as the brothels and taverns of Southwark. A high percentage of Shakespeare's patrons would have been familiar with the appearance and behavior of bears, and it would have been easier for the King's Men to acquire a bear skin and build an authentic-looking costume than it would have been for them to build, say, Roman armor. It then remained for an athletic actor to develop a believable bear's movement and sound: challenging, but possible with some observance and practice.

The Bear's first appearance, looming up out of nowhere behind Antigonus, should frighten the audience. There is a moment when primal fears grab us, triggering the "run or fight" response. He forgets Perdita and moves away from the Bear. The Bear then considers its choices for dinner. It is tempted to eat the baby, but being a good mammal at heart, it makes the moral choice and decides, instead, to punish the old man for deserting the baby. Exit Antigonus and Bear.

Saved by the Bear: a faerie tale improbability that rescues the play from tragedy. The storm is over, the sun comes out, and this mean, nasty tragedy has become a comedy in the blink of an eye. The stage is only empty for a moment, and the Shepherd speaks. The Folio doesn't give him an entrance either, but suddenly he's there, chattering on as if he were continuing an earlier conversation. The Shepherd takes no note of either Antigonus' screams or the Bear's roars. Addressing the audience as if they were his cronies at a local pub, he complains of the vicissitudes of young men, accusing them of lechery, disrespect for their elders, stealing, fighting, hunting, scaring away sheep. Then he discovers the infant Perdita.

What an astonishing moment of grace that this child, cursed, vilified by her father, torn from her mother's arms, abandoned and left to die, should be rescued by the Bear and blessed to grow up with ewes and laughter in the loving care of shepherds, Shakespeare's simplest, kindest, people. The Bear instantly changes the play from tragedy into comedy and does it without resorting to kids' show shtick. Neither the Bear nor Antigonus have to play for laughs. The actor doesn't even have to change his demeanor or alter his intent in order to go from tragic bear to comic bear. Metamorphosis: in the blink of an eye, the audience will transform him as soon as they realize that the infant Perdita is not going to die.

When my daughter, Shannon, was two or three years old, she taught me an important lesson about theatrical transitions: she could go from the depths of despair, wailing, howling, the end of the world, to wild laughing joy in a split second, and it didn't take much to turn her: a hug, a kiss, a bite of ice cream. She could reverse the process too, but that wasn't as much fun. All kids can do this — I now see the same quicksilver behavior in my grandson, Riggins O'Grady. So it is with the Bear, who goes from monster carnivore to cuddly sleepy-time bear through the magic of laughter. An awful lot is riding on a bear suit and a baby doll, but a lot rides on Yorick's skull as well.

Alan Dessen described an alternative director's choice made in an Oregon Shakespeare Festival production: When the Bear came forward, intent upon eating the infant, Antigonus distracted it with his line, "This is the chase," sacrificing himself to the Bear to save the child. The trouble with this choice it that it pardons Antigonus and deprives the audience of the delightful transformation of murderous tragic bear into comic bear.

I've seen the Bear botched in many a production with projected shadows, stuffed teddy bears manipulated like hand puppets, even a strapping young man in an Inca sunburst mask and a gold lamé g-string. Nothing works but a good actor in a bear suit. Is the need for an actor in a bear suit really much more difficult than an actor in a clown's coxcomb? Or an actor as a half-witch, half-devil Caliban? Or a transformed Bottom, half-man, half-donkey? The audience's belief in all these examples depends on the art and skill of actors and costumers. David Austin-Gruen went to the San Francisco Zoo and watched the bears, talked to them, imitated their movements, developed a great roar, then put on the suit and really played a bear, approaching the scene as he would any other, asking himself, "What does the Bear want? What does the Bear need? What are his objectives, his obstacles, his adjustments?"

The Shepherd's son enters soon after, and father and son do a comic double standup, a burlesque sketch about old men as dinner for bears, tempests, drowning sailors, changeling babies with faerie gold. Funny stuff. Why not?

At the end of Act III, the Old Shepherd and his son take up the infant and carry her off to raise her as their own. Even if the producer wants an intermission here (where else would it make sense?) we go into the intermission already ashore in the joyful land of Bohemia, a place of hope, love, and tolerance. The winter is over. Spring is here, and the voice of the turtle is heard in our land. All hail the Bear. The theatre's concession stand can join in the festivities.

When we return, Father Time comes on to tell us that 16 years have passed, and he presents the lovers to us. The next movement in this strange symphony of a play is a celebration, a sheep shearing, a country fair, and the betrothal party of Perdita, now a beautiful teenager, and her country swain, who is really Prince Florizel, son of Polixenes, in disguise. We spend almost an hour frolicking with the country folk before taking ship back to Sicilia.

I think Autolycus, the Rogue, was an afterthought, probably added when early performances proved too heavy, simply not funny enough. Like Feste in *Twelfth Night* or the Fool in *King Lear*, he's almost pure comic relief. Almost. He's not really essential to any of the plots, but serves as a bit player, a comic or a straight man. Also, he's the only entertainer in the play. It's a difficult role to play.

The Winter's Tale is profoundly Judeo-Christian in its morality, yet the only gods mentioned are Greek. We expect the old Shepherd to say some kind of a prayer before he tells Florizel and Perdita to "take hands, a bargain," but he never gets to it. The Bohemia scenes are fun, musical, entertaining until Polixenes arrives, forbids the wedding, and the mood changes. We are plot-ridden for a while, and then we leave Bohemia for good. Here's the designer's problem in a nutshell: several scenes in Sicilia, trash the set, go to Bohemia for spring time, fun and games, then back to the ruined and desolate kingdom of Leontes.

Unkempt, filthy, dressed in a hair shirt and the rags of his first act uniform, Leontes has kept his promise. He hasn't even bathed or changed since he cursed the Oracle 16 years earlier. He leans against a ruined throne that nobody has sat on for all this time: it's rotted, rusted out, covered with cobwebs. He carries a scourge, a cat-o'- nine-tails, to whip himself. He has totally ignored his kingly responsibilities. Apparently, the bureaucrats have kept the kingdom functioning, but Leontes has done nothing, nothing but pray and weep over his dead wife and son, for all this time.

And Paulina is still there, still berating Leontes after 16 years. Once again, for the 5,840th time, the courtiers beg her to get off his back. This scene is at once agonizing and hilarious. The problem of succession is once again raised, and we are reminded of the Oracle's prophecy: "and the king shall live without an heir if that which is lost be not found." No one doubts that Hermione is dead, Mamillius is dead, Antigonus is dead, all long dead, and everyone in Sicilia believes that the infant Perdita died as well. Only we, the audience, know she has survived: unaware that Leontes is her father, she's on the way from Bohemia to beg him for asylum from Polixenes.

Running out of time, with too many loose ends to resolve, Shakespeare suddenly dumps a lot of information on us in a series of "here comes...." At the conclusion of V.1, Leontes is reunited with his daughter, but he doesn't yet know who she is. We end the scene with this cliffhanger. Leontes needs time to clean up before the final scene of the play, so Shakespeare actually sacrifices the father/daughter resolution to the later mother/daughter reunion.

Leontes, Perdita, Florizel, Paulina, Cleomenes, et al., leave the stage to meet with Polixenes, Camillo, and Perdita's foster family, passing a First Gentleman who meets Autolycus entering from another direction and gives Autolycus (and us) information about an off-stage scene. Another gentleman enters a minute later with more information, soon followed by Paulina's steward with even more news: the three gentleman, purposely ignoring Autolycus, rattle on with the story of Leontes' reunion with Perdita for another four minutes, then exit to see the famous statue at Paulina's gallery. This is an impossible scene to stage, unless we add a mime of the story the three gentlemen relate, but Leontes still needs time to clean up to view the statue.

Do we need to retell the audience all this information in the first half of V.2? Do we need to add new news about the shipwreck of the bark that brought Antigonus to Bohemia? Certainly we need to hear Paulina's steward establish the statue and its sculptor, but do we need to remind the audience once again of the death of Hermione? Judicious cuts may be considered here.

The scene that follows, where the Shepherd and his son are rewarded for their care of the Princess Perdita by being named gentlemen, might give us enough time for the change and clean-up of Leontes without all these recaps. In any case, all cuts considered, all clean-up and other technical problems must be resolved before we get to the incredible last scene.

Stephen Booth contends that the Playwright betrays the audience's trust by convincing them in III.2 and III.4 that Hermione is really dead, then bringing her back to life through the device of the statue. Is it chicanery or magic? After Leontes is reunited with Perdita, after he and Polixenes are reconciled, after Florizel and Camillo are forgiven for their disobedience, after most of the plot strings are tied up, everyone is told that they must see Paulina's statue of Hermione. They all proceed to the gallery, and there is the statue, lifelike, the image of Hermione, but aged 16 years. After considerable admiration, Paulina commands the statue to awake, and it does! It moves, descends from its pedestal, and embraces Leontes. Then comes that incredible moment we haven't believed possible for over two and one-half hours: the reuniting of mother and daughter. Hermione's lines are simple, but the joy is immeasurable. Family hug: Leontes, Hermione, Perdita, Florizel, Polixenes, the Old Shepherd and his son.

What happened? Everything we've heard has convinced both characters and audience that Hermione is dead. Didn't Leontes see the dead body? Was another corpse substituted while Hermione was spirited away? Or did she really die, and did the renowned sculptor, Julio Romano, actually create a statue so lifelike that it inspired an outpouring of love from father and daughter strong enough to bring it to life? The Playwright maintains the ambiguity, just as he did with the endings in *Measure for Measure* and *Love's Labour's Lost*. The technical problems are left up to the director, actors, and designers to solve. It's no big stunt for a healthy actress to hold a pose for four and one-half minutes. She can experiment to find a comfortable position. On the Elizabethan stage, she probably stood upstage of the inner-below curtain until it was opened to reveal her. In our 1987 production, we constructed a movable pedestal that was winched downstage through curtains into position. In 2002, we constructed a sarcophagus based on a pedestal with breakaway sides and back that was carried up onto the stage, set in position, then opened to reveal the statue on cue.

The Watermill/Propeller company employed a third method. Hermione doubled as one of Leontes' courtiers, and the entire company, some 20 actors, arrived at Paulina's gallery, wearing hooded capes. Paulina played her speech at V.3.15 as an incantation while she led the company in concentric and opposing circles, rotating faster and faster until centrifugal force broke the circles apart, leaving the statue standing center stage. It was a great effect, but only worked because all the faces on-stage, including Hermione's, were male, and so we were not able to recognize her. Still, the next time I do this play, I'll add some court ladies in capes, Hermione among them, and see if it works.

This play brings back some touching memories for me. My 2002 San Francisco production, set in Bohemia as California might have been, a 19th-century Mexican Nuevo, had the cooperation of the producer, the costumer, the composer, and a company of actors, singers, dancers, musicians, all willing to substantiate the concept. In one of our last rehearsals, a surprise! Hermione delivered her final speech to Perdita in Spanish,

> Dime, hija mia, Donde te salvaste,
> Donde viviste, como encontraste la corte
> De tu padre?

which effectively reduced us all to blubbering idiots. Amy Mordecai and Allen McKelvey, recently married and very much in love, were the perfect Hermione and Leontes. Like *Othello*, this play must begin with a passionate marriage.

Then, we were blessed with Luis Orapeza as the Shepherd who provides the lost child with the home so often lost in the shuffle of the horror of the play: la preciosa Perdita grows up in a more loving family than her own, and her adopted father and brother each teach her more important things than she would have learned as a princess. More than just the actor's talent, Luis brought a goodness, a humanity to the role. A director can coach and stage and choreograph, but he can't direct soul where there is none. Watching a performance by my side, my daughter told me, tears streaming down her face, "That man playing the Shepherd is heartbreaking. He makes your play work."

A final memory is from my earlier production, at NJSF in 1987, and is not mine, but my wife, Ellen's. Actors always want to feel that they are truly communicating with the audience. On rare occasions, they are hit with a certainty that they have reached that goal. Ellen, playing Hermione, experienced such a moment. Some years earlier, Susan Socolowski, a promising young woman who had grown up at our theatre, working her way from intern to general manager, had died unexpectedly, just before her 30th birthday. We were very fond of her and her parents; the loss of their only child was wrenching. At the curtain call one evening, Ellen, having just completed the wondrous reunion of mother and daughter, suddenly saw Susan's mother Jean in the third row. Ellen burst into tears, finished the call, immediately went home and wrote Jean a letter. Jean had the same response — their letters crossed in the mail, each expressing love and remembrance and, yes, comfort, from the shared experience of mothers who lose daughters.

Chapter 39

All's Well That Ends Well

All's Well That Ends Well is one of my least favorite Shakespeare plays. I've had two unsatisfactory experiences with it. I directed it in 1988 in a rep with *Hamlet* and *Rosencrantz and Guildenstern Are Dead*, and it suffered from my own shortage of vitality and enthusiasm in a difficult year — I was in the midst of a battle with my Board of Trustees, which I eventually lost. Several years earlier I had seen the RSC's touring production, elaborately designed, like a Broadway musical, tons of money spent on many set and costume changes, which I felt still didn't make it work.

In the late 1990s, I played the King of France at a prominent Shakespeare Festival, and the experience was miserable. I was hired in January for June rehearsals, so I had plenty of time to learn the role. In early June, the *All's Well That Ends Well* stage manager called to give me cuts over the telephone. "Cuts?" I protested, "I've memorized the entire role." Nevertheless, she gave me the cuts, and the first two weeks of rehearsals were all about unlearning what I had memorized and patching together the cut text, occasionally begging the director to give me back a line to make sense in a passage. Then, in the third week, after seeing a run-through, the producer concluded that the play was too long. He demanded that the director cut another 20 minutes out of it. Despite my protests, I went back to my cell to relearn the role yet a third time. My memory of that summer was of hours and hours spent drilling various incarnations of the King of France, an unpleasant enough sovereign to begin with.

Is this the worst thing a producer can do to an actor? I'm hard pressed to come up with worse torture. The human mind just doesn't work that way. A director should set a desirable running time, then finish any cutting he may want well in advance. Bill Ball even suggested that actors be supplied with "fair copies," scripts that have been edited, then retyped so that the cuts aren't visible distractions. This may sound like a lot of trouble, but it's worth it.

Why does *All's Well That Ends Well* so seldom work? First, the plot is confusing. The play takes place on the outskirts of a war (a group of French noblemen sign on as mercenaries for the King of Florence against Sienna), the most irrelevant war in the Canon. The director has to carefully pick through the play to determine why the war is waged, when it begins, when it ends, when the armies are dispersed, where the various scenes take place. Although the war itself isn't important, the ideals and contradictions of soldiership are. But that's not what the play is about.

The primary plot is a love story. Helena, intelligent, attractive, delightful daughter of a brilliant physician, has been in love with Count Bertram of Rossillion since childhood. The King of France is dying from a rare disease, and when Helena, using her father's scientific methods, miraculously cures him, he rewards her with her choice of husbands from among

***All's Well That Ends Well*,** New Jersey Shakespeare Festival, 1988: Amelia Prentice as Helena, Geddeth Smith as the King of France, Peter Carlton Brown as Bertram (photograph by Jim DelGiudice).

his nobility. Everyone wants to marry Helena but Bertram, who disdains her because he's a count and she's a commoner. Then he goes off to the wars.

Shakespeare adds some gratuitous comedians to lighten the plot — they're not very funny — and he makes use of that melodramatic staple, the bed trick, to bring the young couple together as he does in *Measure For Measure*, but the big problem in this play is Bertram. How can any man refuse such a prize as Helena, especially since the King of France blesses the marriage and will, no doubt, elevate the young couple to positions of great importance in his kingdom? It's not because his affections lie elsewhere. He's in love with no one but himself. Point by point, line by line, Bertram is an insufferable snob and, ultimately, a hypocrite. Shakespeare is taking a nasty shot at the nobility, all nobility, in this play.

Why does Helena persist in her love for this boorish clod? Because love conquers all, plain and simple. I can find no other reason. The star Playwright is asking the audience to buy this or go to the bearbaiting. Unfortunately, the audience usually spends half the play subconsciously warning Helena to select another husband, and the next half mourning her choice. Perhaps modern manners forbid it, but I don't know why an audience wouldn't rise en masse and scream at her to make another choice.

What is the director to do? Find the nicest, sweetest, most likable actor in America, cast him as Bertram, then teach him to talk, to make the words work. Soften him whenever possible without contradicting the text. The Bertram who ends the play capitulating to Helena's love and turning into a decent human being has to be there from the start, and finding that Bertram is problematic for both actor and director.

CHAPTER 40

Pericles, Prince of Tyre

Pericles, Prince of Tyre, was a collaboration between Shakespeare and George Wilkins, a shady character who kept a tavern and a brothel in London. *Pericles* was first performed in 1607 or 1608, published in quarto in 1609, and showed up in the Third Folio of 1664. This play was not Wilkins' only literary effort; he wrote another that the King's Men produced, *The Miseries of Enforced Marriage*, 1606, and he collaborated with Thomas Dekker on *Jests to Make You Merrie*, 1607. The 14th-century African poet, John Gower, one of the sources for the play, is its Chorus.

My first encounter with *Pericles* was Chris Martin's kabuki-style production at his CSC Repertory in New York, built around a percussionist who accompanied Gower as Chorus. As the play progressed, observers of the action, seated on-stage as in my *Titus Andronicus*, were "cast" as characters then recast as needed. All the actors doubled and tripled except Pericles. The story is a pilgrim's progress, an odyssey, a series of tests over many years that brings the protagonist to a resolution, an epiphany.

Herman Melville wrote:

> Why did the old Persians hold the sea holy? Why did the Greeks give it a special deity, a brother to Jove? Surely this was not without meaning. And still deeper is the meaning of the story of Narcissus, who because he could not grasp the tormenting mild image he saw in the fountain, plunged into it and was drowned. But the same image we ourselves see in all rivers and oceans. It is the image of the ungraspable phantom of life, and this is the key to it all.

This evocation lingered in my mind as I prepared the production. The image of the sea was always there. The play is somber and tedious without it.

Our 1989 production began with its set, inspired by the image of a ruined fishing boat I had seen on a shore in Sicily years before. Our set was a beached sailing vessel, the cast its crew and passengers. The boatswain played Gower, and, as in Martin's production, he cast the play as he went along, using properties you might find on such a boat. We had an especially good-looking intern company that year, both men and women, and the well-built men began as mariners on the boat while other cast members were European and American tourists. Even though our acting company was big enough that doubling was not necessary, I decided to use four of my best character men, Kevin Hogan, Don Perkins, Geddeth Smith, and T. Ryder Smith, for multiple roles, some twelve roles among them. The women did not double. As with many of our productions, the Festival Madrigals provided a bridge for the audience from their arrival at the theatre into the action.

Then Gower sang his prologue — original music by Debbie Martin, a significant contribution to the production — and introduced first the shocking situation, then Pericles.

Antiochus, king of Antioch, is in an incestuous relationship with his daughter. Many suitors have come forth to win her hand, but Antiochus has created a riddle to test each one. Those who fail to solve the riddle are immediately beheaded, yet if they dare to speak the correct answer, they're also killed for the insult. It's a lose/lose situation. To represent the suitors who had lost their heads, our mariners gathered in the stern behind a black blanket with slits that revealed only heads, no bodies.

Pericles kneels and reads the scroll with the riddle:

> I am no viper, yet I feed
> On mother's flesh which did me breed.
> I sought a husband, in which labor
> I found that kindness in a father.
> He's father, son, and husband mild;
> I mother, wife, and yet his child.
> How they may be, and yet in two
> As you will live, resolve it you.

A headsman stands behind him, ready to strike. Although Pericles guesses the answer, he begs for more time to consider it. Antiochus suspects that the prince has guessed correctly, but grants him another 40 days before he must make his answer. Pericles doesn't hesitate, immediately escaping back to his home in Tyre, and Antiochus sends an assassin after to kill him.

And we're off and running on his journey of the soul. I had originally wanted to build on our basic set so that we could create a sea voyage between each episode, but decided that would be too cumbersome. Some voyages take time, others do not. Pericles leaves Tyre in the care of the trusted Helicanus and sets sail. He'll keep running from Antiochus and his assassins until the old pervert dies. First stop is Tarsus, where he delivers a shipload of grain to relieve a famine. Gower keeps up his running commentary, making sure the audience does not forget earlier plot points, and stage directions dictate action. Pericles is warned that the assassin Thaliard is after him — there could be others — so he takes ship again. A storm comes up, which Pericles and our mariners played actively, hurling themselves back and forth to suggest the pitch of a ship at sea, and struggling to hold on to the mast. The tempo of their mime was independent of Gower's speech, but there were a couple of points where he needed to pause and allow the mime to play out. The next storm, the movement quickened to match the tempo of the speeches.

The boat wrecks, and Pericles is thrown up on the beach near Pentapolis, where he encounters a trio of comic Fishermen. Stretching their nets across the set, our fishermen changed the stage picture again, simply but effectively. The Fishermen do a vaudeville turn comparing the life of fish and men, and then they produce Pericles' armor, dragged in with their nets. They tell him he's arrived just in time to fight in a tournament. Surprise! The winner gets the hand of the princess Thaisa. I tried to find a moment for the two of them to fall in love, but the formality of the tournament got in the way.

We put this tournament on-stage, rather than off — the six knights fighting a round robin, using short swords, circular shields, and pectoral armor. Pericles is proclaimed the winner by King Simonides, and the banquet celebrating his victory gave us an excuse to bring out the pretty girls for a dance. After a bit of foot-dragging, wooing dance, father/daughter/suitor plot nonsense, a match is made and Thaisa and Pericles are married. I suppose I shouldn't knock this scene, and in production we took it seriously, though there were wisecracks galore. The humor that Shakespeare and Wilkins have given us here is silly, but charming in its own way. The next time we see Thaisa, several months have passed, she's significantly pregnant, and word has come that the people of Tyre are clamoring for the return of their prince, threatening revolt if he stays in Pentapolis.

Gower takes over again to tell us that the rebellious Tyrians are threatening to crown Pericles' loyal caretaker Helicanus as prince. Another mime was added to accompany the description. Despite Thaisa's condition, she and Pericles set sail for Tyre. It's not an especially long journey, and Thaisa is optimistic about it. For the storm that comes up here, we again employed the thunder and rolling sea effects. We used sails of a very light material with several fans to make them flap and appear to tear. Again, the mariners and Pericles collectively mimed the pitching of the boat. Extra rehearsal time was necessary to drill the give and take of actors and effects. A good athlete must be cast as Pericles, perhaps even an acrobat.

Thaisa gives birth. Pericles argues with the gods, challenging their wisdom in delivering his infant daughter Marina at such a time as this. His speech, III.1.1 to 14 is significant, because it's the first time we are shown a susceptible human being, rather than a plaster hero. The storm pauses for a moment, so we can listen to it, then Lychordia, the nurse, enters from below with the infant and the news that Thaisa is dead. Pericles takes a moment to mourn and welcome the child, but the Mariners insist that Thaisa's body must be thrown overboard to appease the gods and quell the storm. Our coffin was built out of the lightest durable material, securely seamed. Thaisa's body was handed up from below through the stage trap and laid in it together with jewels and identification. If it washes ashore, Pericles hopes for a decent burial. The Mariners muscled the coffin upstage to the stern and over the edge, as Pericles, holding the infant, watched. The scene and the storm resolve, as the boat makes way for Tarsus.

The coffin washes ashore in Ephesus, where Lord Cerimon, a physician, revives Thaisa. As written, the scene is interrupted with a cutaway to Tarsus, and is then continued three minutes later. Instead, I juxtaposed scenes III.3 and III.4 to establish Thaisa's retirement in Ephesus as a vestal of Diana before the temporary resolution of the father/daughter plot. After the new combined scene of III.2 and III.4, we returned to Tarsus in III.3 and

Pericles, Prince of Tyre, New Jersey Shakespeare Festival, 1989: Eric Kramer as Pericles, Don Perkins as Antiochus (photograph by Jim DelGiudice).

characters introduced earlier, Cleon and his wife Dionyza, who also has given birth to a daughter since we last saw her. Fearing that his countrymen will revolt without him, Pericles leaves the infant Marina with them and returns to Tyre. For those who prefer an intermission, here's the perfect — in fact, the only — place for it. As in *The Winter's Tale*, 16 years pass and for the same reason: the heroine must grow from an infant to a young woman.

Why am I going to the trouble of tracking this play scene by scene? Because it's obvious that there's another hand at work here besides that of Shakespeare, and because the complexity of the plot and the multitude of characters give the actors little opportunity to develop and give depth to their roles. Even Pericles himself scarcely has time to express himself, much less tell the audience how he's feeling, since he spends the first 60 percent of the play getting into and out of scrapes. Unlike most of Shakespeare, this play is all action. Pericles is an action figure, not a cartoon, but more like the boilerplate lead of a Saturday matinee cliffhanger than Shakespeare's other heroes.

Further, the playwrights contrive a whole new story about Dionyza's daughter, her jealousy of Marina, the plot to murder Marina, and the ex machina arrival of pirates who carry Marina off and sell her to a brothel in Mytilene. But first there are a few laughs in a burlesque turn with a pimp, a pander, and a bawd, Marina protecting her virtue by using her wit and lawyer skills that recall Portia and Isabella. Then we're aiming toward the conclusion of the play.

If we could avoid comparing Shakespeare with Shakespeare, this might be an interesting evening in the theatre. The audience that hangs on until the end sees a hero turned into a vegetative recluse, totally lost in despair over the supposed death of his child. Never mind the fact that he seems to have ignored her, even forgotten her, for 16 years. It made no sense for him to leave his daughter with Cleon and Dionyza all that time, never returning to bring her home. For all his daring-do and hairbreadth escapes, we don't know him at all, and we know little about her. As in *Cymbeline* and *The Winter's Tale*, we have a little girl lost, then found by her father.

Doubt about the value of doing this play is removed by examining their reunion scene, V.1, which leads us into a *Winter's Tale*-like rejoining of parent and child. It feels, sounds, in its power and delicacy, like Shakespeare wrote it all. The conclusion of this strange odyssey, with all its turbulent, storm-drenched sea journeys, is a family reunion. What could be more pedestrian, more familiar, more commonplace? Fathers who mistreat and are near oblivious to wives and daughters for years are taken back into the family and forgiven in an instant. No apologizes are demanded, no retributions exacted, no repentance ordered. There's only forgiveness. Is this the master lesson that Shakespeare tried to teach, the final sermon of his last few plays? Forgive, live and let live? I think so.

Chapter 41

King John

This is it: the completion of the Canon, the 38th Shakespeare play directed, scheduled to open in August of 1990.

King John is an excellent example of the dissimilarity of Shakespeare's work: no one of his plays is like any other. Even *Henry IV, Parts 1 and 2* are different from one another. While it is true that *King John* is one of several plays that examine the dilemma of kingship specifically and the rights and privileges of leadership generally, similarity ends there. Shakespeare used Holinshed's *Chronicles* as his source for *King John*. Holinshed collected material—he didn't write history, but accumulated masses of information, making no attempt to reconcile opposing opinions or conflicting information on the same subject. What passes for the history of the reigns of Henry II's sons is a hodgepodge of myth, rumor, implication, conjecture and cover-your-ass reportage.

With one notable exception, all of the characters in the play are right out of history. By creating the character of Philip Faulconbridge, a bastard son of Richard I, the Lion-Hearted, Shakespeare improved history or possibly improved an earlier play. Philip manages to keep the plot neater, though he gives later historians headaches as they try to find evidence of him elsewhere. Richard Lionheart does not appear in *King John*, but the Bastard's mother describes him as an ardent seducer of women, contradicting modern historians, who label him a homosexual mainly because he produced no heirs to the throne.

Actors who seek psychological consistency in the characters they portray are made neurotic by some of Shakespeare's people, notably Edgar in *King Lear*, Hortensio in *The Taming of the Shrew*, the Bastard and John himself in *King John*, all of whom change personality as their functions change. Actors also have problems with characters who reverse 180 degrees instantly, on a dime, like Bertram in *All's Well That Ends Well*. In *King John*, the Bastard starts out as a wisecracking hot dog, but grows into the image of (the legend of) Richard Lionheart.

John himself is another matter. He begins every inch a king, but as the play progresses, his behavior changes to accommodate anyone in power with whom he comes into contact. He does not grow—he adapts, like a chameleon. He is what and who he is expected to be from moment to moment. Shakespeare might have done something brilliant with *King John*, or he might simply have broken most of the rules of playwriting by giving us a central character who changes from scene to scene. I believe that by play's end, John has become a madman and the evidence is that his enemies poisoned him.

As a result, each scene must be treated as an entity unto itself. This play must be directed one scene at a time, working with the actor in the title role to define the actions and the personality he needs to play that scene. Then you go on to the next scene and allow John to abandon every trait he had in the previous one. Then on to the next and so on through the play. The whole rehearsal time must be used to get through rehearsing the whole play, i.e. *don't* follow the common practice of putting the whole show on its feet and then using the remainder of the rehearsal period for fine-tuning. The actor playing John must be willing to metamorphose from scene to scene, and the longer his solidification of choices is delayed, the better the play will be served.

The play works best with a minimum of scenery and as much space as possible to spread out in, a big stage with multiple entrances and trapdoors, ladders or perhaps some sort of trellis device for actors to climb on, backing the action. The action ranges from wide-open space, the vasty fields of France, to tiny confined rooms where actors can't stand upright. The death of young Arthur, especially, is a tricky scene to design and stage: it has to be approached anew from theatre to theatre; the tricks that make the scene work in one space won't necessarily work in another. Do the play in a void, and spend your money on actors, costumes and properties, not scenery.

Just as Shakespeare ignores the cataclysmic break between the Catholic Church and the Church of England in *Henry VIII*, so too does he ignore the Magna Carta, as significant to the English as our Constitution is to us, in *King John*. For my production I asked the designer to create an enormous multi-colored rectangle of fabric, painted with the text of the Magna Carta, and spread out on the stage. Chris Martin, who played John, first saw it during a dress rehearsal. I watched him the moment it attracted his attention. He looked at me suspiciously, as if it were some kind of animal trap, then asked, "What the hell am I

King John, New Jersey Shakespeare Festival, 1990: T. Ryder Smith as the Bastard, Christopher Martin as King John (photograph by Jim DelGiudice).

supposed to do with *that?*" "You'll figure it out," I said, and he did. He walked around it, walked across it, jumped up and down on it, finally picked it up, spun it around, then wore it like a cape.

King John opens very much like *Henry V*, which can be misleading, but the second act is the key to the play, because here *King John* is like no other play in Shakespeare. The second act goes on forever and involves a score of principals, all coming and going in the debate, but never leaving the stage. A character charges in, proclaims his/her argument for a while, then yields the floor to another. Of all the scenes in Shakespeare, this one will not work simply by turning good actors loose. The director needs to spend considerable time alone, charting the course of the action in the scene.

My wife, Ellen, played Constance, and Shannon played her son Arthur in this production. Mother and daughter are superb actresses in my unbiased opinion, perhaps too good. The lament Shakespeare gives to Constance over the death of Arthur is terrifying, the Playwright punishing himself remembering the recent death of his own son, Hamnet. Life and art imitate each other.

I've seen two excellent King Johns, Kevin Conway and Chris Martin. Conway played the role in Central Park, and he was despicable and wonderful. Chris was obnoxious during rehearsals — he's opinionated and temperamental, but cares deeply about his work — and very exciting in performance.

* * * * * * *

It had taken me 33 years to direct 69 professional productions of Shakespeare, including all 38 plays of the Canon. *King John* completed that journey. What next? After the 1990 season, Ellen and I left the company I had founded 28 years earlier. Our final production was not Shakespeare, but Arthur Miller's *Death of a Salesman*, which involved everyone in my immediate family — the hell with charges of nepotism. I played Willy, Ellen played the Woman, my elder son, Kevin, played Biff, Shannon did the voices of Howard's children, and Timothy helped build the set. After closing night, we struck the play and the season, left the Drew campus, and never looked back. The New Jersey Shakespeare Festival kept producing, but changed its policies, abandoning rotating repertory, and a few years later changed its name: it is now known as the Shakespeare Theatre of New Jersey. The Barrys have kept moving, kept working. The isle is full of noises, and there are plays to be done.

Bibliography

Ardrey, Robert. *African Genesis*. New York: Dell Publishing, 1961.

Asimov, Isaac. *Asimov's Guide to Shakespeare*. New York: Avenal Books, 1978.

Ball, William. *A Sense of Direction*. New York: Drama Book Publishers, 1984.

Barton, John. *The Wars of the Roses*. London: British Broadcasting Corporation, 1970.

Bicheno, Hugh. *Crescent and Cross: The Battle of Lepanto, 1571*. Bristol, UK: Phoenix Press, 2005.

Bloom, Harold. *Shakespeare, the Invention of the Human*. New York: Riverhead Books, 1998.

Booth, Stephen. *Shakespeare's Sonnets*. New Haven: Yale University Press, 1977.

Bowmer, Angus. *Acting and Directing on the Ashland Elizabethan Stage*. Ashland, OR: O.S.F. Association, 1979.

Brook, Peter. *The Empty Space*. New York: Avon Books, 1968.

Burgess, Anthony. *Shakespeare*. New York: Alfred A. Knopf, 1970.

Cook, Ann Jennalee. *The Privileged Playgoers of Shakespeare's London*. Princeton, NJ: Princeton University Press, 1981.

Costain, Thomas B. *The Last Plantagenets*. Garden City, NY: Doubleday, 1962.

Dessen, Allan C. *Elizabethan Stage Conventions and Modern Interpreters*. Cambridge, UK: Cambridge University Press, 1984.

Flavius, Josephus. *The Antiquities of the Jews*. William Whiston, translator. Cirencester, UK: Echo Library, 2005.

Gibson, William. *Shakespeare's Game*. Saddle Brook, NJ: American Book–Stratford Press, 1978.

Grebanier, Bernard. *Then Came Each Actor*. New York: David McKay, 1975.

Greenblatt, Stephen. *Will in the World: How Shakespeare Became Shakespeare*. New York: Norton, 2004.

Gurr, Andrew, with John Orrell. *Rebuilding Shakespeare's Globe*. New York: Routledge, Theatre Arts Books, 1989.

Hobbs, William. *Stage Fight*. New York: Theatre Arts Books, 1967.

Holden, Anthony. *William Shakespeare: The Man Behind the Genius*. New York: Little, Brown, 1999.

Huggett, Richard. *The Supernatural on Stage*. New York: Taplinger Publishing, 1975.

Keegan, John. *The Face of Battle*. New York: Viking Press, 1976.

Kermode, Frank. *Shakespeare's Language*. New York: Farrar, Straus and Giroux, 2000.

Keyishian, Harry. *The Shapes of Revenge: Victimization, Vengeance, and Vindictiveness in Shakespeare*. Atlantic Highlands, NJ: Humanities Press, 1995.

Kirschbaum, Leo. *Character and Characterization in Shakespeare*. Detroit: Wayne State University Press, 1962.

Marius, Richard. *Thomas More*. New York: Alfred A. Knopf, 1984.

Morris, Desmond. *The Naked Ape*. New York: McGraw-Hill, 1967.

Ridley, Jasper. *Statesman and Saint: Cardinal Wolsey, Sir Thomas More and the Politics of Henry VIII*. New York: Viking Press, 1982.

Rosenbaum, Ron. *The Shakespeare Wars*. New York: Random House, 2006.

Saccio, Peter. *Shakespeare's English Kings*. New York: Oxford University Press, 1997.

Schoenbaum, Samuel S. *Shakespeare, the Globe and the World*. New York: Oxford University Press, 1979.

Shakespeare, William. *Complete Works*. Printed in the First Folio of 1623; edited in the Riverside Edition; individual editions by Arden and Folger.

Shapiro, James S. *A Year in the Life of William Shakespeare, 1599*. New York: HarperCollins, 2005.

Taylor, Gary. *Reinventing Shakespeare*. New York: Weidenfeld & Nicolson, 1989.

Tuchman, Barbara W. *A Distant Mirror*. New York: Alfred A. Knopf, 1979.

Weir, Alison. *The Six Wives of Henry VIII*. New York: Grove Weidenfeld, 1991.

Wescott, Roger W. *The Divine Animal*. New York: Funk & Wagnalls, 1969.

Bibliography

Index

Numbers in ***bold italics*** indicate pages with photographs.

Abbott, George 125, 131
Abbott and Costello 20, 37, 64, 70
ACTER 123
Adler, Jacob 117
Albee, Edward 3, 11, 145
Ali, Son of Suleiman 102
All's Well That Ends Well 228–229, ***229***
Anderson, Mary 220
Anderson, Maxwell 163
Anne of Bohemia 136
Anne of Cleves 211
Anne of Denmark 118
Anouilh, Jean 163, 213
Antony and Cleopatra 89–92, ***91***
Arena Stage 129, 132
Aristotle 33
Armin, Robin 64, 123, 124
Arnez, Desi 64
Arthur, Prince 208, 211
As You Like It 123–125, ***124***
Asimov, Isaac 133
Austin-Gruen, David 224

Ball, Lucille 64
Ball, William (Bill) 69, 228
Bancroft, Anne 10
Barnes, Lisa ***164***, 178
Barry, Clement Stanley 65
Barry, Ellen vi, 2, 107, 150, 178, 179, 200, ***221***, 227, 236
Barry, Kevin 236
Barry, Shannon 2, 54, 73, 188–189, 200, 217, 220, ***221***, 224, 236
Barry, Timothy 11, 146, 200, 236
Barrymore, John 38
Barton, John 138, 162
Beckett, Samuel 25, 198
Berber 99
Berle, Milton 29, 109, 124
Berry, Eric 146
Blackfriars Playhouse 7–9
Blake, Kathleen 166
Bloom, Harold 146–147
Blount, Bessie 209

Boccaccio 80, 215
Boleyn, Mary 209
Bolt, Robert 208, 218
Booth, Eric 35, 159
Booth, Stephen 196, 226
Boothby, Victoria 179
Borscht Belt 109
Boston Herald-Traveler Repertory 61
Bowmer, Angus 17, 60
Branagh, Kenneth 38, 159
Brando, Marlon 10
Brans, Madylon ***18***, 20
Braugher, Andre 99
Brecht, Bertolt 140, 163
Brook, Peter 5, 9, 199
Brooks, Mel 107, 117
Burbage, Cuthbert 5
Burbage, James 5, 8, 29, 57, 161, 173, 184, 220
Burbage, Richard 7, 37, 201
Burdman, Stephen 25, 56, 123
Burke, Brendan 35
Burlesque 28, 58, 65, 113, 156, 224, 233
Burns and Allen 64
Burton, Richard 16, 89
Bush, George W. 137

Caesar, Sid 64, 109
Campbell, Joseph 42
Cannon, J.D. 138
Cape May, New Jersey 1, 42
Carnovsky, Morris 109
Castro, Fidel 86, 201
Central Park, New York City 25, 47, 56, 236; *see also* New York Shakespeare Festival
Cervino, Marilyn 161
Chaplin, Charlie 20–21
Chapman, George 80
Charles I 64
Charles II 8, 64
Charles V, Holy Roman Emperor 93–94, 100
Charney, Maurice 179
Chaucer, Geoffrey 80, 215, 218
The Chronicle Plays 133–136

Clement VII, Pope 209
Coca, Imogen 64
Coleridge, Samuel Taylor 21, 55, 61, 102–103
Colicos, John 188, 201
The Comedy of Errors 53–56, ***54***
Commedia dell'arte (commedia) 21, 53, 55, 59, 65
Condell, Henry 7, 118
Conway, Kevin 236
Coralian, Ron 20
Coriolanus 126–128, ***127***
Costain, Thomas B. 142
Crab 21
Cranmer, Thomas 208–209, 211–212, 214
Cromwell, Oliver 64, 117, 209
Cromwell, Thomas 208, 211–212
Cronyn, Hume 35
CSC Repertory 86, 230
Curtain Playhouse 9
Cymbeline 205–207, ***206***
Cyprus 99, 100, 102–103, 105

Dekker, Thomas 230
Demonic, demons 24, 45–46, 50, 69, 91, 133, 170
Demonology 45, 170
Dennehy, Ed 179
Derby, Sixth Earl of 23
Dessen, Alan 224
Devane, William 43
Divine right of kings 16, 45, 86, 137
Dorian, Phil 177
Drake, Alfred 35
Drake, Sir Francis 212
Drew University 1, 115, 183, 236
Durning, Charles 43

East Stroudsburg University 41
Edward I 117
Edward II 138
Edward III 133, 135–136, 140, 169, 171
Edward VI 133, 211, 214
Edward the Black Prince 135
Elizabeth I 5, 36, 40, 60, 84, 86,

94–95, 108, 129, 133, 141–142, 170, 208–209, 211–212, 214
Elizabeth of York 133
Elizabeth Vere 23
Elizabethan Playhouses 4, 7, 8–9, 196
Ellington, Duke 201
Emory, Margaret 217
Erasmus 208
Essex, Earl of 86, 108, 142, 212

Felder, Clarence 26, 146
Ferdinand I, King of the Two Sicilys 95
Ferdinand V 208
Fields, W.C. 120
Finnegan, Ed 51
Fisher, Bishop John 209, 211
Fitter, Chris 142
Fitzroi, Henry 209, 211
Fletcher, John 7, 208, 215–216
Florio, John 59
Folio 4, 7, 10, 31–33, 43, 46, 49, 60, 69, 72, 80, 85, 87, 118, 141, 150, 183, 199, 200–201, 215, 223, 230
Il Fulmine (the Thunderbolt) 19, 67, 68, 131, 209; *see also* thunderbolt
A Funny Thing Happened on the Way to the Forum 58, 109

Gaiety Burlesque 65
Gallagher and Sheen 64
Gibson, William 33
Gielgud, John 16, 36
Giordano, Sal 68
Globe Playhouse 7–9, 40, 157–158, 183, 215, 223
Gorilla Rep 43
Gower, John 230
Graham, Richard 100, 182, 188, 220
Greenblatt, Stephen 112
Gregory VIII 212
Grey, Lady Jane 211
Guinness, Alec 176

Haiken, Jerry 188–89
Hall, Davis 178
Hall, Edward (director) 200–221
Hall, Edward (historian) 133
Hall, Elizabeth 205
Hall, Dr. John 205
Hall, Peter 162
Hall, Susanna Shakespeare 205
Hamlet (film) 157
Hamlet (play) **6**, 31–42, **32**
Hanson, Philip 129
Hecklers, heckling 29, 34–35, 56, 64, 123–124, 136, 148, 156, 170
Heminge, John 118
Henry IV, Part 1 143–149, **144**
Henry IV, Part 2 150–153, **151**

Henry V (film) 157–159
Henry V (play) 157–161, **158**
Henry VI, Part 1 162–167, **164**
Henry VI, Part 2 168–171, **169**
Henry VI, Part 3 **134**, 172–174, **173**
Henry VII 87, 94, 133–134, 138, 163, 168, 175, 177, 208–209
Henry VIII 208–214, **210**
Hersey, David 87
Hertzler, John 178
Hindman, Earl Warren 120
Hitler, Adolf 87, 109, 116–117, 133
Hogan, Kevin 230
Holbein 213
Holinshead, Raphael 133, 234
Hollmann, Heidi 201
Holy Roman Empire 100
Homer 9, 75, 80, 82, 84
House of Commons 134, 138, 141
Howard, David 146
Hoyt, J.C. 35, 179
Hundred Years' War 134–136, 152, 168–169

The Iliad 80, 83
Islam 45, 99

Jacobean Playhouses 4, 9
Jacobson, Deirdre 179
James I/VI 5, 21, 43, 45, 84, 86, 99, 118, 129, 170, 205, 212, 214
James V 94
Jefferies, Annalee 178
Jefferson, Thomas 55
Jenkins, Harold 32
The Jew of Malta 108
Jewish Anti-Defamation League 107
Joan of Arc (la Pucelle) 12, 78, 163–170, 178–179, 213
John of Austria, Don 94–95, 102
Jones, Herman LaVerne 105–108
Jones, Inigo 118
Jones, James Earl 70, 104
Jonson, Ben 118
Judas Iscariot 142
Julius II, Pope 208–209
Julius Caesar 84–88, **85**

Karloff, Boris 206
Kean, Edmund 117
Keegan, John 77, 161
Kempe, Will 29, 56–58, 64, 72, 123–124, 148, 154, 161
Kent, Donald, Dr. 178
Keweenaw Playhouse 17, 23, 31, 42
Keyishian, Harry 3–4, 108, 180
King John 234–236, **235**
King Lear 188–200, **190**
King's Men 5, 8, 118, 223, 230
Kirschbaum, Leo 17, 20, 33, 43, 65, 86, 104, 109
Klein, Susan 47
Kline, Kevin 146–148

Knell, Dane 179
Kott, Jan 24, 37

Lahr, Bert 27
Laine, Addyse 17
LaMar, Diana 182
Lamb, Charles and Mary 132
Langham, Michael 188, 201–202
Laughton, Charles 10, 213
Laurel and Hardy 20, 64
Leary, Robin 63, 92, 182
Lepanto, Battle of 94–95, 98, 102
Levene, Sam 109
Levy, Adam 221
Lithgow, Arthur 69
Little, Guy 17
Lloyd, Christopher 18, 49, 66
Logan, Joshua 42
Lord Chamberlain's Men 5, 16, 142
Lord Hunsdon's Men 5
Lopez, Dr. Roderigo 108
Love's Labour's Lost 184–187, **185**
Luhrmann, Baz 87
Luther, Martin 36, 208–209

Macbeth 43–52, **44**
Machiavelli, Nicoli 175, 207
MacLean, Peter 50–52, 104, 126
Man for all Seasons, A 208, 213
Mangravite, Ron 69
Mankiewicz, Joseph L. 89
Marius, Richard 211
Marlin-Jones, Davey 10, 200
Marlow, Christopher 108, 172
Martin, Christopher 86, 230, 235–236
Martin, Deborah 15, 215, 231
Marx Brothers 65, 120–121
Mary Stuart 86, 94–95, 212, 214
Mary Tudor 94, 117, 133, 208, 211, 214
Marywood University 189
Massinger, Phillip 215
Matthews, Dakin 146
McCarter Theatre 123
McKelvey, Allen 226
Measure for Measure 129–132, **130**
Melville, Herman 230
Mendelssohn, Felix 30
The Merchant of Venice 107–117, **108**
Merciless Parliament 136
The Merry Wives of Windsor 154–156, **155**
Metamorphoses 84
Meyers, Ronald 41
Micas, Joseph 108
Middleton, Thomas 43, 46, 50, 118, 201
A Midsummer Night's Dream **23**, 23–30
Mielziner, Jo 72
Miller, Arthur 3, 145, 236
Miller, Jonathan 87, 89, 109, 115

Miller, Scurvy 65
Mitchell, Warren 109
Moor 99, 100, 102
Mordecai, Amy 226
More, Sir Thomas 133, 175, 208–209, 211
Morton, Thomas Cardinal 133
Mostel, Zero 58, 107, 109–110
Much Ado About Nothing 93–98, **94**
The Murder of Gonzago 31, 129
Muslim 99, 100, 102, 116

Nabokov, Vladimir 91–92
Namath, Joe 52
Napoleon 75, 87, 95, 133
Nastasi, Frank 17, 21
Neale, Grant 56
Nelbach, Daniel 189, 196
New York Shakespeare Festival 42–43, 67, 1107, 138, 162; *see also* Central Park, Public Theatre
Nichols, Mike 185–186
Nissan, Peter 64
Nixon, Richard 137
Norman Conquest 133
North, Sir Thomas 84, 126

O'Brien, Jack 146–147
O'Casey, Sean 3, 38
Occhiogross, Frank 115, 180
The Odyssey 80
O'Grady, Riggins 224
O'Grady, Shannon Barry *see* Barry, Shannon
Olivier, Laurence 10, 40, 50, 100, 102–103, 109–110, 115, 157–159, 182, 220
O'Neill, Eugene 3, 31, 173
Orapeza, Luis 227
Oregon Shakespeare Festival 17, 60, 115, 129, 188, 189, 222, 224
Orff, Carl 30
Osborne, John 2, 3, 208
Othello 99–106, **101**
Ottoman Turks 93–95, 100–103, 108
Ovid 84

Padala, Maureen 68
Papal States 102
Papp, Joseph 42–43, 67, 70, 95, 107
Parallel Lives 84, 126
Partridge, Eric 65
Pasco, Richard 138
Patton, George 75–76
Peak, Charlie 21
Pericles, Prince of Tyre **76**, 230–233, **232**
Perkins, Donald 230
Philip II 93–94, 102
Phillips, Augustus 142
Phillips, Robin 123

Pinter, Harold 25, 52
Pitts, William 54–55, 179
Pius V 211–212
Plummer, Christopher 50
Plutarch 84–85, 93, 126, 201
Polan, Nina 47
Pope, Thomas 148
Porter, Cole 17, 65
Prestamo, Phyil 171
Preston, William 46
Primogeniture 16, 19, 36, 41, 134, 136, 180, 189
Prokoviev, Serge 70
Providential theory of history 16, 45, 78, 86, 142, 145, 212
Public Theatre 42, 47; *see also* Central Park, New York Shakespeare Festival
Puritans 45, 64, 114, 211
Pyramus and Thisbe 25–26, 29

Quarto 4, 7, 31, 33, 43, 72, 150, 183, 199, 200, 215, 230
Quayle, Anthony 50

Raleigh, Sir Walter 212
Reinhardt, Ray 188
Richard I (Lionheart) 133, 138, 234
Richard II 137–142, **139**
Richard III 175–179; **177**
Richardson, Ian 138, 184
Rivers, Leslie Ann 125
Robinson, Roger 104–105
Romano, Julio 226
Romeo and Juliet 67–74; **68**
Rooney, Mickey 27, 58
Rooney, Tracey 68
Rose, George 50
Rose Playhouse 7, 9
Rosenbaum, Ronald 32, 117, 146–147
Rosencrantz and Guildenstern Are Dead 35, 40, 228
Roth, Philip 117
Royal Shakespeare Company (RSC) 123, 138, 184, 219, 228
Ryan, Mitchell 104
Ryland, Jack 35, 84, 92

Saccio, Peter 12, 179, 208
Saint Paul 113, 205
Salinger, J.D. 187
Sams, Eric 31
San Francisco Shakespeare Festival 188, 200, 220–21, 226
Sandoe, Jim 129
Schiff, Daniel C. 109
Schoenbaum, Sam 179
Schulte, Genn 123
Scofield, Paul 50, 188
Scott, George C. 107
Scott, Hal 99
Seinfeld, Jerry 65, 124
Selim II, Son of Suleiman 108

Seymour, Jane 211
Shakespeare, Hamnet 47, 145, 189, 236
Shakespeare, Susanna *see* Hall, Shakespeare Susanna
Shakespeare at Santa Cruz 107
Shakespeare Theatre of New Jersey 236
The Shakespeare Wars 32, 117, 146
Shaw, George Bernard 2, 3, 89, 163, 165, 213, 215
Shaw, Margery 35, 179, 182
Sicily 20, 93, 95, 100, 230
Sidonia, Don Medina 212
Simon, Neil 3, 56
Sixtus V 212
Smith, Geddeth 35, 182, 230
Smith, T. Ryder 35, 131, 230
Smith and Dale 64
Smoots, Jonathan 20
Southampton, Henry Wriothesley, 3rd Earl of 59
Spanish Armada 107
Stanley, Audrey 107
Steelman, Ron 57
Stewart, Patrick 99
Stoppard, Tom 35, 40
Storch, Arthur 107
Stromboli 119
Stukeley, Thomas 95
Suleiman, the Great 100, 102, 108
Swander, Homer 123, 179
Syracuse Stage 107

The Taming of the Shrew 17–22, **18**
Tavaris, Eric 146
Taylor, Elizabeth 59, 89
The Tempest 118–122, **119**
Thomas à Beckett 142
Thomas of Woodstock 135–136, 140
Three Stooges 65
Thunderbolt 19, 67–68, 70, 89, 131, 186, 209; *see also* Il Fulmine
Timon of Athens 201-204, **202**
Titus Andronicus 180–183, **181**
Tolaydo, Michael 178
Troilus and Cressida 80–83, **81**
Troyes, Treaty of 161–163, 166, 172
Tuchman, Barbara 77
Twain, Mark 209
Twelfth Night 60–66, **61**
The Two Gentlemen of Verona 57–59, **58**
The Two Noble Kinsmen 215–219, **216**
Tuchman, Barbara 77

United Scenic Artists 23
Ur-Hamlet 31, 40

Variorum 32
Vaudeville 37, 54, 65, 120–121, 231
Vaughan, Gladys 43

Vaughan, Stuart 162
Venice 59, 100, 102–103, 105, 108–109, 111–115, 129
Verdi, Giuseppe 100
Vere, Lady Elizabeth 23
Vienna (Wien) 34, 129, 132, 222
Virgil, Polydore 80, 84

Walsingham, Sir Francis 212
Waterston, Sam 95

Welles, Orson 86, 146
Wesker, Arnold 109–110
West Side Story 67, 70
Widdoes, Kathleen 95
Wien *see* Vienna
Wilkins, George 7, 230, 232
William the Conquerer 75, 134
Williams, Tennessee 2, 3, 38
Winn, Cal 110, 115
Winslet, Kate 38

The Winter's Tale 220–227, **221**
Wittenberg University 36, 41
Wolfitt, Donald 188
Wood, Charles T. 179

York, Allan 177
York, Y 146
Youngman, Henny 29, 109

www.ingramcontent.com/pod-product-compliance
Ingram Content Group UK Ltd.
Pitfield, Milton Keynes, MK11 3LW, UK
UKHW050534150426
5217IPUK00026B/1936